D0895168

AFRIKA-STUDIEN No. 51

Publication series "Afrika-Studien" edited by Ifo-Institut für Wirtschaftsforschung e. V., München, in connexion with

IFO-INSTITUT FÜR WIRTSCHAFTSFORSCHUNG MÜNCHEN
AFRIKA-STUDIENSTELLE

Studies in Production and Trade in East Africa

with contributions of

H. Helmschrott
W. Kainzbauer
W. Lamade
H. Laumer
T. Oursin
H. Reichelt
G. Rötzer
K. Schädler

Edited by Paul Zajadacz

WELTFORUM VERLAG · MÜNCHEN

SPONSORED BY THE FRITZ THYSSEN-STIFTUNG, KÖLN

Library of Congress Catalog Card Number 76—101980
ISBN 3 8039 0035 2
Print: Druckerei G. J. Manz AG, Dillingen/Donau
Printed in Germany

Review of Published and Forthcoming Studies within the African Research Programme

The entire research programme being conducted up to January 1970 by the African Studies Centre of the Ifo Institute – partly by the Centre itself, partly in conjunction with other institutes and researchers – covers the studies listed below (see also introductory remarks in vols. 1 and 2 of "Afrika-Studien").

For readers' information on changes, supplements, and forthcoming publications, each volume of "Afrika-Studien" will contain a review of the programme as a whole.

Vols. 1–18 have been issued by Springer Publishing House, Berlin–Heidelberg–New York, subsequent volumes by Weltforum Publishing House, Munich, in co-operation with publishing houses in the United Kingdom and the United States. The studies published as mimeographs (African Research Reports) can be obtained through the African Studies Centre of the Ifo Institute for Economic Research (early editions only); the more recent editions (from 1968 onwards) are available through the Weltforum Publishing House, Munich.

A chronological list of published and forthcoming studies is attached at the end of this book.

General Economic Studies

a) Tropical Africa

N. Ahmad / E. Becher, Development Banks and Companies in Tropical Africa (printed as volume 1), in German

R. Güsten / H. Helmschrott, National Accounting Systems in Tropical Africa (printed as volume 3), in German

N. Ahmad / E. Becher / E. Harder, Economic Planning and Development Policy in Tropical Africa (mimeograph), in German

H.-G. Geis, The Monetary and Banking Systems of the Countries of West Africa (printed as volume 20), in German

Africa-Vademecum (Basic Data on the Economic Structure and Development of Africa), prepared by F. Betz (series Information and Documentation, vol. 1), in German, with additional headings in English and French

H. HARLANDER / D. MEZGER, Development Banks and Institutions in Africa (Series Information and Documentation, volume 2), in German

K. ERDMANN, Development Aid to Africa – with Special Reference to the Countries of East Africa (mimeograph), in German

H. AMANN, Operational Concepts of the Infrastructure in the Economic Development Process (mimeograph), in German

b) East Africa

L. SCHNITTGER, Taxation and Economic Development in East Africa (printed as volume 8), in German

R. GÜSTEN, Problems of Economic Growth and Planning: The Sudan Example (printed as volume 9), in English

P. v. MARLIN, The Impact of External Economic Relations on the Economic Development of East Africa (mimeograph), in English

R. VENTE, Planning Processes: The East African Case (printed as volume 52), in English

F. GOLL, Israeli Aid to Developing Countries with Special Reference to East Africa (mimeograph), in German

W. FISCHER, Problems of Land-Locked Countries: Uganda (printed as volume 41), in German

H. HIEBER, Economic Statistics in Developing Countries: The Example of Uganda (printed as volume 40), in German

G. HÜBNER, Importance, Volume, Forms and Development Possibilities of Private Saving in East Africa (mimeograph), in German

M. YAFFEY, Balance of Payments Problems in a Developing Country: Tanzania (printed as volume 47), in English

E.-J. PAUW, Money and Banking in East Africa (Kenya, Tanzania, Uganda) (printed as volume 35), in German

D. BALD, Administration and Economic Exploitation of German East Africa before 1914 (being printed as volume 54), in German

M. BOHNET / H. REICHELT, Applied Research in East Africa and Its Influence on Economic Development (in preparation), in English

P. v. MARLIN and Contributors, Financial Aspects of Development in East Africa (being printed as volume 53), in English

Agricultural Studies

a) Tropical Africa

H. KLEMM / P. v. MARLIN, The EEC Market Regulations for Agricultural Products and Their Implications for Developing Countries (mimeograph), in German

H. PÖSSINGER, Agricultural Development in Angola and Moçambique (printed as volume 31), in German

J. O. MÜLLER, The Attitude of Various Tribes of the Republic of Togo, Especially the Ewe on the Plateau de Dayes, towards the Problem of Commissioned Cattle Herding by the Fulbe (Peulh) of West Africa (printed as volume 14 in German, mimeographed in French)

E.-S. EL-SHAGI, Reorganization of Land Use in Egypt (printed as volume 36), in German

H. THORWART, Methods and Problems of Farm Management Surveys in Africa South of the Sahara (in preparation)

B. MOHR, Rice Cultivation in West Africa – A Presentation of the Economic and Geographical Differences of Cultivation Methods (printed as volume 44)

R. BARTHA, Fodder Plants in the Sahel Zone of Africa (in German, English and French), (printed as volume 48)

b) East Africa

1. Basic Studies

H. RUTHENBERG, Agricultural Development in Tanganyika (printed as volume 2), in English

H. RUTHENBERG, African Agricultural Production Development Policy in Kenya 1952–1965 (printed as volume 10), in English

H. DEQUIN, Agricultural Development in Malawi (mimeograph), in English

H. KRAUT/H.-D. CREMER (ed.), Investigations into Health and Nutrition in East Africa (printed as volume 42), in English

H. BLUME, Autonomous Institutions in East African Agricultural Production (completed), in English

2. Studies Concerning Grassland Use and Animal Husbandry in East Africa

H. LEIPPERT, Botanical Investigations in the Masai Country/Tanzania (an Example from the Semi-Arid Areas of East Africa), (mimeograph), in German

H. KLEMM, The Organization of Milk Markets in East Africa (mimeograph), in German

K. MEYN, Beef Production in East Africa with Special Reference to Semi-Arid Areas (completed), in English

H. SPÄTH, Development Possibilities of the Pig and Poultry Industry in East Africa (in preparation)

WALTER/DENNIG, Comparative Investigations into the Efficiency of Utilizable Ruminants in Kenya (in preparation)

3. Studies in the Organization of Smallholder Farming in East Africa

D. v. ROTENHAN, Land Use and Animal Husbandry in Sukumaland/Tanzania (printed as volume 11), in German

H. PÖSSINGER, Investigations into the Productivity and Profitabilility of Smallholder Sisal in East Africa (printed as volume 13), in German

S. GROENEVELD, Problems of Agricultural Development in the Coastal Region of East Africa (printed as volume 19), in German

V. JANSSEN, Agrarian Patterns in Ethiopia and their Implications for Economic Growth (in preparation), in German

H. RUTHENBERG (ed.), Smallholder Farming and Smallholder Development in Tanzania – Ten Case Studies (printed as volume 24), in English

M. ATTEMS, Smallholders in the Tropical Highlands of East Africa. The Usambara Mts. in the Transition Period from Subsistence to Market Production (printed as volume 25), in German

F. SCHERER, Vegetable Cultivation in Tropical Highlands: The Kigezi Example (Uganda) (mimeograph), in English

v. HAUGWITZ/THORWART, Farm Management Systems in Kenya (in preparation)

W. SCHEFFLER, Smallholder Production under Close Supervision: Tobacco Growing in Tanzania. A Socio-Economic Study (printed as volume 27), in German

H. RABE, Crop Cultivation on the Island of Madagascar with Special Reference to Rice Growing (mimeograph)

E. BAUM, Traditional Farming and Land Development in the Kilombero Valley/Tanzania (mimeograph), in German

R. GOLKOWSKY, Irrigation in Kenya's Agriculture with Special Reference to the Mwea-Tebere Project (printed as volume 39), in German

4. Other Studies Concerning Agricultural Development

M. PAULUS, The Role of Co-operatives in the Economic Development of East Africa, and Especially of Tanganyika and Uganda (printed as volume 15), in German

N. NEWIGER, Co-operative Farming in Kenya and Tanzania (mimeograph), in English

J. VASTHOFF, Small Farm Credit and Development – Some Experiences in East Africa with Special Reference to Kenya (printed as volume 33), in English

F. DIETERLEN / P. KUNKEL, Zoological Studies in the Kivu Region (Congo-Kinshasa) (mimeograph), in German

W. ERZ, Game Protection and Game Utilization in Rhodesia and in South Africa (mimeograph), in German

M. Bardeleben, Co-operatives in the Sudan: Their Characteristics, Functions and Suitability in the Socio-Economic Development Process (in preparation)

Studies in Commerce, Trade and Transport

H. Helmschrott, Structure and Growth of the East African Textile and Garments Industry (printed as volume 45), in German

H. Kainzbauer, Trade in Tanzania (printed as volume 18), in German

K. Schädler, Crafts and Small-Scale Industries in Tanzania (printed as volume 34), in English

K. Schädler, Manufacturing and Processing Industries in Tanzania (mimeograph), in English

H. Reichelt, The Chemical and Allied Industries in Kenya (mimeograph), in English

R. Güsten, Studies in the Staple Food Economy of Western Nigeria (printed as volume 30), in English

G. W. Heinze, The Role of the Transport Sector in Development Policy – with Special Reference to African Countries – (printed as volume 21), in German

H. Amann, Energy Supply and Economic Development in East Africa (printed as volume 37)

R. Hofmeier, Problems of the Transport Economy in Tanzania with Special Reference to Road Transport (in preparation), in English

P. Zajadacz and Contributors, Studies in Production and Trade in East Africa (being printed as volume 51), in English

T. Möller, Mining and Regional Development in East Africa (in preparation)

H. Milbers, The Requirements for the Means of Transport in East Africa with a View to the Economic Expansion of these Countries (in preparation)

Sociological and Demographic Studies

A. Molnos, Attitudes towards Family Planning in East Africa (printed as volume 26), in English

O. Raum, The Human Factor in the Development of the Kilombero Valley (mimeograph), in English

O. Neuloh a. o., The African as Industrial Worker in East Africa (printed as volume 43)

H. W. Jürgens, Contributions to Internal Migration and Population Development in Liberia (printed as volume 4), in German

I. Rothermund, The Political and Economic Role of the Asian Minority in East Africa (printed as volume 6), in German

J. Jensen, Continuity and Change in the Division of Labour among the Baganda (Uganda) (printed as volume 17), in German

W. Clement, Applied Economics of Education – The Example of Senegal – (printed as volume 23), in German

H. W. Jürgens, Examination of the Physical Development of Tanzanian Youth (mimeograph), in English

H. W. Jürgens, Investigations into Internal Migration in Tanzania (printed as volume 29), in German

A. v. Gagern, The African Settlers and How They Organize Their Life in the Urambo-Scheme (Tanzania) (printed as volume 38), in German

Gerken / Schubert / Brandt, The Influence of Urbanization upon the Development of Rural Areas – with Special Reference to Jinja (Uganda) and Its Surroundings (in preparation)

E. C. Klein, Social Change in Kiteezi (Buganda), a Village within the Sphere of Influence of the Township of Kampala (Uganda) (printed as volume 46), in German

U. Weyl, Population Trends and Migration in Malawi with Special Reference to the Central Region of Lake Malawi (in preparation)

M. Meck, Population Trends in Kenya and Their Implications for Social Services in Rural and Urban Areas (in preparation)

Staewen/Schönberg, Cultural Change and Anxiety Reaction among the Yoruba of Nigeria (printed as volume 50), in German with English Summary

J. Muriuki, The Mau-Mau Movement: Its Socio-Economic and Political Causes and Implications upon British Colonial Policy in Kenya and Africa (in preparation), in English

H. Desselberger, Education's Contribution to Economic Development of a Tropical Agrarian Country – the Example of Tanzania (in preparation)

Legal Studies

H. Fliedner, Land Tenure Reform in Kenya (printed as volume 7), in German

H. Krauss, Land Legislation in the Cameroons 1884–1964 (printed as volume 12), in German

G. Spreen, The Present State of Legislation in East Africa (in preparation)

K. v. Sperber, The Implications of Tanzania's Administrative System for Her Economic Development (completed), in English

F. v. Benda-Beckmann, Development of Law in Malawi (completed), in German

Studies in Economic Geography

W. MARQUARDT, The Interrelationship between Man, Nature and Economy: the Example of Madagascar (in preparation)

H.-O. NEUHOFF, Gabun: History, Structure and Problems of the Export Trade of a Developing Country (printed as volume 16), in German

H. D. LUDWIG, Ukara: A Special Case of Land Use in the Tropics (printed as volume 22), in German

R. JÄTZOLD/E. BAUM, The Kilombero Valley/Tanzania: Characteristic Features of the Economic Geography of a Semihumid East African Flood Plain and Its Margins (printed as volume 28), in English

A. J. HALBACH, The Economy of South West Africa (a Study in Economic Geography) (mimeograph), in German

J. A. HELLEN, Rural Economic Development in Zambia 1890–1964 (printed as volume 32), in English

K. ENGELHARD, The Economico-Geographical Pattern of East Africa (in preparation)

J. SCHULTZ, Iraqw Highland/Tanzania: Resource Analysis of an East African Highland and its Margins (in preparation)

K. GERRESHEIM, Evaluation of Aerial Photography in East Africa (an Inventory) (mimeograph), in German

Bibliographies and Others

D. MEZGER / E. LITTICH, Recent English Economic Research in East Africa. A Selected Bibliography (mimeograph), in German

A. MOLNOS, Annotated Bibliography of Social Research in East Africa 1954–1963 (printed as volume 5), in German

B. HEINE, Status and Use of African Lingua Francas (printed as volume 49), in English

M. BOHNET, Science and Development Policy: The Problem of Applying Research Results (mimeograph), in German

Preface

The task of the African Studies Centre of the Ifo Institute, which was founded in 1961, is to elucidate the theoretical and practical aspects of the economic development process of the African developing countries. Within the framework of the Africa Research Programme 50 studies have been published so far in the series "Afrika-Studien" dealing with economic, agricultural, social, geographical and other phenomena of African life. The present compilation "Studies in Production and Trade in East Africa" contains specific economic studies which have been published in extended form earlier, either in German or in English. The investigations by KAINZBAUER (Trade in Tanzania) and HELMSCHROTT (East African Textile Industry) have appeared as no. 18 and 45 respectively of "Afrika-Studien" in German, the one by SCHÄDLER (Crafts and Small-scale Industries in Tanzania) as no. 34 in English. The other contributions were so far available only as mimeographs or manuscripts. The articles in this compilation are extracts of the extended studies mentioned. It is the aim of the African Studies Centre to make available to readers in the English speaking world the larger part of its numerous studies published in the course of the past five years, even though only in abridged form. This is the very purpose of these compilations of which two have already been published: one on agriculture (Afrika-Studien No. 24), one on nutrition (Afrika-Studien No. 42). A compilation of articles entitled "Financial Aspects of Economic Development in East Africa" (including banking, public finance, balance of payments) will be published soon as no. 53.
The field research upon which these studies are based was carried through in 1964, 1965, 1966 and 1967. More recent developments could not in all cases be considered in the analyses.
On account of their large number, neither the various ministries and other official agencies of the East African states nor the countless individuals as well as institutions in and out of Africa which have extended every kind of help to the authors during their investigations and work, can be mentioned by name. The authors would like to extend here their thanks to all of the above. A special word of thank is owed to the editor Paul ZAJADACZ who had the laborious job of revising and — where necessary and possible — co-ordinating the different contributions. Mention must also be made of the generous financial assistance of the Fritz Thyssen Foundation, which rendered possible the various investigations as well as the publication of this compilation.

Dr. Wilhelm MARQUARDT

Contents

STRUCTURE AND GROWTH OF THE EAST AFRICAN TEXTILE INDUSTRY

by

Helmut HELMSCHROTT

Contents

List of Tables

List of Maps

The following treatise by Helmut HELMSCHROTT summarizes the most important results of a study of the East African textile industry. His statements are based on official statistics, information from authorities and financing institutions and, in particular, on the results of a poll of entrepreneurs carried out by the author with the support of EAISR (East African Institute of Social Research), Kampala, Uganda, in the three East African countries from mid-1966 to mid-1967.
The chief points of interest were the economic preconditions for the textile industry, the achieved output level, planned expansion and possibilities for future growth. The consequences arising from the expansion of the textile industry and their significance for sectors of trade and industry on other levels were also investigated.
H. HELMSCHROTT, who studied economics at the University of Munich, is a member of the research staff of the Ifo Institute in Munich. For some years he has devoted himself to economic problems of African developing countries. The results of his work are described in a publication on national accounting problems in tropical Africa (together with R. GÜSTEN) and in several development studies and reports on various countries.
We are indebted to Mr. John FOSBERRY of Munich for translating this treatise into English.

A. INTRODUCTION

Up to a few years ago, the three East African countries Kenya, Uganda and Tanzania were under British colonial rule. The prevailing trade relations can be characterized as follows: the motherland imported raw materials (agricultural and mining products) from the colonies and supplied them with industrial finished products. So the manufacturing industry was concentrated in the mother country. At best, dressing and processing plants such as installations for ginning cotton, hulling coffee, drying tea, smelting and refining copper ore, etc., were established in the colonies.

After World War II, when there was no further doubt that the East African countries could not be denied independence in the long run, the former concept was given up. Thereafter Britain endeavoured to establish industries in East Africa to improve the area's economic basis in the light of impending independence. Industrialization was started about 1950 and rapid growth was achieved very soon in Kenya, at the end of the fifties in Uganda, and only in the middle of the sixties in Tanganyika.

In many cases the industrial products of developing countries are unable to compete on the world market. Their outlets are usually restricted to the home market, which is then shielded off from abroad by high customs barriers and import quotas. Under these circumstances it is logical for industry in developing countries to start out by producing those products which can be readily sold on the home market. One of the most important of these pioneer industries — apart from industries producing beverages, cigarettes, footwear, etc. — is the textile industry.

The first spinning and weaving mill in East Africa (Nyanza Textile Industries Ltd.) was established in 1955 in Jinja, Uganda. This company is owned by the Uganda Development Corporation (UDC), a government development corporation, and is managed by a British firm. With a production capacity of about 45 mill. square yards of fabric it is still by far the largest textile enterprise in East Africa. Between 1955 and 1960 only two other mills were set up: a weaving mill in Dar es Salaam (Tanganyika Textile Industries Ltd.) and a spinning mill in Nairobi (Nath Brothers Ltd.), to which meanwhile a weaving mill has been added. Not until 1960 did a stormy development set in, which will be intensified in the coming years and should persist up to about 1975. Among the most important firms[1] which have started

1 Firms with a production capacity exceeding 10 mill. square yards of fabric per annum.

production since 1960 are the Tasini Textile Co. Ltd. in Dar es Salaam (1960), United Textile Industries Ltd. in Thika (1964), Kenya Rayon Mills Ltd. in Mombasa (1964), Kisumu Cotton Mills Ltd. in Kisumu (1965), Mulco Textiles Ltd. in Jinja (1965), Kilimanjaro Textile Co. Ltd. in Arusha (1967), Friendship Factory Ltd. in Dar es Salaam (1968) and Patel Ltd. in Mbale (1968).

In addition, a number of blanket weaving mills were set up in East Africa after 1960. Mention should be made of the Blanket Manufacturers (Tanzania) Ltd. in Dar es Salaam (1962), Nakuru Industries Ltd., by far the biggest blanket factory in East Africa, in Nakuru (1963), Shah Bhagwanji Kachra (E.A.) Ltd. in Mombasa (1965), Uganda Blanket Manufacturers Ltd. in Kampala (1965), Blanket Manufacturers (Kenya) Ltd. in Mombasa (1966) and Kilimanjaro Blanket Comp. Ltd. in Tanga (1967).

Furthermore, several further spinning and weaving mills and blanket factories are planned or under construction, some of them of quite considerable size. Especially in Tanganyika, there is lively investment in the textile sector.

The stages through which Europe's industry passed are being by-passed, at least partly if not completely, by the developing countries. The entire wealth of technological knowhow slowly and laboriously accumulated in Europe in the space of 100 or 150 years is immediately available to the developing countries. Naturally different economic conditions prevail there than in the industrial countries at the present time, so the most up-to-date production techniques cannot be applied. On the other hand, however, they do not resort to the primitive techniques of the nineteenth century. Hence, the textile industry of the developing countries can make a technological leap over a number of stages and immediately attain a higher starting level.

B. THE ECONOMIC PRECONDITIONS FOR THE EAST AFRICAN TEXTILE INDUSTRY

Even under British colonial rule, there was close economic co-operation among the three East African countries, which was continued after the attainment of independence. The East African railways and ports, the postal and communications systems, and the levying of customs and excise duties and income taxes were controlled by a joint administration. Moreover, there was a uniform currency and also completely free exchange of goods among the three partner countries. This co-operation has meanwhile become less close. The various countries have founded their own central banks and there are hindrances to the exchange of goods among them. Nevertheless, even today the economies of the three East African countries are closely interlaced, which entails that some economic decisions do not lie with the national authorities, but are made by supranational authorities which are combined in the East African Common Services Organization (EACSO). For all that, there is a trend towards limiting the jurisdiction of the supranational authorities more and more, and in this way enabling the scope of national economic policy and, above all, of national industrial policy, to be broadened.

I. Supranational Preconditions

1. The Common East African Market

The Common East African Market, which was established as far back as the twenties, was an important precondition for the setting up of the East African textile industry. For it secured for that industry what for African conditions is a remarkably large home market of 20 mill. consumers. Uniform external tariffs protected this home market from third countries, while among the three constituent countries yarns and fabrics could be traded completely freely — there were neither internal customs duties nor quantitative trade restrictions. Kenya's advantages (central location, higher development level than her two partners on attaining independence, a large number of white and Asiatic settlers, head offices of the banks and insurance companies operating in East Africa, etc.) took full effect under this liberal conception of the Common East African Market, with the result that industry became concentrated primarily in that country. This development gave rise to serious disadvantages for Uganda and even more so for Tanzania. The weak growth of industrial output in these two countries meant a small income and employment effect. In Uganda and Tanzania, the industrial products coming from Kenya ousted imports from other countries and thus caused a perceptible drop in import duties. Since the world market prices for agricultural exports declined and the revenue accruing from duties on exports shrank considerably, these losses were politically painful.
This situation became a danger to the continued existence of the Common East African Market only after three independent states had come into being in East Africa. Tanzania and Uganda, as sovereign states, were not prepared over the long term to belong to a common market which hindered their industrial development. So especially Tanzania urged a reform of the Common East African Market which would ensure each of the three coun-

tries an appropriate share in the industrialization of East Africa. These endeavours led to the Kampala Agreement, which was signed in April 1964.
Since the Kampala Agreement did not improve Tanzania's situation to the desired extent, from mid-1965 onwards Tanzania hampered the free exchange of goods in East Africa by imposing import quotas on interterritorial imports (imports from partner countries). This unilateral intervention by Tanzania was extended to an ever larger proportion of interterritorial exports and threatened to destroy the Common East African Market. For this reason the three national governments appointed a commission of experts, the so-called Philips Commission, which prepared a new agreement on the economic co-operation of the East African countries, and this agreement came into force on December 1, 1967. The common external tariffs, which for yarns and fabrics (incl. blankets) are 40 per cent of the cif value[2], were retained. But it was impossible to restore completely the free exchange of goods among the three partner countries. It is true that the import quotas in interterritorial trade were eliminated, but countries that have a deficit in interterritorial trade (trade among the three East African countries) are entitled to impose on interterritorial imports transfer duties of up to 50 per cent of the corresponding external tariffs, that is, 20 per cent of the producer's price for fabrics and yarns.
Tanzania, whose interterritorial trade showed a deficit of almost £10 mill. in 1967, has meanwhile taken advantage of this right and has imposed transfer duties reaching up to the permissible upper limit, among other things on imports of fabrics and blankets (of cotton and synthetic fibres) from Kenya and Uganda. Uganda, who likewise suffered deficits (approx. £3 mill.) in interterritorial trade, though substantially smaller ones than Tanzania, has subjected imports of rayon fabric and blankets from Kenya to transfer duties which also amount to 50 per cent of the external tariffs.
So the textile industries of the three East African countries have to face up to quite different conditions in exporting their products to partner countries. Fabrics can be exported transfer-duty-free only from Tanzania to Kenya and Uganda, from Uganda to Kenya, and — though this applies only to cotton fabric, and not rayon fabric — from Kenya to Uganda. All other export flows (from Uganda to Tanzania, from Kenya to Tanzania, and in the case of rayon fabric from Kenya to Uganda) are subject to a 20 per cent transfer levy. Hence only Tanzania's textile industry, which in addition to its home market also has free access to the markets in Uganda and Kenya, is in a favourable situation corresponding to former conditions in East Africa.
On the other hand, by far the most important textile industry in East Africa, that of Uganda, is faced with substantial difficulties. This industry, which

2 For cheap fabrics they go up to 1 E.A.sh. per square yard.

came into being at a time when the free exchange of goods in East Africa was still ensured, sold roughly a third of its output in each of Uganda, Kenya and Tanzania. On account of the import quotas introduced by Tanzania in mid-1967 and the transfer duties which replaced them at the end of 1967, Uganda's possible sales to Tanzania have been considerably reduced.
Since that time, Uganda's textile industry has been constrained to sell more of its products on the home market and in Kenya. Although exports to Kenya could be expanded, on the whole Uganda's textile industry can probably offset the decline of sales in Tanzania only by supplying more to the home market. And there it has to compete with imports from third countries, against which it can defend its position in some instances only with great difficulty. If more stringent import quotas or higher import duties formed a stronger barrier to imports from third countries, Uganda's textile industry could very well operate at full capacity again[3].

2. The Production Licence System

Since 1948, a production licence is required for the production of cotton yarns, cotton fabrics, cotton blankets, woollen materials and woollen blankets. In 1953, licences were made compulsory also for all yarns and fabrics of soft fibres. These production licences are issued by the East African Industrial Council, a supranational authority within the framework of EACSO (East African Common Services Organization). The legal basis for this licence system is the East African Industrial Licensing Ordinance of 1953, as amended in 1962, which has statutory force in all three East African countries.

a) Objectives and Adopted Measures

There were two motives for the introduction of compulsory licences: first of all, it was intended to stimulate private investment activity. For it was feared that if the textile industry was freely accessible, the private entrepreneur would expect keen domestic competition and would therefore move into this field, if at all, only with great hesitation. Furthermore, with the building up of the textile industry it was desired to attain the biggest possible employment and income effect.
In order to attain these objectives, the following points are considered in issuing production licences:

3 In this respect see also Chapter D on the Growth Possibilities for the East African Textile Industry.

- A licence is issued only if full utilization of the additional production capacity will not seriously impair the sales chances of already existing and planned undertakings. This requires that the increased output be absorbed by growing home consumption or replace imports from third countries.
- The applicant must undertake to effect vertical integration of the production programme. The firm may comprise only a spinning mill, but a weaving mill must be combined with a spinning mill. The latter can be dispensed with only if it is not essential for technical reasons, i.e. if synthetic endless fibres are processed. Without compulsory vertical integration, it is assumed that primarily weaving mills would be set up to utilize foreign yarns. Under these circumstances the employment and income effect inherent in the spinning mill would be lost for East Africa.

During the first few years the principle of vertical integration was strictly adhered to. Later, requirements were eased slightly when weaving mills up to an output capacity of three mill. square yards (annually) were exempted from compulsory integration. Only rarely are textile enterprises already vertically integrated when production is started. Usually they first operate only a weaving mill (incl. finishing plant), to which a spinning mill is added after one, two or sometimes only after three years.

Prevention of Overproduction

As far as the consumption estimates made by the East African Industrial Council can be relied on, licensing prevents aggregate overproduction of fabric. On the other hand, it does not preclude partial overproduction such as was observed in 1966 in the case of some types of fabric, since the production licences do not specify the production programme exactly. Despite this, there is no cause to depart from this system. Exact fixing of the production programme by the licence deprives the entrepreneur of the opportunity to benefit from favourable market situations. Moreover, the textile industry can change the production programme without any great difficulty, so partial overproduction can be overcome relatively quickly.

Vertical Integration

Compulsory vertical integration may result in an uneconomical combination of spinning mill and weaving mill. According to entrepreneurs, the minimum capacity of a weaving mill is about 3 mill. square yards (annually), while that of a spinning mill is roughly 6–7 mill. lbs. of yarn (annually), that is a quantity of yarn sufficient to make about 20 mill. square yards of fabric. Therefore every vertically integrated undertaking with an output capacity of less than 20 mill. square yards of fabric (annually) is an uneconomical combination of spinning and weaving mill, since the minimum capacity of the spinning mill is not attained. The profit rate of the integrated enterprise is necessarily lower than that of a weaving mill operated on its own. The consequent microeconomic and macroeconomic losses could be avoided, if vertical integration were aimed at, not on the basis of the individual firm, but on the basis of the textile industry of a country or of the whole of East Africa. Such procedure would by all means ensure attainment of the objective of achieving the greatest possible employment and income effect in building up the textile industry.

Without compulsory vertical integration, first of all weaving mills would be established, which would cover their yarn requirements mainly abroad. By high customs duties on yarn imports, however, it would be possible to induce several fairly large weaving mills to seek a combination with a spinning mill in the interests of improved profitability, and the spinning mill would supply yarn, not only to the firm's own weaving mill, but also to other smaller and medium-sized weaving mills. In this way the textile industry would be vertically integrated without any direct compulsion, and in the case of small firms uneconomical combinations of weaving and spinning mills would be avoided.

b) Scope of Issued Licences

Although it is intended to control the scope of production with the aid of the licensing system, Nyanza Textile Industries Ltd. in Jinja, Uganda, is in possession of a licence authorizing unlimited production of cotton and synthetics fabrics. Apart from this, at the beginning of 1967 licences had been issued for a production capacity of altogether 248 mill. square yards of fabric: in Uganda for 59.0 mill. square yards, in Kenya for 62.0 mill. square yards and in Tanzania for 127.5 mill. square yards. Only a production capacity of altogether 17.0 mill. square yards allocated to several small weaving mills was exempted from vertical integration.

Also in the field of blanket manufacture, two firms, Nakuru Industries Ltd. in Nakuru, Kenya, by far the biggest blanket factory in East Africa, and Blanket Manufacturers (Tanzania) Ltd. in Dar es Salaam, received unrestricted production licences. Additional licences issued by the beginning of 1967 permit production of 6.9 mill. blankets annually.

It is often asserted that the generous issuing of licences will result in overcapacity in the near future. In our opinion the East African Industrial Council has probably overestimated the growth of fabric consumption in East Africa, but a number of planned spinning and weaving mills will not go into production until considerably later than originally assumed. There is therefore no cause to fear overcapacity in the near future (1971/72).

Such a development can certainly be prevented also in the following years. By the time the already issued production licences are utilized to the full, fabric consumption will have increased so much that the created production capacities can also be fully utilized. So if the East African Industrial Council pursues a cautious policy in issuing licences in the coming years, overcapacity can certainly be avoided also in the distant future.
In the blanket industry, however, which has expanded greatly since 1966, there will probably be substantial overcapacities. The generous issuing of licences in the blanket industry was followed by lively investment activity. The planned production capacities far exceed the consumption capacity of the East African market, so in a short time the blanket industry will be faced with considerable sales difficulties.

II. National Preconditions

Nowadays it is generally an uncontested objective of developing countries to build up an extensive industry. It may be objected that a country can also attain prosperity by stepping up agricultural output. So why the demand for industrialization?
Development of a country solely by expanding agricultural production can be succesful only if it has good chances of exporting its agricultural products. But the only large-scale buyers worthy of consideration are the industrial countries, and they offer the developing countries only limited outlets. On the one hand this is connected with the fact that the income and price elasticity of demand for agricultural products is relatively rigid, and on the other with the fact that the industrial countries cover a large proportion of their requirements for agricultural goods themselves, and in the case of some products even suffer from overproduction, for which the policy of agricultural protectionism pursued in the industrial countries for decades is chiefly responsible.
A clear indication of the weak position of the agricultural countries on the world market is given by the continual deterioration of their terms of trade. While in the developing countries imports of industrial finished products grow more expensive, the prices of agricultural exports are in many instances declining or stagnating. On account of this deterioration of the terms of trade, the developing countries suffer substantial losses, which for several countries and in certain periods were greater than the inflowing development aid.
In this situation it becomes a necessity for the developing countries not to base their economic development solely on agriculture, but in addition to

press forward with industrialization. It has proved, however, that the advanced industrial nations offer many products at prices lower than the cost at which they can be manufactured in the developing countries. So in many instances the developing countries are faced with the alternative of continuing to buy cheap industrial products from abroad or — large-scale subsidization being out of the question — of raising the domestic price level to such an extent that it is possible to build up profitable industries at home, a procedure that is applied in East Africa by all three countries. What economic policy instruments are available to this end?

The raising of the domestic price level can be achieved only by hindering imports, for which quantitative import restrictions and protective duties are suitable instruments. The fixing of duties for third countries, i.e., countries outside East Africa, is of course a matter for the individual countries, but experience has shown that they do not act independently in this field, but consult each other with the result that — apart from a few, unimportant exceptions — uniform external tariffs could be preserved. So the national instruments that are left are only quantitative import restrictions as towards third countries and, under certain conditions, as towards partner countries. These national instruments for the promotion of industry are supplemented by fiscal concessions and finally by public investments, which attained great significance especially for the textile industry.

The transfer duties — which were dealt with in more detail in the preceding section — can be used as an economic policy instrument only to a limited extent. Only a deficit country has any right to impose transfer duties on interterritorial imports. Moreover — apart from other restrictions — these duties may not exceed 50 per cent of the common external tariffs.

One of the most important measures for the promotion of industry is the quantitative restriction of imports from third countries. The East African textile industry, too, owes its existence largely to intervention of this nature, which is directed mainly against imports from the Asian area, i.e., from Japan, Hongkong and India. From this it can be perceived that there are no chances for the East African textile industry to export to third countries. As soon as the demand on the East African market is largely satisfied by domestic products, the growth of the textile industry will be limited by the growth of home consumption, that is, by endogenous forces. For the time being, there is no question of exogenous forces having any effect.

Among the fiscal promotion measures, which do not differ essentially from each other in the three East African countries, quite apart from the occasionally generous provision of industrial land, emphasis should be placed on tax concessions. Under the act for the promotion of investment, such concessions are granted only to industries that are of special importance for the country's economic development, to which category the textile industry belongs.

Finally, the public authorities participate to a considerable extent in the financing of the East African textile industry. By far the biggest spinning and weaving mills in East Africa, Nyanza Textile Industries Ltd., Jinja, Uganda, which were opened in 1955, were set up by the government-operated Uganda Development Corporation. Public authorities have also had a notable share in building up other textile enterprises in East Africa[4].

C. THE STRUCTURE OF THE EAST AFRICAN TEXTILE INDUSTRY

I. Choice of Location

In the matter of choice of location interest attaches not only to the locations actually taken up, but above all to the considerations on which choice of location was based.

1. The Locations

In early 1968 the East African textile industry (excl. blanket factories) numbered 19 textile plants. Six further plants were under construction or planned. The centre of the East African textile industry is Jinja, the second largest city in Uganda and simultaneously the focal point of the country's industry, which lies where the White Nile leaves Lake Victoria. The two firms located here, Nyanza Textile Industries Ltd. and Mulco Textile Industries Ltd., produced more yarn and fabric in 1966 than all the other spinning and weaving mills in East Africa together. In addition, during recent years great importance has been attained by Dar es Salaam, which will probably grow even more in importance in the years to come. Other locations in East Africa which should be mentioned are: Kampala and Mbale (both in Uganda), Kisumu, Nairobi, Thika, Mombasa, and Limuru (all in Kenya), and Moshi, Arusha, and Mwanza (all in Tanzania) (see Map 1).

The biggest East African blanket factory, Nakuru Industries Ltd., is situated in Nakuru (Kenya). Two blanket factories are located in Mombasa, one each

4 These brief statements are deemed sufficient at this juncture, as the financing of the textile industry is described more thoroughly in Chapter C.

Map 1. *Distribution of Locations of the East African Textile Industry*

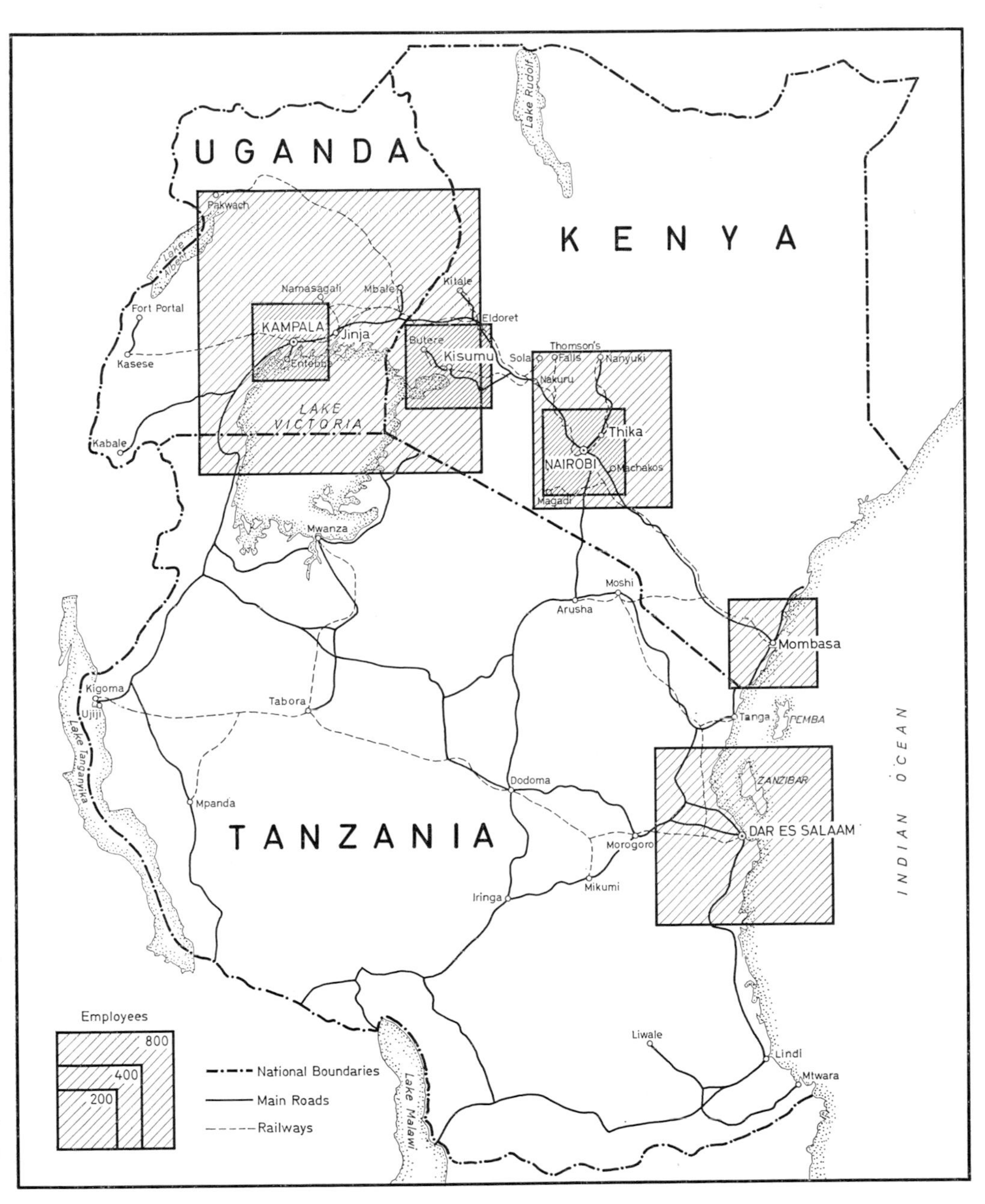

Note: Only those plants in operation in 1967 are shown. The towns marked in the squares indicate the exact locations of the textile industry. The areas of the squares indicate the labour force at the various locations.

Map 2. *Distribution of Locations of the East African Blanket Industry*

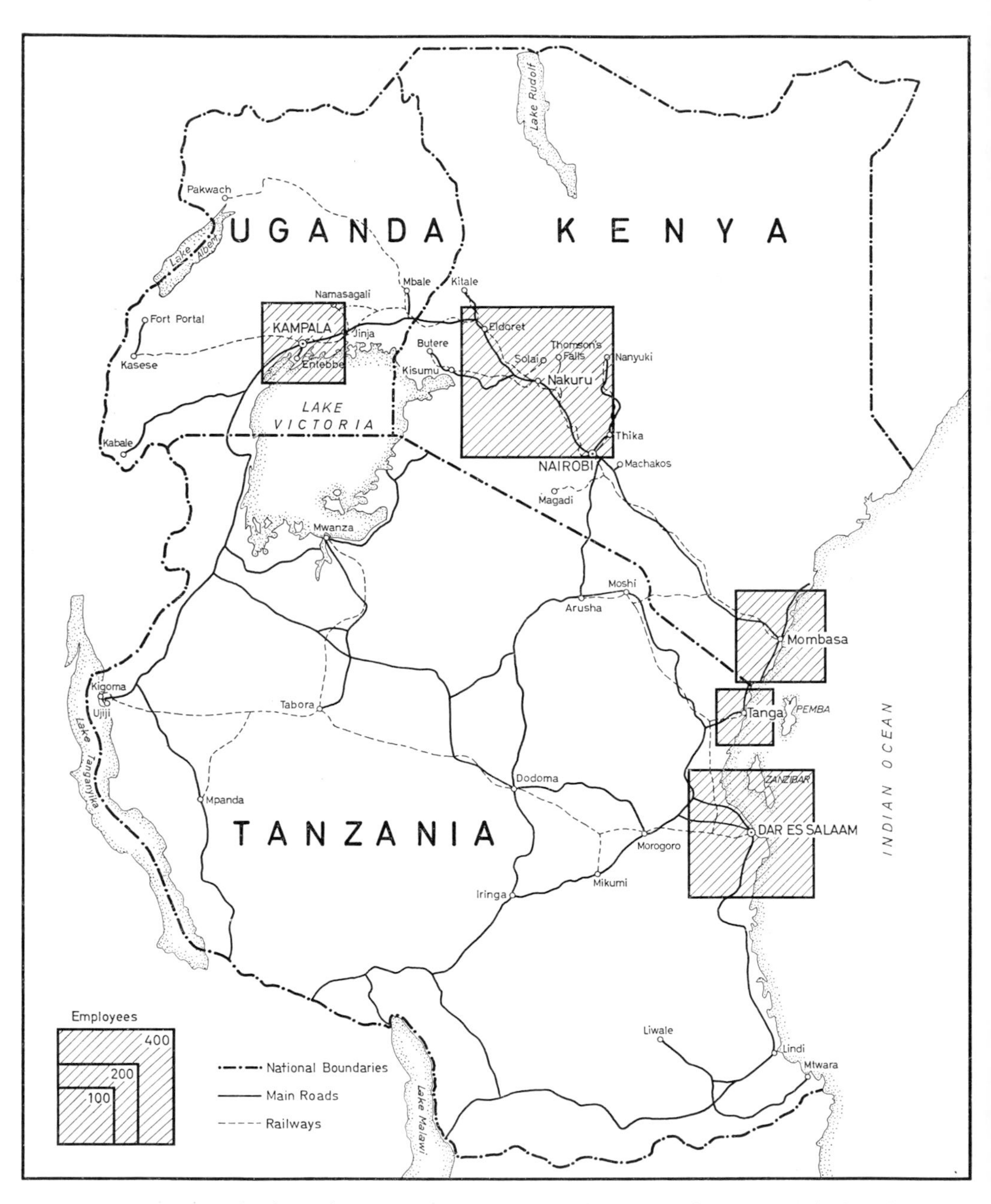

Note: Only those plants in operation in 1967 are shown. The towns marked in the squares indicate the exact locations of the blanket industry. The areas of the squares indicate the labour force at the various locations.

in Dar es Salaam, Kampala and Tanga (Tanzania). Other factories are planned in Mombasa, which is developing more and more to a centre of the East African blanket industry, and in Kisumu and Limuru (see Map 2).
The locations of the textile industry (incl. the blanket industry) are characterized by good traffic routes and by good power and water supplies. They are in the middle or in the immediate vicinity of large consumption centres such as the areas of Jinja-Kampala, Thika-Nairobi, Mombasa, Dar es Salaam, Moshi-Arusha, and Mwanza, which simultaneously guarantees a plentiful supply of labour.
The greater part of the East African textile industry processes domestic cotton, and the smaller part imported raw materials such as rayon, shoddy wool, etc. For the second group, especially the seaports Mombasa and Dar es Salaam, where several textile enterprises of this type have been established, are favourable locations with regard to raw material supplies. On the other hand, the imported raw materials for the mills in Nairobi and Thika have to be transported about 450 km and for the mills in Kampala roughly 1,000 km. For the mills processing domestic cotton, the locations at Jinja, Kisumu, and especially Mwanza offer the advantage of short transport distances, while Nairobi, Moshi, Arusha, and Dar es Salaam are more or less fairly distant from the cotton growing areas.

2. Motives for Location Choice

The economic problem in selecting an industrial location consists in determining the production costs and the earnings for alternative locations — in a given economic area – and choosing those locations which permit the biggest profit. Theoretically any point in a given economic area can be considered as an industrial location. On the basis of certain general previous knowledge, a large proportion of those points can be eliminated as potential locations from the outset, since the comparative disadvantages are obvious at first glance. In this way the infinitely large number of theoretically conceivable locations is reduced to a manageable number worth practical consideration. In this connection it is typical of developing countries that the number of locations worth considering is relatively small as compared with developed countries. Vast areas of East Africa are still not opened up as far as transport routes are concerned, and have no power, water, etc. Consequently, from the very start they are out of the question as industrial locations, and all that remains is a quite small group of locations that are worthy of consideration.
Whether, in choosing locations, the economic area considered embraces all three East African countries or just one country depends on various conditions. If a government development corporation sets up a textile plant,

only a location within the national territory can be considered. In the case of private investors, on the other hand, location choice extends in principle to the entire East African area, although the crisis-like trend in the Common East African Market is restricting the scope of choice more and more. For example, a textile enterprise may prefer as its location the country in which it sells the major part of its products, even though a neighbouring country (on the whole) offers more favourable location conditions. Such action reduces the risk to which the enterprise may be subject in the event of the dissolution of the Common East African Market.
The various location factors such as the position relative to raw materials, the position relative to consumers, the cost of power and water, etc., often have a widely differing influence on location choice for varying branches of industry. The East African textile enterprises stated almost without exception that their primary consideration was to find a location which ensured an adequate supply of power and water at moderate cost and which had good traffic connections. These considerations are just as applicable to spinning and weaving mills as to blanket factories.

II. Production

1. The Production Programme and Quantitative Output

The production programme of the East African textile industry (excl. the blanket industry) is essentially limited to the manufacture of coarse cotton fabrics and, though to a considerably smaller extent, rayon fabrics. The latter materials are chiefly coloured woven goods which are used for traditional apparel (Kikoys and ghingams). The cotton fabrics, mainly bleached and dyed, serve as bed linen, curtain materials and table linen, for the making of women's and girl's dresses, and in the form of khaki cloth for jackets and trousers (incl. shorts) for men and boys.
The output of yarn and fabrics increased substantially in 1966 (as against the previous year), and this trend probably continued in 1967. For example, the output of yarn and fabrics rose from 16.0 mill. lbs and 47.6 mill. square yards in 1965 to 25.9 mill. lbs and 78.1 mill. square yards in 1966. In consequence of the quantitative import restrictions introduced by Tanzania in the second half of 1967, the output planned for 1967 (38.4 mill. lbs of yarn and 108.7 mill. square yards of fabric) was probably not attained (v. Tables 1 and 2).
Synthetic-fibre fabrics, comprising almost exclusively rayon fabrics, accounted for about 20% of East Africa's total fabric output. However,

Table 1. *The Fabric Output of the East African Textile Industry (excl. the Blanket Industry)*
(in 1,000 square yards)

Type of fabric	Country	1965	1966	1967
Cotton fabrics	Kenya	–	3,000	12,250
	Uganda	31,700	50,000	59,200
	Tanzania	6,500	10,500	14,750
	Total	38,200	63,500	86,200
Rayon fabrics	Kenya	4,200	6,000	10,300
	Uganda	–	2,500	3,750
	Tanzania	5,245	6,050	8,500
	Total	9,445	14,550	22,550
All fabrics	Kenya	4,200	9,000	22,550
	Uganda	31,700	52,500	62,950
	Tanzania	11,745	16,550	23,250
	Total	47,645	78,050	108,750

Note: The data for 1967 are businessmen's forecasts.
Source: Own survey.

Table 2. *The Yarn Output of the East African Textile Industry (excl. the Blanket Industry)*
(in 1,000 lbs)

Type of yarn	Country	1965	1966	1967
Cotton yarn	Kenya	600	2,000	6,400
	Uganda	12,180	18,900	22,500
	Tanzania	–	600	3,360
	Total	12,780	21,500	32,260
Rayon yarn	Kenya	3,200	4,400	5,930
	Uganda	–	–	–
	Tanzania	–	–	170
	Total	3,200	4,400	6,100
All yarns	Kenya	3,800	6,400	12,330
	Uganda	12,180	18,900	22,500
	Tanzania	–	600	3,530
	Total	15,980	25,900	38,360

Note: The data for 1967 are businessmen's forecasts.
Source: Own survey.

this ratio varies greatly in the individual countries: while the production of synthetic-fibre fabrics in Uganda is insignificant, in Tanzania and above all in Kenya, which as maritime countries offer favourable location conditions for the processing of imported rayon yarns, it is of great importance.
The blankets, which are made chiefly of shoddy wool and cotton linters, are for the most part of poor quality. Their ex-factory price ranges from 6 to 35 E.A. shs and averages 9 E.A. shs. Like the rest of the textile industry, the East African blanket industry is currently passing through a phase of vigorous growth. Output rose from 2.8 mill. blankets in 1965 to 4.8 mill. in 1966. The 1967 output probably lay substantially below the target of 6.8 mill. blankets set for that year, because — as in the case of cotton and rayon fabrics — interterritorial trade was considerably disturbed and the sales prospects of the blanket industry — this is especially true of the blanket factories in Kenya — were estimated far too optimistically (v. Table 3).

Table 3. *The Output of the Blanket Industry*

Product	1965	1966	1967
Blankets (1,000 units)	2,795	4,823	6,820
Yarn (1,000 lbs)	1,000	1,000	11,250

Note: The data for 1967 are businessmen's forecasts.
Source: Own survey.

With the exception of a single enterprise, up to the end of 1966 the East African blanket factories did not operate spinning mills, but only weaving mills. Accordingly the yarn output of roughly 1 mill. lbs in both 1965 and 1966 — this quantity is sufficient to make about 0.3 mill. blankets — was extremely low. Not until 1967 was the spinning mill in Nakuru (Kenya), which has been in existence for some time, substantially extended and a spinning mill opened in Kampala (Uganda). As a result, yarn output rose considerably in 1967. The plans provided for an output of about 10 mill. lbs, a quantity equivalent to roughly half of the yarn consumed by the East African weaving mills.
The blanket industry, too, which cannot stand up to the competition from Japan, India, and Italy on the export markets, has to rely exclusively on the East African market. But whereas blanket manufacture has already nearly reached the limit set by the consumption capacity of the domestic market, yarn production has good growth chances up to the complete vertical integration of the blanket factories. Hence the future development of the blanket industry will be characterized less by horizontal than by vertical expansion of production.

2. Business Size Structure

At the beginning of 1967, the East African Textile Industry employed a labour force (incl. the blanket industry) of approx. 10,500. Of this number 3,400 were employed by the biggest textile enterprise in East Africa, the Nyanza Textile Industries Ltd. in Jinja, Uganda. In the great majority of textile plants the labour force numbered less than 500, the largest number being in the 200 to 500 employee category, which included 10 enterprises. The small-firm category (less than 200 employees) was chiefly made up of blanket factories which had gone into production only a short time previously and had therefore not yet reached their final work force figures.
Business size structure will shift in the coming years in favour of the larger firms. Some plants that were opened only recently are still in the "running-in" phase, and in addition several enterprises intend to expand their businesses considerably. In addition, the textile factories now under construction or being planned are mainly large plants.

3. The Degree of Integration

As already mentioned, weaving mills (incl. blanket factories) with a licensed production capacity in excess of 3 mill. square yards — roughly equivalent to 1 mill. blankets — are obliged to have their own affiliated spinning mill. Among the weaving mills existing in East Africa at the beginning of 1967, there were 12 affected by this requirement. Of those 12 mills 9 already possessed their own spinning mills, which covered part or all of the weaving mills' yarn requirements. Of course, domestic yarn production has already attained greater importance than these figures seem to indicate, for thanks to their own spinning mills the big East African textile enterprises are already completely independent of yarn purchases.
The non-integrated textile firms at the beginning of 1967 comprised chiefly small rayon weaving mills and most of the blanket weaving mills. While the blanket weaving mills covered their yarn requirements almost without exception with foreign yarns, the rayon weaving mills also purchased notable quantities of domestic yarns. This was possible because some spinning mills produced more yarn than was needed in their affiliated weaving mills and knitwear factories. However, these inter-company flows of yarn are not very voluminous as yet, and also in future they will not attain any great importance as a result of the required vertical integration and the ever greater importance assigned to medium and large textile enterprises.
At the beginning of 1967, there was still only one textile plant in East Africa with its own fabric printing department. The great popularity of colourfully

printed materials among the African, and especially the rural, population induced the textile industry to pay more attention to fabric printing. For example, at the beginning of 1967, two to three firms were intending to set up fabric printing departments. An argument often used to oppose the large investments involved is that the African population's demand for printed fabrics embraces an extremely broad spectrum (as regards patterns and colours) and therefore, with the still limited aggregate demand, the individual articles account for only very small quantities which make profitable manufacture dubious. This broad spectrum of demand, however, is not an invariable factor. If a number of patterns are produced at home and at the same time imported patterns are subjected to high duties, it is to be expected that the demand will be directed to an increased degree to the few domestically produced patterns. In this way the attainable sales of the various patterns would be increased to such an extent that profitable production becomes possible.
As yet the textile industry is only loosely associated with the garments industry[5]. It is true that knitwear and hosiery factories are already purchasing a notable proportion of the necessary yarns, particularly rayon yarns, from domestic spinning mills, but the rest of the garments industry (predominantly shirt manufacture) uses foreign materials almost exclusively. This is because the coarse fabrics offered by the East African weaving mills are not suitable for shirt-making. Not until early 1967 did some of the weaving mills reluctantly extend their production programme to fine poplin shirting, with the result that, in so far as domestic products can compete with imports as far as quality and price are concerned, the East African garments industry will rely more on domestic fabrics in the future. Consequently the degree of integration of the textile and garments industries will increase.

4. The Applied Production Techniques

In planning the production programme, the investor has a choice of production techniques which are the results of current engineering know-how. From among these production techniques, each of which has a characteristic cost function, the entrepreneur interested in profit maximization chooses the one involving the lowest aggregate cost for the production of the desired quantity of products (optimal production technique).
The combination of labour and capital, gauged by the capital input per work station, depends (for a given output quantity) decisively on the ratio of the factor prices. The low wages of local labour, the scarcity of capital and the high prices for capital goods (heavy burden of transport costs)

5 In this study knitwear and hosiery factories are included in the garments industry.

permit the conclusion that very labour-intensive production techniques can be expected in East Africa. Is this a valid assumption?

Labour-intensive production techniques in the East African textile industry are found only in the small rayon weaving mills and occasionally also in the medium-size cotton weaving mills, which use semi-automatic and in rare cases also non-automatic looms. In the big weaving mills, however, modern and hence capital-intensive production techniques dominate in the form of fully automatic looms, some of which are housed in air-conditioned rooms. Capital-intensive production techniques are likewise provided for in the case of almost all plants now being planned or under construction.

Hence the arguments put forward at the beginning in respect of the future prove to be largely false, and in respect of the present and the past only partly correct. What is this attributable to? The question arises of whether the assumed premises are unrealistic or whether the investment decisions are influenced by prejudice against technologically outdated production methods.

The wage costs of African enterprises are usually not so low by a long way as the low wages (time-rates) of African workers seem to indicate. Particularly in the case of operations with little mechanization, the productivity of African labour is often very low by European standards. In addition, jobs requiring high technical or clerical proficiency are frequently held by skilled European personnel. The latter not only draw very high wages, but also cause substantial incidental costs such as travelling expenses for the journey from Europe and back, rent allowances, etc.

The lack of capital from which developing countries usually suffer frequently does not find expression in high factor prices (interest) for industrial enterprises. Not infrequently, branches of industry deemed worthy of support receive low-interest credits from public authorities or within the framework of development aid from abroad. Interest for such credits is often considerably lower than the interest which has to be paid by an industrial firm in highly developed countries. The East African textile industry, too, has received a notable volume of low-interest credits, which has undoubtedly reduced the tendency to select labour-intensive production techniques.

Furthermore, firms to which the investment promotion act is applicable can write off up to 120 per cent of the purchase value of new capital goods (machinery and mechanical equipment). This cheapening of the factor of production "capital" as compared with the factor of production "labour" similarly favours capital-intensive production methods.

Finally, the tendency towards capital-intensive production techniques is increased by prejudices and extra-economic causes. Without having made any calculations, many entrepreneurs are convinced that modern production techniques such as are found in America or Europe are the most profitable in developing countries, too. Not infrequently they also choose the capital-

intensive production methods out of a desire to avoid too much dependence on the unions, some of which are quite radical, and that dependence naturally increases with the number of employees.
The reason given for labour-intensive production techniques used in some places is the lack of firm-owned capital. As compared with the planned production capacity, the affected investors had only limited funds of their own and were not prepared or felt they were not in a position to broaden their financing basis with borrowed or equity capital.
Quite apart from the high foreign-exchange expenditures, precisely the small employment effect of capital-intensive production methods in East Africa must be assessed as macroeconomically very unfavourable. As the result of vigorous population growth and the flight from the land, in all three countries there is a high degree of unemployment, which especially in Kenya is very marked. This could be combatted by the application of more labour-intensive production techniques.
The available possibilities in this respect are very great precisely in the textile industry. It is currently one of the foremost growth industries in East Africa and, furthermore, the number of jobs created in this branch of industry depends to a particularly great extent on the selected production technique. For example, an African worker can operate only about four semi-automatic looms, but can tend up to 20 fully automatic looms.

5. The Question of Second-Hand Machinery

At a symposium on industrialization problems in Africa held in spring 1966 in Cairo by the UN Economic Commission for Africa (ECA), Addis Abeba, the use of second-hand machinery in African developing countries, a theme which is also of special concern to the East African textile industry, was thoroughly discussed. The result of these discussions was that — apart from a few exceptions — experience hitherto makes more extensive use of second-hand machinery in Africa seem inadvisable. "A United Nations expert (Centre for Industrial Development) stated that the conclusions arrived at in a study made by the centre were that in the case of certain types of machines, use of second-hand machinery could be recommended. It was, however, felt that it would be not advisable to encourage in Africa the use of second-hand machines, but in view of the conclusions in the United Nations report referred to, it was suggested that ECA might examine the question further." [6]
In the blanket factories and small rayon weaving mills in East Africa, many of which have only limited funds of their own, second-hand machinery is

6 ECA (UN Economic Commission for Africa): *Report of the Symposium on Industrial Development in Africa.* Addis Ababa, 1966, p. 45.

found frequently, but in the medium and especially the big cotton spinning and weaving mills very rarely. Not infrequently European textile firms which replace old looms and spindles with new ones in the course of rationalization enter into a financial engagement in developing countries with the object of disposing of equipment which has been made redundant in this way and is difficult to sell in Europe, and obtaining relatively good prices. So also in the case of the East African textile plants many of the second-hand machines which are in use come from such sources, foreign enterprises having granted long-term credits to African firms or acquired an interest in them in exchange for the contribution of second-hand equipment to the new factory

According to most of the entrepreneurs, second-hand machines cause high maintenance costs and great difficulties in spare-part procurement. Moreover, the use in East Africa of second-hand looms which were previously subjected to different climatic conditions involves a high and incalculable risk. Furthermore, the favourable depreciation allowances which the investment promotion act permits for new capital goods cannot be taken advantage of for second-hand machinery. It is generally asserted that these disadvantages outweigh the low write-offs and low interest as far as costs are concerned. This opinion is usually shared also by entrepreneurs who use second-hand machines; as justification for their decision they cite insufficient funds of their own, etc.

In addition, capital goods brought to East Africa from America or Europe are burdened by high transport costs, which are roughly identical for new and second-hand machines. Owing to the long transport distance, the advantage of second-hand machinery, namely the low procurement price, loses its relative importance, so that in developing countries which are a long distance from industrial countries the use of second-hand machinery would no longer seem to be lucrative.

If the difficulties that are mostly involved in the procurement of spare parts could be reduced by better management precautions and the discrimination of second-hand machines under the investment promotion act was given up, the use of second-hand machinery could presumably be made more advantageous again in many places, also from the management standpoint. This would also result in very significant macroeconomic benefits: the demand for foreign exchange triggered by investments would decline, and since the use of second-hand machinery usually also entails labour-intensive production techniques a greater number of jobs would be created.

III. Raw Material Consumption

Although a very large proportion of the East African textile industry is vertically integrated, the raw material consumption of the weaving mills (yarns) and spinning mills (staple fibres) will be presented separately. Apart from the amount and structure of consumption, interest in this connection attaches above all to the question of whether it is macroeconomically expedient to compel East African spinning mills to process local cotton.

1. Yarn Consumption of the Weaving Mills

As a result of the rapid growth of fabric production, East Africa's yarn consumption has increased substantially. It rose from 17.4 mill. lbs in 1965 to 28.4 mill. lbs in 1966. The mills processed predominantly cotton yarns and in addition, though to a much smaller extent, rayon yarns. The importance of other synthetic yarns such as nylon, polyester yarns etc., is so slight that they can be neglected. In 1965 and 1966, cotton yarns accounted for a bare 85 per cent of total yarn consumption (see Table 4).

Table 4. *The Yarn Consumption of the East African Textile Industry (excl. the Blanket Industry)*
(in 1,000 lbs)

Type of Yarn	Source	1965	1966	1967
Cotton yarns	Local	12,180	20,700	30,690
	Foreign	2,170	2,900	1,790
	Total	14,350	23,600	32,480
Rayon yarns	Local	970	1,160	3,200
	Foreign	2,110	3,640	3,940
	Total	3,080	4,800	7,140
Cotton and rayon yarns	Local	13,150	21,860	33,890
	Foreign	4,280	6,540	5,730
	Total	17,430	28,400	39,620

Note: The data for 1967 are businessmen's estimates. "Foreign" includes all countries outside East Africa.

Source: Own survey.

The yarn consumption of the blanket weaving mills was also stepped up considerably, namely from 7.7 mill. lbs in 1965 to 13.7 mill. lbs in 1966. By far the largest proportion of the yarns processed was imported from Japan and Italy.

Despite the increasing blanket output, yarn imports in 1967 probably declined because — as already indicated in the foregoing — in that year one firm opened a spinning mill and another added a substantial extension to its already existing spinning mill (v. Table 5).

Table 5. *The Yarn Consumption of the East African Blanket Industry* (in 1,000 lbs)

Source of Yarn	1965	1966	1967
Foreign	6,690	12,700	10,060
Local	1,000	1,000	1,190
Total	7,690	13,700	11,250

Note: The data for 1967 are businessmen's estimates. "Foreign" includes all countries outside East Africa.

Source: Own survey.

2. Fibre Consumption of the Spinning Mills

Owing to the waste that occurs during spinning, the fibre consumption of the spinning mills is 5 to 10 per cent higher than the yarn output. In 1965 it was 17.1 mill. lbs and in 1966 27.4 mill. lbs. The great majority of the fibres processed was cotton produced by domestic growers. As there is still no synthetic fibre industry in East Africa — and there will be no change in this situation in the coming years — the rayon staple fibres were imported from abroad, almost exclusively from Japan.
In comparison, the fibre consumption of the East African blanket industry, amounting to 1.1 mill. lbs in both 1965 and 1966, was extremely low, which is due to the fact that — as already mentioned — at the end of 1966 there was still only one blanket weaving mill with its own integrated spinning mill. In 1967 this situation had changed considerably in so far as the investment plans and resulting production plans of the blanket industry had successfully been put into effect. It can be expected, therefore, that in 1967 yarn output increased perceptibly and fibre consumption rose to a good 10 mill. lbs.

3. Processing of Domestic Cotton

The most prolific cotton growing areas in East Africa lie on the southern banks of Lake Victoria in Tanzania and in the eastern part of Uganda. In 1966 the two countries each contributed about half of the total East African cotton crop, which amounted to roughly 165,000 tons. By 1971 the cotton crop is to be stepped up to 224,000 tons, primarily by means of intensive pest control, better fertilization, and the introduction of varieties giving a higher yield. The quality of East African sorts of cotton (S 47, BP 52, UK 51, and SATU) corresponds to the world average and in part is even better. The staple length ranges from 1 2/32 to 1 6/32 inches and permits yarn counts of up to 35 and 60 (British system) respectively. The latter is still quite suitable for making fine poplin shirting.

As in nearly all developing countries, in East Africa, too, the governing principle is that as far as possible home industry should process domestic raw materials. So as far as the East African textile industry is based on cotton, it is compelled to resort to East African cotton, as it is refused licences to import cotton from third countries.

However, at this stage the domestic textile industry still takes only a very small proportion of the cotton produced in East Africa, which after coffee and sisal is East Africa's most important export. The domestic industry processed 10,100 tons, i.e., only about 6 per cent of the local cotton, in 1966. By 1970, however, its rising consumption will increase this proportion to about 10 per cent despite the concomitant rapid growth of cotton output.

The requirement of processing domestic cotton is often opposed with the argument that East African cotton is of too high quality for the needs of the local spinning mills and hence too expensive. The conclusion is then drawn that it would be better to export all East African cotton and give the domestic textile industry the opportunity to procure cotton of suitable quality from abroad. In this way it would be possible not only to cut the spinning mills' raw material costs, but also to save foreign exchange, since the additional foreign exchange earnings from the export of cotton would exceed the additional foreign exchange expenditures for cotton imports.

Undoubtedly, for making the coarse yarns with yarn counts between 12 and 20 (British system) which are predominantly produced in East Africa, middling cotton from Pakistan or Brazil would also be suitable. This sort of cotton costs (c.i.f. East African seaport) about 6 per cent less than local cotton ex ginning plant. Although the processing of short-staple imported cotton would involve more waste and for some spinning mills also higher transport costs (from seaport to spinning mill), the East African textile industry could cut raw material costs perceptibly, if it changed over from domestic to foreign cotton. This advantage would be greatest at the coast and would diminish as the spinning mill's distance from the coast increases. Hence the location conditions of places near the coast would improve, giving rise to a tendency to transfer the textile industry more towards the coast in future. However, this is not intended by any means to indicate that Uganda's textile factories situated far from the coast could not also extract noteworthy benefits from the use of foreign cotton.

The foregoing arguments still have said nothing about whether the use of

foreign cotton would also be justified from the macro-economic angle. In the final analysis, the answer to this question depends on the possibility of exporting East African cotton. The world market supply of medium-long cotton, which comes mainly from the USA, is a multiple of the East African output. Consequently the slight increase in East African exports by the quantity currently consumed by the domestic textile industry would have no perceptible effect on the world market price.
Hence domestic cotton growing would not be adversely affected in any way[7]. One aspect that should be assessed as beneficial is that on balance East Africa's foreign exchange receipts would rise slightly. The changing over of the textile industry from domestic to foreign cotton can therefore be recommended from both the microeconomic and the macroeconomic standpoint.

IV. Financing

1. Sources of Finance

An important contribution to the financing of the East African textile industry is made by the public authorities. The most important financing institutions that should be mentioned are the three government development corporations (Uganda Development Corporation in Uganda, Industrial and Commercial Development Corporation in Kenya, and National Development Corporation in Tanzania) and the three semi-public finance companies (Development Finance Company of Uganda, Development Finance Company of Kenya, and Tanganyika Development Finance Company). For the financing decisions of the government development corporations, macroeconomic considerations dominate, while for those of the semi-public finance companies[8], microeconomic principles (great security of investments, high dividends for participations, and fair market interest on credits) are of primary importance.
Up to the beginning of 1967, these financing institutions had provided the textile industry with roughly £5.4 mill. in the form of equity capital and long-term credits. The most important projects were the spinning mill and weaving mill of Nyanza Textile Industries Ltd. in Uganda and the Friendship Textile Mills Ltd. in Tanzania. Especially the government development corporations will continue in future to be an important source of capital for

7 See also below, p. 59 et seq.

8 Equal interests in these companies are held (£0.5 mill. each) by the respective country, the German Development Corporation, the British Commonwealth Development Corporation, and the Netherlands Overseas Finance Company.

the textile industry. In Kenya and particularly in Tanzania several fairly large projects were under consideration.
A very large proportion of the funds made available by the government and semi-public financing institutions comes in the final analysis from foreign development aid (capital aid). In addition, private foreign investors have formed an important source of capital for the East African textile industry. For this remarkable inflow of capital, particularly from Japan, India, Italy, the Federal Republic of Germany, and recently also France, there are probably two main reasons:

- Since East Africa is building up ever stronger barriers to imports, former suppliers can retain their markets only by investments in East Africa itself.
- Particularly the European textile industry is interested in disposing of superfluous second-hand machines abroad on account of its overcapacity, which in some instances is extensive. Not always, but in most cases this also demands financial engagement.

Despite the weight of government and semi-public financing institutions and of foreign private capital sources, domestic private capital is also of considerable importance. These funds are raised primarily by the Indian minority resident in East Africa, which can be regarded as the only reservoir of private capital that is of any real significance. The Indian minority, which was formerly engaged almost exclusively in trade (import trade and wholesale and retail business), has recently been turning its attention to an increasing extent to the industrial sphere, in which connection the accumulated profits from many years of business activities form the basis for industrial investments. The private East African entrepreneur finds his way to industry as a general rule via commerce, while in Europe a different route was taken, that is, the crafts and their more advanced form, the manufactories, formed the nucleus of industrial development to a great extent.
The greater interest of the Indian minority in industry is not solely due to the chances of profit it offers, but is also a consequence of political pressure. In Tanzania, for example, the Indians were forced out of some branches of commerce by semi-public trading companies. But even where there was no such intervention, the trading activities of the Indian minority are becoming more and more the target of African politicians' criticism. They regard such activities as exploitation of the African population and are convinced that commerce can largely be taken over by the latter. In the industrial field, on the other hand, the East African countries have to rely to a high degree on the entrepreurial initiative of the Indian minority, for which reason their activity in this sphere meets with no criticism.

2. Capital Requirements

In the industrial countries, the capital input per employee in the textile industry has to a large extent increased in recent years so much that this sector has become one of the most capital-intensive industries. According to an OECD survey[9], it is surpassed only by the iron and steel industry, the petrochemical and the chemical industry (including the synthetic fibres industry).

This development favoured the view, which was partly inspired by self-interest, that the industrialization process in developing countries should not be initiated with the textile industry, since with the capital employed only relatively few jobs could be created. This argument is tacitly based on the idea that in the developing countries, too, the textile industry must be operated on a highly capital-intensive basis, and that thanks to other industrialization chances the building up of a textile industry could be waived for the time being.

As the industrial products of the East African countries cannot in many instances compete on the world market with the industrial products of the developed countries, there is no question of building up export goods industries of any notable extent. The industrialization possibilities of East Africa are therefore practically limited to industries for which the home market ensures adequate sales. However, the low consumption capacity of that market means that the industrialization possibilities are very limited. In view of this situation, it will prove a necessity for East Africa to take advantage of every chance that presents itself and develop an extensive textile industry.

The capital intensity of the East African textile industry is probably higher than might first be expected in the light of the low wage level for African labour, but is substantially lower than the level in the modern textile industry of America or Europe, and also lies below the average of the other industries established in East Africa. For a textile plant comprising a spinning mill, weaving mill, and finishing department (bleaching and dyeing plant), the historical cost of fixed assets per job averaged 26,000 E.A. shs and per output capacity of 1,000 square yards of fabric annually 2,100 E.A. shs.

Different production techniques, the varying importance of second-hand machinery, and the different procurement dates of the machines result in the capital input of the individual plants deviating in some cases considerably, i.e. up to 25 per cent above and below the average. In the coming years the average capital input will increase, because the planned plants will use capital-intensive production techniques and new machines to an even greater extent than the existing ones, and because in some cases more extensive finishing of the materials (fabric printing) is intended.

9 OECD: *Modern Cotton Industry, A Capital-Intensive Industry.* Paris 1966, p. 95.

D. THE GROWTH OF THE EAST AFRICAN TEXTILE INDUSTRY

I. Growth Chances

The growth chances of the East African textile industry, which will hardly open up any export opportunities in the forseeable future, are governed exclusively by endogenous growth forces, that is, by the increase of the population and the rise in per capita income. So in the long run the textile industry can grow only as rapidly as domestic consumption. Over the short and medium term, however, substitution for imports permits a substantially higher growth rate.

1. Fabric Consumption in 1965

The fabric consumption in 1965 was determined — separately for the three East African countries — with the aid of the foreign trade statistics and of the poll of firms carried out by the author. Since the interterritorial trade (trade among the three East African countries) cannot be covered by the statistics as accurately as the trade of the East African countries with third countries, the consumption figures for East Africa as a whole are presumably more reliable than the consumption figures for the individual countries.

Table 6. *East African Fabric Consumption in 1965*
(in 1,000 square yards)

	Kenya		Uganda		Tanzania		East Africa	
	C	S	C	S	C	S	C	S
Import surplus in trade with third countries	38,365	31,303	34,413	24,497	54,239	16,063	127,017	71,863
Import surplus in interterritorial trade	4,898	–8,251	–12,653	5,478	7,755	2,773	–	–
Output	–	4,200	31,700	–	6,500	5,245	38,200	9,445
Consumption	43,263	27,252	53,460	29,975	68,494	24,081	165,217	81,308

Symbols: C = Cotton fabrics
S = Synthetic fabrics

Source: EACSO: Annual Trade Report 1965. Mombasa, 1966.
Own surveys (v. Table 1).
Own estimates.

In 1965, 246.5 mill. square yards of fabric (excl. blankets) were consumed in East Africa. Of this quantity, 165.2 mill. square yards were cotton fabrics and 81.3 mill. square yards synthetic fabrics (chiefly rayon fabrics). Tanzania, the biggest of the three East African countries, took 92.6 mill. square yards, Uganda 83.4 mill. square yards, and Kenya 70.5 mill. square yards of the total East African consumption.

The annual per capita fabric consumption of the population which in 1965 was 11.0 in Uganda, 9.1 in Tanzania, and 7.5 square yards in Kenya, shows marked regional differences. These differences cannot be explained by regional differences in per capita income — in Uganda the per capita income is only slightly higher than in Kenya, while it is by far the lowest in Tanzania — or by regional differences in climatic conditions or the degree of urbanization. On the contrary, the decisive factor is probably the clothing habits, which to some extent are still rooted in African traditions and vary quite a lot from region to region (v. Table 7).

Table 7. *Per Capita Fabric Consumption of the Population of the East African Countries in 1965*

Country	Fabric consumption (in 1,000 sq. yards)	Population (in 1,000 persons)	Per capita consumption (in sq. yards)
Kenya	70,515	9,400	7.50
Uganda	83,435	7,600	10.98
Tanzania	92,575	10,200	9.08
East Africa	246,525	27,200	9.06

Source: See Table 6.

Compared with West African countries, East Africa's average per capita consumption of 9.0 square yards per annum is very low. According to ECA estimates[10], in 1964 per capita consumption on the Ivory Coast was 51.6, in Gambia 35.5, in Senegal 35.1, in Liberia 29.8, in Ghana 25.5, and in Sierra Leone 24.1 square yards. With the exception of Nigeria (9.7 square yards) and Dahomey (8.7 square yards), the per capita consumption of the other West African countries also lies substantially above that of East Africa. To a great extent these differences are also probably due to regional variations in clothing habits. In any case, per capita income differences can be eliminated as a reason, for in West Africa the per capita income is not substantially higher than in East Africa.

In 1965, blanket consumption in East Africa was 5.9 mill. The high annual consumption in Kenya and Uganda (0.29 and 0.24 respectively) as com-

10 ECA (UN Economic Commission for Africa): *The Textile Situation in West Africa: Markets – Industries – Prospects.* Addis Ababa 1966, p. 88.

pared with Tanzania (0.14) is probably mainly due to the fact that in these two countries a relatively large proportion of the population lives in the highlands and are therefore exposed to cool nights (v. Tables 8 and 9).

Table 8. *East African Blanket Consumption in 1965*
(in 1,000 blankets)

	Kenya	Uganda	Tanzania	East Africa
Imports from third countries	1,253	1,093	801	3,147
Exports to third countries	14	–	4	18
Import surplus in interterritorial trade	–34	598	–564	–
Output	1,500	95	1,200	2,795
Consumption	2,705	1,786	1,433	5,924

Source: EACSO: Annual Trade Report 1965, Mombasa 1966.
Own surveys.

Table 9. *Per Capita Blanket Consumption of the Population of the East African Countries in 1965*

Country	Total Consumption (in 1,000)	Population (in 1,000)	Per capita consumption (in units)
Kenya	2,705	9,400	0.29
Uganda	1,786	7,600	0.24
Tanzania	1,433	10,200	0.14
East Africa	5,924	27,200	0.22

Source: See Table 8.

2. The Growth of Consumption

The forces governing the growth of fabric consumption are population growth and the increase in per capita income. For estimating future fabric consumption it is assumed that, ceteris paribus, fabric consumption will increase proportionally with the population, and that the growth of per capita consumption will lag behind the growth of per capita income. The value of the income elasticity of the demand for fabrics, which is a constant factor linking the development of per capita consumption with the development of per capita income, is therefore less than 1.

Population growth can be reliably predicted for the relatively short period from 1965 to 1970. On the other hand, difficulties are encountered in forecasting the growth of per capita income and, above all, in determining the income elasticity of demand. The information obtainable for advance estimation of these magnitudes is so meagre and incomplete that the coefficients selected for East Africa can be regarded only as rough approximations.

a) Population Growth

Very different population growth rates are expected for the three East African countries. The national development plans are based on a growth rate of 3 per cent for Kenya, 2.5 per cent for Uganda, and 2.2 per cent for Tanzania. This is equivalent to a weighted average of 2.5 per cent for East Africa. Hence the population will increase in Kenya from 9.4 to 10.9 mill., in Uganda from 7.6 to 8.5 mill., and in Tanzania from 10.2 to 11.4 mill. (see Table 10).

Table 10. *Population Growth in East Africa from 1965 to 1970*
(in 1,000 inhabitants)

Country	1965	1966	1967	1968	1969	1970	Growth rate in %
Kenya	9,400	9,700	10,000	10,300	10,600	10,900	*3.0*
Uganda	7,600	7,700	7,900	8,100	8,300	8,500	*2.5*
Tanzania	10,200	10,400	10,600	10,900	11,100	11,400	*2.2*
East Africa	27,200	27,800	28,500	29,300	30,000	30,800	*2.5*

Source: 1. Kenya, Development Plan 1966–1970, Nairobi 1966.
2. Uganda, Uganda's Second Five-Year Plan 1966–1971, Entebbe 1966.
3. Tanzania, Tanganyika Five-Year Plan 1964–1969, Dar es Salaam 1964.

b) Growth of the Real Per Capita Income

The income of an African household is made up of money income and income in kind, the latter sometimes being quite substantial. Provided that a household does not dissolve earlier savings and does not take up credits, household spending for the purchase of goods will be limited solely by the amount of the money income. However, it cannot be concluded from this that a change in income in kind could not influence expenditures for the purchase of textiles.

If there is no saving — which is a quite realistic assumption for peasant households in Africa — consumption expenditures necessarily equal the total money income. Under these circumstances a change in the income in kind may affect not the amount, but the structure of expenditures, and in this way also affect the sale of textiles. For example, increased food purchases made necessary by a reduction of the income in kind can be offset only by reduced expenditures for the purchase of other consumer goods.

However, these effects, the extent of which is very difficult to determine, should be so insignificant that the per capita fabric consumption can be made dependent solely on the money and real per capita income. For statistical reasons the monetary gross per capita domestic product at constant prices must be used as an indicator for this variable. Although not necessarily the case, there is usually a close connection between these two magnitudes, so this procedure would seem to be justified.

In the event that the objectives set in the national development plans can be attained, the monetary gross per capita domestic product at constant prices will grow between 1965 and 1970 by annual 3.9 per cent in Kenya, 3.7 per cent in Uganda, and 6.0 per cent in Tanzania. The weighted average for East Africa will reach a figure of 4.6 per cent. It has repeatedly proved, however, that the sights of the development plans of the African countries have been set too high. So it is possible that in East Africa, too, actual economic development will lag behind the planned or expected development. But this discrepancy should not be very great, as the development plans concerned have been conceived throughout very cautiously and realistically (v. Tables 11 and 12).

Table 11. *The Growth of the Monetary Gross Domestic Product at Constant Prices* (in mill. £)

Country	1965	1970	Average growth rate in %
Kenya	227.9	321.8	*7.1*
Uganda	193.6	259.5	*7.1*
Tanzania	173.1	259.8	*8.5*
East Africa	594.6	841.1	*7.1*

Note: The constant prices on which the gross domestic product is based relate to 1964 and 1965.

Source: 1. Kenya, Development Plan 1966–1970, Nairobi 1966.
2. Uganda, Uganda's Second Five-Year Plan 1966–1971, Entebbe 1966.
3. Tanzania, Tanganyika Five-Year Plan 1964–1969, Dar es Salaam 1964.

Table 12. *The Growth of Real (Monetary) Per Capita Income* (in £)

Country	1965	1970	Average growth rate in %
Kenya	24.3	29.5	*3.9*
Uganda	25.4	30.5	*3.7*
Tanzania	17.0	22.8	*6.0*
East Africa	21.9	27.3	*4.6*

Note: The real monetary per capita income is the quotient of the monetary gross domestic product at constant prices and the population.

Source: See Table 11.

c) The Income Elasticity of Demand

The relation between the growth rates of per capita consumption and per capita income, that is, the income elasticity of demand, depends decisively on the income level. At a low income level the per capita consumption of textiles grows more rapidly and at a high level more slowly than per capita income. Although the East African countries, as compared with those of western Europe, have as yet attained only a very low per capita income, they are already in a phase in which the growth rate of per capita textile consumption lags behind the growth rate of per capita income.

Now, what methods can be considered for the quantitative determination of the income elasticity of demand? A cross-section analysis based on the African countries south of the Sahara can be eliminated from the outset, since only in a few countries are reliable data on textile consumption available. On the other hand, a time-series analysis could be undertaken for the three East African countries, whose textile consumption back to 1953 has been estimated by the East African Common Services Organization. It proved that the growth rate of per capita consumption is largely independent of the growth rate of per capita income. However, in the light of general experience some interdependence between these two magnitudes would appear to be so certain that the result obtained is presumably due to the very faulty initial data and therefore need not be taken into consideration. Hence, as the regression-analysis approach produced no plausible results, the income elasticity of demand can be determined only hypothetically.

The ECA (UN Economic Commission for Africa) points out in a study of the West African textile industry[11] that expenditures for the purchase of textiles grow appreciably more slowly than total consumption spending. A 1 per cent increase in total consumption spending is reportedly accompanied in countries with an annual per capita consumption of up to 15 square yards of fabric by an increase in expenditure on textiles of 0.5 per cent, and in countries with a higher per capita consumption by an increase of only 0.36 per cent. The coefficient of 0.5 taken into consideration for the three East African countries, however, is not identical with the income elasticity of demand for textiles. For on the one hand there is the question of the dependence of textile expenditures on total consumption spending, and on the other that of the dependence of the consumed quantity of fabric on income. Hence this coefficient is not directly applicable to the following projection.

Income elasticity should be less than 0.5 for two reasons: consumption spending grows more slowly than income, and the increase in the quantitative consumption of textiles is less than the expenditures for textiles, since to an

11 ECA (UN Economic Commission for Africa): *The Textile Situation in West Africa: Markets – Industries – Prospects.* Addis Ababa 1965, p. 86 et seq.

ever greater extent better and therefore also more expensive qualities are demanded. If it is assumed that the propensity to consume in East Africa is 0.9 and that the price level for textiles rises about 5 per cent annually on account of improved qualities, the coefficient 0.5 is equivalent to an income elasticity of 0.43. This value is used in the following computations.

3. Fabric Consumption in 1970

Now that the growth of the population and the per capita income and also the income elasticity of demand for textiles are known, we have all the magnitudes required to determine fabric consumption in 1970, taking fabric consumption in 1965 as the point of departure. To this end the following estimator was used[12]:

$$C_{1970} = B_{1965}\,(1 + b)^5 \cdot C^K_{1965}\,(1 + f \cdot e)^5.$$

Using this estimator — the inserted values can be taken from the preceding tables — fabric consumption in 1970 will reach 87.8 mill. square yards in Kenya, 101.1 mill. in Uganda, and 116.3 mill. in Tanzania. Fabric consumption shows a particularly marked increase (in 1970 as against 1965) as a result of the vigorous growth of income in Tanzania (up 26 per cent) and the rapid population growth in Kenya (up 25 per cent). In Uganda, on the other hand, fabric consumption in 1970 will be 21 per cent higher than in 1965 (v. Table 13).

Table 13. *Fabric Consumption of the East African Countries in 1970*

Country	Per capita consumption (in square yards)	Population (in 1,000)	Fabric consumption (in 1,000 sq. yards)
Kenya	8.06	10,900	87,854
Uganda	11.89	8,500	101,065
Tanzania	10.20	11,400	116,280
East Africa	9.91	30,800	305,199

Source: Own computations.

Even in 1970, the home consumption of some types of fabric will still be so low that they cannot be profitably manufactured domestically. In the

12 Symbols:
- C total fabric consumption
- C^K per capita consumption
- B population
- b average population growth rate
- e average growth rate of monetary per capita income at constant prices
- f income elasticity of demand for fabrics.

opinion of the textile firms operating in East Africa, this will probably be true of about 20 per cent of the aggregate fabric consumption of roughly 305 mill. square yards. Hence in 1970 the East African textile industry can reckon with maximum potential sales of 244 mill. square yards.
East Africa's blanket consumption, for which advance estimates were made by the same method as used for the other textile consumption, should amount to approximately 7.5 mill. blankets in 1970. Of this number, Kenya will account for 3.5 mill., Uganda for 2.2 mill., and Tanzania for 1.8 mill. Since blankets are quite homogeneous merchandise in comparison with the other fabrics, roughly 90 per cent of the total consumption, or 6.7 mill. blankets, should be suitable for manufacture in East Africa (v. Table 14).

Table 14. *Blanket Consumption of the East African Countries in 1970*

Country	Per capita consumption (in units)	Population (in 1,000)	Blanket consumption (in 1,000 units)
Kenya	0.32	10,900	3,436
Uganda	0.26	8,500	2,207
Tanzania	0.16	11,400	1,813
East Africa	0.24	30,800	7,456

Source: Own computations.

4. Export Chances

The fabric and blanket exports of the East African textile industry to third countries were extremely low in 1965 and also in the ensuing years. This alone, however, does not prove that East African products cannot compete on the world market, for possibly exports have hitherto been neglected owing to the very favourable sales opportunities on the home market.
It is a fact, however — as repeatedly emphasized — that the East African textile industry is protected from imports by high duties and incisive quantitative import restrictions. This protection has proved absolutely necessary for its existence and continued growth, since according to several entrepreneurs the cost price of East African products not infrequently exceeds the c.i.f. price of comparable imported goods by up to 25 per cent. From this it should be clear that, apart from exchange of goods among the partner countries, the East African textile industry has no export chances.
Undoubtedly the East African textile industry, which as yet can look back over only a brief history, still has vast scope for rationalization investments and its competitiveness will doubtless improve in the coming years, but its

inferiority especially to Asian competitors is currently still so serious that no notable export successes can be expected in the forseeable future.
Limited export opportunities might open up only if several African countries formed a customs union, as proposed at the Lusaka conference (1965). The efforts made in this direction, which at the time met with general approval, have so far, however, not led to any tangible results. The difficulties recently encountered by the Common East African Market, which has already been in existence for years, also do not hold out any promise of rapid and decisive success. So it is certainly realistic for the East African textile industry to preclude the possibility of any notable exports to third countries during the coming years, especially since there can be no question of subsidizing exports at the present time.

II. Planned Expansion

According to the foregoing computations, in 1970 the East African textile industry has chances of selling 244 mill. square yards of fabric and 6.7 mill. blankets. Can these requirements by covered by domestic products as early as 1970? This depends not only on the existing production capacities, but also on the planned extensions.

1. Planned Production Capacity of the Textile Industry (excl. the Blanket Industry)

In so far as the extension plans of the textile industry are put into effect, which is to be expected, in 1970 it will have a production capacity of roughly 171 mill. square yards of fabric. Consequently the domestic consumption of 244 mill. square yards — reference is made here and in the following, not to total domestic consumption, but only to that portion thereof which can be covered by the home industry — will still be substantially higher. It follows from this that the production facilities available in 1970 will be able to operate at full capacity, and that even after 1970 the textile industry can still expand considerably. In this connection we have assumed for the time being that fabrics produced in East Africa can be traded unhindered among the three partner countries. But how would the situation have to be assessed if the Common East African Market were to be dissolved into three separate national sub-markets?
Since the production capacity planned for 1970 does not exceed the consumption capacity of the home market in any of the three East African countries, the textile industries of the individual countries can attain their planned objectives even if they have to depend exclusively on the national

markets. Of course, this would require that in each country the structure of production be adapted to the structure of demand.
This would compel particularly Uganda's textile industry, which in contrast to the textile industries of Kenya and Tanzania exports a substantial part of its output to the partner countries, to carry out incisive conversion measures, which would naturally also involve a certain amount of loss. Uganda's textile industry has been in difficulties of this nature since mid-1967. In the latter half of 1967, Tanzania drastically cut down fabric imports from Uganda with the aid of quantitative import restrictions, and since the end of 1967 has imposed transfer duties on them. The consequence of this hampering of interterritorial trade was that Uganda's textile industry could no longer operate its production facilities at full capacity and even had to work short time temporarily. Over the medium term, however, these consequences can be overcome, since Uganda's home consumption is still higher than the domestically available production capacities and the production programme of Uganda's textile industry can be adapted to the changed sales situation. This may possibly make it necessary for Uganda's government to impose heavier restrictions on imports from third countries.
Under the hypothetical assumption that the only outlet channels open to the textile industries of the East African countries are the national markets, the growth chances after 1970 vary greatly. In 1970, fabric output will probably reach 38 per cent of home consumption in Kenya, as much as 77 per cent in Tanzania, and the even higher figure of 89 per cent in Uganda. After 1970, therefore, Uganda's textile industry will be able to expand essentially only in pace with the growth of home consumption. On the other hand, the growth possibilities of Tanzania's textile industry will be more favourable, and those of Kenya's textile industry will be especially favourable.
The licenses issued by EACSO by mid-1967 for almost 300 mill. square yards of fabric annually will probably not be utilized to the full until 1973, if experience so far can be relied on. Since that portion of domestic consumption, which can be covered by local production, will probably have increased meanwhile to about 280 to 290 mill. square yards per annum, the licensed production capacity remains just within the limits of domestic consumption. However, if the generous licensing policy — a result of EACSO's too optimistic consumption estimates — is continued, there is a risk that over-capacities may be created in the East African textile industry.

2. Planned Production Capacity of the Blanket Industry

The production capacity of 10.1 mill. blankets intended to be reached in 1970 will probably be faced with a consumption in East Africa of only

6.7 mill. Under these circumstances the blanket industry will have to revise some of their investment plans; nevertheless it can be expected that in 1970 production capacity will lie above the consumption level. Since a substantial proportion of the planned extensions will have been completed in the near future, the East African blanket industry will probably enter a phase of serious overproduction even before 1970.

At the beginning of 1968, production capacity in Kenya was already considerably in excess of consumption in that country, and this discrepancy will be aggravated still more by the projects which at that time were planned and in some cases already under construction. In Uganda and Tanzania, on the other hand, production capacity will still be less than the level of demand in 1970 despite the planned extensions. However, this gap is much smaller than the surplus production capacity in Kenya. If Uganda and Tanzania use transfer duties to control blanket imports from Kenya so that the planned objectives of their own blanket industries are not jeopardized, substantial overcapacities in Kenya will be unavoidable.

The situation is more favourable with regard to yarn production. About 20 mill. lbs are needed to make 6.7 mill. blankets, the equivalent of East African consumption in 1970. So in this case, too, with an intended production capacity of 23 mill. lbs the entrepreneurs have overestimated the future sales potential, but not so badly as in the case of blanket manufacture. This is explained by the fact that some blanket-making firms have planned no spinning mill for 1970, or quite generally no spinning mill at all, but only a weaving mill. In these cases it is intended to procure the required yarn from other domestic spinning mills or to import it. Since yarn output will be completely adequate to supply East African blanket weaving mills in 1970, it will be possible to do without yarn imports from third countries.

E. THE CONSEQUENCES OF EXPANSION

The generally available information permits determination only of the direct consequences; secondary and tertiary effects necessarily have to be neglected.

I. The Financial Requirements

In the section on the financing of the textile industry it was pointed out that in East Africa investment in capital assets averaged 2,100 E.A. shs for an annual production capacity of 1,000 square yards of fabric. However, in some instances there were considerable differences among the firms polled: the upper limit was 2,500 E.A. shs and the lower limit 1,700 E.A. shs. These data refer to vertically integrated enterprises comprising a spinning mill, a weaving mill, and a bleaching and dyeing department. Since the planned production facilities will be more capital-intensive than the already existing ones, in future the average capital input for plant should be very close to the upper limit (2,500 E.A. shs). Hence the expansion of production capacity by about 123 mill. square yards between 1965 and 1970 will require capital investments of roughly £15.4 mill.

A substantial proportion of these capital requirements, very probably more than two thirds, will presumably be raised by foreign countries, i.e. chiefly in the form of development aid from national and international financing institutions and in part also by private persons. In this connection, investment expenditure involving the need for foreign exchange is frequently taken over by foreign countries, while the so-called local costs are assumed by domestic investors.

II. Growth of Labour Force

Between 1965 and 1967, the output of fabric grew much more rapidly than the number of employees. So the productivity of labour in terms of output per worker increased perceptibly. In a vertically integrated enterprise in 1965, an average of 137 employees was required to produce 1 mill. square yards of fabric. In 1966, this figure dropped to 114 and — if the firms' expectations are realized — should have been reduced again (to 99) in 1967. It would be wrong to ascribe this development solely or predominantly to the increasing proficiency of African labour. The situation was probably considerably influenced by the fact that the new, additional plants were as a rule more capital-intensive than the already existing ones.

The plants in the planning stage at the beginning of 1967 will differ considerably from each other as far as the productivity of labour is concerned. According to the statements of the entrepreneurs, in some plants provision has been made for 110 employees for the annual production of 1 mill. square yards of fabric, while others hope to manage with only 50 employees. 80 workers was the most frequently cited required labour force. If calculations are based on this figure, the expansion of production capacity by 123 mill. square yards (between 1965 and 1970) will create about 10,000 new jobs. So in 1970 the entire East African textile industry (excl. the blanket industry) should reach an employment level of roughly 16,000 employees.

III. Consumption of Yarn and Fibres

The specific yarn consumption, i.e. yarn consumption per square yard of fabric, of the East African weaving mills, which produce almost exclusively coarse fabrics, averaged roughly $^{1}/_{3}$ lbs in the years 1965–66. In the coming years, however, finer fabrics, e.g. poplin shirting, will be included in the production programme to an increasing extent. Regardless of this structural shift, however, in 1970 the production of coarse fabrics will be so predominant that specific yarn consumption should still lie very little below $^{1}/_{3}$ lb. Consequently the fabric output of 171 mill. square yards planned for 1970, of which 141 mill. square yards will be cotton fabrics and 30 mill. square yards rayon materials, will require a yarn input of 47 mill. lbs of cotton yarn and 10 mill. lbs of rayon yarn.
The cotton spinning mills, which also supply knitwear and hosiery factories with yarn, though in very small quantities, plan for 1970 a yarn output of 49 mill. lbs, which slightly exceeds the yarn consumption of the weaving mills. Allowing for 5 per cent wastage, this yarn output presupposes an input of 52 mill. lbs of cotton. Since East African cotton is perfectly suitable for making the yarn qualities in question and the textile industry is required to process domestic cotton, the demand for cotton will be satisfied exclusively from domestic sources. Hence in 1970 it will process a good 10 per cent of the total East African cotton crop, which is estimated in the development plans at 495 mill. lbs for 1970.
Government agencies often point out that the growing consumption of rayon fibres will soon justify the establishment of a synthetic fibre industry. In the judgment of experts, however, this view is much too optimistic, as for years to come the East African consumption of synthetic fibres will not attain the minimum capacity of a synthetic fibre industry. The result is that in 1970 the rayon spinning mills will still have to procure their rayon fibre requirements entirely from abroad. On the basis of the rayon spinning mills' planned yarn output of 10.4 mill. lbs, fibre imports of approximately 11 mill. lbs can be expected in 1970.

IV. The Linkage Effects

Special credit is due to A. O. Hirschman[13], for having called attention to the impetus imparted by an expanding sector of an economy to preceding

13 A. O. Hirschman: *The Strategy of Economic Development.* New Haven 1958, p. 98 et seq.

and succeeding sectors (backward and forward linkages). In the sphere of economic policy he arrived at the conclusion that, in developing countries, as far as possible those sectors of the economy should be promoted which have especially marked effects on other sectors of the economy, in order to thus initiate a cumulative development process. What significance does the East African textile industry have in this respect?

1. Backward Linkages

The most important sectors of the economy preceding the textile industry are agriculture as a cotton supplier and the chemical industry as a supplier of man-made fibres.

a) Agriculture

The East African textile industry can stimulate domestic cotton growing only if its additional cotton purchases raise the price of East African cotton. For various reasons, however, this cannot be expected.
The medium-long sorts of East African cotton have a very close substitution relationship with the medium-long cotton sorts of other producing countries such as the USA, Pakistan, Brazil, etc. If a surge of demand first hits market A and pushes the price up there, after a certain time lag this price movement is also transmitted — the process can be compared with a system of communicating tubes — to the other markets. Simultaneously the price reaction first triggered by the surge of demand on market A is attenuated again. So the resulting definitive price increase on market A depends less on the ratio of additional demand to supply on market A than on the ratio of additional demand to supply in the entire market system.
The East African textile industry currently processes only 6 per cent of the cotton harvested in East Africa, and even in 1970 it will take no more than 10 per cent of the crop. These quite small quantities relative to the total crop are of negligible significance if the cotton consumption of the East African textile industry is compared with the world market supply of medium-long cotton. This means that the purchases of the East African textile industry can have no notable effect on the price of East African cotton, and therefore no stimulus for domestic cotton growing can be expected from this source. The only consequence will probably be that East Africa's cotton exports will be reduced by the quantity of cotton consumed by the textile industry.
The situation would have to be judged entirely different in the case of such products as sugar and coffee, which are subject to export quotas under international market regulations. Once the export quota is completely

exhausted, only an increase in domestic consumption can open the way for increased production. As far as cotton is concerned, which can be traded freely on the world market, such deliberations are quite meaningless.

b) The Chemical Industry

If the possibility of exports is excluded, synthetic fibres will be worth producing in East Africa only when home consumption permits full utilization of the minimum capacity[14]. In the case of the part of the textile industry processing synthetic fibres — at present demand for man-made fibres comes only from industry — this presupposes a certain output level, the height of which depends on the minimum capacity for synthetic fibre production and on the share of synthetic fibres in the final product (yarn or fabric). Here it becomes clear that an expanding branch of industry can usually not result immediately in the building up of ancillary industries, but only after it has attained a certain output. The greater the consumption capacity of the home market, the more rapidly and certainly it will reach that output level. Consequently the linkage effects which initiate the creation of an industry are stronger in big countries or on extensive common markets than in small and nationally oriented countries.
It has already been pointed out that experts are of the opinion that for years to come synthetic fibre consumption in East Africa will remain so low that synthetic fibre production in East Africa cannot be considered. So in the forseeable future the rapidly growing textile industry will not allow a synthetic fibre industry to be built up in East Africa. Hence synthetic fibre requirements will continue to have to be covered abroad.

2. Forward Linkages

The tailoring trade and to some extent also the garments industry in East Africa are older than the textile industry. Even today they still procure a large proportion of their materials from abroad. This demonstrates that the tailoring trade and the garments industry by no means owe their existence to the textile industry.
They were rather placed at a disadvantage than benefited by the building up of a domestic textile industry. It has repeatedly been stressed that a large-scale textile industry in East Africa could be established only because the domestic price level for fabrics was raised sharply with the help of high

14 Minimum capacity is that capacity which with optimal utilization promises just the amount of profit which can induce the entrepreneur to make the necessary investments.

duties and quantitative import restrictions as towards third countries. So the materials purchased by the tailoring trade and the garments industry — regardless of whether they are imported or domestic materials — have become more expensive. From this it follows that the building up of a textile industry in East Africa had no stimulating effects on the tailoring trade and the garments industry.

3. The Development Phases of the Textile Industry

G. B. BALDWIN supports the view that in developing countries spinning mills are set up first, and weaving mills only later: "Few needs are more essential to man than covering his nakedness and keeping warm. These needs call for the building of textile plants — usually spinning first, then weaving — . . ."[15] It will be recalled that in East Africa vertical integration is compulsory for the larger textile plants. It is true that a spinning mill may be operated permanently on its own, but a weaving mill must add a spinning mill within three years. The textile enterprises for which vertical integration is not compulsory operate only weaving mills. In the case of the larger textile enterprises it is found that they rarely put their spinning mill and weaving mill into production simultaneously, but usually begin with weaving and take up spinning only later. So BALDWIN's theory is not confirmed in East Africa.

As long as there is no textile industry in a developing country, there is a demand not for yarn, but essentially only for fabric, which is procured from abroad. Since there is initially no market for yarn, it is absolutely inconceivable for the building up of the textile industry to begin with the setting up of spinning mills. Weaving mills must necessarily be built first, for they create a market for yarn and also the preconditions for the establishment of spinning mills. At best, the two stages can be built up simultaneously.

BALDWIN's view can be relevant only for developing countries in which the craft of weaving has been preserved to a great extent. In such countries, of course, even before the establishment of weaving mills – that is, industrial plants — there is already a demand for yarn from craftsmen weavers and hence a basis for the building up of spinning mills. Such deliberations may have a certain amount of significance for West African countries, but they are immaterial for East Africa.

---

15 G. B. BALDWIN: *Industrialization: A Standard Pattern in Finance and Development.* The Fund and Bank Review, published by the International Monetary Fund and the International Bank for Reconstruction and Development. Washington 1966, p. 275.

F. CONCLUDING REMARKS

Ragnar NURKSE[16] raises the question of whether the development process in the USA and Canada in the 19th century offers any clues as to how developing countries may develop economically. The industrial revolution in Britain triggered such a strong flow of food and raw material imports that the countries affected were able to step up their production of export goods substantially, and in this way a development process was started which also resulted in the industrialization of those countries. For most of the present developing countries this route is blocked; frequent exceptions are found only among those countries which have exploitable deposits of mineral raw materials or petroleum. In the case of raw agricultural products, however, the world market has only a limited capacity, since such products are faced with low price elasticity and low income elasticity of demand. In addition, the advanced industrial nations are also important producers of farm products and — it would appear — will remain so. So for many developing countries the chance of profiting to any great extent from the export of agricultural raw products is extremely small, and this likewise forces them to set out on the road to industrialization.

Nowadays a number of economists support the view that in the developing countries the industrialization process must be iniated on a broad basis. "The solution seems to be a balanced pattern of investment in a number of different industries, so that people working more productively, with more capital and improved techniques, become each other's customers."[17]

The demand for balanced development of industry from the outset is understandable only under the assumption that prior to the outset of the industrialization process there is a complete lack of demand for industrial finished products in developing countries. Under these circumstances the demand must first be created by the industrialization process itself. If the possibility of exporting is disregarded, this requires that from the very beginning the output structure of the emerging industry largely coincides with the structure of the demand it creates.

However, there can be a complete lack of demand for industrial finished products only in a developing country which, prior to industrialization, maintained no economic relations to the industrial countries, and the economy of which is based almost exclusively on subsistence production. But in reality the developing countries were engaged in trade with industrial countries before the former's industrialization. Consequently when indus-

16 R. NURKSE: *Equilibrium and Growth in World Economy.* Cambridge (Massachusetts) 1961, p. 242 et seq.

17 R. NURKSE: *op. cit.*, p. 247.

trialization set in in the developing countries a market for industrial finished products already existed.

This did away with the necessity of initiating balanced industrial development from the outset. On the contrary, it was possible for industry to turn to the production of products for which there was already a brisk demand on the home market, and for the manufacture of which the technical requirements were not all too high. Apart from food, beverages, footwear, garments, etc., this class of products also includes fabrics, with the result that — as already mentioned at the beginning — in the developing countries the textile industry became a pioneer industry.

Nowadays the industrialization of most developing countries is based on the substitution of domestic products for goods previously imported. As soon as these possibilities have been largely exhausted, the idea of balanced development of industry regains importance. For from this point onwards, industrial development must fit into the framework of domestic consumption growth. It must adapt not only to the respective level of consumption, but also to its structure. Then the income elasticities of demand for the various goods decide which industries belong to the growth industries and which to the stagnating ones.

Bibliography

A. Books

AKINOLA, R. A.: *Factors affecting the Location of a Textile Industry – The Example of the Ikeya Textile Mill.* Nigerian Institute of Social and Economic Research. Ibadan 1965.

British Colonial Office: *Report of the Economic and Fiscal Commission* (under the direction of Jeremy RAISMAN). London 1961.

DONALD, J. R., LOWENSTEIN, F., and SIMON, M. S.: *Demand for Textile Fibres in the United States,* Technical Bulletin No. 1301. Washington D.C. 1963.

GATT: *A Study on Cotton Textiles.* Geneva 1966.

HIRSCHMAN, A. O.: *The Strategy of Economic Development.* New Haven 1964.

NDEGWA, Ph.: *The Common Market and Development in East Africa.* Kampala 1965.

NURKSE, R.: *Equilibrium and Growth in the World Economy.* Editors: Gottfried HARBERLER and Robert M. STERN. Cambridge (Massachusetts) 1961.

OECD: *Die moderne Baumwollindustrie, eine kapitalintensive Industrie.* Paris 1965.

SUNARAJAN, T. V.: *The Textile Industry in the North African Sub-Region: Present Situation and Growth Prospects* (A Pre-Feasibility Study). UN Economic Commission for Africa. Addis Ababa 1966.

SPINDLER, J. v.: *Das wirtschaftliche Wachstum der Entwicklungsländer.* Stuttgart 1963.

United Nations: *Report of the United Nations Interregional Workshop on Textile Industries in Developing Countries.* New York 1966.

—: *Industrial Growth in Africa.* New York 1963.

—: *A Study of Industrial Growth.* New York 1963.

UN Economic Commission for Africa: *The Textile Situation in West Africa: Markets – Industries – Prospects.* Addis Ababa 1966.
—: *Report on the Symposium on Industrial Development in Africa.* Addis Ababa 1966.

B. Articles and Papers

Van Arkadie: Import Substitution and Export Promotion as Aids for Industrialization in East Africa. *East African Institute of Social Research.* Kampala 1964.
Baldwin, G. B.: Industrialization: A Standard Pattern. In: *Finance and Development, The Fund and Bank Review.* The International Monetary Fund and the International Bank for Reconstruction and Development. Washington D.C. 1966.
Baryaruha, A.: Factors affecting Industrial Employment – A Case Study of Nyanza Textile Industries Ltd. *East African Institute of Social Research.* Kampala 1965.
Haddon-Cave, C. P.: Real Growth of the East African Territories, 1954–1960. In: *The East African Economic Review.* Nairobi 1963.
Newlyn, W. T.: Gains and Losses in the East African Common Market. *East African Institute of Social Research.* Kampala 1965.
Nixon, F. I.: Location Theory Applied to Industrial Development in East Africa. *East African Institute of Social Research.* Kampala 1966.
—: Normal Patterns of Industrialization in East Africa. *East African Institute of Social Research.* Kampala 1966.
UN Economic Commission for Africa: *Textile Industries in the East African Sub-Region.* Addis Ababa 1965.
—: *Clothing Industries in the East African Sub-Region.* Addis Ababa 1965.
UN Economic Commission for Africa and Centre for Industrial Development: *Textile Industries in Africa.* Addis Ababa 1966.

C. Official Publications

1. Kenya

Development Plan 1966–1970. Government of Kenya. Nairobi 1966.
Statistical Abstracts of Kenya (annual). Government of Kenya. Nairobi.
Annual Reports of the Commercial and Industrial Development Corporation, Kenya.
Annual Reports of the Development Finance Company of Kenya, Kenya.

2. Uganda

Work for Progress, Uganda Second Five-Year Plan 1966–1971. Government of Uganda, Entebbe 1966.
Statistical Abstract of Uganda (annual). Government of Uganda. Entebbe.
Annual Reports of the Uganda Development Corporation, Uganda.
Annual Reports of the Development Finance Company of Uganda, Uganda.

3. Tanzania

Tanganyika Five-Year Plan for Economic and Social Development 1964–1969. Government of Tanzania. Dar es Salaam 1964.
Statistical Abstract of Tanzania (annual). Government of Tanzania. Dar es Salaam.
Annual Reports of the National Development Corporation, Tanzania.
Annual Reports of the Tanganyika Development Finance Company, Tanzania.
Investment Opportunities in Tanganyika. The Economist Intelligence Unit for the Government of Tanzania. Dar es Salaam.

4. East African Community

Treaty for East African Co-operation. East African Common Services Organization. Nairobi 1967.

Customs and Excise Tariff Handbook. East African Common Services Organization. Nairobi 1966.

Document: The Kampala Agreement. In: *East African Journal.* The East African Institute of Social and Cultural Affairs. Nairobi 1965.

Annual Trade Report of Tanganyika, Uganda and Kenya 1965 and 1966. East African Common Services Organization. Mombasa 1966 and 1967.

The East African Industrial Licensing Ordinance. Government of Kenya. Nairobi 1962.

D. Other Sources of Information

By far the greater part of the information on which this study is based was obtained in interviews with private firms, government authorities and semi-public finance companies. The investigation material and documents provided by these agencies are classified as confidential and can therefore not be cited.

FORESTRY AND SAWMILLING IN EAST AFRICA

by

Gerhard Rötzer

Contents

List of Tables

List of Maps

Abbreviations Used

cm	centimetre (0.3937 inch)
fm	Festmeter (35.31 cubic feet of solid timber)
ha	hectare (2.471 acres)
kg	kilogram (2.205 lbs)
m	metre (3.281 feet)
mm	millimetre (0.0394 inch)
sq. km	square kilometre (0.3861 square mile)
sq. m	square metre (10.76 square feet)
Shs	shillings
t	metric ton (0.9842 long ton)
Kshs	Kenya shillings
Tshs	Tanzania shillings
Ushs	Uganda shillings

The following article consists of extracts from a study on forestry, sawmilling, and timber sales in Kenya, Uganda, and Tanzania.
Kenya, Uganda and Tanzania are faced with the urgent problem of how to bring their forestry and timber production up to such a level as will enable it to cover the rapidly rising consumption of timber in the three countries. In that connection there must be far-sighted planning, harmonised between the three states, of the measures required for improving the situation as regards the supply of timber. One precondition for such planning is, however, accurate knowledge of the facts and of the conditions in which the countries are at present supplied with timber. It is not only the separation of governmentally organised forestry from the sawmilling industry, which is exclusively in private hands, that makes this difficult. At the present time there is little understanding of the difficulties facing the sawmilling industry, which attends to logging operations and sales. Mr. RÖTZER's investigation was directed to affording a preliminary idea of these difficulties. In particular he has tried to describe the flow of timber in, and between, the three East African countries.
The unabridged report was presented as a paper to the State University of Agriculture and Forestry at Vienna.
Diplom-Ingenieur Gerhard RÖTZER has studied forestry at the Universities of Vienna and Hamburg. Since 1965 he has been working in the forest administration in Austria, Germany, England, and Turkey. During 1966/67, with the financial support of the Fritz Thyssen Foundation, the author carried out field research into the forest industry in East Africa. Presently he is working in a forestry project of the Food and Agriculture Organisation in the Iran.
We are indebted to PATRIA Translations, Ltd., in Dorchester, England for translating this article into English.

A. FORESTRY IN EAST AFRICA

The aims and principal aspects of forestry policy differ, as between the East African countries, according to the importance which they respectively assign to forestry as an element within their economies. The organisation of forestry has accordingly reached levels which differ as between Kenya, Uganda and Tanzania.
In Kenya the Forest Department has already existed since 1902[1]. During the time of British colonial government up till 1962, the year of independence, it was built up into a properly working system, which now manages all areas in the country that have been declared to be forest reserves. It looks after not only the central (state-owned) forests but also the county council forests.
At the time when the British began to exercise their colonial government, in 1895, the greater part of the highlands (where the climate is moderate, and where Kenya's main forest areas lie) was hardly inhabited. The highlands were simply areas through which nomadic Masai and large herds of wild animals used to pass. These forests could therefore be easily protected. On the other hand the difficulties were greater in the more densely populated areas, where devastation of the forests through shifting cultivation and cattle had already begun long before the white man's arrival.
Kenya at the present day is only about 3 per cent wooded. Apart from small afforestations the forest area is not increasing. The main function of the forests in Kenya is to preserve and improve the climate so as to ensure the country's water supply. This function is more important than the provision of firewood and commercial timber.
In Tanzania, on the other hand, the organisation of forestry has in many respects not gone so far as it has in Kenya. The size of the country alone, with its endless open woodlands, gives rise to difficulties which either do not exist at all or are not so serious in Kenya and Uganda. It is true that land has been reserved for forestry since the time before the first world war, when the greater part of the mountain forests and the mangroves as well as limited areas of open woodland were so reserved. But the creation of forest reserves, that is of areas which are permanently managed as forests

1 K. P. W. Logie: *Forestry in Kenya. A Historical Account of the Development of Forest Management in the Colony.* Nairobi, Government Printer, 1962, p. 6.

and which at the same time have as a main function the regulation of water supplies in the country, has not yet been brought to an end in Tanzania. The Forest Division is at present directing its efforts to determining what growing stock of timber does exist in these legally protected areas, mostly extensive open woodlands, and what measures are required for managing them on a sustained yield basis.
In Uganda, like the other two East African countries, the first main function of forestry is to supply the country with the necessary forestry products; the second is to safeguard water reserves, to prevent soil erosion and to ensure continuance of the climatic conditions needed for agriculture. Hence in Uganda, which by reason of its climate is excellently suited for farming, only the land absolutely essential for the performance of those tasks has been declared to be forest reserves. The creation of forest reserves, which are the only forest areas permanently managed as such, has been largely concluded in Uganda.

I. The Forest Areas

1. Kenya

Except for a few hundred square kilometres, within African tribal areas, all the forests in Kenya have been declared to be reserves. The total area of such reserves is 17,438 sq. km, that is approximately 3 per cent of Kenya's total area (see Map 1). As regards types, out of Kenya's total forest area productive high forest accounts for 22 per cent, protection forest (high forest) for 30 per cent, bushland for 21 per cent, bamboos for 11 per cent, grassland for 13 per cent, and mangroves for 3 per cent[2]. The Catalogue of the Forests of Kenya, compiled in 1964 by the Forest Department at Nairobi, says that of the total forest area 61.6 per cent is in the Rift Valley Region, 23.8 per cent in the Central Region, 5.8 per cent in the Eastern Region, 1.6 per cent in the Western Region, 7.0 per cent in the Coast Region, and 0.2 per cent in the Nairobi Region[3].
The Rift Valley Region includes not only the area of the Rift Valley, but also, in particular, the forest areas in the Western highlands up to the mountain forests of Mount Elgon; it also includes the forests in the North, roughly between Lake Rudolf and Mount Kenya, those in the Samburu district, and the Marmanet forests near Thomson's Falls. The area comprises 99 island-like forest areas, separated from each other by cultivation or

2 Republic of Kenya, Forest Department: *Annual Report, 1964*. Nairobi, Government Printer, 1965, p. 29.
3 —: *Catalogue of the Forests of Kenya*. Nairobi 1964.

Map 1. *Forest Reserves in Kenya*

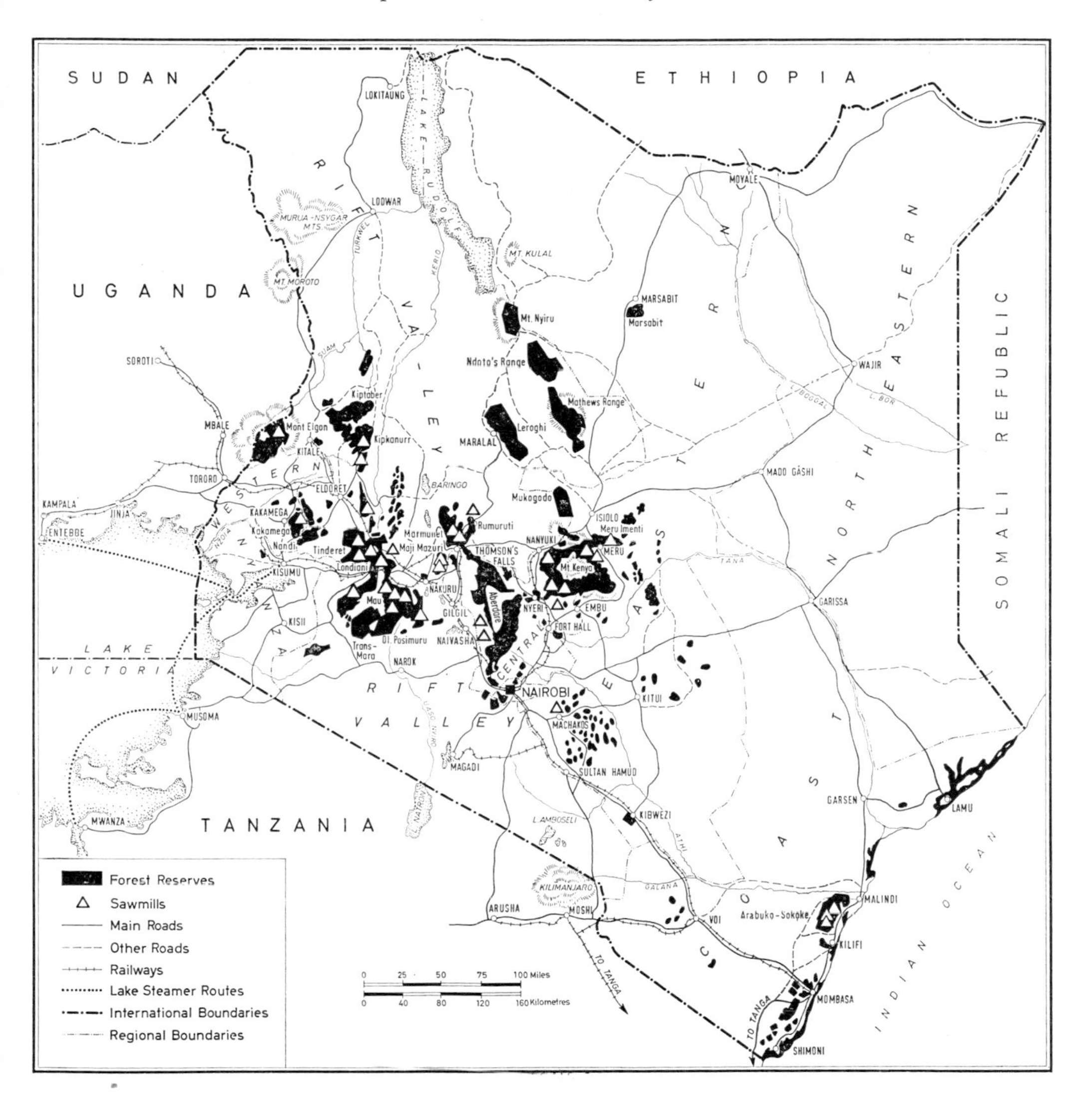

bushland. In the larger forests the timber is usually worked on an industrial basis. Only the forest reserves located in the Samburu district of the North are regarded, because of their remote, poor and dry locations, as not being timber production areas in the proper sense. But their beneficent effect, especially their water storage function in these dry areas of North Kenya, is of the highest importance.

The largest forest areas in the Central Region are those covered by the mountain forests of Mount Kenya and the Aberdares, the biggest being the Aberdare Forest, the Kikuyu Forest and the Mount Kenya Forest. The forests of Mount Kenya, unlike those in the Aberdare region, are used by a considerable number of sawmills. The timber is mostly Podocarpus and Juniperus.

From the forestry point of view the majority of the 60 existing forest areas are in extremely poor locations. To the Eastern Region there also belongs a part of the Eastern Mount Kenya forests, although geographically these are contained in the Mount Kenya Forest of the Central Region. There are moreover in this region a large number of small and ultra-small forest areas which, because of their dispersion and small extent, are of only local signifigance. Forest areas of considerable extent are to be found only in Machakos and northwards in Meru.

The Western Region includes the Kakamega Forest, covering almost 24,300 ha, and four further small isolated forests. This area differs essentially from the other forests in Kenya inasmuch as it is the country's only forest area consisting of genuine tropical rain forests, of the kind widely found in the Congo and in West Africa as well as in Uganda. High-grade tropical hardwoods, like the Elgon Olive, are utilized in this area, although the latter contains only one single sawmill worth mentioning.

Of the forest areas covering 117,450 ha in the Coast Region 44,955 ha are mangrove belts. The largest forest area is the Arabukosokoke Forest, covering 39,119 ha. Although already to a large extent over cut, it still contains 32,400 ha rich in Muhuhu (Brachylaena hutchinsii). The second largest wooded area is the Shimba Forest; this, however, has been declared to be a protected area for the purpose of ensuring Mombasa's water supply. These coastal forests supply no timber apart from firewood and the Muhuhu species.

In the immediate neighbourhood of Nairobi there are about 2,430 ha of forest, but this is of minor importance as regards timber production.

Nearly all Kenya's productive natural forests are between 1,800 m and 2,600 m above sea level. According to Whimbush[4] a distinction can be drawn in this context between two types of forest, the occurrence of which depends on the amount of rainfall; one is mountain rain forest, the other

4 S. H. Whimbush: *Catalogue of Kenya Timbers.* Nairobi, Forest Department, 1957 (Second Reprint).

being mountain conifer forest. The former is found on the Eastern and South-Eastern slopes of the mountains, for instance of Mount Kenya and the Aberdares; these slopes receive the North-Eastern and South-Eastern rain-bringing trade winds, and therefore have rainfalls between 1,400 mm and 2,300 mm per annum. They produce many kinds of timber, among which Podocarpus gracilior and milanjianus, Ocotea usambarensis, Apodytes dimidiata, Strombosia scheffleri and Casearia battiscombei are the most important. Mountain conifer forest is mainly found on the Western slopes of the mountains, where the annual rainfall amounts to only something between 890 mm and 1,400 mm. Typical for this area are Juniperus procera (pencil cedar), Podocarpus milanjianus and gracilior, Olea hochstetteri, Rapanea rhododendroides, Pygeum africanum and many other species, which are hardly used. At the present time, just as in the past, Kenya's natural forests are not managed with a view to sustained production of indigenous timber species; the reason is that the annual growth obtainable from these natural forests is much too small to meet the demand for timber either now or in the future. In addition the existing natural forests are not big enough. Forestry policy therefore aims at using these forests, so far as possible, for straightforward exploitation of the commercial timbers. The object is to clear the forest areas completely, so that they can afterwards be afforested with fast-growing exotic softwoods in the form of plantations. The areas now afforested do, however, include some plantations of indigenous timbers and foreign hardwoods[5]. According to figures published by the Forest Department at Nairobi some 81,983 ha of artificial forests had been planted up to the end of 1963. Since about 4,450 ha are afforested each year, Kenya's afforested area amounted in 1967 to approximately 100,000 ha. The greater part of the plantations is not yet mature.

2. Uganda

In Uganda nearly all the country's larger and more important forest areas are protected. In 1964 the forest reserve totalled 15,061 sq. km[6]; since the area of the whole country is 204,185 sq. km[7], this means that the proportion under forests is 7.4 per cent (see also Map 2). Uganda's forest reserves, classified according to the character of the vegetation, consist of closed high forests (46.6 per cent), open woodlands (47.8 per cent), and open areas together with grassland (6.5 per cent). Of the whole area, totalling 15,061 sq.

5 See also p. 83 et seq.
6 Uganda Government: *Annual Report of the Forest Department, 1963–1964.* Entebbe, Government Printer, 1964, p. 31 (subsequently quoted as Uganda Government: *Annual Report, 1963–1964).*
7 Excluding water.

Map 2. *Forest Reserves in Uganda*

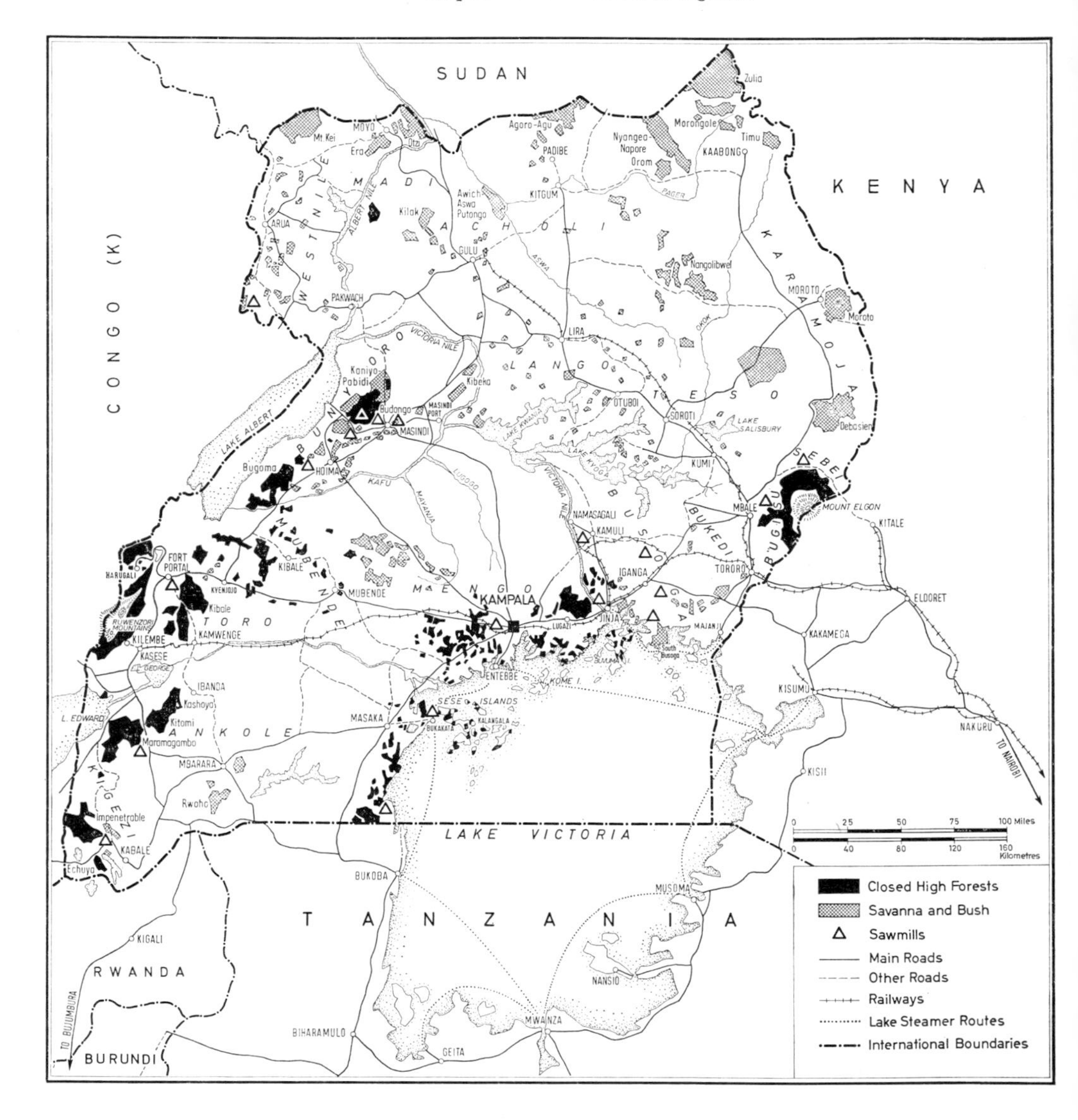

km, 5,869 sq. km (39 per cent) are productive forests, while 9.192 sq. km (61 per cent) are protection forests. Of the high forests, amounting to 7,032 sq. km, the proportion protected is 2,349 sq. km, or 33 per cent. The remaining 4,683 sq. km are the areas from which the greater part of Uganda's sawnwood production originates. They all consist of tropical, evergreen rain forest. The open savannah woodlands, which account for more than 50 per cent of the forest reserves, supply almost exclusively firewood and poles for the rural population. For administrative reasons the wooded area of Uganda is divided into two categories of forest reserves, namely the central forest reserves (12,075 sq. km) and the local forest reserves (2,986 sq. km). The former comprise forests of national or regional importance. They are administered by the Government Forest Department. The latter are of only local significance. They are subject to the Local Government Service. It is thought that these forest areas, with adequate capital expenditure on silviculture and afforestation, will suffice to provide Uganda in future with the necessary forest products as well as with surpluses for export.
Besides the forest reserves Uganda still has about 75,110 sq. km of unreserved forests, fully conforming to the savannah woodlands type. These, and some 1,154 sq. km of private forest, are not managed on a sustained yield basis. The said areas will in the near future be exploited, after which it will be possible to supply timber only from the forest reserves.
In Uganda, unlike Kenya, chief importance has hitherto been laid on management of the natural forests. The existing afforestation programme provides for fast-growing exotic softwood plantations, but at 225 to 365 ha per annum the rate of afforestation is very low (in Kenya the area annually afforested is 4,455 ha). Since the first plantations were not laid out until 1946, Uganda still has no mature artificial forests.
The afforestation programme is implemented chiefly by the Central Government Forest Department, and only to quite a small extent by the Local Government Forest Service. In Uganda, like Kenya, the tree species used for afforestation are Cupressus lusitanica, Pinus patula and Pinus radiata. Up till 1966 about 6,278 ha had been afforested. With regard to the afforestation so far done it must be stated, however, that the present rate of not more than 365 ha per annum is much too low to cover the country's future timber consumption.
The rural population is supplied only in small part with firewood and poles for hut building from the forest reserves, because these are for the most part not located near the areas of concentrated population. Firewood and poles are taken either from the surrounding unreserved bushland or from plantations, these having been laid out for that purpose, in the neighbourhood of settlements, either by the Central Government or the local forest authorities or by private enterprises.

3. Tanzania

The greater part of Tanzania's interior consists of a high plateau which, because it is sheltered by peripheral mountains, receives only 750 mm of rainfall each year. Drought consequently prevails over wide areas. It is thus only in isolated places where the rainfall is considerable (for instance on mountain slopes), or along rivers or in areas with ground water, that a closed high forest can be formed. Almost the entire remainder of the country is covered with the open Miombo forest, which is typical of Tanzania, and by bush vegetation (see Map 3). Grassland and semi-deserts likewise cover wide areas.

Among the types of forest in Tanzania a distinction can be drawn between those with a loose canopy (these include open Miombo woodlands, bushland, thickets and wooded grassland) and those with a thick canopy. These latter can be subdivided into upland rain forests, dry or mist forests, groundwater and littoral forests, freshwater swamp forests and finally the mangrove areas[8].

The "open woodland" covers wide areas incompletely wooded with trees of a low diameter class. Some of these species are very valuable. Timbers of the Brachystegia, Isoberlinia, Pseudoberlinia, Acacia, Combretum, and Upaca types predominate. The largest such forest areas, declared to be forest reserves, are located in the West of the country. The economic value of this type of forest lies at the moment in the valuable Muninga timber (Pterocarpus angolensis). Equally characteristic and economically important are the two types of Brachystegia spiciformis (Miombo and Mtundu) and, above all, Brachylaena hutchinsii (Muhuhu).

More than 50 per cent of the bushland is covered by bush and by individual small trees, mostly of the acacia type. This kind of vegetation is most widespread in the coastal region and in the Umba steppe to the North of the West Usambara Mountains.

The woodland steppe can be taken to include wide areas on which there are isolated trees, or groups of trees, mostly acacias or Borassus palms, together with intervening grass areas.

Alongside these kinds of vegetation there are at many places grassland steppes, permanent swamps or semi-deserts. The mountain rain forests are as a rule productive, and may be classified among forests of the type with a full crown closure. They are found at a height of between 1,800 m and 2,600 m on the slopes of mountains, like the Usambara, the Para, the Nguru and the Uluguru, as well as on the Southern slopes of Kilimanjaro. The most important tree species which are utilised on a large scale are Podocarpus, Ocotea usambarensis and Cephalosphaera usambarensis. Podocarpus and

8 As regards the types of forest with a loose canopy see H. J. von Maydell: Die Forstwirtschaft Tanganyikas, in: *Holzzentralblatt,* No. 126 (1962), p. 2029.

Map 3. *Forest Reserves in Tanzania*

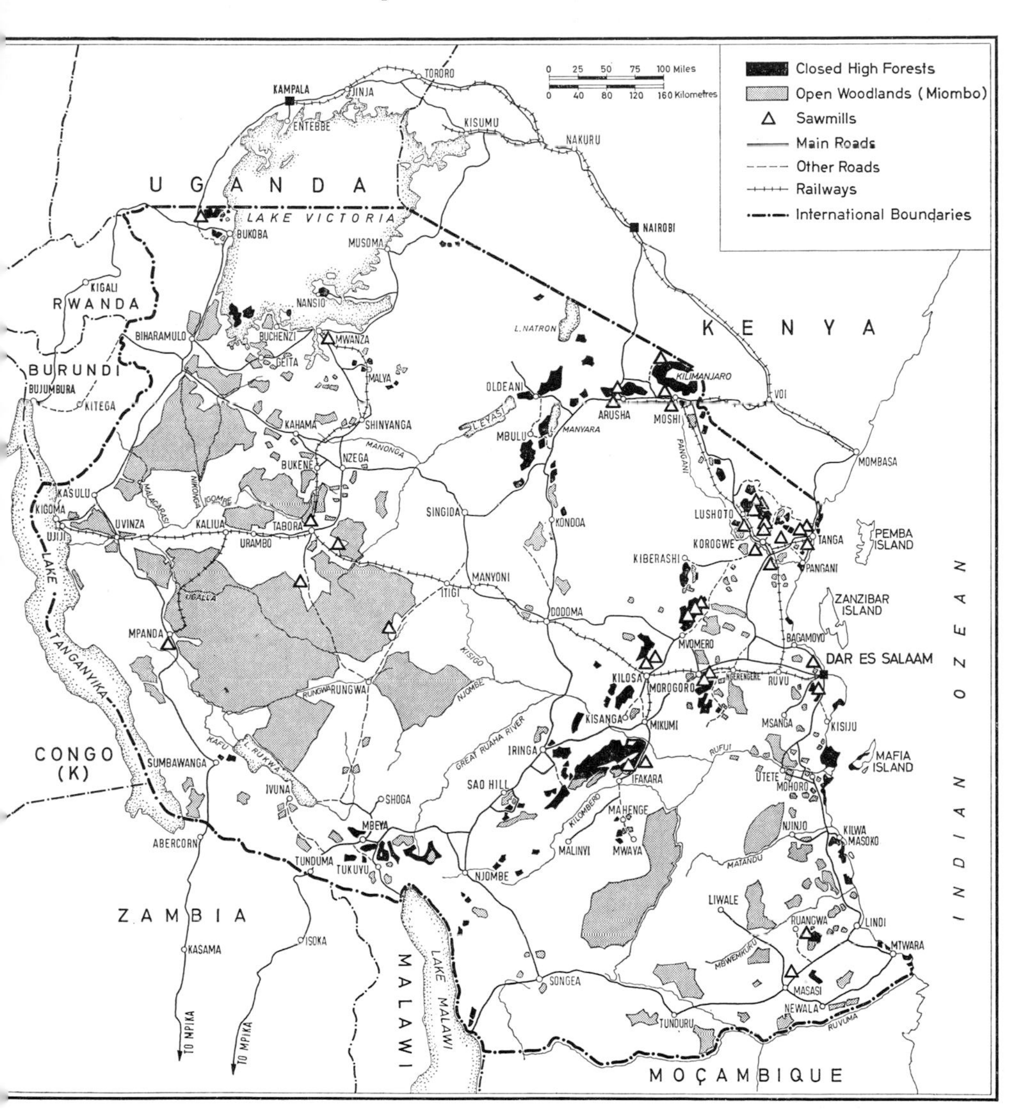

Ocotea rank second and fifth, respectively, in regard to the quantities felled in Tanzania.

The semi-dry woodlands consist of mist forests, on the upper slopes of the mountains, where the rainfall is relatively low. They are chiefly located in the Northern part of the West Usambara Mountains, in the Para Mountains, on the North slopes of Kilimanjaro, on Mount Meru and in the Crater Highlands. Economically important types of timber are Juniperus procera (the African pencil cedar), Juniperus cassyporrea and Ocotea usambarensis (camphor wood).

The groundwater forests and littoral forests are of great economic importance because of their accessibility and their valuable species like Khaya and Chlorophora. Some fine forest stands can be found along the large rivers, on the foothills of the Usambara Mountains, in some parts of the Eastern Para Mountains, in the Rau Forest, on the Eastern slope of the Nguru Mountains and on South-Eastern Kilimanjaro.

The economic importance of forests in the permanent swamps is small, and they are not widely dispersed. They are to be found on a major scale only in the Bukoba district in the North-West of the country.

The mangrove forests cover extensive coastal belts, especially in the Rufiji delta and about Tanga. In the economic sense the mangrove forests are important for the production of mangrove poles and for the extraction of tannins.

The forest reserves declared in Tanzania up till 1965 amounted to 130,728 sq. km[9], of which 114,047 sq. km (87.2 per cent) were Central Government Forest Reserves, while 16,681 sq. km (12.8 per cent) were Local Authority Forest Reserves. In addition there are on "open land" 245,050 sq. km of forest areas which, although they are not forest reserves, are governmentally controlled by the forest authority. Approximately 600 sq. km are private forests.

As regards the types of vegetation the forest reserves, covering 130,728 sq. km, comprise closed high forests (7.1 per cent), Miombo (89.6 per cent), mangroves (0.6 per cent) and grassland (2.7 per cent). Of the total area 119,365 sq. km, out of which 113,610 sq. km are accessible, could be used for producing sawnwood. Some part of the reserved grassland is suitable for afforestation with fast-growing conifers.

In order to meet the rising demand for cheap timbers there is an afforestation programme for exotic softwoods. The most important of those used for afforestation are Pinus patula, Pinus elliottii, Pinus caribea and Cupressus lusitanica. The area afforested in 1966 amounted to 2,543 ha. According to

9 The United Republic of Tanzania, Ministry of Agriculture; *Annual Report of the Forest Division, 1965*. Dar es Salaam 1965, Survey Division of the Ministry of Lands, Settlement and Water, p. 4 (subsequently quoted as: The United Republic of Tanzania: *Report of the Forest Division, 1965*).

the Forest Department at Dar es Salaam there are at the present time 18,040 ha of exotic softwood plantations, divided between fourteen afforestation projects. The biggest afforested area is in the Sao Hills of the Southern Highlands; it is well in the lead with an annual afforestation rate of 810 ha. With the exception of some plantations in the Usambara Mountains all the country's afforested areas are still not mature. According to the afforestation plan the intention is to plant between 2,500 and 2,800 ha of fast-growing softwood plantations per year[10].
With a view to simpler supply of Dar es Salaam there is a plan for afforesting a coastal area, covering 60,750 ha, with exotic softwoods. In the course of pilot plantings it has been found that Pinus caribea is well suited to the sandy soils found in that area. This project is also designed to ensure the supply of a future paper mill in that area with pulpwood.
It has been found in the course of trial plantings, effected with a view to the growing of high-grade timber, that afforestation with Tectona grandis (teak) holds out a good prospect of success in areas with deep soils and relatively large rainfall. Up till now there are a few teak afforestations, of which the largest (360 ha) is near Mtibwa, roughly 250 km to the North-West of Dar es Salaam. This plantation is seven years old; it grows well, and about 80 ha are added to it each year. The 1965–69 five-year afforestation plan provides for planting 400 ha with teak in 1967 and 1968, and 600 ha in 1969.

II. Timber Consumption in the East African Countries

According to a FAO study there is information about the consumption of timber, as well as of timber and paper products, during the period from 1956 to 1960, and there are similar forecasts covering the years 1980 and 2000, for the individual East African countries. According to this source the consumption of timber (only sawnwood and poles) in the East African countries during the 1956–60 period exceeded 1 million fm. The breakdown of such consumption as between countries, and according to the nature of the products, can be seen from Table 1.
Although no forecasts are made about the future consumption of all wood and paper products, the following tendencies in consumption are discernible. By the year 2000 the consumption of sawnwood in all three countries will increase by at least three times the average annual consumption for the 1956–60 period. The demand for poles, which will remain the rural population's most important building material, will increase only in accordance with the growth of population. By 2000, however, the total demand for

10 The United Republic of Tanzania: *Report of the Forest Division, 1965*, p. 1.

Table 1. *Annual Consumption of Wood, as well as of Wood and Paper Products, 1956–60, 1980 and 2000*

	Sawnwood fm	Poles fm	Plywood and veneer sq. m	Fibreboard sq. m	Paper and cardboard t	Firewood mill. fm
Kenya						
1956–60 average	94,522	291,226	678,900 [a]	398,750 [a]	15,150	.
1980	217,000	426,000	2.33 mill.		40,600	.
2000	473,000	747,000	6.50 mill.		112,800	.
Uganda						
1956–60 average	70,000 [b]	.	.	.	.	.
1980	.	.	.	.	.	.
2000	250,000	.	.	.	.	.
Tanzania						
1956–60 average	87,730	486,760	.	.	.	10.5
1980	280,000	753,000	.	.	.	13.5
2000	570,000	1,136,000	.	.	.	17.0

[a] Imports
[b] 1965–66

Source: J. E. M. ARNOLD, M. F. E. DE BACKER, S. L. PRINGLE: *Present Wood Consumption and Future Requirements in Kenya.* Food and Agriculture Organisation of the United Nations, Rome, 1962, p. VII; —: *Present Wood Consumption and Future Requirements in Uganda.* Food and Agriculture Organisation of the United Nations, Rome, 1962, p. V; —: *Present Wood Consumption and Future Requirements in Tanganyika.* Food and Agriculture Organisation of the United Nations, Rome, 1962, p. IV–V.

poles will grow to something less than three times the average annual consumption in 1956–60. Much the same applies to firewood, which in all three countries will remain the principal fuel. The per capita consumption of firewood will, however, rather decrease. In the case of plywood, veneer and paper products the rate of growth will exceed that for sawnwood. Since the per capita consumption of paper products at present still remains higher in Kenya than in Uganda and Tanzania, this rate will on a long view probably increase faster in the two countries last mentioned than in Kenya. Although forecasts of demand over such lengthy periods cannot be made with great precision, it must be assumed that in the long run the future demand for wood in all three countries will not be such that it can be met from the natural forests. The extremely rapid growth of demand for timber will thus have to be primarily met through large-scale afforestation.

III. Management of the Forests

1. Kenya

It has already been indicated that in Kenya the importance of the natural forests, as a source of timber supply, is decreasing in comparison with that of planted forests. It is true that up till a few years ago Kenya's wood consumption was still met almost exclusively from natural forests. As the fast-growing plantations become ready for felling, however, the proportion of the country's timber supply for which the artificial forests account is rapidly growing. By now more than 50 per cent of all the timber felled comes from plantations.

For half a century it was merely three kinds of timber which accounted for 80 per cent of the felling in natural forests, namely Juniperus procera (the East African pencil cedar), Podocarpus gracilior and Podocarpus milanjianus. The remaining 20 per cent comprised a number of other indigenous hardwoods. Further hardwoods, the majority of which are exported, are Brachylaena hutchinsii (Muhuhu), Olea hochstetteri (East African olive), Olea welwitschii (Elgon olive) and Aningeria adolfii (Muna). Other valuable species, although the amounts available are extremely limited, are Chlorophora excelsa, Vitex keniensis (Meru oak), Cordia abyssinica (Muninga) and Fagara macrophylla (East African satinwood). Besides these timbers there are a number of other species which, because of their sporadic distribution or their poor qualities, or because they have not yet been established in the market, are of no economic importance.

According to estimates[11] the commercial timber output per ha varies, in the case of most podocarpus, juniperus or camphor-bearing forests, between 100 and 150 fm per ha. Yields of up to 200 fm per ha are mentioned in exceptional cases. This means the quantity of commercial timber actually usable. For natural forests in the tropics, it is true, these figures represent quite high yields. These, however, are not typical tropical rain forests with the latter's extreme distribution of tree species and only a low proportion of exploitable timber; they rather tend to be upland forests, between 1,800 m and 2,700 m above sea level, which do not contain a great number of species, and in which certain types like podo and cedar (juniperus) predominate.

The first afforestations were already started in Kenya before the first world war. The present artificial forests contain areas planted with indigenous and exotic tree species, of which the former account for about 10 per

---

11 At the time of the author's investigation the results obtained from a census of natural forests, carried out in Kenya by a Canadian working party, were not yet available.

cent. The indigenous trees planted are for the most part Juniperus procera (pencil cedar), the planting having been done between thirty and forty years ago. Because of their extremely slow growth such plantations are no longer being continued. The conclusion from many experiments is that four kinds of timber have established their position as suitable for afforestation in Kenya. All of them are exotic, fast growing conifers from Central America, namely Cupressus lusitanica, Cupressus macrocarpa, Pinus patula and Pinus radiata. Since it has recently been found that Cupressus macrocarpa are prone to a form of canker and to boring insects, while Pinus radiata are similarly susceptible to a fungus (Dothistroma pini), recent afforestations have been confined to Cupressus lusitanica and Pinus patula. Promising experiments have been carried out with Araucaria cunninghammia and angustifolia as well as with several kinds of pine, especially with Pinus elliottii.
Further tree species which were introduced in Kenya are Eucalyptus, Grevillea robusta (silky oak) and Acacia mollissima. After their introduction between 1919 and 1929 various kinds of eucalyptus served to supply fuel for the newly built railway, leading into the interior of the country. Nowadays eucalyptus are of no importance for the production of sawnwood, but they are used for firewood. Because of their perfect shape of growth, they are also suitable for producing transmission poles. Both Grevillea robusta and the eucalyptus were introduced from Australia, and were originally used only to provide shade in coffee plantations. Not until later was Grevillea robusta used for producing relatively cheap sawnwood. In order to supply a large tannery at Eldoret with bark for the extraction of tannin some 40,500 ha have been afforested with Acacia mollissima.
As early as 1967 the new census, conducted by Canadian experts, had provided precise figures with regard to the growing stock of merchantable timber in planted forests so far as certain areas were concerned. According to this census the average volume per hectare for fellable cypress stands 33 years old is 533 fm[12], a figure which may also be regarded as an indicator for the whole of Kenya.

2. Uganda

In Uganda the main emphasis in forestry is on the natural forests, and those which are productive are almost exclusively evergreen, tropical rain forests. The silvicultural treatment is primarily directed to producing cheap but serviceable timbers. These natural forests contain a high proportion of very valuable species, such as Entandophragma (mahogany).

12 This figure is based on data for four plantations; in these, like the rest of the plantations in Kenya, Cupressus accounts for the greater part of the timbers planted.

Up till 1957 the aim of silviculture as treatments was to create an uneven aged stand with several crown layers — in fact a selection forest, with a rotation of 30 years. This polycyclic system was later abandoned because it was found that, when trees which had for a long time been growing under suppression are released from it, they no longer achieve optimum growth. It was further found that, with such selection, considerable logging damage occurs, while moreover the light available for the next generation of trees is not good. The authorities accordingly changed over to a monocyclical system, the aim of which is to produce an even aged stand under a rotation of 60 to 80 years. This change, however, cannot be carried out all at once; an intervening period of about 30 years is in each case required for removal of the undesired and over-matured stems. The fellings conform to the principle of a sustained yield, and are based on a previous volume determination of the growing stock of timber.
A special problem in the management of Uganda's forests is created through the damage done by elephants, these being found in particularly excessive numbers in the rain forests of West Uganda. The damage done to the forest is frequently so great that a proper forest stand can no longer be said to exist. Despite the damage done by elephants the authorities hope, through suitable treatment[13], to raise the annual increment of the productive rain forests from 0.35–0.42 fm per ha to 1.75–2.0 fm per ha. This, however, will take at least one rotation, that is roughly 80 years.
A census of Uganda's forests was carried out by CAHUSAC in 1957 and by DAWKINS in 1958. Aerial photographs and sample plot systems were used in all forest areas in the country. Their census gives an idea of how much timber there is in the individual areas[14]. It indicates that as between the different forest areas the stock of timber per ha varies from 133 fm in the Budongo Forest down to 3 fm in some small areas, which hardly deserve to be called forest[15]. The Budongo Forest covers 378 sq. km, which is only 6 per cent of the country's forested area, but it contains 28 per cent of all the timber in Uganda. Unfortunately 50 per cent of this forest is Cynometra timber, for which there is no broad market because of its extreme hardness. On the other

---

13 Normal treatment includes poisoning of the undesired trees and isolating of those desired, by which means considerable acceleration of growth can be achieved. Action of this kind has been taken since 1954. Up till 1964 some 21,475 ha of natural forest had been so treated, including 20,732 ha in Central Forest Reserves. Since approximately 4,860 ha are so dealt with each year, the improved area amounted in 1966 to about 31,185 ha. See Uganda Government: *Annual Report, 1963–1964*, p. 35.

14 See L. LANGDALE-BROWN, H. A. OSMASTON and J. G. WILSON: *The Vegetation of Uganda and its Bearing on Land Use.* Margate, Kent, Eyre and Spottiswood Ltd., 1964, p. 83 et seq.

15 In the volume determination only trees of more than 50 cm breast-height diameter were measured.

hand this forest area is very rich in mahoganies, such as Entandophragma and Khaya.
Calculation of the average total volume, weighted by the areas of the forests concerned, results in a figure of 32 fm per ha. Of this timber the proportion which is usable, being in fact now used by sawmills, is 49 per cent, or about 16 fm per ha.
This average value does not include Mvule (Chlorophora excelsa), because that timber does not occur in the tropical rain forest. Because there are only isolated Mvule trees, a sawmill using this species must obtain its roundwood from distances of up to 130 km. The upper limit to the growing stock of this valuable timber in the Busoga district would appear to be 0.7 fm per ha.

3. Tanzania

The aim is management and sustained yield basis of indigenous tree species in the mountain rain forests, in the moist rain forests of the foothills, in the areas where Mvule (Chlorophora excelsa) predominates, and in the extensive Miombo areas, which are mostly managed with a view to production of the predominant and valuable timber called Muninga (Pterocarpus angolensis).
In the mountain rain forests on the slopes of Kilimanjaro, and in the West Usambara Mountains, the object of management is to preserve the forests through natural regeneration. Attention is chiefly directed to the first-class species Ocotea usambarensis (East African camphor). This tree can be easily regenerated through the coppice system. The treatment is confined to poisoning of over-mature stems, to removal of the thick undergrowth, and to keeping a free space for the suckers, which soon spring up in large numbers around the tree stumps after felling. The treatment is applied three years and one year before, as well as one year and five years after the tree has been cut.
The type of timber chiefly found in the damp forests of the foothills is Cephalosphaera usambarensis. The treatment suitable for this species has not yet been determined, although the species has been exploited since a long time. It is still an open question whether natural or artificial regeneration offers the better prospect of success.
The Miombo areas are chiefly valuable because of the Muninga (Pterocarpus angolensis). The measures adopted for the preservation of this tree have so far been directed only to removing a quantity which corresponds to the natural growth. Inquiries designed to investigate the means by which more Muninga could be made to grow in the Miombo areas, at present only very poorly stocked by nature, are still in their initial stage.
The largest occurrence of Mvule is in the South-East of Tanzania on the Rondo plateau. Individually, however, the tree is very widespread in the

country. Regeneration is achieved on the Rondo plateau through root suckers, just as it is in the case of Ocotea usambarensis in the mountain rain forests.
Besides the types of timber mentioned Tanzania has other species which, although they are exploited, are not managed on a sustained yield basis. Once their natural locations have been exploited their regeneration is no longer assisted. This is partly because they are replaced by species which grow faster, but partly also because no methods of preserving them are yet known. The species to which this applies include Podocarpus milanjianus (podo), Juniperus procera (cedar), Khaya nyasica (East African mahogany), Dalbergia melanoxylon (East African blackwood) and Brachylaena hutchinsii.
Only scanty data about the stock of timber and the yearly increment in Tanzania's forest reserves are available. Through a sample census of 15 forest reserves, comprising large Miombo areas on which Muninga chiefly grew, the Forest Department worked out a rough weighted average of 12 fm per sq. km. No data are to hand concerning the stock and increment of the podo and camphor forest reserves in the Usambara Mountain forests. Only for one area in the Usambara Mountains was the usable stock of Cephalosphaera usambarensis found to be approximately 2,850 fm on 30 ha. That corresponds to 95 fm per ha. These figures for growth relate, however, only to the main species in each area. Other species are in all cases exploitable in addition. In some places the volume of these other species would be as much as twice the amounts stated above, or more.

IV. Forest Protection

Besides being used for timber production the forest areas in all three East African countries are of great importance for the supply of water.
Kenya, in the parts where natural forests are found, is a mountainous country. The basic principle followed is that removal of timber on slopes of over 40 per cent inclination is not permitted. On slopes of between 30 per cent and 40 per cent the removal of single stems is allowed. The maximum slope on which clear cutting is permitted is 30 per cent.
A great danger to the forests in Kenya is cattle. It is kept in the lower areas, it is true, but they increasingly penetrate into the forests at higher levels. The Kenyan Forest Department is trying to prevent this through suitable regulations.
Protection of forests in Uganda is confined to those on the mountains in the West and South-West, as well as to the arid hilly regions in the North and

North-East of the country, since Central and Southern Uganda on the whole receive sufficient rainfall besides being adequately provided with water-courses and marshes. In the water catchment areas the mountains and hills have been declared to be protected areas. The object of the protective measures is to preserve and improve the vegetation coverage through regular supervision of the forests, through regulations forbidding agricultural cultivation and removal of timber (apart from the removal of single stems, which is allowed in certain areas), and through controlled burning of the bush and savannah grasslands at the proper time.
In Tanzania it is important to have an adequate supply of water because the whole of agriculture, with the inclusion of coffee, tea and sisal growing, depends on this. Many Tanzanian rivers have their catchment areas in the mountain rain forests, which are moreover rich in valuable tree species. The foremost aim of forestry is to make use of this timber without destroying the capacity of the forests to store water. The Forest Department has excluded those forests which lie on steep slopes, and are in danger of erosion, from the timber concessions. The total protected Miombo areas are of small extent. The protective measures there are confined to controlled burning, at suitable times, so as to prevent damage to the standing trees, which are in any case scarce.

B. THE SAWMILLING INDUSTRY

I. Features of the Sawmills

1. Number and Location of the Mills

In Kenya there are a total of something like 60 sawmills. Most of these, however, are extremely small, and their sawnwood output forms only an insignificant part of the total production. Essentially there are 35 sawmills which have their felling concessions in Government forests, and which account for the bulk of the country's sawnwood output. In Uganda there are about 20, and in Tanzania between 35 and 40 similar mills.
The greatest concentration of sawmills in Kenya is in the highlands to the West of the Great Rift Valley, and in the areas of the Mau, Tinderet, Londiani and Maji Muzuri forests. Other sawmills are concentrated in the Charangani Hills (North of Eldoret), in the Kakamega Forest (North of

Kisumu), in the Marmanet Forest (North of Thomson's Falls), in the South-Western Aberdare region and, above all, on the slopes of Mount Kenya. Stretching roughly eastward from the line Mount Kenya-Nairobi as far as the coast is a dry bush area which, except for a few isolated woodlands in the Machakos district, is without forests and has no sawmills. Except for Muhuhu sawnwood and parquet timber the coastal forests produce no quantities of commercial timber worth mentioning.

In Uganda, like Kenya, the distribution of the sawmills corresponds to that of the forests. Since the most productive forest areas are in the West of the country, lying roughly along the line from Masindi through Hoima to Fort Portal and Lake George, and southward of this line, the largest sawmills are in that area.

There is a concentration of four mills around Masindi in the Bunjoro district, together with the Budongo, Siba and Busaja forest reserves. To the South of Masindi, likewise in Bunjoro, there is one sawmill in Hoima and another in the Bugoma forest reserve. A further large sawmill is located at Fort Portal, with a concession to work parts of the Kibale forest reserve in the Toro district. The large Kalinzu forest reserve lies to the South of the waterway serving Lake George, and in it is the timber concession of the only large sawmill in that area. All the sawmills so far mentioned fell their timber exclusively in natural tropical rain forests.

The only Ugandan sawmill which operates in a softwood plantation is located in Southern Ankole, in the Mafuga forest reserve, this being the country's only significant conifer plantation. Two further large sawmills occupy a special position, inasmuch as they are located actually within the country's two most important towns, namely Kampala and Jinja. The Kampala sawmill's concession areas are to be found in the small isolated woodlands of the West Mengo forest reserve; those of the Jinja sawmill are in the larger Mabira forest reserve between Kampala and Jinja.

Two Mvule sawmills are located in the Busoga district to the East and North-East of Jinja. Since Mvule trees occur only rarely, for the most part in densely populated areas, in villages and surrounding agricultural lands, the area from which these sawmills obtain their timber is very extensive. Some further small sawmills are located around Mount Elgon in the Bugisu district and Sebei.

Numerous small sawmills, now mostly closed down, are located in the Buganda province. They obtain their roundwood, in many cases Mvule, from privately owned areas.

The Forest Department of Tanzania states that the country's sawmilling industry comprises between 25 and 30 significant firms, which operate approximately 35 to 40 sawmills. In addition there are an unknown number of small bush sawyers who, in wide areas of the country, are the only producers of sawnwood apart from the pit sawyers.

If Tanzania is divided into regions from the forestry point of view[15a], the distribution of its 35 largest sawmills is as follows:
In three areas there is a definite concentration of sawmills. The first is the Tanga region, including the Usambara Mountains, with 13 mills; the second is the coastal region including Dar es Salaam, the Morogoro-Kilosa area and the Northern Kilombero valley, with 11 mills; and the third is the Kilimanjaro-Arusha-Moshi region, with 6 mills. In each of these three areas there are, in addition, a number of smaller sawmills.
A further sawmill concentration is found in the West region, around Tabora and the great Muninga woodlands. In this remote part of Tanzania, however, certain sawmills have had to cease operation during recent years. In the West region during 1967 four or five minor sawmills were operating. A high proportion of the sawnwood produced in this area consists in pit sawyers' crude products, which are locally marketed in the Tabora, Singida, Dodoma and Kigoma districts.
There are no further significant sawmills in the South region, except for two, on the Rondo plateau and at Masasi, which work almost exclusively for export.
In the forests of the Southern highlands is not a single sawmill. Sawnwood is supplied exclusively by ultra-small establishments, using bush circular saws, and pit sawyers.
The Mwanza district, where timber is scarce, is practically dependent on supplies of sawnwood coming from Kenya or from the hinterland. There are only a few small mills.
The only considerable sawmill in North-West Tanzania is located near Bukoba, but it sends the greater part of its output to Uganda.

15a Tanzania can be subdivided into regions as follows:

Title of region	*Areas comprised*
Tanga region	The area around Tanga and Muheza, as well as the Usambara Mountains
Arusha-Kilimanjaro-Moshi region	The Kilimanjaro area plus the area of Moshi, Arusha (Olmotonyi), Mount Meru and the Mbulu area
Coastal region	Dar es Salaam and the Rufiji area, the area about Kilosa, Morogoro and Ulanga (North Kilombero)
West region	The Tabora region and Western Tanzania between the Mwanza district in the North and the Southern highlands
South region	The areas South of the Rufiji as far as the Mozambique frontier between the Southern highlands and the Indian Ocean
Lake region	The Mwanza district and the areas about the Southern Lake Victoria, including Bukoba
Southern highlands region	The highlands between Iringa and Mbeya in the Southern part of the country.

2. Output

Of all three East African countries it can be said that the production of sawnwood is spread between an excessive number of mills, which are too small and are for the most part antiquated. This applies less to Uganda than to Kenya and Tanzania.
The average annual output of a sawmill in Kenya was about 2,200 fm of sawnwood in 1966. This average figure was calculated from data concerning 34 mills, which produced 77 per cent of Kenya's total output. The rest of the mills would hardly appear to produce more than 250 to 300 fm per annum.
In Uganda 70 per cent of the sawnwood is produced by eight sawmills. Their average annual sawnwood production in 1965–66 was 5,020 fm, which is large by African standards. The remaining 30 per cent came from 12 smaller mills. Their average annual output is about 1,500 fm.
In Tanzania 31 sawmills produce 66 per cent of the sawn timber. The rest is produced by bush circular saws and by pit sawyers. The average annual output of these 31 sawmills is 1,200 fm of sawnwood per mill (in 1966), this being lower than the corresponding figures for Kenya and Uganda.
In all three countries most of the sawmills do not work on full capacity. If they would their output could be two or three times as much.

3. Ownership

All Kenya's sawmills are in private ownership; the majority belong to Asians, and a minority to Europeans. Except for three sawmills owned by Timsales, Ltd. (a timber-selling organisation at Nairobi) and one European sawmill, in which several providers of capital are interested, all of them are family enterprises. The position is similar in Uganda and Tanzania, where the sawmilling industry is almost entirely in private Indian hands.
Attempts have been made in Uganda to promote the setting up of sawmilling firms by Africans, but they failed. One reason why they did so was that the timber trade requires not only technical and vocational knowledge but also, and in the first place, commercial skill. Another was that Indian competition makes it difficult for an African, even with Government support, to establish a footing in the timber trade.
In Tanzania the Indian minority are in a particularly uncertain situation because of the Government's efforts to Africanise and nationalise the various industries. For this reason certain sawmills, owned by Indians, have acquired African partners in the hope of safeguarding their position.
In remote parts of the country, however, many small bush circular saws hardly deserving the name of a sawmill are also operated by Africans. African interests are primarily considered when new licences for the opera-

tion of sawmills are granted. Since Africans have neither sufficient capital nor the required vocational skills, however, these licences are frequently after all transferred to immigrant Indian firms.
Finally in Tanzania there are some African cooperative societies which hold timber concessions. They either sell the roundwood to Indian sawmill owners or, as in the case of the timber known as Dalbergia melanoxylon, they export roundwood. A few Indian sawmills obtain their supplies from private forests; this is for example done by one mill in the East Usambara Mountains, which owns a large and highly productive forest area. The forest stands there consist almost exclusively of Cephalosphaera usambarensis. A similar case, except that the mill is of smaller size, is to be found in the Uluguru Mountains not far from Morogoro.

4. Equipment and Power Supply

Only four mills in Kenya, three in Tanzania and six in Uganda could be regarded, in 1967, as modern and well equipped. The majority of East African sawmills have machinery and equipment which is both antiquated and insufficient.
Apart from numerous small sawmills, using only circular saws, it is the gang saw which predominates in Kenya; such saws are frequently manufactured by Pini & Key, of Vienna, and they are suitable for the small stems of the plantation timber. In Uganda it is mostly band saws which cut the large timber, most of it coming from natural forests. In Tanzania, alongside the band saw, the horizontal frame saw is frequently found. It is also found in Uganda. In spite of its small output the horizontal frame saw is used for cutting valuable timbers like Mvule for export because of the outstanding quality of its cut.
Only a few sawmills are supplied with electricity from the public system. Most of them, because of their remote location, have to produce the necessary power themselves. The majority produce it by means of old portable steam engines, while others use diesel engines taken from crawler tractors which have become unusable. The power is directly transferred, by belt drive, to the sawing machines.
Besides the inadequate machinery there are many mills where inappropriate and ill-devised arrangement of the machines gives rise to hold-ups of the work. The reason is frequently that successive machines are of unequal capacity, that there is too little space for intermediate storage, and that conveyance of the goods (invariably by hand) between the individual processes is badly organised.

5. Sawnwood Recovery

Sawnwood recovery of course varies according to the quality and size of the roundwood; it also varies according to the nature of the sawing machines employed, as well as according to the dimensions of the sawnwood produced. Accurate measurements for the purpose of precisely determining the recovery are not generally available, but can only be estimated. Generally it can be said that because of the inadequate sawing machines, and above all because the saw blades are poorly maintained, the percentage of sawnwood recovered is small. The proportion ranges, according to the type of timber, between 25 per cent and 60 per cent.

In Kenya the proportions stated for 1967 by way of reply to the questionnaire varied in the case of Juniperus procera between 25 per cent and 40 per cent, in that of Podocarpus between 40 per cent and 60 per cent, and in that of Cupressus between 40 per cent and 50 per cent. According to accurate measurements in a Cupressus sawmill, which used a Pini & Key gang saw, the recovery amounted to 47 per cent. Taken as a whole, the proportion of sawnwood recovery in Kenya is probably between 40 per cent and 50 per cent.

Inquiries conducted from 1964 to 1966 in six Ugandan mills, which were equipped with band saws and were processing large timber from natural forests, showed that the recovery averaged 42 per cent. The proportions for mills using circular saws are likely to be well below these levels.

In Tanzania, according to the sawmills, an average sawnwood return of 45 per cent can be assumed. The figures given for extraction from the larger stems of the podo, camphor, khaya, mvule, and other varieties were between 50 per cent and 60 per cent.

II. Concessions for, and Organisation of, Roundwood Supply

In Kenya, Uganda and Tanzania the greater part of the forests are owned by the Government; the latter grants licences to fell timber in certain areas which lie within the forest reserves. Private forests are in practice of no importance. During the term of the concession only the concessionaire is allowed to fell timber on the area covered by the concession.

In Kenya the Forest Department, which manages not only the national but also the county council forests, grants felling licences to the sawmills. The period of concession amounts to five, or frequently to ten years. Prolongation of that period is possible.

Except in the case of ultra-small sawmills on private land the sawmills in Uganda obtain their supply of roundwood from concession areas in the forest reserves; the licences for these areas are granted in the case of the central forest reserve by the Forest Department at Entebbe, and in that of the local forest reserves by the local forest authority concerned. Here again the concessions are valid for five, or in most cases even for ten years, and can be prolonged. In Uganda the areas covered by the concession are as a rule greater than in Kenya, so that they meet the greater average capacity of the sawmills.

In Tanzania, unlike Kenya and Uganda, a high proportion of the roundwood used for sawnwood production does not come from operation of long-term concessions in forest reserves, but results from short-term licences to fell timber on unreserved land, either forest or open woodland, which has not been declared a forest reserve. Such casual licences are in many cases granted to individual Africans, who then often fell only a few trees for their own requirements, or may perhaps fell timber on a somewhat larger scale and sell the roundwood to sawmills.

As a general rule the larger sawmill firms have concession agreements with the forest authorities, and these agreements assure them of the right to cut the timber in a given area for between five and ten years. This is always the case in the closed high forests of the forest reserves, which are spread over the country like islands. Frequently, however, the firms obtain additional roundwood from forests, not declared as reserves, which are open to anybody who receives a felling permit from the Forest Department. This is especially so in the case of those sawmills which supply their need for timber of the Muninga (Pterocarpus angolensis), Muhuhu (Brachylaena hutchinsii) and Miombo (Brachystega spiciformis) in open woodlands alone, and have no concession areas of their own. In the Rufiji area, which lies to the South of Dar es Salaam and is especially rich in Muninga, a concession was granted to an African logging company which fells the timber on a large scale, and then conveys it to Dar es Salaam, where it sells the roundwood to private sawmills. In Tanzania, therefore, the operation of a sawmill is not necessarily dependent on a concession area belonging to that sawmill, as is the general rule in Kenya and Uganda.

The concession agreements, at least those at longer term, usually lay down a maximum and minimum annual cut, the minimum stem diameter according to the species of tree, the limit below which no tree may be felled, the planted areas which will be made available for clear cutting, and all other conditions required in order to ensure careful felling and extraction. The felling, the transportation, and in most cases the building of forest roads as well, have to be done by the sawmill operator.

The felling is controlled by the local forest departments. In particular the felled timber is measured on the spot, or at a log yard, by forest department employees. On the basis of such measurement the operator pays the state forest authorities.

In point of fact the system of granting licences is to no small extent responsible for certain difficulties which beset the sawmilling industry. Delaying of agreements already concluded frequently creates a strained relationship between the Government department, which grants the licences, and the operators, mostly Indian, who receive them. As an aid to Africanisation of the sawmilling industry, and owing to official dislike of the mainly Indian sawmill operators, these latter are often left until the last moment in doubt about whether their concession will be prolonged, and if so for how long. Although there are hardly any properly qualified Africans with adequate financial resources, the authorities are quite reluctant to grant or prolong Indians' licences. This produces an extremely unfortunate effect on the willingness of the operators concerned to incur capital expenditure[16]. It is quite understandable that, towards the end of a concession period and in view of the uncertainty about whether their licences will be prolonged, the operators postpone or no longer incur capital expenditure on replacements or new fixed assets, the result frequently being considerable impairment of their operations.

III. Production and Timber Species Used

Timber production in the East African countries, including the output from private forests and farms, can be estimated to amount to roughly 500,000 fm of roundwood per annum (see also Table 2).

Table 2. *Roundwood Production in the East African Countries*

Country	Year	Quantity fm
Kenya	1966	195,700
Uganda	1965–66	126,900
Tanzania	1966	141,900
Total East African Countries		464,500

Source: Statements by Forestry Departments at Nairobi, Kampala and Dar es Salaam.

16 In Tanzania, where the sawmilling industry is largely in Indian hands, the Government is trying to promote the influence of Africans through the granting of concessions. The most valuable kind of timber in Tanzania is, for example, the African blackwood (Dalbergia melanoxylon). In all cases where licences are granted to Indian sawmill operators this species is excluded; it is reserved for small African purchasers, like wood carvers, of for African cooperative societies, which are granted regular blackwood concessions. These cooperatives export a large part of their output in the form of roundwood.

Of the total roundwood production recorded for the three countries, namely 464,000 fm, Kenya accounted for 43 per cent, Uganda for 27 per cent and Tanzania for 30 per cent. The main features and breakdown of the output, according to tree species and groups of species, differ quite widely as between the three countries.

Almost half of the roundwood felled in Kenya comes from exotic softwood plantations. The rest comes from natural forests, chiefly mountain rain forests around Mount Kenya, the Aberdares and Mount Elgon, as well as from the Mau, Nandi and Kakamega natural forests. The plantations are almost all located in the highlands of South-West Kenya, largely to the West of the Great Rift Valley, but also on Mount Kenya.

A characteristic feature of Kenya's forestry is that it is increasingly based on only a small number of tree species. These comprise two indigenous trees, Podocarpus and Juniperus, as well as exotic fast-growing plantations containing Cupressus lusitanica, Pinus patula and Pinus radiata. Among these trees the Cupressus, in particular, occupies a prominent position. During the period from April, 1965 to March, 1966, according to the Forest Department at Nairobi, roughly 73,100 fm of sawnwood were produced. At 33,700 fm, or 46.1 per cent, the proportion for which Cupressus accounts is far the greatest. Next come Podocarpus with 35.8 per cent, Juniperus with 9.8 per cent, Ocotea with 3.2 per cent, Pinus with 1.5 per cent, Olea with 1.3 per cent, and Brachylaena with 0.9 per cent. Altogether nearly 20 different kinds of tree are used, although the greater part are used only to an insignificant extent. The seven types of timber mentioned together made up 98.6 per cent of the total sawnwood output for 1965–66.

Forestry in Uganda is almost exclusively directed to the managing of natural forests. These, it is true, are distributed only like islands throughout the country; but they do represent a type of tropical rain forest which is both productive and rich in high-grade timbers. As is natural with this type of forest there are a great many different kinds of timber, and these are marketed in the form of "mixed hardwoods", except for that which comes from areas where — as a result of natural causes or silvicultural treatments — one kind of merchantable timber predominates.

Given the distribution of the individual species in this wide-ranging mixture it is as a rule not possible in Uganda permanently or adequately to keep the individual species separate so far as regards felling them and offering them for sale. There are exceptions in the case of some concession areas, like the Budongo forest reserve, the Siba forest reserve and the Banjoro district, which are exceptionally rich in mahoganies such as Entandophragma and Khaya (the African mahogany). Timber species with similar qualities, and above all with similar specific gravities are therefore combined in groups and so marketed. The timbers felled in Uganda, although no precise data are available regarding their respective shares of total production, are classified in the following groups of tree species:

- Mvule; this, as the most valuable type of timber, forms a group of its own, and is often felled by sawmills which specialise exclusively in Mvule.
- Furniture wood.
- Heavy construction timber (all woods with a specific gravity greater than 753 kg/fm at 12 per cent humidity).
- Medium-weight construction timber (all woods with a specific gravity between 753 and 481 kg/fm at 12 per cent humidity).
- Light construction timber (all woods with a specific gravity less than 481 kg/fm at 12 per cent humidity).
- Conifers.

Although a high proportion of the timbers are individually of great value, it is a disadvantage, by comparison with uniform timber, to use mixed timbers for building purposes. This is because of their differing properties in regard to shrinkage, weight, breaking strength, proneness to attack by fungus and insects, colour, and so forth. The market, if it could, would primarily call for uniform and cheap mass-produced timber; but in Uganda up till now, owing to the lack of fast-growing plantations, not enough such timber is produced.

For 1966 the amount of roundwood felled in Tanzania was announced to be 141,900 fm. Of this amount the largest part, namely 36.1 per cent, came from the Tanga region[17], 13.7 per cent from the Arusha-Kilimanjaro-Moshi region, 13.2 per cent from the coast region, 13.1 per cent from the West region, 9.8 per cent from the South region, 9.4 per cent from the lake region and 4.7 per cent from the Southern highlands region.

The type of wood most used in Tanzania is Muninga (Pterocarpus angolensis), which in 1966 accounted for 21.4 per cent of all the roundwood felled. Next came Muhuhu (Brachylaena hutchinsii) with 17.6 per cent, Podocarpus with 15.8 per cent, Brachystegia spiciformis with 10.5 per cent, Cupressus with 5.8 per cent, Ocotea with 5.6 per cent, Cephalosphaera with 3.4 per cent, Khaya with 3.3 per cent, Chlorophora with 2.3 per cent, Bukea with 1.4 per cent, and Albicia with 1.1 per cent. These types of timber accounted for 88.2 per cent of the roundwood fellings. Altogether more than 40 species were utilised.

Muninga, Muhuhu and Brachystegia are species of the open woodlands; Podocarpus, Ocotea and Cephalosphaera are typical of the mountain forests, especially those on Kilimanjaro, Mount Meru and the Usambara Mountains. The only locality where they are found is a forest, not far from Bukoba on Lake Victoria; this locality is in a flat area, which is marshy during the rainy season, and which almost exclusively contains Podocarpus.

---

17 As regards the division of Tanzania into regions see footnote 15a on p. 90.

The figures given above do not include the production from private forests and farms. The owners of the former confine themselves to appreciable cuttings of Mtambara (Cephalosphaera usambarensis) in the Usambara and Uluguru Mountains; those of the latter confine themselves to small plantations of Cupressus and Grevillea, the latter frequently to provide shade in coffee plantations.

IV. Logging Operations

Note: While investigating forestry and sawmilling in the three East African countries the author studied methods and techniques of felling, extraction, roundwood loading and roundwood transportation, and analysed the costs. The following paragraphs, however, state only the most important results of this investigation, which was concerned rather with operation and management.

1. Felling

Apart from a few quite progressive mills, which use power saws, the felling is done in all three East African countries by means of dragsaw and axe. Although the dragsaw has been generally adopted in preference to axe felling, the primitive chopping of trees, including those of the largest size with breast-height diameter of up to 2 m, is not uncommon. Even the crosscutting into transportable logs is still done by axe at many places. The output is low, not only because of defective working methods and poor maintenance of the tools, but also owing to the poor labour discipline of the African workers employed at the sawmills, which are usually owned by Indians. Because the African worker is so little interested in earning more, or producing more, piece-work has been adopted in only a very few cases. Good outputs cannot be obtained without supervision and control by reliable supervisors.
The wages of forest workers are laid down by official regulation. The minimum wage for a forest worker in 1967 was about Shs 90 per month; in addition the employer also as a rule provides free lodging, for the worker and his family, as well as a ration — for the most part weekly — of ground maize.

2. Extraction

In all three countries the extraction of the stems from the stump as far as the road, practicable for trucks (lorries), is done by crawler tractor. In a few plantation areas agricultural wheeled tractors are also used. There is an exception in the case of Tanzania's extensive bush and open woodlands, as well as in Uganda's areas devoted to extraction of Mvule (Chlorophora excelsa), where four-wheeled trucks (lorries) normally drive up to the isolated fellable trees. Use is made everywhere of primitive ground skidding, frequently combined with employment of winches fitted on the crawler tractors. Yarding arches are rare exceptions. The only example of modern extraction methods is afforded by the Kenya Forest Department's Logging Unit; this has undertaken the extraction of plantation timber for certain sawmills, and uses the Canadian articulated wheeled skidder known as the "Timber Jack".

Not only in Kenya but also in Uganda and Tanzania the vehicles employed are for the most part old, the sawmills having bought them second-hand. Since engines which have become unusable are available for purchase at very low prices, after which they can be used for removal of spare parts, the vehicles are constantly repaired in the sawmills' own workshops and are thereby kept on the road for an extremely long time. The age of the vehicles in use is correspondingly great. The average age of the logging vehicles, as recorded in the course of the investigation, was about 12.5 years in Kenya; this compared with 10.5 years in Uganda, and with 11.5 in Tanzania.

The State Forest Departments of all three countries require the concessionaires not to exceed a maximum extraction distance of 400 yards (365 m) for ordinary ground skidding, and of 800 yards (730 m) if a yarding arch is used. But measurements of extraction distances at about 50 mills in East Africa frequently revealed average distances greater than the maxima permitted. Only in the Kenyan plantation areas was the average less than the distance allowed. The average extraction distances were as follows:

Kenya	399 m in natural forest and
	179 m in plantations;
Uganda	391 m in natural forest;
Tanzania	422 m in natural forest.

The performance of the vehicles used for extraction is poor at nearly all the mills. The reasons for this are that the organisation is bad, that the aged vehicles often need repair, that the per capita productivity of the forest workers and drivers is low, that the forest roads and skid tracks are defectively and inefficiently constructed, and that tractor capacities are insufficiently employed.

For the individual countries the following average annual performances per extraction tractor were worked out:

Kenya	1,949 fm		
in fact	2,022 fm	in	natural forest;
	1,815 fm	in	planted forest (the large annual output of the three state-owned Timber Jacks, namely 6,600 fm each, not being counted);
Uganda	4,100 fm	in	tropical rain forest;
Tanzania	1,075 fm	in	closed high forest, and
	886 fm	in	open woodland.

The relatively great average performance in Uganda is due to the large stems (up to 85 fm per tree), easy ground, stronger tractors and shorter extraction distances. Reasons for the poor performance in Tanzania include longer skidding distances (both in open woodland and in mountain forests), difficult ground and unduly small sawmills; these employ too many tractors, and moreover their capacity is even less fully employed than it is, for example, in Kenya.
Also the average volume per tree is smaller in Tanzania.

3. Loading of Roundwood

Because of the heavy logs found in natural forest, mechanical aids have to be used for loading. In planted forest, as well as in open woodlands and the bush, the most frequent method of loading is on the other hand to roll the logs up by hand. Loading devices fitted on the truck (lorry), such as winches or cranes, are generally unknown. Owing to the high cost of up-to-date loading equipment, together with the extreme cheapness of labour and the present unwillingness of Indian sawmill operators to incur heavier capital expenditure, use is in many cases made only of simple appliances like a tripod and chain hoist, primitive cranes made in the owner's own workshop, cheap loading devices from old military stocks that are hardly capable of use for loading timber, direct loading by bulldozer and loading ramp, and hauling up the logs by winch and tackle.

4. Transportation of Roundwood to the Sawmill

Forest road construction

Together with the concession the sawmill operator also undertakes the construction of roads required for operation in the area concerned. Although planning of the road system is supposed to be done by the forest administration, the practice especially in the natural forests is to leave the lay-out and construction to the concessionaire. Since the latter as a rule has no

employees skilled in such matters, and is moreover interested only in getting the work done as cheaply as possible, many operators build roads which do not meet the requirements.
Mostly only temporary roads are built. Once they have been used, they fall into disrepair again. Only in isolated cases do the forest departments take over roads, which are maintained even after felling has been completed. Only in the planted forests of Kenya are the conditions better, because the Kenyan state forest administration itself undertakes the building of roads in the districts. Apart from a few exceptions the road density is too low.

Transport facilities for transportation of logs to sawmill

In all three East African countries the transport is normally done by means of trucks (lorries) owned by the sawmills. The only exceptions in Kenya are found at two sawmills, which are supplied with logs by the Logging Unit of the Forest Department; similarly in Tanzania there is a mill to which roundwood is supplied through an African cooperative society which has its own felling concession and its own vehicles. In Tanzania, more frequently than in Kenya or Uganda, Africans who have obtained casual licences from the Forest Department bring their timber to the Indian sawmills for sale; the timber is in fact brought either by hired contractors or on the Africans' own lorries.
The vehicles used for timber transportation in Kenya, Uganda and Tanzania are in many cases too old and too decrepit for smooth operation. In particular their loading capacity is too small. Use is mostly made of old, second-hand military vehicles which the sawmills have bought cheaply. The conditions are somewhat better in Uganda, where the sawmills are larger than in Kenya or in Tanzania and also more highly capitalised. More new lorries are bought.
With regard to the age of the vehicles employed for logging the questionnaire showed the following:

Kenya	12 years;	
Uganda	9 years;	
Tanzania	11 years	in the case of vehicles used for bringing timber out of closed high forests;
	7 years	in that of vehicles for bringing timber out from open woodland and bush.

The following average distances between the sawmills and their felling areas were found:

Kenya	13 km	for sawmills felling in natural forest;
	6.5 km	for sawmills felling in plantations;

Uganda	34	km	for sawmills felling in natural forest;
	72	km	for sawmills principally felling Mvule;
Tanzania	19	km	for sawmills felling in natural forest;
	79	km	for sawmills felling in open woodland.

The vehicles observed in the individual countries carry the following average quantities of roundwood to the sawmills:

Kenya	1,999 fm,	per lorry per year. (Average number of lorries per mill: 2–3)
Uganda	2,377 fm,	per lorry per year. (Average number of lorries per mill: 3–4)
Tanzania	820 fm,	per lorry per year. (Average number of lorries per mill: 2–3)

The low performance of the vehicles in Tanzania is mainly due to the long transportation distances (79 km) to the sawmills, which obtain their timber from the poorly stocked open woodland area.

V. Roundwood Prices

In all three countries the concessionaire has to pay, to the state forest departments, prices which differ according to the timber species.
Payment is made in Kenya per fm of roundwood, according to the type of timber, and in the case of plantation timber according to the size. The various prices for timber are laid down annually by the Forest Department. They vary according to the market value of the species in question. During 1965–66, for example, the price — known as the stumpage rate — ranged between Shs 18.85 for Podocarpus gracilior and Shs 68.35 for Vitex kenyensis, in the case of wood from natural forests; in that of logs 54.4 cm in diameter the stumpage rate for Cupressus was Shs 23.10, while for Pinus it was Shs 17.40 and for Juniperus Shs 24.90 per fm.
In Kenya the stumpage rate applies to all forest areas. It constitutes practically the only revenue of the Forest Department. Reductions or increases are not applied where forest areas are more or less favourably located for transportation, nor for differences in the nature of the site. This in many cases handicaps concessionaires, who have to compete with mills working in more favourable conditions. Up till 1966 this handicap was made good, for mills located a long way from the nearest railway station, inasmuch as the Forest Department granted a kind of mileage allowance; this allowance, however, has been discontinued.

The costs which the sawmill incurs through payment of stumpage on the roundwood to the Forest Department appear at first sight low. But the proportion recovered in the form of sawnwood, the salable product, is only 40 per cent to 50 per cent; and in the light of this fact the expense of stumpage appears relatively large in relation to the proceeds of sale. The proportion of stumpage to the selling price for sawnwood in 1965–66 was, for example, about 22 per cent in the case of podo.
Measurement of the roundwood taken by the concessionaire, and payment of the stumpage, are effected in Uganda and Tanzania according to the same principles as in Kenya. In Uganda the stumpage is paid according to the tree species or group of species. A certain burden is imposed in that country by the heavy stumpage rate on mahogany and mvule (in 1967 the charge on mahogany was for instance Shs 78.75 per fm); the burden is especially heavy for those sawmills which principally fell timber of these kinds. In Tanzania the various tree species are classified, according to their value, in six classes for which the roundwood price is laid down by Government order.

C. TIMBER SALES IN EAST AFRICA

I. Supply and Flow of Timber

The frequent gap between the needs of the areas producing and selling sawnwood in East Africa, on the one hand, and the facts of the communications system on the other, create the specific sales and supply situation which exists in the individual East African countries.
Because of its relatively good railway system Kenya has communications better than those, for example, in neighbouring Uganda. But, since the island-like distribution of forests in Kenya does not sufficiently coincide with the wood-consuming areas, some long hauls are required before the sawnwood can be sold. This is especially so in the case of Mombasa, which is one of the largest sawnwood markets, but which lies on the coast far from all the timber-producing forest areas. The neighbouring coastal forests are not capable of meeting the demand for sawnwood and construction timber.
The forest areas lie for the most part in South-West Kenya, this being the part of the country which has been opened up by the railway from the port of Mombasa to Uganda, and by the various branch lines. All the larger

sawmills, which supply not only their own local region but also distant markets, are on or near a railway line. Most of the sawnwood transportation to neighbouring countries or to the seaport, as well as to destinations inside the country, is therefore done by rail. This is so even though Kenya's road system is by African standards in a reasonable state, and is also quite dense. North Kenya, with its extensive dry savannahs, its small undeveloped population and its rudimentary road system, is neither a timber production area nor a market for sawn timber.

Uganda's largest and most productive forest reserves lie, island-like, in the West of the country; they extend roughly South-West, along a line from the North point of Lake Albert as far as the frontier of Rwanda. But since the country's important timber markets lie principally in the East and South-East (the largest being at Kampala and Jinja), as well as in the North central part of the country (where there are markets at Soroti, Lira and Gulu), the sawnwood has to be carried for quite long distances, much as it has in Kenya. There is an exception only in the case of timber produced from the forest reserves to the West of Kampala, and between Kampala and Jinja, since these reserves are located close to the markets for their timber.

The important forest areas in the West are opened up for traffic almost exclusively by roads; thus the situation there differs fundamentally from that in Kenya, where almost all the sawmills and markets lie on a railway line. The railway which leads to West Uganda (with its terminus at Kasese) does not actually touch any forest area, so that it is not used for carrying timber to the East. The same applies to the country's second railway line, which runs to the North. This line is used for imports of timber from Kenya, it is true, but hardly for delivering wood from production areas inside Uganda. All the work of carrying sawnwood — with the exception of deliveries from Kenya, of those to Kenya and Tanzania, and of exports going overseas — is accordingly done by truck (lorry). Uganda's roads are asphalted to only quite a small extent, but in other respects are relatively well developed as an all-weather road system.

Tanzania's sawmills are concentrated in only three of the country's regions; the first is the Tanga region including the Usambara Mountains, the second the Kilimanjaro-Arusha region, the third the coastal region around Dar es Salaam, including the hinterland around Morogoro, Kilosa and the northern Kilombero valley. Up till a few years ago there was a fourth concentration of sawmills in the Western muninga areas around Tabora. Of late, however, the majority of these mills have suspended operation, so that in this area the production and conveyance of timber are important only for local requirements.

Only small quantities of sawnwood, much of it roughly converted, go West to Kigoma (terminus of the railway from Dar es Salaam), to Mwanza in the North, and to the distant Dar es Salaam. These regions are of course supplied from the sawmills located in their respective areas. Thus each of them has enough timber markets of its own. Consequently there is no great long-distance flow of timber to very remote markets, as might have been expected in a country so large as Tanzania.

Only the country's capital city, being the largest centre for consumption of sawnwood, receives not only timber imported from Kenya but also some from the sawnwood-producing areas in the North of the country around Kilimanjaro and the Usambara Mountains. The Southern region abutting on Mozambique, and the wooded Southern highlands region, have as yet no developed sawmilling industry; they obtain the necessary supply of sawnwood exclusively from small bush sawyers. These produce by means of primitive circular saws on the spot. Pitsawyers produce also small quantities for local requirements. Normally the timber is not transported for any considerable distance.

The poorly wooded area in the North-West, around Mwanza, is supplied to a small extent from a few sawmills in the Tabora region to the South, but largely from Kenya, either by ship across Lake Victoria or by lorry along the road which runs to Kenya on the eastern side of the lake. The only large sawmill in North-West Tanzania is at Bukoba; but its market is mainly in Uganda and Burundi.

Tanzania's exports of sawnwood, at more than 20,000 fm in 1966 and almost 29,000 fm in 1965, are the largest for any of the three East African countries [18]. But the sawmills which at present export are mostly located near the coast, or not too far inland, and they export through three ports, namely Tanga, Dar es Salaam and Mtwara. Consequently the distances for conveyance of timber to the respective ports are short.

It will be seen, from what has so far been stated, that there is a certain flow of timber between the three East African countries; each of them, in fact, supplies both its neighbours. The quantities of timber exchanged between the individual countries differ quite widely. The questionnaire, which also covered the interterritorial movement of timber over a period of one year, revealed that Kenya sells to its two neighbours much more wood than it receives from them. Thus about 13,000 fm of sawnwood were sent from Kenya to Uganda, and 8,000 fm to Tanzania. Kenya bought some 2,200 fm from Uganda and 4,250 fm from Tanzania. The timber shipments between Uganda and Tanzania were even smaller. Uganda sold roughly 1,500 fm to Tanzania, while Tanzania sold approximately as much to Uganda [19].

In Uganda and Tanzania there is a shortage of timber in the cheap ordinary grades. Kenya, with its fast-growing plantations of exotic conifers, and its

18 The figures relate only to the sawmills covered by the questionnaire, which account for two-thirds of the total sawnwood production.

19 Data covering deliveries from Kenya and Uganda for 1965–1966, and from Tanzania for 1966.

still abundant stands of Podocarpus, has enough such timber. One reason for the interterritorial timber trade is that certain areas short of timber in Tanzania and Uganda are, for purposes of transport, closer to timber-producing areas in Kenya than to those in their own country. One example of this in Tanzania is the area around Mwanza on the southern part of Lake Victoria; this area produces almost no timber of its own, and is further away from the wooded areas of Tanzania in the South and East than from the forests in Western Kenya. Conveyance by ship between Mwanza and Kisumu in Western Kenya moreover provides good communication. Much the same applies to the timber sent from Kenya to markets in the East and North-East of Uganda; these markets are better connected by rail with the West Kenyan timber-producing areas than with their own country's forest areas, most of which lie in West Uganda.
Thus, despite the long distances (about 1,250–1,500 km) between the sawmills in Kenya and Dar es Salaam, it is the Kenyan sawmills which supply the Dar es Salaam market. This is due to the acute shortage of cheap softwoods. It therefore seems absurd that sawmills in North Tanzania, for instance on North Kilimanjaro, sell their podocarpus timber to Nairobi. This is no doubt understandable from the point of view of the sawmills concerned, because they are closer to the Kenyan than to the Tanzanian market; it is not understandable, however, if the object is to ensure the most efficient possible supplying of the country with its own timber.

II. Marketing

Just as the production of sawnwood is in the hands of private sawmilling firms, so in the East African countries the marketing of timber and its conveyance to the purchaser are carried out, or at least organised, by those same firms. There are no wood merchants in the proper sense.
In Kenya there is an exception in the shape of Timsales, Ltd., a timber marketing company with its registered office at Nairobi. This company itself operates three sawmills of its own. For ten other private sawmills, which are independent of each other, Timsales does the marketing. The mills receive, from the central sales agency at Nairobi, orders telling them where they are to deliver. Thus the sawmills send their products directly to the consumer.
A further exception is found in the case of a few Tanzanian timber exporters, who buy from the sawmills and then export the timber overseas [20].
Some Kenyan mills which are located in forest areas, and are consequently a

20 In 1937 a timber marketing company called Uganda Timber Sales, Ltd. was formed; all the sawmills which received concessions from the Forest Department had to belong to it. The marketing was done on a cooperative basis. In 1959, the activity having become insufficient, the company was liquidated.

long way from the consuming markets, maintain a timber yard at the largest buying centres; this yard carries a suitable stock of sawnwood for sale. Where this is the case, the producer conveys the timber from his sawmill to the yard either with his own vehicles or by public transport. Similarly in Uganda and Tanzania the larger sawmills located at the principal markets, for example at Kampala, Jinja and Dar es Salaam, operate timber sales agencies which carry a suitable stock of sawnwood; at these agencies, in general, better qualities are offered.

The problem of supplying the market with air-seasoned timber arises, above all, in Uganda. Despite the forestry authorities' efforts to ensure more efficient use of the various types of timber, as well as of preserved and seasoned goods, it is mainly fresh unimpregnated timber that is offered for sale[21]. So as to correct this abuse the Forest Department at Entebbe has established a department of its own, one function of this department being to conduct publicity in favour of optimum and efficient use of timber.

Purchasers' requirements in regard to quality are often low. They attach prime importance to low prices. Thus for example in Uganda, owing to the many different tree species and also because buyers are not exacting, most of the sawnwood is merely sold as "mixed hardwoods" in a barely seasoned state. Still, progress is being gradually made towards more suitable use of the different species, chiefly by the large consumers. Especially the public authorities, in connection with their building activity, are more and more conforming to the conclusions reached by modern timber research.

One general marketing problem is presented in East Africa by the fact that, with progressive development and a rising standard of living, the population even outside the larger towns want sawnwood to an extent which exceeds that sold in the town markets, while the sawmills take little trouble to provide such goods. Up till now the low purchasing power of the small African customer has made such business unprofitable for the sawmills. Yet precisely this demand for preferably cheap goods, with few requirements in regard to quality, might help the sawmills to sell their poorer grades, shortenings and part of the wood waste. At present the majority of mills have in stock much sawnwood of a quality and size such that it cannot be sold in the financially stronger markets. Thus the economies of the countries concerned lose highly valuable assets, because blue stain and insects make the wood really unusable after it has been incorrectly stored for a short time. Even somewhat better

---

21 There are in Uganda five wood preserving plants, two of which are operated by the Electricity Board solely for the purpose of impregnating poles. The other three belong to sawmills; two of these impregnate the greater part of their production for the Kilembe copper mines. The impregnation is done by a compression process, using copper-chromium salts soluble in water. The sawmill in 1967 charged a supplement of Shs 63 per fm; but many buyers find this price too high.

and dearer timber could be sold to the numerous small village cabinet makers, who are to be found spread about everywhere, and who mostly suffer from shortage of sawnwood while such wood is rotting at the sawmills only a few miles away.
In Tanzania the sawmills take even less trouble than do those in Kenya and Uganda to supply timber to the population in the interior of the country. Their demand for sawnwood, even of lower quality, is however smaller than that in the other two East African countries. The majority of the rural population in the remote areas of the South and West, with poor traffic facilities, buy practically nothing except poles for building huts, and these are obtained as and when required from the bush and the open woodlands. So far as sawnwood is required for making primitive furniture, hut doors and shutters, it is cut by hand when needed. The necessary licences for this felling, mostly of single trees from areas not declared to be forest reserves, are granted by the district forest authorities.

III. Markets for Sawnwood

1. Sawnwood from Kenya

In 1966 the sawmills covered by the questionnaire produced sawnwood amounting to 68,400 fm, representing 77 per cent of the country's total production. Of this quantity there was sold:

inside Kenya	35,900 fm (= 52 per cent)
in Uganda	13,300 fm (= 19 per cent)
in Tanzania	7,900 fm (= 12 per cent)
outside East Africa	11,300 fm (= 17 per cent)

The largest market in Kenya is at Nairobi. Of the 35,900 fm sold inside Kenya, Nairobi took 20,200 fm. It was followed by Mombasa with 4,000 fm, Kisumu with 3,600 fm, Nakuru with 1,900 fm, Meru with 1,600 fm, Thompson's Falls with 1,100 fm, and the Embu reservoir with 1,000 fm. The rest went to Eldoret, Kericho, Kinangop, Naivasha, Kisii, and Kakamega. Each of the places here named is only the centre of a sales area; this applies especially to Nairobi. The list cannot be regarded as complete, however, because the total production of sawnwood is not included.
The most important buyer of sawnwood and construction timber is the building industry, which is confined to relatively few centres. While it is true that the demand for sawnwood in the villages is rising, such demand still

represents a small proportion of the whole. The African rural population's traditional method of building huts does not require processed timber of good quality; the builders make do with simple posts and poles which, like the firewood, are obtained from the neighbourhood of the settlement areas. The rural population's sawnwood requirement is mainly confined to timber for doors, shutters and simple furniture, produced in small joiners' shops throughout the country. The people obtain their supplies locally from ultra-small sawmills or even from pit sawyers. The larger sawmills covered by the questionnaire are generally interested in customers with more purchasing power, and take little care to supply the small customers found in villages and in the country.

A special problem affecting Kenya's forestry and sawmilling industry lies in the fact that the entire area to the East of Nairobi contains no productive forests, and that consequently Mombasa, the country's second largest market, lies at a great distance from any area producing timber.

From Kenya's point of view Uganda is an important market for cheap plantation timber and uniform podocarpus wood; the reason is that Uganda possesses almost solely high-grade hardwoods, from natural forests, which are relatively dear and which, because so many species are comprised, do not represent cheap goods of uniform quality. Kenya's deliveries of timber to Uganda are distributed between five market areas. Among these the country's largest city, Kampala, comes by a long way first with 6,800 fm. It is followed by Jinja with 2,200 fm, Mbale with 2,100 fm, Soroti with 1,800 fm, and Tororo with 400 fm. The timber is carried exclusively by rail. Only cheap ordinary grades of Cupressus and Podocarpus softwoods are sold.

Tanzania, like Uganda, has hardly any mature softwood plantations. The productive felling areas in natural forests are located more in the eastern, north-eastern and southern parts of the country. Tanzania's three most important areas for sale of Kenyan sawnwood are Mwanza (which takes 4,200 fm per annum), Musoma (1,400 fm) and Dar es Salaam (2,300 fm). The timber for Mwanza and Musoma is normally conveyed by rail to the port of Kisumu, and then by ship across Lake Victoria; a minor proportion goes directly by lorry. Dar es Salaam is supplied only by rail.

In Kenya's exports of sawnwood to destinations outside East Africa the greatest share is taken, in terms of value, by Juniperus procera, known in the trade as "pencil cedar". It is exported either as normal sawnwood in the form of boards or else (and this applies to a large proportion) in the form of ready-made pencil slats. The chief customer countries are the United Kingdom, the Netherlands and the Federal Republic of Germany. Muhuhu (Brachylaena hutchinsii) is sold exclusively from the coastal forests, in the form of parquetry, to the United Kingdom and the Federal Republic of Germany. Good qualities of knotless Cupressus wood are exported to Réunion, Kuwait, Israel, the United Kingdom, Denmark, and even Norway.

Small quantities of Podocarpus are sent to the United Kingdom, the Federal Republic of Germany, Denmark, Réunion, and Madagascar. Walnut (Lovoa swynnertonii), Elgon olive (Olea welwitschii) and Muna (Aningeria adolfii friderichi) are exported in smaller quantities to the United Kingdom, Norway, Belgium, and the Federal Republic of Germany. Of these timber species walnut is the only one shipped partly as roundwood. The timber is conveyed from the interior to Mombasa, the port for export, by rail; in the case of Muhuhu wood from the neighbouring coastal forests the transportation is done by lorry.

2. Sawnwood from Uganda

In Uganda during 1965–66 the sawmills covered by the questionnaire produced and sold about 43,600 fm of sawnwood, that is 83 per cent of the total sawnwood production. The sawnwood sales, thus recorded, were made up as follows:

inside Uganda	37,400 fm	(= 86 per cent)
in Kenya	2,200 fm	(= 5 per cent)
in Tanzania	1,400 fm	(= 3 per cent)
outside East Africa	2,600 fm	(= 6 per cent)

The largest market inside Uganda is Kampala, which took 12,400 fm, that is, in terms of quantity, approximately one-third of all the sawnwood sold in Uganda. Next in order as customers or markets come the Kilembe copper mines with 8,200 fm, Jinja with 4,700 fm, Lira with 2,200 fm, Soroti with 2,100 fm, Mbale with 2,000 fm, Arua with 1,500 fm, Gulu with 1,300 fm, and Fort Portal with 1,100 fm. Sales are not confined only to the towns, but are also effected in the surrounding areas. In 1966 moreover, as already mentioned, Kampala, Jinja, Soroti and also Tororo received from Kenya substantial sawnwood deliveries amounting to 13,300 fm, of which roughly half went to Kampala alone.

Uganda's deliveries of timber to Kenya are appreciably smaller than its timber imports from that country. However, by reason of the fact that Uganda chiefly sells valuable timber species like mahogany and mvule, the value of its exports is more than one-third that of its imports; this is so even though, in terms of quantity, the imports from Kenya are seven times as great as Uganda's exports to that country. The only important market in Kenya for sawnwood from Uganda is at Nairobi; smaller quantities are sold at Eldoret, Kisumu, Nakuru, Kitale, and Kericho.

Finally Tanzania, which takes about 1,400 fm of sawnwood each year from Uganda, is of no importance as a customer for that country. Tanzania, in contrast to Kenya, takes the cheaper grades. The largest market is at Mwanza,

which takes 71 per cent of all the sawnwood sold. Smaller markets for sawnwood from Uganda are at Bukoba, Musoma and Mwadui.
Although the Government of Uganda is much interested in promoting timber exports, such exports are small. In 1965–66 they comprised only about 2,600 fm of sawnwood (roundwood is not exported). One reason lies in the great distances from Mombasa, the port for export; another is that the domestic demand is continuously increasing, including that for valuable types of timber, and that the home market even offers better prices than foreign markets. Because of the strong competition by other timber-exporting countries, especially West African, which have not such long hauls to their seaports, and owing to the burden of freight charges, high prices cannot be obtained for Ugandan export timber sold ex sawmill. For this reason it is possible to export only timber of the very highest grade, for which suitably attractive prices can be obtained.
The timbers chiefly exported are mvule (Chlorophora excelsa) and mahogany (Entandophragma and Khaya), both being in strong demand on the world market. Apart from the Netherlands almost the sole buyer is the United Kingdom. Rwanda is the only African country, outside East Africa, which takes cheap cypress plantation timber; this is supplied on quite a small scale by Uganda's only sawmill operating in a softwood plantation in the South. In general the planning of Uganda's forestry, given the rapidly growing consumption of timber due to the increase in population, is not directed in any considerable degree to the promotion of exports.

3. Sawnwood from Tanzania

The questionnaire covered 31 sawmills, which in 1966 produced 42,100 fm of sawnwood, this being two-thirds of all the sawnwood produced in Tanzania. (The remaining third, not covered by the questionnaire, is mostly produced by small bush sawyers or pit sawyers to meet the demand in their respective localities.) The sawnwood sales, recorded as a result of the inquiry, were made up as follows:

inside Tanzania	22,100 fm	(= 52 per cent)
in Kenya	4,200 fm	(= 10 per cent)
in Uganda	1,500 fm	(= 4 per cent)
outside East Africa	14,300 fm	(= 34 per cent)

The most important wood consumption areas in Tanzania, according to the quantities of sawnwood sold, are Dar es Salaam (8,500 fm), Moshi (2,700 fm), Mwanza (2,200 fm), Tanga (1,800 fm), and Dodoma (1,700 fm); there are also smaller markets like Arusha, Morogoro, Mikumi, Kilosa, and Korogwe. Mwanza and the surrounding country also receive sawnwood delivered from Kenya and Uganda. Sawnwood from Kenya likewise reaches Musoma and Dar es Salaam; it chiefly consists of cheap cypress plantation wood.

Tanzania's timber exports to Kenya go almost exclusively into two areas, namely Nairobi and Mombasa. The sawnwood sales in 1966 to those areas amounted, respectively, to about 2,900 and 500 fm; in addition some 900 fm of roundwood was supplied to Nairobi. The greater part of the sawnwood exported from Tanzania to Kenya comes from a single sawmill on North-West Kilimanjaro. This sawmill sells to Nairobi practically the whole of its podo production, amounting in 1966 to about 2,600 fm. That appears strange, since Kenya is itself the greatest producer of this kind of timber in East Africa. But the distance from the said sawmill to Nairobi is only 270 km, comprising 129 km by lorry and 141 km by rail; that is less than the distance from many sawmills in West Kenya, which can deliver to Uganda more cheaply than to Nairobi. The roundwood comes for the most part from the northern Kilombero valley. The haul from there is 1,350 miles by rail. The timber is sold to the East African Railways and Harbours at Nairobi. Mombasa is linked with Tanga by the coastal road, only 198 km long; in 1966 it obtained roughly 500 fm of sawnwood from the Tanga area and from the Usambara Mountains. The distance from Mombasa to the forest areas in North-East Tanzania is shorter than to those in West and North-West Kenya.

Table 3. *Tanzania's Timber Exports, 1966*

Timber Species	Quantity fm
Brachylaena hutchinsii (Muhuhu)	7,248
Pterocarpus angolensis (Muninga)	4,199
Podocarpus spp. (Podo)	2,817
Cephalosphaera usambarensis (Mtambara)	2,274
Chlorophora excelsa (Mvule)	979
Dalbergia melanoxylon	905
Ocotea usambarensis (Camphor)	857
Combretum schumannii	365
Olea welwitschii	142
Newtonia buchananii	129
Afzelia quanzensis	119
Khaya nyasica	107
Albicia	36
Others	98
Total	20,275

Source: Personal Communication by the Forest Department, Dar es Salaam.

Uganda is hardly worth mentioning as a buyer of sawnwood from Tanzania. In 1966 it took only about 1,500 fm, which were exclusively sold to the two main markets in Uganda, namely Kampala and Jinja, and which came exclusively from one sawmill at Bukoba in North-East Tanzania.
Of the three East African countries Tanzania is the greatest exporter of timber[22]. Table 3 shows its exports in 1966, classified according to types of timber; the exports include those to Kenya and Uganda.
As regards the principal timber exports the countries taking the largest quantities in 1966 were as follows:

Brachylaena	Federal Republic of Germany (2,595 fm), Italy (1,890 fm), the United Kingdom (1,551 fm) and the Netherlands (921 fm).
Pterocarpus	Belgium (2,087 fm), the United Kingdom (1,281 fm), Norway (249 fm) and the Netherlands (224 fm).
Podocarpus	Kenya (1,878 fm), Zambia (722 fm) and Burundi (249 fm).
Cephalosphaera	United Kingdom (1,656 fm) and Zanzibar (319 fm).
Chlorophora	Zambia (365 fm), Kenya (332 fm), the United Kingdom (131 fm) and Greece (77 fm).
Dalbergia	Japan (790 fm) and France (90 fm).
Ocotea	Kenya (791 fm) and Zambia (63 fm).

The remaining types of timber go to the same customer countries as well as to Rwanda, Mauritius, Somalia, the Lebanon, Sweden, and Finland. Brachylaena hutchinsii (Muhuhu) is exported almost exclusively in the form of parquetry.
In Tanzania there are three ports available for the export of timber, namely Tanga, Dar es Salaam and Mtwara. In 1966, of the timber exported, 8,322 fm went through Tanga, 1,281 fm through Dar es Salaam and 2,965 fm through Mtwara.
Thus Tanzania is in a much more favourable position as compared with Kenya, and especially as compared with Uganda, inasmuch as the transportation distances between the sawmills working for export and the ports are considerably shorter. This does not apply to the open woodlands in the West of the country; but at the present time those areas hardly supply any timber for export.

---

22 In 1966, according to statistics from the Forest Department at Dar es Salaam, exports of sawnwood amounted to about 20,300 fm. This figure included the timber sold to Kenya and Uganda. Differences from the figures on page 112 are due to rounding off.

IV. Characteristics of Timber Sales

An idea of the transport and sales situation in East Africa can be obtained from analysis and comparison of the distances, means of transport, freight costs and timber selling prices in the individual countries. The result is to reveal for the three countries a picture which varies, in some cases quite appreciably, as between the markets to which they sell.

1. Home Sales

Table 4 indicates the average distances for timber shipments inside Kenya, Uganda and Tanzania, the average freight costs which arise in this connection and the average selling prices obtainable free at sawmill.

Table 4. *Average Transportation Distances, Freight Costs, and Selling Prices on Domestic Timber Sales, 1967* [a]

Country	Transportation distance Truck	Rail	Total	Freight costs Truck	Rail	Total	Selling price free at mill
	km			Shs [b] per fm			Shs [b] per fm
Kenya	32	256	288	11	26	37	211
Uganda	198	–	198	42	–	42	355
Tanzania	114	116	230	28	12	40	310

[a] The figures relate to the mills covered by the questionnaire.
[b] Kshs, Ushs and Tshs.
Source: The author's own findings and calculations.

The largest mean transportation distance is in Kenya, where the average is 288 km between the sawmills and their markets. This results in part from shipments to Mombasa, which is Kenya's second largest timber-using centre, but which has no woods near by from which timber for building and construction purposes can be obtained. If Mombasa had not been taken into account in calculation of the average distance between mills and markets, the figure would drop by 53 km, to 235 km.
It will be seen that in Tanzania, despite its size and its extensive open woodland areas, the average distance between mills and markets is shorter than in Kenya. The reason is that large areas of Tanzania still have no sawmills, and that those mills which do exist are close to their markets. As the remote forest areas become increasingly opened up, the position in this respect will doubtless change.
Finally in Uganda, the smallest East African country, the average distance for sawnwood transportation is the least. This is so even though most of the

productive forests lie in the West, while the chief consuming areas are in the East of the country. Up till now Uganda has hardly any planted forests for production of sawnwood. There are, however, plans to start them because of the growing demand for cheap softwood, which at present has to be imported from Kenya. If such plantations are started near the consuming areas, the distance between mills and markets will further decrease.

Table 4 further reveals that the conveyance of timber to market is done in Kenya almost exclusively by rail, in Uganda only by truck, and inside Tanzania by truck and rail in approximately equal degrees.

The questionnaire addressed to the sawmills also covered the trucks (lorries) which are used for conveying sawnwood to the nearest railway station, or direct to market.

Thus in Kenya 34 sawmills kept 34 trucks for conveyance of sawnwood. The age of these vehicles was about eight years, and their average capacity around 5 t. These trucks were employed only for short distances, mostly between the sawmill and the nearest railway station.

In Uganda 13 sawmills had 36 trucks in use for carrying sawn timber. The average age of the trucks was 2½ years, and their average capacity 6.3 t.

Of 28 sawmills, questioned in Tanzania, only 11 had their own trucks for carriage of sawn timber. The rest employed carriers to convey the timber shipped, or occasionally used trucks otherwise employed for bringing out the roundwood. The 11 sawmills were employing 21 trucks, roughly three years old. The average load for which they had capacity was approximately 6.5 t.

Freight charges in the individual countries depend not only on the transportation distance, but also on the method of transport. Kenya, where the average distance between mills and markets is greatest, has the lowest freight costs. The reason lies in the high proportion of timber carried by rail, which is cheaper. Uganda, where the average transportation distance is shortest, has the highest freight costs; this is because timber is delivered only by truck and, given the relatively long distances and the poor roads, transport by that means is risky and dear.

The extent to which freight costs increase the price of timber depends on the level of the selling price obtainable. Kenya, unlike the other two countries, chiefly produces cheap softwood from plantations, and podocarpus from its natural forests. On the average therefore, as can be seen from Table 4, it obtains only low prices for its timber. The average prices paid not only for the high-grade timbers from Uganda's tropical rain forests, but also for timbers from Tanzania's open woodlands, littoral forests and bushland, are appreciably greater than those paid for Kenyan timber. If freight costs are set in relation to selling prices, it becomes apparent that at almost 18 per cent the proportion of transport charges to the selling price is highest in Kenya; it compares with 12.6 per cent in Tanzania and 12 per cent in Uganda.

2. Interterritorial Sales

We come now to interterritorial timber sales, that is to the movement of timber between each of the East African countries. In this connection Table 5 contains data concerning the average transportation distance, freight charges and average selling prices.

Table 5. *Average Transportation Distances, Freight Costs, and Selling Prices on Interterritorial Timber Sales, 1967* [a]

From . . . to . . .	Transportation distance km				Freight costs Shs [b] per fm				Selling price free at mill Shs [b] per fm
	Truck	Rail	Ship	Total	Truck	Rail	Ship	Total	
Kenya–Uganda	13	425	–	438	8	26	–	34	211
Uganda–Kenya	171	655	–	826	32	49	–	81	478
Kenya–Tanzania	35	562	224	821	12	28	12	52	191
Tanzania–Kenya	122	378	–	500	30	27	–	57	313
Tanzania–Uganda	155	–	267	422	37	–	20	57	284
Uganda–Tanzania	142	–	328	470	30	–	27	57	378

[a] The figures relate to the mills covered by the questionnaire.
[b] Kshs, Ushs and Tshs.

Source: The author's own findings and calculations.

Timber Shipments between Kenya and Uganda

The timber shipped from Kenya to Uganda comes from sawmills in the West of Kenya, and goes to markets in the East of Uganda; but Uganda's deliveries to Kenya come from the forests in West Uganda, and go to markets in the central part of Eastern Kenya. Consequently the distances for timber shipped from Kenya to Uganda are much shorter, in fact roughly half as great, as in the case of Uganda's shipments to Kenya. A remarkable feature of timber movements between the two countries is moreover that the proportion of more expensive truck transport is greater in the case of Uganda's sales to Kenya than in that of Kenya's sales to Uganda. The average price obtained on sales of timber from Uganda is something more than double the price obtained for the softwood which Kenya sells to that country. This higher price approximately makes good the disadvantages of longer distance and higher freight costs on deliveries from Uganda to Kenya, so that at 17 per cent the proportion of freight costs to selling price is only a little higher, in the case of timber from Uganda, than the corresponding proportion of 16 per cent for timber from Kenya.

Timber Shipments between Kenya and Tanzania

Most of the timber sold from Kenya to Tanzania goes to Mwanza, the rest to Dar es Salaam. The resulting average transportation distance is 821 km. More than half of Tanzania's shipments to Kenya (2,600 fm) come from one mill on North Kilimanjaro. At 270 km the transportation distance to Nairobi is much shorter than that of 650 km to Dar es Salaam. Small quantities of timber are moreover sent from the Tanga district, and from the eastern Usambara Mountains, along the coast road to Mombasa. The distance is between 200 and 360 km. It would therefore seem more natural to supply the area short of timber around Mombasa from the forests in North-East Tanzania than from those in West Kenya, from which the timber now comes. Timber is also sent to Kenya from Southern Tanzania, from the district about Ifakara, mostly in the form of Khaya roundwood. Since all this timber is sold to East African Railways and Harbours at Nairobi, the fact that the haul by rail is as long as nearly 1,300 km is not so important.
The average price of Shs 191, obtainable on timber shipped from Kenya to Tanzania, is mostly for cypress; the timber sold from Tanzania to Kenya, at an average price of Shs 313, is mostly podo as well as some khaya and mvule. At 27 per cent the proportion of freight charges to selling price for shipments from Kenya to Tanzania is unfavourable by comparison with that of only 19 per cent for sales from Tanzania to markets in Kenya.

Timber Shipments between Tanzania and Uganda

The quantities of timber shipped between these two countries are very small, amounting to only about 1,500 fm of sawnwood per annum in each direction. Tanzania's sales to Uganda come exclusively from a podocarpus sawmill at Bukoba. The haul to the markets at Kampala and Jinja amounts to 422 km, of which 155 km are done by truck and 267 km by ship across Lake Victoria. Uganda, for its part, supplies the Mwanza district with construction timber. The average distance in this case is 470 km, comprising 142 km by truck and 328 km by ship. In the case of deliveries from Tanzania to Uganda the freight costs amount to 20 per cent, and in that of deliveries from Uganda to Tanzania they amount to 15 per cent of the selling price.

3. Export

The following remarks relate only to the sale or transport of timber as far as the ports from which it is to be exported. Data similar to those compiled for domestic and interregional timber sales will be found in Table 6.

Table 6. *Average Transportation Distances and Freight Costs to Ports for Export, as well as Prices obtained on Export of Timber, 1967* [a]

Country	Transportation distance Truck	Rail	Total	Freight costs Truck	Rail	Total	Selling price free at mill
		km			Shs [b] per fm		Shs [b] per fm
Kenya	29	729	758	12	39	51	316
Uganda	164	1,098	1,262	39	58	97	519
Tanzania	130	36	166	27	5	32	557

[a] The figures relate to the mills covered by the questionnaire.
[b] Kshs, Ushs and Tshs.

Sources: The author's own findings and calculations.

Tanzania, where the sawmills working for export lie not far from the coast, is in the most favourable position for exporting timber; Uganda, with a transportation distance of more than 1,000 km to the seaports, is in the least favourable position. A further advantage enjoyed by Tanzania is that it has three ports available for export. Kenya and Uganda, on the other hand, depend on only a single port, Mombasa.
In Uganda and Kenya, because of the great distance to the coast, the railway accounts for the greatest proportion of the total traffic carried. In Tanzania the sawmills for the most part despatch the timber directly to the seaports by truck.
According to the differences in transportation distance between the sawmills and the ports for export the average freight costs also differ widely from each other. In Uganda they amount, per fm, to roughly three times those arising in Tanzania. Owing to the heavy cost of transport for its exports Uganda is in many cases hardly able to compete in the world market with other timber-exporting countries, especially those located on a coast; it can hardly compete, for example, with Tanzania or with the West African countries. Tanzania moreover achieves an average export price of Shs 556 per fm ex sawmill. Uganda's exports fetch on the average Shs 519, and Kenya's only Shs 316 per fm. When the proportion of freight costs to the timber selling price is calculated, Tanzania's favourable situation in regard to the export of timber becomes even clearer; the cost of freight to the port for export is indeed only 6 per cent of the selling price in the case of Tanzania, against 16 per cent in that of Kenya and 19 per cent in that of Uganda.

D. CONCLUSIONS

The chief object of this study was to analyse the forestry and sawmilling industry instead of working out a plan designed for all three East African countries.
Nevertheless it appears desirable to offer some remarks which may help to solve problems connected with this industry, and to ensure a better supply of timber in East Africa.

Assistance for the Sawmilling Industry

Immediate measures should be directed not only to improving the structure of the sawmilling industry, but also to improving sawmill operation through provision of credit as well as through advice and training. Thus:

- After investigation of raw material supplies, of the terms of transport and the sales situation, the numerous, mostly unprofitable small firms should be amalgamated into larger up-to-date operating units.
- Modernisation of the sawmilling industry should moreover be promoted through capital development loans, granted on favourable terms to finance the purchase of vehicles and machinery, in which connection the Forest Department should help with advice.
- In connection with action on these lines it appears desirable to establish model sawmills with foreign technical aid kow-how. These should employ modern methods of operation; at the same time they should undertake the duty of advising as well as training managers and skilled workers. Another task for such model sawmills might be to test new machines, so as to find out whether they are suitable for use in East African conditions. The model mills should also attach importance to making sure that the felling, extraction, loading, transport, and forest roadmaking are carried out on modern lines. Kenya is setting an example to the two other East African countries, inasmuch as the Forest Department at Nairobi has such a project on the stocks under a bilateral agreement with the support of New Zealand.

Logging operations, in particular, could be improved through action as follows:

- Improved methods of operation in connection with felling and primary conversion. The most effective way to do this might be through showing up-to-date appliances, as well as through providing advice about maintaining the equipment and about modern methods of felling. Advanced training facilities should also be provided for skilled forest workers.

- Improved forest road building. It would be best if road and track building could be done not by the concessionaire, but by the state forest administration. Since this would save the sawmill operator the cost of building roads, the stumpage rate could be correspondingly increased. Forest road building should in the first place be concentrated at the mills which are most important and most productive from the forestry point of view. In the other woodland districts the planning of the road system, and the supervising of the work done, should be assisted by experts from the state forest department. The creation of a fuller and denser road system would in general shorten the extraction distances.
- For extraction of timber in natural forest, where the ground is not too steep, it would be necessary to use rubber-tyred yarding arches; use could be made, on difficult ground, of special tractors with a device fitted for hoisting the stems. For extraction in planted forest it would be desirable to use modern wheeled tractors, articulated like the Timber Jack and the Tree Farmer, instead of crawlers.
- Improved methods of loading, and use of up-to-date trucks with capacity for loads between 10 and 20 t, to bring out the timber.
- Establishment of adequate stocks of roundwood so as to tide over any shortfalls in the supply of timber during the rainy season.

Improvement of Timber Supplies

On a long view the establishment of fast growing plantations near the major markets is the only possible way to reduce the difficulties, of supply and transport, which will steadily increase in the future. The effect would be greatly to reduce the present long transportation distances between areas where there is an excess of timber and those where there is a shortage. Since the demand is chiefly for the cheaper timbers of ordinary quality, it should suffice to plant the fast-growing exotic conifers, like Cupressus lusitanica, Cupressus macrocarpa and Pinus patula, which have already proved their value in East Africa. Various trial plantings near the coast about Mombasa and Dar es Salaam have shown that fast-growing plantations can be established even in the damp, tropical climatic conditions which prevail at the coast. Pinus caribea, which can stand the sandy coastal soils and the high, humid temperature, was found especially promising in that connection.
East Africa's principal areas of timber shortage, near which afforestations on a large scale would be required, are as follows:

In Tanzania

- The Mwanza district to the South of Lake Victoria; this district is at present supplied with timber from Kenya.

- Dar es Salaam, the timber for which now comes from remote forest areas in North Tanzania, from the Tanzanian interior and from Kenya.

In Kenya

- The coastal area around Mombasa. Timber for this now comes from West Kenya.

In Uganda

- Kampala and Jinja. Most of the timber comes at present from West Uganda and Kenya.
- The nothern consuming centres Mbale and Soroti. These now obtain their timber from West Uganda and from Kenya.

In the immediate neighbourhood of Dar es Salaam an area of about 60,000 ha has already been reserved for afforestation with Pinus caribea. This plantation project is designed not only to ensure the supply of wood for a future paper mill, but also to provide Dar es Salaam with cheap sawnwood.

Unfortunately much too little attention has been paid up till now, in the laying out of softwood plantations, to the problem of how they are to ship the timber to their future markets. Afforestation has been carried out in many areas which, while suitable in terms of silviculture, are too small and too scattered for efficient logging.

The fact should not be overlooked, however, that one of the essential preconditions for a better supply of timber is to create timber marketing organisations in all three East African countries. This applies, above all, to Uganda and Tanzania. At present every individual sawmill arranges its own marketing. The result frequently is that timber is sent for long distances to purchasers who could be supplied more easily, and at lower cost, from sawmills nearer to their location. A timber marketing organisation, to which all the sawmills in the country would belong, and which would be better able than the individual firms to gain an overall view of the market, could ensure optimum marketing of the timber in an efficient manner. A further result of joint timber marketing should be to ensure that the prices for timber are unified. At the present time there is only one such organisation; it is in Kenya, and it handles the sale of timber for 13 sawmills.

A further problem in this context is how to use the felled timber and timber products more economically and more efficiently, for instance through industrial processing. At the present time large quantities of rejects are rotting at the sawmills, even though they could well be sold in the villages to small purchasers, thus making it relatively easy to supply the rural population with cheap sawn timber. On the other hand it frequently happens that valuable high-grade timbers are not used or processed in a manner befitting their value

and their quality. Timbers with inferior properties ought, on the other hand, to be offered for sale as cheaper goods for ordinary use. Such timber can be made usable by impregnation. Even relatively small stem sizes could be used if they were glued up to make construction timber.
Nor have all the possibilities yet been anywhere near exhausted as regards industrial processing of timber products in the East African countries. Firms, amalgamated to form larger units, could process their waste matter into chipboards. For example one large Ugandan sawmill, which has waste material equivalent to some 30,000 fm of roundwood each year, and which obtains various woods (largely mahogany) from primary tropical rain forest, has set up a small plant on such lines. Similar opportunities for processing must also exist in other areas.
It is further possible in East Africa to produce cedar wood oil. This is in great demand as a perfume in the soap and toilet preparations industry, as well as for treating high-grade leathers, and it could be exported. Sawdust accumulates in large quantities on the production of pencil slats from Juniperus procera. From this sawdust, and from other wood waste, two sawmills in Kenya have found it possible by a simple distillation process to make high-grade cedar wood oil.

Bibliography

Arnold, J. E. M., de Backer, M. F. E., and Pringle, S. L.: *Present Wood Consumption and Future Requirements in Kenya.* Rome. Food and Agriculture Organization, 1962.

—: *Present Wood Consumption and Future Requirements in Uganda.* Rome, Food and Agriculture Organization, 1962.

—: *Present Wood Consumption and Future Requirements in Tanganyika.* Rome. Food and Agricultural Organization, 1962.

Kenya, Republic of, Forest Department: *Annual Report, 1964.* Nairobi, Government Printer, 1965.

—: *Catalogue of the Forests of Kenya.* Nairobi, 1964.

Langdale-Brown, L., Osmaston, H. A., and Wilson, J. G.: *The Vegetation of Uganda and its Bearing on Land Use.* Margate, Kent, Eyre and Spottiswood Ltd., 1964.

Logie, K. P. W.: *Forestry in Kenya. A Historical Account of the Development of Forest Management in the Colony.* Nairobi, Government Printer, 1962.

Tanzania, The United Republic of, Ministry of Agriculture: *Annual Report of the Forest Division, 1965.* Dar es Salaam, Survey Division of the Ministry of Lands, Settlement and Water, 1965.

Uganda Government: *Annual Report of the Forest Department, 1963–64.* Entebbe, Government Printer, 1964.

Von Maydell, H. J.: Die Forstwirtschaft Tanganyikas, in: *Holzzentralblatt,* No. 126 (1962).

Whimbush, S. H.: *Catalogue of Kenya Timbers.* Nairobi, Forest Department, 1957 (Second Reprint).

THE CHEMICAL AND ALLIED INDUSTRIES IN KENYA

by

Hans Reichelt

Contents

List of Tables

The following study is based on research on the structure of the East African manufacturing industries, in particular the chemical and allied sector[1]. It was undertaken by the author in co-ordination with the East African Institute of Social Research (EAISR) (now Makerere Institute of Social Research – MISR) at Kampala in Uganda.

The need for a more detailed information on the existing manufacturing industries in Kenya has been felt most urgently by foreign businessmen who are interested in starting a manufacturing activity in Kenya as well as by importers and exporters abroad who are looking for new sources of supply or for new markets for their products. Besides, also the Kenya Government needs better information on the existing manufacturing industries if it wants to apply effective measures to accelerate the economic development of the country, particularly in the field of industrial development.

The purpose of the research was to give an analysis of some of the manufacturing industries in Kenya, namely the chemical and allied sector which constitutes a sizable part of the total manufacturing sector. This analysis included a survey of the market situation in the different branches, a discussion of the structure of the existing firms and a projection of future demand until 1970. Since Kenya is industrially the most advanced among the three East African countries data on the industries of the other two countries, Uganda and Tanzania, were included in certain instances in order to allow comparisons. One source of information for this study was material published, the main source of information, however, being interviews which were conducted in particular with members of the business community, but also with Government officials and officers of parastatal organizations. The author conducted his field studies in East Africa from March 1966 to April 1967.

H. Reichelt studied economics and business administration at the universities of Heidelberg and Munich, at the Hochschule für Welthandel, Vienna, at the Bologna Center of the Johns Hopkins University and at Southern Illinois University, Carbondale, USA. His past work includes a study on the economic development of Southern Italy within the framework of the European Economic Community, an abstract on the role of education in the economic development of the emerging nations and a handbook for business people on the general economic situation in Kenya. From October 1967 to December 1969 H. Reichelt has been working in the Uganda Ministry of Planning and Economic Development at Entebbe under the Technical Assistance Programme of the Federal Republic of Germany. Later he became a staff member of the World Bank in Washington, USA.

1 See H. Reichelt: *The Chemical and Allied Industries in Kenya* (Preliminary Report). African Studies Centre of the Ifo Institute for Economic Research, München 1967 (mimeo.).

A. GENERAL STRUCTURE OF THE ECONOMY AND THE POSITION OF THE CHEMICAL AND ALLIED INDUSTRIES

The structure of the Kenyan economy shows that the primary and the services sectors are in many respects of greater importance than the manufacturing and contruction sectors. In 1964, the primary sector (including the monetary sector of agriculture, livestock, fishing and hunting, forestry, and quarrying as well as the non-monetary sector) contributed 41.7 per cent to gross domestic product (GDP) of £281.3 million, and the services sector 46.3 per cent, whereas manufacturing and construction totalled only 12.0 per cent (manufacturing 10.4 and construction 1.6 per cent)[2]. In 1964, the primary sector employed 86.5 per cent of the total labour force of 3.2 million persons, the services 10.6 per cent, while only less than 3 per cent of the labour force worked in the manufacturing and construction sectors. These figures show the high productivity of labour in manufacturing relative to the primary sector which is not surprising if one notes that the largest part of the labour force in the primary sector is engaged in subsistence agriculture where the rate of open and disguised unemployment is high.
The dominating importance of agriculture in Kenya is less evident from export statistics. In 1967, exports of manufactured goods took up about 44 per cent of total exports, the rest being little processed agricultural products, mainly coffee, tea and sisal. Without the products of the oil refinery, manufactured goods during the last few years contributed about one third to overall exports. Among domestic exports[3] of manufactured goods of a total value of about £15.6 million[4] in 1967, the most important items were petroleum products (£7,406,000), pyrethrum extract (£2,423,000), cement (£1,006,000), soda ash (£806,000), and wattle extract (£861,000). The share of manufactured goods in exports to Uganda and Tanzania[5] is especially

2 Republic of Kenya: *Development Plan for the Period 1965/66 to 1969/70.* Nairobi 1966, p. 83 (quoted in the following as Republic of Kenya: *Revised Development Plan*).

3 "Domestic exports and imports" or "international trade" refers to trade with countries outside East Africa while "interterritorial trade" refers to the trade among the three East African countries.

4 "£" in the following is used as equivalent to 20 KShs which is valued, at present rates of exchange, US$ 2.80 or £Sterling –/17/–.

5 In the following all figures refer only to "Mainland Tanzania" unless special mention is made.

large and reached 78 per cent in 1966, and 74 per cent in 1967. Kenya's export trade is, therefore, fairly well diversified and it is particularly here where the importance of the manufacturing industries for the whole economy is most apparent.

An examination of the changes in the structure of the economy which are projected in the Development Plan reveals, in particular, a projected reduction in the share of the traditional and non-monetary sectors in GDP (from 24.4 per cent in 1964 to 20.5 per cent in 1970; most of the reduction being accounted for by a sharp fall in the share of subsistence agriculture and livestock holding). At the same time, the manufacturing and construction sectors are to increase their joint share in GDP from 12.0 per cent to 14.5 per cent over the same period (an increase from 10.4 per cent to 11.6 per cent from the manufacturing sector alone). This advance of the contribution of the manufacturing sector as against the non-monetary primary sector may be regarded as an indicator for the general economic development planned. As regards employment by the end of the Development Plan, it is estimated that out of a total labour force of 3.8 million persons, about 85 per cent will still be employed in the primary sector. The percentage of manufacturing and construction will increase from 2.8 to 3.7 per cent while the labour employed in the services is supposed to increase from 10.6 to 11.6 per cent during the Plan period.

The position of the chemical and allied industries group within the manufacturing sector can be derived from the data available on the manufacturing industries published in the Kenya Census of Industrial Production 1963[6]. In 1964, the chemical and allied industries contributed about 24 per cent to the total net output[7] of the manufacturing sector (table 1). In terms of gross output the share of the chemical and allied industries was, with about 30 per cent of the total, even bigger, while its share in the total employment was only about 10 per cent[8].

The discrepancy between its share in total employment and its contribution to the output of the manufacturing sector indicates that (in the chemical and allied industries) the productivity of labour is much higher than the average for the manufacturing sector.

In assessing the importance of the manufacturing sector in Kenya one could note that its contribution to total exports is much greater than its share in

6 Republic of Kenya, Statistics Division, Ministry of Economic Planning and Development: *Census of Industrial Production, 1963.* Nairobi 1965 (quoted in the following as Republic of Kenya: *Industrial Census, 1963*).

7 Net output is defined as gross production less all current costs other than labour costs, interest, bad debts and depreciation. It basically corresponds with the value-added concept in national income statistics.

8 Republic of Kenya: *Industrial Census, 1963,* p. 109, adjusted figures. Without the refinery the shares of the labour force would have been 9 per cent, of gross output 18 per cent and of net output 17 per cent.

Table 1. *Structure of the Manufacturing Sector*[a], *1964*
(in per cent of total net output)

Industry Group	%
Food processing	*18.6*
Beverages, tobacco	*17.2*
Textiles, clothing, footwear	*9.8*
Wood, paper, print	*15.8*
Chemicals and allied products	*24.4*
Metal working industries (excluding the railway workshops)	*12.0*
Miscellaneous	*2.2*
Total	*100.0*

[a] Excluding small-scale industries under 5 employees, not covered in the 1963 Industrial Census.

Source: Republic of Kenya: *Revised Development Plan,* p. 251; Republic of Kenya: *Industrial Census, 1963.*

Table 2. *Contribution of the Chemical and Allied Industries to the Total Exports of Manufactured Goods, 1965–1967*
(in per cent unless otherwise stated)

Goods	Domestic Exports 1965	1966	1967	Interterritorial Exports 1965	1966	1967	Total Exports 1965	1966	1967
Petroleum Products	*38.0*	*40.9*	*47.6*	*22.1*	*20.7*	*22.5*	*27.7*	*28.6*	*33.8*
Pyrethrum Extract	*16.4*	*16.4*	*15.6*	*0.0*	*0.0*	*0.0*	*5.8*	*6.5*	*7.0*
Cement	*7.9*	*5.8*	*6.5*	*4.3*	*3.9*	*3.6*	*5.5*	*4.7*	*4.9*
Soap	*0.1*	*0.0*	*0.0*	*5.1*	*5.2*	*6.6*	*3.3*	*3.2*	*3.6*
Soda Ash	*6.7*	*7.6*	*6.6*	*0.1*	*0.1*	*0.2*	*2.5*	*3.1*	*3.1*
Wattle Bark Extract	*6.0*	*10.0*	*5.5*	*0.0*	*0.0*	*0.0*	*2.1*	*3.9*	*2.5*
Paints	*0.1*	*0.1*	*0.1*	*2.6*	*1.6*	*1.2*	*1.7*	*1.0*	*0.7*
Insecticides	*0.4*	*0.5*	*0.4*	*1.4*	*1.9*	*2.4*	*1.0*	*1.4*	*1.5*
Glassware	*0.5*	*0.8*	*0.3*	*1.0*	*1.2*	*1.0*	*0.8*	*1.0*	*0.7*
Matches	*0.0*	*0.0*	*0.0*	*0.4*	*0.5*	*0.3*	*0.3*	*0.3*	*0.2*
Total	*76.1*	*82.1*	*82.6*	*37.0*	*35.1*	*37.8*	*50.7*	*53.7*	*58.0*
in £1,000,000	9.1	12.0	12.8	8.2	7.9	7.2	17.3	19.8	20.1
Total Exports of Manufactured Goods (in £1,000,000)	11.9	14.6	15.6	22.2	22.4	19.1	34.1	37.0	34.7

Source: East African Common Services Organization, East African Customs and Excise Department: *Annual Trade Reports of Kenya, Tanganyika and Uganda.* Mombasa (quoted in the following as EACSO: *Annual Trade Reports).*

output or employment. The same can be observed of the chemical and allied industries within the manufacturing sector (table 2).
In 1967, the chemical and allied sector contributed almost 58 per cent[9] to total manufactured exports and 82.5 per cent to the exports of manufactured goods outside East Africa. Among Kenya's exports of manufactured goods, products of the chemical and allied sector are therefore by far the most important.

B. INDUSTRIAL POLICIES OF THE GOVERNMENT

The Kenya Government recognizes the development of a local manufacturing industry as an essential condition for rapid and sustained overall economic growth[10]. It uses mainly indirect means to stimulate and accelerate the industrial development of the country leaving the ownership and the management of industrial enterprises to private business which is usually willing to take the risk to invest, because the general investment climate is favourable. In most cases, at least as regards the modern and large-scale manufacturing sector, the capital for new ventures as well as the managerial and part of the technical skills to run them has to come from abroad.

I. Protection of Private Investments

The Government encourages private investment from foreign sources by a number of legal safeguards and regulations:

Guarantee against Nationalization

The right of private ownership is guaranteed in Section 19 of the Kenya Constitution. Nationalization of private property is recognized as a tool of public policy only in certain cases[11].

9 Table 2 does not take into account exports of "other chemicals" like pharmaceuticals, polishes, etc. which are of considerable importance among interterritorial exports.
10 Republic of Kenya: *Revised Development Plan,* p. 235.
11 See Republic of Kenya: *African Socialism and its Application to Planning in Kenya,* Sessional Paper No. 10. Nairobi 1965, p. 27.

Has the property of a private person or organization been nationalized prompt and full compensation is granted and the person or organization affected has the right to bring the case directly before the Supreme Court. The person or organization whose property has been nationalized is after a reasonable space of time permitted to transfer the compensation granted to another country freely and without deductions.

Economic and not political considerations determine decisions concerning nationalization. The Sessional Paper on African Socialism stresses the point that nationalization of private property, if this is utilized fully, brings no economic advantage to the country. It is clearly recognized that nationalization discourages the inflow of additional private capital and thus slows down the overall economic development of the country. In accordance with these principles, nationalization in Kenya has not been of any practical importance.

Foreign Investments Protection Act

The Foreign Investments Protection Act (1964) guarantees the foreign investor the right to transfer out of Kenya profits (after taxation), his investment of foreign assets, and the principal and interest on any foreign loans, irrespective of any exchange restrictions which might otherwise apply. These guarantees are given if the investor has applied for and has been granted by the Treasury an Approved Status Certificate[12]. The Certificate of Approved Enterprise is conceded if the planned investment furthers the economic development of Kenya or if it is of general benefit to the country[13].
The possession of a Certificate of Approved Enterprise is not an essential condition for a foreign firm to operate in Kenya and in the past there were little difficulties for foreign-owned enterprises in transferring their profits abroad. In future, when more stringent exchange control regulations than those at present in operation may be introduced, it is likely that the Certificate of Approved Enterprise will be of greater value than it is now.

---

12 The transfer of profits out of Kenya of enterprises which do not possess an Approved Status with respect to this Ordinance must be endorsed by the Treasury. In granting these approvals the Treasury has in the past been rather generous.

13 Enterprises not only in the manufacturing sector but also in building and construction, in agriculture, mining, tourism and financial institutions, but in general not firms primarily concerned with trading can receive an Approved Status. The Approved Status is in general not granted for investments which entail a change of ownership of an existing enterprise or of land into foreign hands, or speculative investments of any kind which do not add to the productive capacity of the country.

II. Other Indirect Aids to Industry

Many raw materials imported for further processing by local industries are listed in the customs duties schedule with a zero tariff. In order to increase the competitiveness of local industries with respect to imported goods a number of branches of the manufacturing sector may claim refunds of customs duties paid on imported raw materials on which tariffs have been levied. The industries concerned are listed in the Local Industries (Refund of Customs Duties) Ordinance of 1962 and the Amendments to this Ordinance. Among the industries to which this concession is granted are the insecticides and the soap industries. The Ordinance and its Amendments list not only the industries concerned but also the kind of raw materials and the names of the firms to which the concessions apply as well as the percentage of the refund in each individual case.

The most frequently applied devices for the protection of local industries, however, are import tariffs and quantitative restrictions through import licensing on competing imports. Customs duties are in general uniform in all the three East African countries. Compared with other developing countries the tariff protection in East Africa is relatively low.

For many locally produced goods an additional protection is deemed necessary in the form of quantitative import restrictions. In these cases, import licenses are required prior to importation. The goods the importation of which requires import licenses are listed in the Imports, Exports and Essential Supplies (Imports) Order (1964) and its Amendments. The list includes (as at January 1966) those oil refinery products which are produced in Kenya, all kinds of paints and allied articles, soaps, mosquito coils and aerosol insecticides, cement, glass tumblers, and matches. Quantitative restrictions on imports from foreign countries may also in the future be imposed separately by each member State of the East African Community (Art. 5 of the Treaty for East African Cooperation).

Further aids to the investor are the modest corporation tax levied and the investment allowances granted. The corporation tax on company income in East Africa is shs 7/50 per £ or 37.5 per cent on the profit made which is considerably lower than in most other countries. In addition, an investment deduction is granted at a rate of 20 per cent on the capital cost of constructions of new factory buildings and new machinery installed in these buildings. This is an incentive for the entrepreneur to undertake such investments because they help to reduce his corporation tax obligations[14].

14 He can thus write off in the first year 24 per cent of the costs of new factory buildings and 32.5 per cent of the costs of the new plant and machinery and 4 or 12.5 per cent, respectively, in the following 24 or 7 years until the total of 120 per cent of the original costs is reached.

III. Direct Government Intervention

Although in the manufacturing sector in Kenya the Government can, in general, limit itself to indirect means to encourage the establishment of local industries, in certain cases these indirect means are not sufficient to attract a private person or group to undertake a desirable investment in the manufacturing sector because the investment project is either too risky or only marginally profitable.

For a direct financial engagement in the manufacturing sector the Government has two organizations at its disposal, the Development Finance Company of Kenya (DFCK)[15] and the Industrial and Commercial Development Corporation (ICDC). Both the DFCK and the ICDC provide equity as well as loan capital mainly for manufacturing enterprises where the majority of the capital is furnished by private sources. In the chemical and allied sector, ICDC has an equity interest in East Africa Industries, Kenya's largest soap manufacturer, and owns the African Diatomite Industries while the DFCK gave loan and equity capital to Windmill Fertilizers Ltd.

IV. The East African Common Market

It has to be taken into consideration that the Kenya Government's industrial policy is today to a large extent determined by regulations agreed upon in the framework of the East African Common Market. The three East African countries Kenya, Uganda and Tanzania have for a long time been members of a de-facto common market although there had not been a legal common market agreement. Since independence, in Tanzania and Uganda a growing dissatisfaction had been spreading, the main reason for which was the uneven industrial development which had taken place in the three countries and which had favoured Kenya. Uganda and Tanzania were pressing for quite a while for their fair shares in the industrial development of East Africa.

The Kampala Agreement of 1964 attempted to solve this problem, at the same time maintaining the advantages of the large unified market comprising all three countries. Its various provisions, sought to adjust industrial production of the individual member country to her respective demand, to allocate new big industries to only one of the countries from where they could serve the whole of East Africa, and to allow the imposition of quantitative

15 In the DFCK participate also the British and the German development corporations (Commonwealth Development Corporation and Deutsche Entwicklungsgesellschaft) and, since 1967, the Dutch Development Corporation.

restrictions on imports from the other two East African countries failed, or rather were never completely accepted by all three Governments.
The new Treaty for East African Co-operation which came into force on December 1st, 1967, can be considered the first concise legal framework for East African cooperation[16]. It does not attempt a renewed allocation of industries like the Kampala Agreement but aims at an even industrial development in East Africa by more indirect means.
For this purpose, interterritorial tariffs, "transfer taxes", may be imposed on manufactured goods by "a Partner State which is in deficit in its total trade in manufactured goods with the other two Partner States"[17].

Only those goods which the importing country is itself producing (or expects to produce within 3 months) can be liable to the imposition of transfer tax. On the basis of the previous year's trade statistics, the value of imported goods from any partner state on which transfer tax is imposed may not exceed the deficit in trade in manufactured goods with that state. The transfer tax must not exceed 50 per cent of the external tariff. With the present rates of customs duties the transfer tax rates rarely exceed 15 to 20 per cent at valorem.

Quantitative restrictions by licensing may not be imposed on interpartner state trade except in certain determined cases (overall imbalance in the external payments position in the importing country, contractual obligations into which the Government of the importing country has entered with certain firms, etc. — Art. 12 of the Treaty). Contractual obligations will enable the Tanzania Government to use quantitative restrictions to protect its oil refinery at Dar es Salaam and the Kenya Government to protect the oil refinery and the nitrogenous fertilizer plant to be constructed, both at Mombasa (Annex II of the Treaty). As will be pointed out in detail later on, Tanzania has until the new Treaty came into force extensively used a system of quantitative restrictions to protect its young local industries against imports of Kenya-made products.
It seemed that the regulations of the Treaty concerning interpartner state trade improved the situation for the manufacturing industries in Kenya, at least as far as their exports to Tanzania are concerned which in the past had suffered as a result of quantitative restrictions and the prevailing insecurity about the future of interpartner state trade. Also, tariffs are always preferable to quantitative restrictions for the regulation of foreign trade as they do not exclude the working of the price mechanism. It will not, however, be possible to assess the effects of those transfer taxes imposed on certain goods by Tanzania and Uganda shortly after the Treaty came into force for some time yet.

---

16 With respect to Tanzania, the East African Common Market includes also the island of Zanzibar.

17 Art. 20, paragraph 3 of the Treaty. See East African Common Services Organization: *Treaty for East African Co-operation.* Nairobi, Government Printer, 1967.

In the Treaty for East African Co-operation, the allocation of industries to individual member countries as it was provided for in the Kampala Agreement has not been attempted.
In certain branches of the manufacturing sector, however, new industries have to have a license before they are allowed to start production. This license is issued by the East African Industrial Council after consultation with the respective Ministries of Commerce and Industry, and after receiving possible comments or protests from the established business community. Among the chemical and allied industries only the production of glassware and of sheet glass is liable to a license from the East African Industrial Licensing Council.

C. ANALYSIS OF THE CHEMICAL AND ALLIED INDUSTRIES

I. Production and Markets of Individual Industries

The industries of the chemical and allied sector in Kenya can be divided into two groups

- Industries using predominantly local raw materials; and
- Industries using predominantly imported raw materials.

Industries of the chemical and allied sector using predominantly local raw materials have, in general, a strong export orientation. Only the glass and cement industries, which belong in this group, sell an appreciable part of their output on the local market.
The fertilizer industry has been dealt with here, too, although the largest existing plant in East Africa, a phosphate fertilizer factory, is located at Tororo in Uganda. This factory sells most of its output to Kenya and has close ties through its management to a Kenya firm[18].
The industries which are predominantly based on imported raw materials are producing goods mainly for the local market with exports to the Partner States in the East African Community, and are protected against imports from outside East Africa by customs duties and quantitative restrictions. Some of these goods, like soap or matches, are finished consumer goods, while

18 In treating the future prospects of the fertilizer industry in Kenya the projected nitrogenous fertilizer plant at Mombasa has been included in this chapter although it will be based for a long time to come on imported raw materials.

others are used as intermediate goods or as fuel, mainly in other manufacturing industries or in building and construction.

Several industries which would normally be introduced in this group and which are represented in Kenya, have been excluded, partly because the information available showed too many important gaps, and partly because there were only one or two firms dominating the local market. Among the industries omitted are the medical products and pharmaceutical industries, the shoe, furniture and floor polish industries and also production of printers ink and of medical and industrial gases. In their internal structure these industries show very similar characteristics to those other industries using predominantly imported raw materials which are discussed in greater detail.

1. Industries Using Predominantly Local Raw Materials

a) The Soda Ash Industry

One of the oldest manufacturing activities in Kenya is the mining and processing of soda at Lake Magadi.

The lake is situated about 60 miles south-west of Nairobi in the Rift Valley and contains large deposits of trona (sodium sesqui-carbonate, $NaHCO_3$). The main deposit is about 12 1/2 miles long and 1 1/2 to 2 miles wide. It is estimated to contain the equivalent of at least 100,000,000 tons of soda [19].

The present Magadi Soda Company was formed in 1924 as a subsidiary of Imperial Chemical Industries Ltd. which took over part of the capital equipment and installations from an unsuccessful predecessor [19].

The trona is mined from the surface of the lake basin by a bucket dredger, crushed, mixed with lake liquor, and pumped to the nearby factory for processing. The main part of the processing is the roasting in two calciners through which the washed trona is moved. The calciners are rotary kilns heated by fuel oil. During roasting, the trona is broken down from sesqui-carbonate ($NaHCO_3$) to the normal sodium carbonate (Na_2CO_3), the finished soda ash. The calcined ash is then ground and sieved and filled in paper bags for despatch. It contains on the average 97.55 per cent Na_2CO_3, 1.28 per cent NaF, and 0.5 per cent NaCl.

The annual production of soda ash after the take-over of the Company by ICI in 1924 until the end of World War II fluctuated between 25,000 tons and 70,000 tons without showing any clear trend [20]. It was only after the war that sales went up markedly, and production rose to a level of over 140,000 tons in 1959 and 1961. In the years after 1961, there was again a marked decline in sales and production partly as a result of the ban on the exportation to South Africa, which had hitherto bought about half of

19 For a detailed history see M. F. Hill: *The Story of the Magadi Soda Company.* Birmingham 1964.

20 Geological Survey of Kenya, Report No. 42, Geology of the Magadi Area, by B. H. Baker, Nairobi 1958, p. 69.

Magadi's output. The Company is presently recovering from this blow by opening up alternative markets mainly in the Soviet Union and Japan. Table 3 shows the development of production and exports during the last ten years.

Table 3. *Production and Exports of Soda Ash, 1958–1967*

Year	Production (1,000 tons)	Domestic Exports Quantity (1,000 tons)	Domestic Exports Value (£1,000)	Interterritorial Exports Uganda tons	Uganda £1,000	Tanzania tons	Tanzania £1,000
1958	111.0	104.0	1205	419	4	723	8
1960	124.5	115.2	1317	849	8	891	9
1961	142.4	142.7	1587	975	9	1029	10
1962	122.1	111.2	1241	1426	13	1020	10
1963	101.9	106.9	1234	1363	13	732	8
1964	80.4	64.0	708	54	1	235	3
1965	81.9	73.5	806	2234	23	718	8
1966	110.6	105.1	1111	1845	19	1343	15
1967	103.1	96.8	1022	1698	18	1740	20

Source: EACSO: *Annual Trade Reports.*

As can be seen from table 3, the company has always operated well below its full production capacity of 200,000 tons per annum. It was only in the best years of the Company's history (1959 and 1961) that the capacity utilisation reached about 75 per cent.

While about half of exported output went to South Africa in 1962–1963 (these exports ceased completely in 1964) the structure of domestic exports has changed considerably since. In 1967 (1966) the main buyers outside the East African market were Japan 29.8 per cent[21] (20.6 per cent), U.S.S.R. nil (18.9 per cent), Thailand 14.8 per cent (12.4 per cent), and New Zealand 12.4 per cent (9.8 per cent).

The sales of Magadi soda to the East African market are on the increase as a result of the growing demand by new industries and the expansion of existing industries. Table 4 shows the direction of the sales in East Africa during the last few years.

About 70 per cent of the soda sold in East Africa went to the Kenya market in 1965–66. The glass factories at Nairobi and Mombasa are the largest local consumers of soda.

The future sales of Magadi soda ash are largely dependent on the development of export markets outside Africa. Even though the East African market is expanding, over 90 per cent of sales are still exported outside East Africa, mainly to markets in Asia. The development of exports is determined by external factors which are difficult to forecast.

The internal market, in this case covering the whole of East Africa, has

21 Of domestic exports only.

Table 4. *Main Industries in East Africa Buying Magadi Soda, 1961–62 to 1965–66*
(in tons)

Industry	1961—1962 [a]	1962—1963	1963—1964	1964—1965	1965—1966
Glass Making	2,180	1,760	2,489	2,417	3,468
Soap Manufacture	768	705	672	861	895
Water Purification	1,171	1,080	1,201	1,100	1,460
Silicate of Soda Manufacture	2,564	2,506	2,572	2,676	2,818
Sundries	458	764	853	1,223	1,111
Total	7,141	6,815	7,787	8,277	9,752
% of total sales	*5.7*	*6.1*	*9.2*	*10.8*	*9.4*

[a] Financial years.

Source: Magadi Soda Company.

expanded quite fast during the last few years, due mainly to the rapid growth of the glass industry and also the less rapid growth of the soap industry. The growth of the glass and soap industry in East Africa will probably soon slow down as there is little room left for further import substitution and the growth of these industries will be determined only by increases in incomes in East Africa. It can be assumed, considering past developments and expected growth rates, that the sales of soda ash in East Africa in 1970 will be in the range of 13,000 to 15,000 tons.

The domestic market for soda ash would be greatly increased if the production of caustic soda on the basis of soda ash would be started in East Africa. Caustic soda (NaOH) is a basic inorganical chemical with a wide application in a large number of industries which are already established in East Africa, like the textile, soap, petroleum and vegetable oil milling industries. Caustic soda is also used in the pulp and paper industry where a factory will be in operation in Kenya by 1970[22]. In 1965, imports of caustic soda into East Africa exceeded 8,000 tons, and the average price c.i.f. port was about £35 per ton. The manufacture of caustic soda from soda ash is technically possible, but, from the economic point of view, the production of caustic soda by the electrolysis of common salt is, according to a recent study, more advantageous[23].

22 Republic of Kenya: *Revised Development Plan,* p. 262; a delay of at least 2 years in implementing this project is likely.

23 United Nations, Economic and Social Council, Economic Commission for Africa: *Recherche sur l'industrie chimique et sur celle des engrais en Afrique de l'Est, élaboration de données concernant la planification,* Report submitted at the Conference on the Harmonization of Industrial Development Programmes in East Africa, Lusaka, 27. 9.–5. 10. 1965, document E/CN. 14/INR/83. July 1965 (mimeo.), pp. 9–11 (quoted in the following as ECA: *Recherche sur l'industrie chimique*).

b) The Diatomite Industry

Diatomite is an accumulation of the silicious remains of microscopic aquatic plants. Deposits of diatomite are found at different places in Kenya but there is only one company exploiting two of them on a larger scale at a processing plant about ten miles south-west of Nakuru. The diatomite found at the larger of these two quarries contains about 85 per cent of SiO_2 and small quantities of NaO_2, Fe_2O_3, Al_2O_3 and CaO.

The first materials were quarried during World War II and the product was sold as a filler to local soap manufacturers. After the war, the operations expanded and in 1954 the production of calcined materials at a site close to the quarries commenced. The original company continued production until 1965. Difficulties, partly because of the loss of the South African market after the introduction of the embargo in 1963, forced the company into receivership. In September 1965, the company was taken over by the Kenya Government through the Industrial and Commercial Development Corporation. Negotiations to return it into private ownership were underway in 1967.

Diatomite comes in two main grades on the market, an uncalcined grade and a calcined grade. For the uncalcined product the processing consists mainly of cleaning. It is the lower-value product and it is sold as a filler, especially to the soap and insecticides industries. It is also used as an insulation material. For the calcined product the processing is more complicated.

The raw ore is fed together with a five-per-cent addition of a fluxing agent through a milling and drying system. The dried fluxed material then passes through a rotary kiln where it is heated to 1100 degrees centigrade with a passage time of about 25 minutes. The outcoming clinker is again milled into a powder and is then air-separated into the different grades of the final product.

About 10 per cent of the calcined product, consisting of broken diatoms and small fragments, is sold as filler grade. About 80 per cent is of filter-aid quality. It has been found to have an extremely high absorption capacity of about 3 to 3.5 times its own volume of water[24]. Besides the diatomite ore, the main raw materials for the calcined product are soda ash and salt, both bought from the Magadi Soda Company.

The diatomite industry in Kenya is predominantly an export industry, even though the local market for uncalcined products is important. Table 5 shows the exports of diatomite during the period from 1961 to 1967.

According to information from the Company about 45 per cent of sales in East Africa in 1966–67 went to the local Kenya market (about 250 to 300 tons). Outside East Africa, the United Kingdom is the most important

---

24 W. Pulfrey: *The Geology and Mineral Resources of Kenya* (Revised), Geological Survey of Kenya, Bulletin No. 2, Nairobi 1960.

Table 5. *Exports of Diatomite, 1961–1967*

Year	Domestic Exports		Interterritorial Exports Uganda		Interterritorial Exports Tanzania		Total Exports	
	t	£	t	£	t	£	t	£
1961	1,185	21,373	141	1,485	578	5,138	1,904	27,996
1962	1,210	20,527	154	1,192	462	3,422	1,826	25,141
1963	1,929	31,843	103	802	265	2,005	2,297	34,650
1964	1,646	26,095	128	1,231	138	1,204	1,912	28,530
1965	1,161	19,908	35	483	153	1,461	1,349	21,852
1966	763	13,375	143	1,352	190	2,155	1,096	16,882
1967	723	13,753	138	1,401	199	2,036	1,060	17,190

Source: EACSO: *Annual Trade Reports.*

customer having purchased 94 per cent of the exported product in 1966, and 85 per cent in 1967.

It was only in 1962–63, when South Africa became a major buyer, that the Company utilized a large part of its capacity, producing about 2,500 t of finished goods during 1963. In 1967, the kiln was operating at about 50 per cent of capacity on a one shift basis.

The two main industries buying diatomite in East Africa are the soap industry, which takes over 50 per cent of the quantity sold, and the insecticide industry, which takes about 25 per cent. A considerable part of the diatomite exported outside East Africa is of the calcined filter grade (about 25 per cent in terms of quantity, but about 40 per cent in terms of value) while only about 5 per cent in quantity terms of the products sold in East Africa are calcined. The price differences between the different grades are considerable. The lowest grade (coarse fillers for roof insulation) costs £5 per ton and the highest grade (filter aids) £40 per ton. Filler for the soap industry is sold at £8/10/0 per ton ex factory, and filler for insecticide manufacturing at £6 per ton.

As the diatomite industry is predominantly an export industry and as there is little likelihood that a sufficient domestic market for the higher and more profitable grades will develop for many years to come, its future will almost entirely depend on the expansion of exports. The way to achieve this expansion would be to aim at a diversification of export markets, which would require a considerable amount of additional finance. Another possibility would be for the Company to seek a close organizational and also financial liaison with an overseas company which could secure sales. The negotiations undertaken with an American interest which resulted in a marketing contract signed at the beginning of 1968 showed that the Company went this second way.

c) The Cement Industry

Kenya's cement industry consists of two firms, The Bamburi Portland Cement Company Limited with its factory at Bamburi near Mombasa, and The East African Portland Cement Company Limited with a factory at Athi River, south of Nairobi. Both are associate companies of large European concerns, which have commercial connections.

The older of the two companies is the E.A. Portland Cement which was incorporated in 1933 and started operating a grinding plant on the basis of imported clinker in Nairobi shortly thereafter. In 1958, the company took up the production of cement from local raw materials in its new factory at Athi River. The factory uses the wet production method and operates a modern rotary kiln. It has an annual production capacity of 120,000 tons.
The formation of the Bamburi Portland Cement Company Ltd., which before September 1st, 1966, was called British Portland Cement Company Ltd., was approved under special ordinance No. 61 of 1951, for the purpose of constructing a cement factory at Bamburi. The company commenced production in 1954, and during its first financial year of operation sold 23,000 tons of cement. The first two shaft kilns[25] installed gave the factory an annual capacity of over 100,000 tons. Later, the capacity was progressively increased. In 1961 the total capacity was 400,000 tons. The dry production method is used. The Company has a Subsidiary in Mauritius and Associate Companies in Tanzania and Réunion which operate storage and bagging plants. In 1966, the Associate in Tanzania opened up a production unit at Wazo Hill near Dar es Salaam with an initial production capacity of about 150,000 tons p.a.
The Bamburi factory is located in the middle of very large deposits of Pleistocene coral limestone and close to Jurassic shales. In addition the gypsum which is added to the ground clinker at a proportion of 3 to 5 per cent is found not too far away at Roka, south of Malindi. The Athi River factory has to transport its requirements of limestone from Sultan Hamud[26] where an unusually magnesia-low crystalline limestone is quarried[27]. Nearby deposits of calcrete are also used (cunkar, an impure superficial limestone which is used as secondary source of limestone). The larger part of the gypsum used is supplied by the gypsum quarries around Garissa from where it is transported by road over a distance of about 220 miles to Athi River via Thika and Nairobi, a distance of about 220 miles.

Table 6 shows the development of production and consumption of cement in Kenya and the country's domestic and interterritorial trade in cement.
The consumption of cement is closely related to the building and construction activity of the economy and this, in turn, depends on the level of investment in general. The advent of independence brought about a high degree of insecurity among the business community which consisted — and consists today — nearly entirely of European and Asian firms. There was therefore a sharp

---

25 Shaft kilns are vertical kilns as opposed to rotary kilns. They are usually smaller than rotary kilns.

26 Sultan Hamud is 64 miles by rail from Athi River.

27 W. Pulfrey: The Geology and Mineral Resources of Kenya, Geological Survey of Kenya, Bulletin No. 2, Government Printer, Nairobi 1960, p. 21.

drop in business investment and in new residential housing developments after 1960. Cement consumption fell to 83,000 tons in 1964 which was less than 50 per cent of the 1960 level. Only in 1965, was there a slow recovery of the Kenya cement market, a trend which has been more pronounced in 1966. The 1967 figures indicate that the trough in the economy immediately before and after Uhuru has been overcome and confidence restored.

Table 6. *Production, Trade and Consumption of Cement, 1958–1967*
(1,000 tons)

Year	Production	Domestic Exports	Interterritorial Exports to Uganda	Interterritorial Exports to Tanzania	Domestic Imports + Re-Exp.	Local [a] Consumption
(1)	(2)	(3)	(4)	(5)	(6)	(7)
1958	236.1	4.0	8.3	59.5	7.6	171.9
1960	335.8	42.4	7.7	104.7	1.1	182.1
1961	324.3	93.6	6.5	106.5	0.7	118.3
1962	338.1	103.9	11.1	100.8	0.9	123.2
1963	338.3	108.9	16.8	97.0	0.8	116.4
1964	415.4	171.4	13.2	148.6	0.5	82.7
1965	476.2	196.3	7.1	176.2	0.0	96.6
1966	462.9	166.9	9.0	143.5	1.7	145.2
1967	485.8	217.7	12.2	73.7	0.0	182.2

[a] Local Consumption (7) = (2) — (3) — (4) — (5) + (6). The estimate for local consumption disregards stock changes.

Source: EACSO: *Annual Trade Reports;* Republic of Kenya: *Kenya Statistical Digest,* published by the Statistics Division of the Ministry of Economic Planning and Development, Vol. I, No. 3 (September 1963) (quoted in the following as Republic of Kenya: *Statistical Digest*); same publisher: *Economic Survey, 1966,* prepared by the Statistics Division of the Ministry of Economic Planning and Development, Nairobi, 1966, p. 46 (quoted in the following as Republic of Kenya: *Economic Survey*).

Looking at the production figures since 1958, one gets quite a different picture from the consumption sequence. Between 1958 and 1967 the production of cement more than doubled. Although imports declined from a very low level to virtually zero during this period the rapid increase in production in the face of stagnant domestic consumption was largely made possible by a rapid expansion in export sales. Domestic exports as well as interterritorial exports increased very considerably. In respect of interterritorial exports Tanzania is much more important as an importer of Kenya cement (see table 7). This is easy to understand if it is remembered that Uganda has its own cement works at Tororo and until the inception of the Treaty for East African Co-operation in December 1967 restricted imports of cement to about 10 per cent of its requirements in order to protect the

Tororo factory against competition from Kenya[28]. Tanzania, on the other hand, did not have its own cement factory until the middle of 1966 when the Tanganyika Cement Company Ltd. started production at its new factory at Wazo Hill. Between 1958 and 1963, cement consumption fell also in Tanzania, although not as abruptly as in Kenya. Despite this fall in consumption, the Kenya sales to Tanzania were increased until 1961 by substituting imports from overseas which in 1958 amounted to about 70,000 tons. By 1965, imports into Tanzania from overseas had dropped to practically zero. After 1963, the Tanzania cement market expanded rapidly, mainly as a result of the vigorous housing program of the Tanzania Government.

Table 7. *Regional Distribution of Cement Exports, 1958–1967*
(1,000 tons)

Country	1958	1960	1961	1962	1963	1964	1965	1966	1967
Total Interterritorial Exports	67.8	113.4	113.0	111.9	113.8	161.8	183.3	152.5	85.9
thereof:									
Uganda	8.3	7.7	6.5	11.1	16.8	13.2	7.1	9.0	12.2
Tanzania	59.5	104.7	106.5	100.8	97.0	148.6	176.2	143.5	73.7
Total Domestic Exports	4.0	42.4	93.6	103.9	108.9	171.4	196.3	166.9	217.7
thereof:									
Mauritius	0.3	24.9	46.5	42.8	31.0	46.9	69.3	52.3	72.1
Réunion	1.0	.	9.6	9.9	12.7	44.9	63.4	64.3	76.2
Seychelles	0.3	0.6	0.7	0.7	0.8	1.0	3.0	3.3	5.5
Madagascar	.	.	4.3	1.6	2.6	2.9	14.0	16.0	7.2
Other Domestic Exports	0.8	5.9	17.4	35.9	41.0	63.2	38.7	16.9	12.9
Total Exports as per cent of Production	*30.4*	*46.4*	*63.7*	*63.8*	*65.8*	*80.2*	*79.7*	*69.0*	*62.5*
Interterritorial Exports as per cent of Production	*28.7*	*33.8*	*34.8*	*33.1*	*33.6*	*39.0*	*38.5*	*32.9*	*17.7*

Source: EACSO: *Annual Trade Reports.*

Exports of Kenya cement outside East Africa rose even faster than exports to Uganda and Tanzania. The domestic exports increased continuously during the period from only 4,000 tons in 1958 to more than 200,000 tons in 1967. An analysis of the direction of domestic exports shows that the islands in the

28 Uganda will start the construction of a second cement factory at Kasese which will have an initial capacity of 100,000 t p.a. and go into production before 1970. It will supply mainly the markets of the Western Region of Uganda and of Rwanda and Burundi, but also the Kampala Area. Since December 1967, quantitative restrictions against imports of Kenya cement have been succeeded by a transfer tax.

Indian Ocean, especially Mauritius and Réunion, are the largest buyers. The Bamburi Cement Company has built up an outstanding sales organization to supply the markets on these islands and also in the mainland countries on the Indian Ocean.

The remarks made so far and the figures in table 7 indicate that the Kenya cement industry as a whole is extremely export orientated. This export orientation increased over the years until 1965 to over 80 per cent of total sales (and close to 90 per cent for the Bamburi factory alone) but dropped back again in 1967 to about 60 per cent. Such a high degree of dependence on exports is rare in manufacturing industries of a developed country. In Kenya it has a counterpart on a similar scale in the soda works of Magadi which has been analysed above.

An approximate indication of the development of export prices of cement during the last ten years is given in table 8.

Table 8. *Total Value and Value per Ton of Cement Exports, 1958–1967* (in £1,000 and E.A. Shs, respectively)

Year	Domestic Exports		Interterritorial Exports: Uganda		Interterritorial Exports: Tanzania	
	Total Value (£1,000)	Value per ton (E.A. Shs)	Total Value (£1,000)	Value per ton (E.A. Shs)	Total Value (£1,000)	Value per ton (E.A. Shs)
1958	33	165	85	205	561	189
1960	207	98	70	182	729	139
1961	418	89	58	178	681	128
1962	470	90	99	178	565	112
1963	503	92	149	177	538	111
1964	802	94	119	180	764	103
1965	939	96	68	191	880	100
1966	843	101	81	179	803	112
1967	1,006	92	162	264	526	143

Source: EACSO: *Annual Trade Reports.*

The average f.o.b. price per ton for cement exports outside East Africa was Shs 165 in 1958. By 1961, it had fallen to Shs 89 and showed a slow increase until 1966. An important factor which made the price decreases after 1958 possible was the introduction of bulk exports by the Bamburi factory. Only in this way could the foreign competition in export markets be met. This came mainly from Eastern Europe countries which often offered their products at very low prices not dictated by profit considerations. The export prices of Kenya cement to Tanganyika showed a continuous decrease until 1965 and were in that year only slightly higher than the average domestic export prices. The export prices to Uganda, on the other hand, were considerably higher during the whole period than the prices for cement sales to other countries (except for similarly situated countries, like Rwanda and

Burundi), because the market in Uganda permitted these higher prices. The reason for this were "imperfections of the market" in the form of de facto quantitative restrictions of imports of cement from Kenya into Uganda mentioned above.

The cement prices for local sales are generally higher than the export prices, partly because the quantities sold are smaller and only a small part is sold in bulk (under 10 per cent of the total local sales), and partly because high transport costs allow a discriminatory pricing policy, so that a greater proportion of overheads is borne by the domestic than by the export market. The ex-factory prices for local sales as per the end of 1966 were Shs 187/- per ton at Bumburi and Shs 222/- at Athi River.

The analysis of the sales of Kenya cement shows that the future development of the industry will be strongly influenced by the foreign demand for its products. The domestic market will not grow fast enough until 1970 to take an appreciably larger share of total production than in the early sixties. According to calculations based on correlations of cement consumption with per-capita incomes and size of the population as well as with capital formation in building and construction[29], the consumption of cement in Kenya will rise to about 260,000–270,000 tons in 1970. The present capacity of Kenya's cement factories, however, is 820,000 tons p.a., having increased considerably when the Bamburi Cement Company brought its total capacity from 400,000 tons p.a. to 700,000 tons p.a. in 1967/68. This means that in 1969 there will be a surplus capacity of about 570,000 tons and in 1970 of about 560,000 tons for exports. Exports in 1965 were of the order of 380,000 tons over 45 per cent of which went to Tanzania. With the new plant at Dar es Salaam it can be expected that this market will be lost for the Kenya producers before the end of this decade.

By then, if the Kenya plants are to work at full capacity, new export markets outside East Africa for a surplus of about 350,000 tons will have to be found, and about two thirds of total production will have to be exported, which is about the same export ratio as during the years 1961–1963 and 1966–1967, but lower than in 1964 and 1965. Whether or not this high rate of exports

29 Analyses by country undertaken by the ECA suggest that cement consumption is correlated with per-capita incomes and the size of the population. It has, however, to be kept in mind that cement consumption is only indirectly connected to per-capita incomes and size of population. There exists a closer correlation between cement consumption and capital formation and here especially with investment in buildings and construction. See also United Nations, Economic and Social Council, Economic Commission for Africa: *L'industrie du ciment et des industries connexes en Afrique de l'Est,* Report submitted at the Conference on the Harmonization of Industrial Development Programmes in East Africa, Lusaka, 27. 9.–5. 10. 1965, document E/CN. 14/INR/ 84. July 1965 (mimeo.), pp. 28 et seq. As to the modes of calculation see H. Reichelt: *op. cit.,* pp. 75–77.

can be achieved depends on the development of demand for cement and the economic policies in the major export markets outside East Africa, questions which are outside the scope of this study.

d) The Glass Industry

There are two glass factories in Kenya, the EMCO Glass Works Ltd. at Nairobi and the Kenya Glass Works Ltd. at Mombasa. Both factories which were founded after World War II, were established originally by Europeans. The Madhvani Group of Companies, the largest Asian business concern in East Africa with headquarters in Jinja, Uganda, purchased the Nairobi plant in 1959, and the Mombasa plant in 1961 [30].

Besides the two Kenya glass factories, the Madhvani Group owns and operates East Africa's third glass factory which is at Dar es Salaam and a fourth plant at Kampala. The Kampala factory will start operation in early 1969 [31].

The two Kenya glass factories which use the most modern techniques of glass manufacture including a thermoplastic process with a two-colour glass printing machine, are producing all types of bottles, including medical flasks and cosmetic glasses, tumblers and lantern globes [32]. Taking into consideration the breakages and the relatively large number of articles the normal capacity of both factories together is in the region of 13,000 tons to 15,000 tons p.a. In 1967, this capacity was utilized at a rate of about 80 per cent.
The production of glass in Kenya has increased since 1961 at an annual rate of, on the average, 10 per cent, from about 7,000 tons in 1961 to over 11,000 tons in 1966. A large portion of the production has been exported, mainly to Uganda and Tanzania, but also to other countries (table 9).
The most important customers of the Kenya glass industry are the breweries, the producers and bottlers of soft drinks, the producers and bottlers of pharmaceutical products and, for tumblers, private households and restaurants. The brewing and soft drink industry in Kenya covers virtually its total demand for bottles from the local glass industry.
In the past, the Kenya glass industry exported about 40 per cent of its production, mainly to Uganda as is shown in table 9. Uganda will not have her own glass industry before 1969. With the new factory at Kampala

30 The Madhvani Group of Companies (ed.): *Enterprise in East Africa.* About 1966.

31 The East African glass industry is producing containers and general glassware only. There was no factory producing sheet glass in East Africa by 1969 nor was there a project in an advanced stage to construct such a factory, because the East African market even taken as a whole does not yet warrant the profitable operation of a sheet glass plant.

32 R. S. Paul and J. Batt (eds.): *Industry in East Africa 1964–65.* Nairobi 1965, p. 339.

Uganda's imports from Kenya are likely to decline. A reduction of sales to Tanzania is also expected, as there are plans for an expansion of the Dar es Salaam factory. Both Uganda and Tanzania have taken increasing quantities of glass containers from Kenya as their local beer and soft drink industries have expanded. Kenya's domestic exports of glass have been directed mainly to the markets adjacent to East Africa in the North West, like Rwanda, Burundi and Congo (Kinshasa), and also to the Indian Ocean countries like Aden, the Sudan, Madagascar, and Mauritius.

Table 9. *Production and Trade of Glassware* [a], *1961–1967*
(in tons)

Year	Local Production	Interterritorial Exports Uganda	Interterritorial Exports Tanzania	Domestic Exports	Imports [b]	Local Consumption
1961	7,000	1,170	610	1,070	1,270	5,420
1962	8,000	870	430	2,040	1,570	6,230
1963	8,800	1,160	910	1,420	1,520	6,830
1964	9,500	1,940	1,160	1,100	2,240	7,540
1965	10,000	2,490	1,340	1,280	1,970	6,860
1966	.	2,660	2,270	1,830	2,380	.
1967	.	2,141	1,275	822	2,523	.

[a] Glass containers of all kinds and household articles.
[b] In some years imports include laboratory, hygienic and pharmaceutical glassware, e.g. in 1964 230 tons, in 1965 140 tons, in 1966 200 tons and in 1967 1,000 tons.
Sources: EACSO: *Annual Trade Reports;* own estimates.

Future prospects of the glass industry do not depend so much on direct private consumption but, in particular, on industrial demand since the main consumers of glassware are breweries, bottling plants for soft drinks, etc., and the development of the production of these industries determines directly the consumption of glassware. The output of the main industries using glass containers as a packing material has increased during the recent years at an annual rate of between 5 and 10 per cent. In addition, new users of glassware are to be found among existing and new industries. An annual increase in the consumption of glassware of an order of 7 per cent until 1970 seems, therefore, rather conservative. This would mean a total prospective consumption within Kenya of about 9,600 tons in 1970.

On the basis of these assumptions, the sales possibilities of the Kenya glass industry until 1970 remain rather stagnant. Decreasing interterritorial exports will probably only slowly be balanced by increasing local demand and domestic exports. Under these circumstances it will not be possible to utilize the existing capacities economically, i.e. with a narrow production programme. A continuous production will, to be sure, only be achieved by extending the variety of articles manufactured in small quantities, but this will influence productivity in a negative way. A higher degree of specialization between the factories not only in Kenya but in the whole of East Africa is, therefore, more than ever before, essential to maintain efficiency.

e) The Pyrethrum Industry

The pyrethrum plant belongs to the chrysanthemum family and the variety grown commercially is Chrysanthemum cinerariaefolium. The flower contains insecticidal ingredients which are called "pyrethrins". The insecticidal properties of pyrethrum have been known for a long time. In the early nineteenth century pyrethrum was used in Persia for the production of an insect powder [33]. Later it was introduced into Europe where it has been grown in Dalmatia since about 1840. Towards the end of the nineteenth century, Japan became the world's largest producer of pyrethrum, and retained its dominant position until it was displaced by Kenya during World War II. In 1965/66 Kenya was supplying 60 per cent of world consumption. Other important producers today are Tanzania, Ecuador, New Guinea, Japan, and Yugoslavia.
Despite its relatively high price and the development of synthetic insecticides, the markets for pyrethrum have not suffered during the past years. This is due to a number of properties which are in general not characteristic of synthetic insecticides.

- Pyrethrum is safe for human beings and for warm-blooded animals. It is, therefore, ideally suited to protect food and can be used without danger in horticulture, industry (food processing industry and warehouses) and households.
- Pyrethrum has an immediate "knock-down" effect on insects.
- Insects do not usually develop a resistance to pyrethrum after frequent applications.

Two developments in recent years have boosted the sales of pyrethrum. First there has been the development of synergists, i.e. chemicals which are not themselves toxic, but, together with pyrethrum, increase its effectiveness. They can be produced at relatively low cost, thus reducing the overall cost of the pyrethrum insecticide. Secondly, the development of aerosols which increased the consumption of insecticides in households, where pyrethrum is especially suitable.

The cultivation of the pyrethrum plant and the pyrethrum industry in Kenya are controlled by the Pyrethrum Board of Kenya (P.B.K.) and the Pyrethrum Marketing Board (P.M.B.). These Boards were established under the provisions of the Pyrethrum Act 1964, which sets out the functions of both Boards as follows [34]:

---

33 G. D. G. Jones: Pyrethrum in Kenya, The Story of a Natural Insecticide, in: *The Times Review of Industry,* April 1962, pp. 5–7.

34 Quoted from The Pyrethrum Board of Kenya and The Pyrethrum Marketing Board: *Report and Accounts for the Period 1st July 1964–30th September 1965,* p. 5.

Pyrethrum Board of Kenya (P.B.K.)

- The licensing of growers in accordance with the annual quota determined by the Marketing Board,
- Investigation and research into pyrethrum agronomic matters.

Pyrethrum Marketing Board (P.M.B.)

- The determination for each Pool Year of the annual quota to be produced,
- The acceptance/grading of pyrethrum covered by the annual quota and payment therefor by means of a Pool system of accounting,
- The appointment of contractors for the manufacture of extract,
- The marketing of pyrethrum products,
- Investigation and research into pyrethrum marketing and processing.

The determination of an annual production quota and the licensing of growers aims at restricting the quantity of flowers produced in accordance with the growth of world demand in order to safeguard prices.
For the processing of the flowers to extract, the P.M.B. has appointed as sole contractor The Pyrethrum Processing Company of Kenya Ltd. (P.P.C.K.)[35]. The P.P.C.K. was formed in 1964 when the pyrethrum industry in Kenya was reorganized. It took over the existing extract plants, one at Nairobi and two at Nakuru. In order to rationalize production, the operation of the Nairobi plant was subsequently stopped so that the pyrethrum is presently processed in two factories. Their respective annual rated capacities are 8,000 and 4,000 tons throughput of dried flowers which were utilized at about 80 per cent in 1966–67. A separate factory at Nakuru, where the dewaxed and decolourized grade "pale" is produced, is rented to the Pyrethrum Board of Kenya which runs it under its own management. The P.P.C.K. receives for its services a processing fee from the P.M.B. which covers the cost of production and a fixed profit per ton of flowers processed. Both the P.B.K. and the P.M.B., are non-profit-making organizations. After deducting the expenses for processing and administration, research and selling, all proceeds are returned to the growers.

The production process[36] commences with picking the mature flowerheads at fortnightly or three-weekly intervals when the pyrethrum fields are in bloom. They are dried in artificially-heated dryers on the larger farms and in co-operatives, and in the sun by the small-scale African farmers, whereby the moisture content is reduced from about 78 per cent to at the most 10 per cent. The dried flower-heads contain in general 1.3 to 1.4 per cent pyrethrins, the insecticidal compound. The dried flowers are then delivered to the factory at Nakuru for further processing.

35 The P.P.C.K. has an authorized capital of £350,000, of which the P.B.K. holds 58 per cent.

36 See A. H. Stedman and B. Irvine: Pyrethrum in Kenya, Flower to Concentrate, in: *The Times Review of Industry,* April 1962, pp. 13–14.

About 80 to 90 per cent of the flowers are processed into pyrethrum extract, the remainder being sold as dried flowers in bales or as powder after grinding. For the production of the extract, the flowers are ground into a coarse powder which is then washed with isohexane, a petroleum product, in a solvent extraction process. When the miscella emerges from the extractor, it contains about 1 per cent of pyrethrins. By evaporation of the solvent, the pyrethrin content is brought up to about 33 per cent. This concentrate is diluted with refined kerosene to a standard 25 per cent content.

The extract is sold in three grades at the following prices[37] (1966):

	Shs per lb.
Crude	58/50
Partially dewaxed	63/50
Dewaxed and decolourized "pale"	77/–

In addition, dried flower-heads and powder with a guaranteed pyrethrin content of 1.3 per cent are sold at £305 and £350 per long ton f.o.b. Mombasa. The exhausted grist which still contains small amounts of pyrethrins is exported as "marc", mainly to the Far East, for the manufacture of mosquito coils, or is sold on the local market as cattle food.

The production of pyrethrum in Kenya goes back to the late 1920's when the plant was introduced into the Kenya Highlands by European settlers. The quantity produced increased steadily during the 1930's until it reached a first peak during and shortly after the Second World War. Production underwent a severe setback in the post-war period when new synthetic insecticides like D.D.T. and B.H.C. came on the market, which were much cheaper than pyrethrum to produce. It took the Kenya pyrethrum industry about 15 years to regain the production level of the war years (table 10). In 1961, pyrethrum production in Kenya reached a record with over 10,000 tons of dried flowers delivered to the Pyrethrum Board. This proved to be more than the world market could absorb. Rigid licensing and decreased pay-outs to the growers from 1961 to 1963 helped to reduce production of pyrethrum flowers and deliveries to the Board. A further reduction occurred as a result of the land settlement scheme which reduced the acreage under pyrethrum further, so that the accumulated stocks of extract were depleted and attempts were made to increase production by increases in payments to the farmers and by granting new licenses. Through these measures the deliveries of pyrethrum flowers to the Board were increased again to 6,200 tons in 1965 and to over 11,000 tons in 1967.

European large-scale farmers provided the bulk of production until a few years ago, although, unlike other cash crops, the growing of pyrethrum was from the beginning open to Africans. Since 1965 the quantity delivered from

37 F.o.b. Nairobi Airport.

Table 10. *Production of Pyrethrum, 1945–1967*
(in 1,000 t of dried flowers)

Year	Quantity	Year	Quantity
1945	7.4	1960	8.5
1946	6.7	1961	10.2
1948	1.6	1962	10.0
1949	1.5	1963	5.7
1951	2.2	1964	4.3
1953	2.3	1965	6.2
1954	2.6	1966	9.3
1956	3.1	1967	11.1
1958	3.8		

Sources: N. HARDY: Pyrethrum in Kenya, The Board and its Functions, in: *The Times Review of Industry,* April 1962, p. 10; Republic of Kenya, Statistics Division of the Ministry of Economic Planning and Development: *Statistical Abstract, 1965.* Nairobi, 1965, p. 58 (in the following quoted as Republic of Kenya: *Statistical Abstract*); same publisher: *Kenya Statistical Digest,* Vol. IV, No. 4 (December 1966), p. 20.

small farms has exceeded that delivered from the large European farms. Most of the pyrethrum flowers delivered to the Marketing Board are processed by the P.P.C.K. to liquid pyrethrum extract. The proportion processed to extract has in recent years reached 90 per cent of all flowers delivered. As less than 1 per cent of total production is sold to local producers of insecticides[38], the sales figures of the marketable product can be taken from the trade statistics (table 11).

Table 11. *Exports of Pyrethrum, 1961–1967*

Year	Pyrethrum Extract		Flowers and Powder	
	tons	£	tons	£
1961	295	2,266,878	2,533	808,483
1962	373	2,723,486	1,521	440,923
1963	334	2,547,929	1,736	481,657
1964	279	2,166,588	925	286,498
1965	270	1,963,671	853	266,074
1966	316	2,396,634	1,339	427,977
1967	322	2,422,957	1,544	487,754

Source: EACSO: *Annual Trade Reports.*

38 The Kenya Government has restricted imports of aerosols and household insecticides, which has induced several manufacturers to start local production. This also increased the local sales of pyrethrum products, although – in relation to exports – these sales are still negligible.

Table 11 reveals falling sales of extract as well as of flowers in 1964 and 1965. This was mostly due to drastic reductions in the production of pyrethrum flowers, the reason for which has been mentioned above.
The most important customer for Kenya pyrethrum is the United States of America. In past years, the U.S. has taken between 35 per cent and 50 per cent of all pyrethrum exports from Kenya, mainly in the form of extract. Other important customers are the United Kingdom for extract and the Far East for dried flowers and marc.
The future of the pyrethrum industry depends on the development of the insecticide industry. Relativ to synthetic insecticidal compounds, pyrethrum is a very expensive material. Its success on the world market in spite of this high price is due to the fact that until today no synthetic material has been developed for low-cost production which has all the properties of natural pyrethrum. But the high price of pyrethrum is a strong inducement to the chemical industry in the advanced countries to develop a synthetic equivalent which can be offered at a lower price. This is a real danger for the pyrethrum industry in Kenya and elsewhere, and many experts claim that it is only a question of time before such a danger materializes. It is highly doubtful whether the pyrethrum industry would be able to survive such an eventuality. A drastic price reduction of the extract would have to be made in order for the industry to be able to compete. The pyrethrum processing industry in Kenya is run mainly on a non-profit basis[39] so that lower prices cannot be allowed by reducing profit margins. The precondition for lower prices is, therefore, lower cost of production.
By far the most important item in the processing of pyrethrum is the cost of the raw material, the payments to the farmers. These payments have been increased considerably during the past few years to stimulate production. If a "synthetic pyrethrum" came on the market, a reduction in the pay-outs to the farmers per lbs of dried flowers delivered would be inevitable, to allow price decreases of the extract. There is no doubt that many of the farmers would be able to absorb lower prices by higher efficiency. Compared with the possibility of lower material prices, all other ways of reducing the cost of production in the pyrethrum industry are of minor importance, because they affect cost items which are of very little weight in the total cost.
The Revised Development Plan anticipates a doubling of pyrethrum production between 1965–66 and 1965–70, to a total of 12,500 tons[40], two thirds of which would come from smallholders. Whether or not this high level can be achieved and sustained depends entirely on the development of world demand for pyrethrum, which, in turn, is determined mainly by

39 Out of the £14 profit per ton of dried flowers processed which is paid to the P.P.C.K., 58 per cent is paid to the P.B.K. and the P.B.K. and the pyrethrum growers.
40 Republic of Kenya: *Revised Development Plan,* p. 374.

competition from synthetic substitutes. The eventual prices of those substitutes and the degree of rationalization and competitiveness that the pyrethrum industry in Kenya will be able to achieve will ultimately decide the future of this industry.

f) The Wattle Extract Industry

Wattle extract is manufactured from the bark of the wattle tree and used for the tanning of leather. The largest producer of wattle extract in East Africa is the East African Tanning Extract Company Ltd. at Eldoret, a subsidiary of the British Forestal Land, Timber and Railways Company Ltd. Besides wattle extract, the Company at Eldoret produces a wide range of wood and agricultural products. The Company started operating in Kenya in 1932[41] and supplies about two thirds of Kenya's production of wattle extract. A second important company in Kenya producing wattle extract is the Asian-owned Kenya Tanning Extract Company at Thika.
Outside Kenya, there is another large East African producer in Tanzania, the Tanganyika Wattle Company Ltd., a wholly owned CDC[42]-subsidiary, operating in the Njombe area of Tanzania.

The wattle bark is chopped into pieces of half an inch size and the extract is derived by treating the bark with hot water (170–240 degrees F) using the counter-current method. Later, the liquors are evaporated and the concentrated extract runs into sacs as solid or into spray dryers where the powder is made. The solid extract has a 60 per cent tannin content, the powder a 56 or 68 per cent tannin content.

As nearly all of the wattle extract is exported, the foreign trade figures roughly coincide with the sales of the industry. Table 12 demonstrates rather marked fluctuations in sales. One of the reasons for these fluctuations is that the supply of wattle extract is rather sensitive to price changes. Another important factor determining production is the weather. Most of the production takes place during the rainy season when the bark has a higher tannin content, and is easier to separate from the stem. The dry weather in most of 1965 was to a great part responsible for the low output in that year.
The main export markets for wattle bark extract are India and Pakistan, which during the last years took over half of total exports, and also the United States of America.
Since the wattle extract industry is highly export oriented, future prospects are not very promising, because the development of world demand for

41 See for the history of the Company: The Revolution of a Local Industry, in: *East African Trade and Industry*, Vol. XI, No. 141 (November 1965), pp. 26–27.
42 CDC = Commonwealth Development Corporation, a British Government organization concerned with the promotion of economic development by participation in commercial activities.

Table 12. *Exports of Wattle Bark Extract, 1955–1967*

Year	Quantity (t)	Value (£1,000)	Price (£/ton)
1955	33,223	2,261	68
1957	26,315	1,522	58
1959	19,261	1,026	53
1960	14,253	730	51
1961	16,994	765	45
1962	16,449	725	44
1963	13,814	638	46
1964	18,154	883	49
1965	13,139	711	54
1966	25,786	1,455	56
1967	15,793	861	55

Source: EACSO: *Annual Trade Reports.*

vegetable tanning extracts is insecure. Synthetic substitutes are more and more taking the place of wattle extract. In most recent years prices have nonetheless been firm and in 1966 the highest value of annual sales for the last nine years was achieved. The high sales of 1966 must, however, be considered exceptional. It is likely that exports will eventually stabilize at a much lower level of about 15,000 tons.

Annex: The Fertilizer Industry in East Africa

In 1966, there were two fertilizer manufacturers in East Africa, only one of which, the Tororo Industrial Chemicals and Fertilizers Limited (TICAF) was based mainly on local raw materials producing a single superphosphate. The Company is exploiting the large deposits of approximately 200 million tons of apatite (a phosphate mineral containing about 42 per cent of P_2O_5) in the Sukulu Hills near Tororo in Uganda. The apatite is processed in a factory to a single superphosphate with a guaranteed watersoluble P_2O_5-content of 20 to 21 per cent and an average content of about 21 per cent. The present capacity of the plant is 30,000 tons of superphosphate p.a. Besides superphosphate TICAF is also producing sulphuric acid, mainly for its own consumption in the fertilizer plant but also to a limited extent for sales to outside consumers. The sulphuric acid plant has a rated capacity of 10,000 tons p.a.

The phosphate bearing soil is mined in the north valley of the Sukulu Hills where it is lying at the surface. It is mixed with water, screened and partially demagnatized in a magnetic separator on the hill. The magnetic residue contains about 80 per cent of Fe_2O_3 and is at present discarded but may later on find use in a local steel industry. The mine is working during daylight only. The semi-product is then pumped down to the factory as a slurry. In a number of processes the slurry is

treated to separate impurities from the apatite. The concentrate of apatite produced contains about 40.5 to 41.5 per cent of P_2O_5 and is one of the world's highest grades of phosphate (e.g. Morocco 33 to 34 per cent, Kola 38 to 39 per cent, Florida 34 to 35 per cent).
For the manufacture of superphosphate, strong sulphuric acid (98 per cent) is brought to react with the apatite slurry in a mixer. The mixer has a capacity of 8 tons per hour, with 75 per cent running time. After the reaction the product is brought to a drum-type granulator where it is formed into the final granulate. After an additional time of reaction in the granualtor the final product is bagged for despatch.

The Company was incorporated in December 1955 with the Uganda Development Corporation (UDC) as principal shareholder. Soon after tests were started in a pilot plant in which about 20,000 tons of soil were treated between October 1956 and July 1958. In 1961, African Explosives & Chemical Industries (E.A.) Ltd. (later as Twiga Chemical Industries Ltd.), a subsidiary of ICI with headquarters in Nairobi, was appointed managing agent and sole selling agent of TICAF. The construction of the factory started shortly afterwards and production commenced in 1962. In 1963, about 7,000 tons of fertilizer were produced.

Table 13. *Sales of Single Superphosphate by TICAF, 1964–1967*

Year	Total Sales		Markets		
	£	t	Kenya t	Uganda t	Tanzania t
1964	146,949	13,500	10,341	456	2,703
1965	369,151	28,953	15,896	2,719	10,338
1966	346,172	23,574	24,655	1,300 [a]	1,041
1967 [a]	.	18,750	16,400	2,000	200

[a] Approximate figures.
Source: TICAF and EACSO: *Annual Trade Reports.*

Of the total sales during the last three years Kenya took about 70 per cent, Tanzania about 20 per cent and the remaining 10 per cent were sold locally in Uganda. Exports outside East Africa are negligible. The recent drop in sales is due to serious marketing difficulties in Kenya arising from a trend towards the utilisation of mixed and compound fertilizers, using imported triple supers, and from structural changes in the Kenyan agricultural sector.
The average ex-factory price (net of sales commission of 5 per cent to Twiga Chemicals) has increased steadily during the last few years from Shs 218/- per ton in 1964 to about 297/- in 1967. The reason for this continuous price increase lies partly in the rising prices of imported sulphur [43]. The price of

43 For the production of 1 ton of super phosphate about 0.1275 t of sulphur is needed.

1 ton of sulphur c.i.f. Mombasa rose from about Shs 395/- per ton in 1964 to about 650/- per ton 1966–67 which increased the manufacturing cost of superphosphates by about Shs 35/- per ton.

The consumption of phosphate fertilizer in Kenya is subsidized by the Government at a rate of Shs 375/– to 385/– per ton of water-soluble nutrient which is about Shs 75/– per ton of a 20 per cent single superphosphate. Most of the sales to Kenya go through the Kenya Farmers' Association which buys the Tororo fertilizer at a price of Shs 308/50 per ton from the sales agent (as per March 1967) for loads over 100 tons.

In spite of the considerable local production of phosphate fertilizers large quantities continue to be imported into East Africa from overseas, mainly in the form of triple supers (sometimes also called double supers) (see table 14). These phosphate fertilizers are bagged and sometimes mixed with other granulates by a plant at Nakuru, Kenya, Windmill Fertilizer Ltd., an associate of a Dutch fertilizer manufacturer[44]. Importation of triple supers into East Africa is still economical in bulk because large consignments ensure relatively low transport costs, especially if charter ships are used.

Table 14. *Imports of Phosphate Fertilizers into East Africa, 1963–1967*

Year		Kenya		Uganda		Tanzania	
		t	£	t	£	t	£
1963	supers	12,079	325,599	647	18,639	630	16,911
	others	1,893	64,434	2	90	15	595
1964	supers	12,126	343,497	1,490	40,896	845	24,126
	others	100	2,003	–	–	33	705
1965	supers	11,400	360,697	1,654	50,453	1,129	34,850
	others	297	8,319	15	316	60	3,018
1966	supers	18,977	586,486	916	29,596	906	28,405
	others	1,591	47,022	2	101	4	147
1967	supers	14,509	427,847	556	15,866	1,168	35,050
	others	640	24,352	401	14,293	1	46

Source: EACSO: *Annual Trade Reports.*

As mentioned above, TICAF is producing its requirements of H_2SO_4 in a sulphuric acid plant located within the fertilizer complex[45].

44 It is capable of mixing economically also small quantities of granulates of different kinds of fertilizers thus offering the appropriate fertilizer mix for various kinds of conditions as to soils, plants, etc. The mixing unit has a maximum hourly capacity of 30 tons.

45 In the production of phosphate fertilizer sulphuric acid is an important material for the transformation of the insoluble phosphate in the apatite into water soluble phosphate which can be used as fertilizer. To produce 1 ton of single superphosphate 0.375 tons of sulphuric acid is necessary. A production of 25,000 tons of single super at Tororo needs, therefore, an H_2SO_4 input in the region of 9,400 tons.

The sulphuric acid plant operates by the contact process with imported sulphur, oxygen from the air and water as the three ingredients. The sulphur is melted, burnt to SO_2 which in turn is burnt to SO_3 with vanadium oxyde (V_2O_5) as catalyser. The SO_3 is passed into diluted H_2SO_4 where it reacts with the free water.

TICAF is producing H_2SO_4 in three grades:

- Commercial grade with a H_2SO_4-content of 98.5 per cent. This grade is the most important one as it is used in the fertilizer production. The remainder is sold mainly to Nyanza Textiles, East Africa's largest textile producer at Jinja.
- Chemically pure grade with a H_2SO_4-content of 96 to 98 per cent. Important consumers are the battery charging plants. About 50 per cent of it is sold to Kenya.
- Creamery grade is chemically pure but diluted with water to a H_2SO_4-content of about 90.5 to 91.5 per cent. It is sold in very small quantities to creameries in Kenya who use it to determine the fat content of milk.

The approximative quantities of H_2SO_4 produced and sold are given in table 15:

Table 15. *Production and Sales of Sulphuric Acid by TICAF, 1964–1967*

Year	Production	Use for fertilizer manufacture	Sales to outside consumers Commercial grade		Chemical pure	
	t	t	t	£	t	£
1964	5,720	5,062	556	21,179	102	3,680
1965	10,122	9,226	805	33,131 [a]	121	.
1966	10,017	9,083	801	36,301 [b]	124	.
1967	7,450 [c]	6,800	570	.	110	.

[a] Includes creamery grade.
[b] Includes pure grades.
[c] Approximate figures.
Source: TICAF.

With regard to the geographic distribution of sales of sulphuric acid to outside consumers, by far the greatest part is sold in Uganda where Nyanza Textiles buy about two thirds of all sulphuric acid sold by TICAF. Of the remainder, Kenya takes about 75 per cent and Tanzania 25 per cent.
The ex-factory prices differ according to the location of the customer so that the price including freight which the customer has to pay is approximately equal all over East Africa. Through this policy the Company can also offer its product at competitive prices in areas close to the coast which are especially vulnerable to imports. In 1966–67, the average ex-factory price for commercial grade was about 820/- Shs per ton whereas for chemically pure grade it was about Shs 670/- because a larger percentage of

total sales (about 50 per cent) was sold in Kenya and was, therefore, affected by higher railage. Imports of sulphuric acid into East Africa in 1961 amounted to 820 tons at a value of about £60,000 c.i.f. port and in 1965 to 120 tons at a value of about £10,000. At the same time, consumption of sulphuric acid in East Africa increased from 820 tons in 1961 (equal to imports) to 10,270 tons, 1,045 tons of which were consumed in industries outside the fertilizer factory.

The future prospects of the fertilizer industry in East Africa depend on the development of demand for fertilizer which, in turn, is less a function of the acreage of cultivated land than of the speed at which the African farmers shift to the production of cash crops and at which fertilizers will be employed by the African farmers.

An ECA report gives some estimates for the prospective demand for fertilizers in East Africa in 1970[46]. The figures suggest that between 1964 and 1970 the consumption of phosphate fertilizers will increase nearly fourfold (from 7,800 tons to 28,900 tons) and that of nitrogenous fertilizer nearly double (from 14,800 tons to 25,600 tons). Developments during the past few years have shown that these forecasts were rather optimistic.

Phosphate Fertilizers

Of the total demand for phosphates in East Africa in 1965 — about 10,000 tons of pure nutrients[47] — the Tororo factory supplied about 50 per cent. If we assume that this ratio of local production to imports remains the same until the end of this decade the consumption of single superphosphate in East Africa in 1970 will be in the region of 70,000 tons and imports of triple superphosphate will be about 40,000 tons to 50,000 tons. These figures are highly tentative because the development of East African capacity and demand by 1970 is very doubtful.

There have been proposals to expand the factory at Tororo to an annual capacity of 63,000 tons of triple superphosphate. Since no definite decision with regard to this project was taken by mid-1968 it seems doubtful that these plans will be realized by 1970.

Tanzania also has plans to establish a factory for the production of superphosphate fertilizers. The Development Plan mentions a plant with a capacity of 40,000 tons p.a.[48]. The location of this factory is not yet decided. Tricalcic phosphate deposits of about 10 million tons have been discovered in the Min Jingu Hills near Lake Manyara. The ECA[49] recommends a concentration of the phosphate bearing soil

46 ECA: *Recherche sur l'industrie chimique,* pp. 32 et seq.

47 Imports in 1965 remained about equal relative to the previous year and Tororo's sales increased by 10,500 tons or about 2,200 tons of pure nutrients.

48 The United Republic of Tanganyika and Zanzibar: *Tanganyika Five-Year Plan for Economic and Social Development, 1st July, 1964–30th June, 1969,* Vol. I. Dar es Salaam, Government Printer, 1964, p. 40.

49 ECA: *Recherche sur l'industrie chimique,* pp. 13, 150, 307.

from 20 per cent to 31 per cent at Arusha and the establishment of a fertilizer factory with a capacity of about 160,000 tons p.a. at Dar es Salaam, producing a single superphosphate of 16 per cent to 17 per cent water soluble content. This factory would also export to the islands in the Indian Ocean including Madagascar. Other proposals suggest that the phosphate deposits should be used for the production of a compound fertilizer at a plant at Dar es Salaam the other ingredients being imported. Similar plants have recently been built at Dakar and on Mauritius with annual capacities of about 60,000 tons.

Any increase in the production of phosphate fertilizers entails a higher consumption of sulphuric acid for which, at present, no sufficient capacities exist. If the Tororo factory should expand to 63,000 tons annual capacity of triple superphosphate an additional capacity for sulphuric acid in the region of 56,000 tons would be required[50]. In order to meet the demand of other local consumers of sulphuric acid, a new acid plant would have to be designed for a capacity of 60,000 tons to 65,000 tons. The question arises whether also this new sulphuric acid plant should be based on imported sulphur. The annual consumption of sulphur for this plant would be in the region of 15,000 tons against about 3,200 tons at present.

Sulphur is found in Uganda in the Kilembe area where sulphur ores are a by-product of the copper production. At Kilembe there are large stock piles of pyrit concentrates which are left over from the first stage of refining the copper ores on the site. In 1965, they consisted of about 360,000 tons of concentrates containing 1.3 per cent of cobalt and 44.9 per cent of sulphur. The investment cost of a plant to extract the cobalt and produce sulphuric acid has been estimated at about £2,000,000[51].

A second possibility would be to utilize the sulphuric gases which are released while roasting the copper ores at the smelter at Jinja and which contain 18,000 tons of sulphur p.a.[52].

The present high world market prices of sulphur make the production of sulphuric acid on the basis of local sulphur appear profitable so that this project will most probably be part of the overall scheme.

While the use of local sulphur for the production of sulphuric acid in Uganda seems more profitable in the long run (even if the price of imported sulphur were much lower than at present), a sulphuric acid industry in Tanzania with a phosphate fertilizer factory at Dar es Salaam would possibly be better off on the basis of imported sulphur. The advantages are mainly in the lower capital investment and capital cost which in a coastal location could overcompensate the higher raw material prices.

---

50 This presupposes that the existing acid plant at Tororo will be obsolete when the new fertilizer factory reaches production stage. The lifetime of a sulphuric acid plant is usually estimated to be about 8 years which makes this assumption realistic.

51 Uganda Government: *Work for Progress, Uganda's Second Five-Year Plan, 1966–1971.* Entebbe, Government Printer, 1966, p. 105.

52 Similar plants based on sulphur dioxide from smelters exist in the Congo (Kinshasa) and in Zambia.

But if the present high sulphur prices are really the result of a persistent shortage of sulphur and high prices can be expected to continue it might also be possible that the Tanzania project would be better off if the local pyrit deposits near Geita in the Lake Viktoria area were utilized. The ECA has estimated the extraction cost for 1 ton of sulphur from this deposit at US$ 66 or about Shs 470/–[53]. This compares favourably with a present import price of about Shs 650/– c.i.f. coast, even if additional transport costs to the sulphuric acid factory are taken into account. Locating the acid plant as well as the fertilizer plant at Arusha or Dodoma could under these conditions be a proposition worth careful consideration, taking into account the costs and benefits of each location and comparing them with Dar es Salaam.
The ECA has also suggested for Kenya the establishment of a large sulphuric acid plant at Mombasa using imported sulphur, with an annual capacity of 160,000 tons[54] which would operate in conjunction with a nitrogenous fertilizer (ammonium sulphate) factory.

Nitrogenous Fertilizers

There were no nitrogenous fertilizer plants in East Africa by 1968, but all three of the East African countries were planning or considering the construction of a plant. The production of nitrogenous fertilizers had in the 1964 Kampala Agreement been allocated to Uganda. As a result of the subsequent developments in the Common Market negotiations this agreement has become obsolete. In the meantime, Kenya came to the forefront with the project of a nitrogenous fertilizer plant at Mombasa the construction of which started at the end of 1967.

The factory will produce over 100,000 tons of calcium ammonium nitrate (CAN – $Ca[NH_3NO_3]_2$) p.a., in the beginning on the basis of imported liquid ammonia, later possibly using refinery gas which is at present burnt as waste or naphta. The project was supposed to be in operation by 1970, but will certainly be delayed by several years.
The second Uganda Development Plan[55] refers to the project in Uganda as a factory with a capacity of 100,000 tons per annum, presumably based on the water electrolysis process for the manufacture of ammonia. The ECA calculated the unit cost of production of ammonia at Jinja at about twice as high as it would be at Mombasa[56]. The Uganda project, therefore, has at least for the time being little chance of realization.

Whether the Mombasa plant will be economic considering the relatively small size suitable for the local market is a question which is not easy to

---

53 ECA: *Recherche sur l'industrie chimique*, p. 151.
54 United Nations, Economic Commission for Africa and Centre for Industrial Development: *Prospects for the Development of the Chemical Industry in Africa*, Paper submitted to the Symposium on Industrial Development in Africa, Cairo, 27th January–10th February 1966, document E/CN. 14/AS/III/22 (10th December 1965), (mimeo.), table 15.
55 Uganda Government, *op. cit.*, p. 88.
56 ECA: *Recherche sur l'industrie chimique*, p. 244.

answer. The prices for nitrogenous fertilizer have gone down continuously during the last years. This was the result of new techniques of production and of larger production units integrated in extensive industrial complexes in the advanced countries where single train units of 1,000 tons of ammonia per day and over are becoming common[57]. Compared with these quantities the demand for nitrogenous fertilizers in East Africa is very small. Imports of nitrogenous fertilizers into East Africa in 1965 were about 70,000 tons (in 1967 about 48,000 tons) half of which was sulphate of ammonia which the Mombasa factory will not produce. The total East African consumption of other nitrogenous fertilizers was only about 35,000 tons in 1965 and only about half of this was calcium ammonium nitrate[58]. For the construction of a local ammonia plant to be justified the consumption of calcium ammonium nitrate in East Africa will have to increase manyfold, much more than projected by the ECA for 1970 or 1980[59] unless the ammonia plant or the calcium ammonium nitrate plant can find export markets for most of their production. Otherwise the advantages of large-scale production of the fertilizer industries in the advanced countries will enable them to offer their products at cheaper prices for a long time to come.

2. Industries Using Predominantly Imported Raw Materials

a) The Soap Industry

The soap industry in East Africa is — with regard to the size of the establishments and the methods of production — a very heterogeneous industry. Altogether there are about 30 full-time soap-producing units and a large number of small manufacturers producing soap intermittently as a side-activity and on a cottage industry basis. Most of the full-time soap manufacturers are small and medium firms with an annual production of under 3,000 tons, generally of low-grade laundry soap. The two largest producers are located at Nairobi, namely East Africa Industries Ltd. (E.A.I.), and Colgate-Palmolive. Unilever holds about 55 per cent of the share capital of E.A.I., the Commonwealth Development Corporation about 30 per cent and the Kenya Government-owned Industrial and Commercial Development Corporation the remaining 15 per cent. Colgate-Palmolive (East Africa) Ltd., is a subsidiary of Colgate-Palmolive International.
In addition to soap, both factories produce other articles; East Africa

57 ECA/Centre for Industrial Development, *op. cit.*, pp. 50–51.
58 ECA: *Industrie Chimique en Afrique de l'Est*, p. 33.
59 The ECA assumes for Kenya an annual increase in consumption of 8 per cent until 1980 which would bring the Kenyan consumption of calcium ammonium nitrate to about 20,000 tons by 1970 and 45,000 tons by 1980.

Industries make non-soapy detergents, toothpaste, glycerine[60], edible fats and oils and Colgate-Palmolive manufacturers toothpaste, a detergent and a cleansing agent. While E.A.I. produce toilet as well as laundry soaps, Colgate-Palmolive manufacture toilet soaps only.
The medium-size soap plants are family businesses and are evenly scattered in the major points of concentration of the population in East Africa, namely at or near Kampala (Nakasero Soap Works Ltd.), Jinja (Madhvani Sugar Works Ltd.), Tororo (Tororo Oil and Soap Factory Ltd.), Kisumu (Baby Soap Factory Ltd.), Nairobi (Elephant Soap Factory Ltd.), Dar es Salaam (Taramal Industries Ltd.), Tanga (Marahaba Ltd. and Nuurami Industries Ltd.), and Mwanza (Lake Soap Industries Ltd.). The largest of these medium size producers are the Nakasero Soap Works Ltd. with an annual production of between 6,000 and 8,000 tons, the remaining medium size firms producing between 3,000 tons and 4,000 tons of soap p.a. each.
The large factories import virtually all of their raw materials[61] from overseas, partly because they are not available locally at all, partly because they are not available in the required quantity and/or quality, and partly because some of the locally manufactured raw materials for the soap industry are offered at prices higher than the world market price. But the smaller factories also import most of their raw materials and buy locally only sodium silicate and some diatomite which is used as a filler for laundry soap. The smaller firms also buy most of their coconut oil requirements locally.
With regard to production methods, there is little difference in principle between the techniques used by the two expatriate Companies at Nairobi and their European counterparts. The main stages of production — milling, extrusion and cutting — are highly mechanized and modern machinery has been used from the beginning. E.A.I. started to produce soap in 1958, Colgate-Palmolive in 1965. Apart from the basic production process, more labour-intensive methods are used. This is true for the wrapping and, in particular, for the packing of the soap into boxes and the transport within the factory. The reasons are partly that unskilled labour can be used for these activities, and partly that the most modern fully-automatic packing and wrapping machines have very large capacities, greatly in excess of the sales possibilities which are limited by the small size of the market. The medium-sized factories also have the core of their production processes today more or less highly mechanized. Some of them grew from small-scale cottage industries into their present size and have only recently started using some

60 Glycerine is a by-product in the manufacture of soap, for which there is no local demand. E.A.I. produces and exports about 700 to 800 tons p.a. at a f.o.b. value of about £70,000 (1966–1967).

61 The main raw materials are tallow, fats or fatty acids and coconut oil, together about 75 per cent in value of the raw materials, and caustic soda. In addition, sodium silicate and diatomite is used in the production of laundry soap and perfumes in the production of toilet soap.

modern machinery. As a larger share of their production consists of laundry soap produced and sold in bars which do not require wrapping, most of the packing can be done by hand and few mechanical devices are used for transport within the plant.

Production statistics were not available in East Africa until the imposition of the excise tax in the middle of 1966 [62]. According to these excise statistics the total soap consumption in East Africa in 1967 was in the region of 45,000 tons, about 7 per cent of which was imported and the rest produced locally. Exports outside East Africa were negligible. Production and consumption were distributed approximately as follows between the three East African countries:

Table 16. *Production [a] and Consumption of Soap in East Africa, 1967*
(in 1,000 t)

Country	Production	Interterritorial Exports	Interterritorial Imports	Domestic Imports	Home Consumption
Kenya	18.3	6.3	3.2	0.8	16.0
Uganda	13.0	3.0	5.1	0.3	15.4
Tanzania	11.0	0.2	1.2	2.2	14.2

[a] Without surface-acting agents and washing preparations, incl. detergents.
Source: EACSO: *Annual Trade Reports.*

Table 16 shows clearly the dominating position of the Kenya soap industry in East Africa. In 1967 Kenya produced nearly half of the total quantity of soap manufactured in East Africa. The market share of the Kenya manufacturers in terms of value is, however, still greater than in terms of quantity because they concentrate on relatively high-quality laundry soaps and produce relatively more toilet soap than their competitors in Uganda and, especially, in Tanzania [63]. This is due to structural differences in the production as well as of the markets for laundry and toilet soap.

Laundry soap has been produced in East Africa for many years. Until the late 1950's the bulk of the production was carried out in small shops on a cottage industry basis. Consequently, the soap was consumed in the vicinity of the place of production and interterritorial trade in laundry soap was very small. This situation changed when E.A.I. entered the field of laundry soaps on a large scale at their factory at Nairobi in 1958. In 1957 Kenya had a net trade deficit in laundry soap

62 Since June 1966, the East African Customs and Excise Department collects figures of stockroom receipts of soap for tax purposes. It can be assumed that not all of the producers declare all of their soap production, so that the figures of the E.A. Customs and Excise probably underestimate the quantities of soap manufactured.

63 In 1967 the average ex-factory price of soap produced in Kenya was about Shs 1/20 per lb. against about Shs 0.75 per lb. in Uganda and Shs 0.60 in Tanzania.

of £120,000. In 1959, the soaring interterritorial exports brought about a net trade surplus of over £150,000 which had increased by 1964 to £785,000, but dropped to £109,000 in 1967. In 1964, Kenya exported £ 1,125,000 worth of laundry soap, about two thirds of which went to Tanganyika. This growth of production was almost entirely due to the rapidly increasing local East African demand for laundry soap and not to import substitution. Domestic imports of laundry soap into East Africa declined only slightly from a value of about £313,000 in 1957 to £279,000 in 1967.

In Uganda the production of laundry soap also increased during this period, but not as spectacularly as in Kenya. Except for the year 1964, Uganda remained a net importer until 1967 with Kenya as its most important foreign supplier.

Tanzania, on the other hand, did not develop its own soap industry until after 1964, when its imports had reached a value of over £1,000,000. In 1965, Tanzania introduced restrictions on imports of laundry soap from Kenya and Uganda to boost its own production, and succeeded in reducing its total imports in 1967 to a value of only £200,000.

The production of toilet soap demands more advanced technical know-how than that of laundry soap. The bulk of production in East Africa comes, therefore, from the two expatriate factories at Nairobi. They offer well-known international brands which are in a very strong position in this more sophisticated market. Again, the rapid development of local production started in 1958 in Kenya, and Kenya is predominant in this field compared to the two other East African countries. In 1967 Kenya's interterritorial exports which had steadily been increasing had a value of £770,000, of which Uganda took about two thirds and Tanzania only one third.

The soap industry in East Africa is protected by a tariff against imports from overseas of $37^{1}/_{2}$ per cent ad valorem or by a specific tariff of Shs 80/- per 100 lbs, whichever is the greater (1966–67). In addition, each of the three countries has imposed quantitative restrictions on imports of soap from overseas so that local production is well protected against foreign competition. Since June 1965, Tanzania has subjected imports of soap from Kenya and Uganda to licences. This affected first imports of laundry soap which, by the end of 1966, had virtually ceased. Licenses for imports of toilet soap from Kenya and Uganda into Tanzania were easily obtainable until the beginning of 1967. After that, more and more applications for import licenses for toilet soap were turned down, so that the Tanzanian soap market will eventually be lost completely for the Kenya and Uganda manufacturers[64]. This was a severe blow, especially for the Kenya producers. The Kenya and Uganda soap producers were fortunate that the losses on the Tanzania market occurred at a time when the home markets were expanding rapidly, so that the overall reduction in sales was small in Kenya and non-existent in Uganda.

This development nevertheless retarded the growth of soap production in Kenya and Uganda at a time when this growth had been anticipated by expansion of capacities. Although the existing capacity of the soap factories

64 Tanzania has after 1st December, 1967 replaced its quantitative restrictions on soap imports from Kenya and Uganda by transfer taxes.

is not known, one can assume that the capacity of the Kenya soap industry in 1966 was far from fully utilized, even on a one-shift basis.

While the reduction in sales on the Tanzania market was most strongly felt by the Kenya producers (and here especially by E.A.I.), the imposition of an excise tax on soap in 1966 of Shs 25/- per 100 lbs applied to all three East African countries and mainly affected the sales of the medium and small manufacturers who have specialized more in the production of the cheaper grades of soap. As a consequence of the price increase which resulted from the imposition of excise duty, regular consumption of soap has become too expensive for the lower-income levels, and the drop in demand forced some of the manufacturers to discontinue the production of their cheapest grades.

According to the Development Plan 1965–66 to 1969–70[65], the soap consumption is estimated to grow by an overall rate of 10 per cent, a rate which is called "conservative" and, thus, may even be higher. When discussing the future prospects of the industry one has, however, to take account of probable diverging developments among the different qualities and types of soaps and cleansing materials. Within soap consumption, a structural change towards better qualities of soap has been noticeable for some time. The manufacturers are following this trend by reducing the production of the cheapest grades, such as blue mottled soap, in favour of better quality laundry soaps and toilet soap. The better quality soaps will therefore probably experience higher growth rates than the annual 10 per cent, while the sales of cheaper grades will increase at a much slower rate or may even decline. This is not only the result of increase in consumer incomes, but also of the excise tax introduced in 1966 and mentioned above.

Soap production in Kenya will not exactly follow the trend of the consumption sequence. It can be expected that the interterritorial exports, which in 1965–66 still accounted for about 30 per cent of total domestic production, will most likely decline not only because Tanzania may be expected to reduce its imports of toilet soap as well, but eventually also because the Uganda market will become more difficult for Kenya producers. It is therefore possible that Kenya's interterritorial trade in soap will be balanced in the future. With regard to domestic imports, there is little room left for import substitution, except maybe for toilet soap in Tanzania[66], and domestic exports of soap in the past have been very small. The Revised Development Plan[67] hopes for increased exports of soap elsewhere in Africa, but the prospects for this are none too bright. The soap industry is among the first industries that a developing country erects, because relatively simple techno-

65 Republic of Kenya: *Revised Development Plan,* p. 265.
66 Present imports include a wide range of products, the quantity of each of which is far too small to warrant major local production.
67 Republic of Kenya: *Revised Development Plan,* p. 265.

logical methods can be used and the minimum economic size of the firm can be rather small. All countries, therefore, will try to supply their domestic soap markets from local production as soon as possible, thus reducing imports. At the same time, on those export markets which are available, the Kenya soap industry has to compete with large overseas producers, which are generally able to offer their products at very low prices to underbid the Kenya manufacturers once they meet them on the open market outside the protected East African market. A further point has to be taken into consideration in this connection, namely that the largest interterritorial exporters in Kenya are affiliated to overseas companies. Their parent companies export themselves a considerable part of their production to Africa, and particularly to those African countries in which they do not have subsidiaries. This means that while the two Kenya producers need not fear competition on the East Africa market from their affiliated companies, they are restricted by company policy from exploring and taking advantage of export possibilities outside their consigned area.
As net interterritorial exports are likely to decline without a significant increase in net domestic exports, the development of Kenya soap production will be more closely connected to the development of consumption in Kenya. For the immediate future, this means that production will stagnate or only increase at a slow rate. After the recent extensions, the existing capacities are sufficient to cope with the increasing local demand until 1970 at the earliest.

b) The Paint Industry

There are five main companies producing paints in East Africa, four of which are exclusively manufacturing paints and allied products and one who produces paints besides several other chemicals. These companies are Berger, Jenson & Nicholson of E.A. Ltd., Leyland Paints (Africa) Ltd., Sadolins Paints (E. A.) Ltd., Walpamur Company (E. A.) Ltd., and Twiga Chemical Industries Ltd.
All paint manufacturers are subsidiaries or associates of large overseas concerns, four from Britain and one from Denmark. Kenya is the main producer of paints in East Africa. Three of the four main producers also have manufacturing or mixing units at Dar es Salaam and Kampala [68], in addition to a plant in Nairobi.

The first paint plant in East Africa was established in 1950 at Dar es Salaam. In 1956, the first factory at Nairobi went into production. This was at a time when East Africa, and Kenya in particular, was witnessing a spectacular economic boom which was to last until 1960. The growth in the building and construction industry

68 See: Paint – A £1 Million Industry in East Africa, in: *East African Trade and Industry,* Vol. X, No. 132 (Febr. 1965), pp. 24–43.

was particularly rapid, and as a result, the market during this period for paints was extremely dynamic. By 1961, the four major paint manufacturers had manufacturing units at Nairobi. Shortly after this time the situation changed. The Kenya economy entered into a severe depression brought about by the insecurity among the largest part of the potential investors about their future. This period lasted until about the end of 1964. In the meantime the economic activity and together with this also the consumption of paints in the other two countries had accelerated so that Uganda overtook Kenya in paint consumption by 1963–1964.
The rapid developments in Uganda and Tanzania still induced some of the Kenya paint manufacturers to establish blending plants at Kampala and Dar es Salaam respectively where certain finished paints are prepared from intermediate products imported from the Kenya factory. There are now three paint factories at Dar es Salaam supplying most of Tanzania's paint requirements.

The range of paints manufactured locally include emulsion paints, enamels, distempers and water paints, ready mixed oil paints, as well as cellulose paints and thinners for automotive and other industries.
In the absence of production statistics, the Annual Trade Reports give a rather good indication about the development of the East African paint industry. Table 17 shows the interterritorial trade in paints, the imports of paints from overseas and the net trade position of each country. The section on Kenya reflects the development of a strong local paint industry in the

Table 17. *Trade in Paints of the East African Countries, 1954–1967* [a]
(in £1,000)

Year	Kenya				Uganda			Tanzania			
	Dom. Imp.[b]	Int. terr. Imp.[b]	Int. terr. Exp.	Net trade pos.[c]	Dom. Imp.	Int. terr. Imp.	Net trade pos.[c]	Dom. Imp.[b]	Int. terr. Imp.	Int. terr. Exp.	Net trade pos.[c]
1954	300	49	12	—337	112	12	—124	121	–	49	— 60
1955	489	24	4	—507	210	31	—241	203	–	50	—144
1957	530	15	26	—519	181	33	—214	128	3	25	—101
1959	445	77	69	—453	182	82	—261	179	7	94	— 87
1960	471	69	94	—446	132	100	—226	166	9	78	— 94
1961	361	21	225	—157	146	155	—301	176	77	28	—223
1962	223	33	232	— 23	94	143	—234	136	92	32	—193
1963	228	40	240	— 24	134	155	—287	117	87	40	—160
1964	100	63	365	+207	123	243	—362	123	126	63	— 82
1965	138	38	580	+411	108	487	—592	84	97	38	—137
1966	179	43	339	+127	72	286	—352	104	54	38	—116
1967	119	41	221	+ 70	54	203	—254	94	19	39	— 70

[a] SITC-groups 533 03 b) until 1963, 533 39 after 1963. This excludes distempers.
[b] Net imports, net of interterritorial transfers and re-exports.
[c] Positive figures indicate export surplus, negative figures import surplus. Domestic exports and, in the case of Uganda, interterritorial exports are not separately shown because of their insignificance but included in calculating the net trade position.
Source: EACSO: *Annual Trade Reports.*

years after 1957. By 1965, Kenya had become a net exporter of paints. Until 1960, when Kenya's economy was still flourishing, local production served mainly to satisfy the Kenya market. Only from 1961 on, when the home market contracted, did interterritorial exports to Uganda and Tanganyika become really important. In this way the Kenya paint manufacturers were able to survive the depression of the early 1960's without too much difficulty, and in some cases even managed to expand their total sales.

There is no doubt that the development of the East African paint industry was only possible because of the strong protectionist policy adopted by the three Governments. In the beginning this protection was directed only against imports from overseas[69]. In addition to levying import duties, all three countries have paints on their lists of products which require licenses from the respective Ministries of Commerce and Industry for importation. For imports from overseas these licenses are in general granted only for certain special paints which are not produced locally. Prior to the inception of the Treaty for East African Co-operation they also had to be obtained for interterritorial imports, although only Tanganyika restricted imports of paints from the other two countries, particularly from Kenya since 1965.

In 1965–66 the total market for all kinds of paints in East Africa was in the region of £1.8 to £2 million per annum. Of this, about 15 per cent was imported from outside East Africa and 85 per cent, the equivalent of about 900,000 gallons, was produced in East Africa. An estimate of the value of production of paints in each of the three countries permits one to calculate the approximate regional distribution of the market (table 18).

Table 18. *Production, Trade and Consumption of Paints in East Africa, 1965–1966* (in £1,000)

	Production [a]	Exports	Imports	Consumption [a]
Kenya	1,000	580	180	600
Uganda	100	–	600	700
Tanzania	450	40	180	590
East Africa Total	1,550	620	960	1,890

[a] Estimates.

Source: EACSO: *Annual Trade Reports;* own estimates.

With respect to the different kinds of paints produced, an approximate breakdown is as follows (percentages in value terms):

69 The import duty on paints, until 1960 only 11 per cent ad valorem, was subsequently increased first to 25 per cent, then, in 1963 to $33^1/_3$ per cent and in 1966 to $37^1/_2$ per cent.

emulsion paints	ca. 25
enamels	20 to 25
distempers and water paints	ca. 15
cellulose paints and thinners	15 to 20
other (primers, undercoats, etc.)	10 to 15.

The largest part of the paints manufactured, (about 80 per cent of the total value) is sold for building and decorating purposes. Of the remainder, about one third each goes to car repair shops, to industrial firms for maintenance, and to industrial firms for use in their production. An important customer of the local paint industry in Kenya and Tanzania is the Government which buys about 25 per cent of the total output of the paint industry in those countries.
It is rather difficult to measure the capacity of the paint industry in East Africa. It depends much on the range of products and of different colours which each factory is manufacturing. The machine capacity is the greater the fewer different products and colours are manufactured. With the present production programme, the factories are on the average working at about 60 per cent machine capacity on a one shift basis. A production at 50 per cent capacity on a one shift basis is still considered "normal".

Some machines at some of the plants are also working at night without supervision so that the overall capacity could not be doubled merely by going to a second shift. Working on two shifts is also considered to be impractical because of the scarcity of supervisory personnel. By reducing the number of products each factory could grossly increase its capacity without any additional investment in plant and machinery.

The future demand for paints will, like that for cement and other building materials, be closely connected with future investment in building and construction. With Kenya just at the beginning of another building boom (in 1966–67), it can, therefore, be expected that its consumption of paints in the next years will rise steeply, probably by more than 100 per cent between 1965 and 1970 to an annual consumption of about 900,000 gallons at a value of about £1.5 million in 1970. The production of paints in Tanzania envisaged in the current Five-Year Plan is given as 3,500 tons (= about 700,000 gallons) at a gross value of £700,000. Allowing for an additional 20 per cent of value for consumption of paints which are not produced locally, total consumption in Tanzania is likely to be about £850,000 by 1970. For Uganda, the consumption of paints by 1970 may increase to over £1,150,000 p.a. so that total consumption in East Africa by 1970 would be worth about £3.5 million of which, with imports at the current rate, about £500,000 would come from outside East Africa.
It is safe to say that the largest part of this increase in local production will take place in Kenya which might well double its production of paints by

1970 to a value of close to £2 million. This assumption seems realistic as the productive capacities are grossly underemployed and most of the increase in production could be handled with the existing fixed capital assets. This would leave Tanzania a value of production of about £700,000 and Uganda about £300,000 to £400,000. These estimated production figures are of course very arbitrary as they are only partly based on the investment plans of the producers and their realization will depend also on the way the new treaty on the East African Common Market will influence the existing flow of goods between the partner states.

c) The Insecticides Industry

Kenya is a predominantly agricultural country with most of its agriculture on a preindustrial stage of development characterized by a very low productivity in terms of output per man and per acre of land under crop cultivation or livestock holding. One of the methods to increase productivity in agriculture is the more intensive use of insecticides and pesticides.
Since the end of the Second World War a number of factories have started the local production of insecticides based mainly on the use of imported toxiphine, DDT and BHC. Local pyrethrum is only added to a very small extent because of its high price. Most of these factories are subsidiaries of overseas concerns. The major local producers of insecticides are Cooper, McDougall & Robertson (East Africa) Ltd., Twiga Chemical Industries Ltd. (ICI subsidiary), Kenya Chemical Industries Ltd. (subsidiary of The Kiwi Polish Co.), Shell Chemical Company (East Africa) Ltd., Murphy Chemicals (East Africa) Ltd., Pfizer Laboratories Inc., East African Aerosols Ltd., and Anffi Ltd. All of these plants — with one exception — are located at or near Nairobi.
The production process in the insecticides industry in Kenya restricts itself to the last stage of production which consists, in general, of a dilution of imported concentrated liquids (or, in the case of powders, of mixing with local filling materials) and packing into small sizes for sale to the final consumer. The range of products includes cattle dip and cattle spray fluids and powders of the control of ectoparasites on lifestock, veterinary products like healing oil for cuts, dairy bacteriacides etc.; plant protective products, especially dusting powders for the protection of coffee and cotton; and household aerosols and disinfectants.
The production and the direction of sales of insecticides and similar products can only be estimated. Production statistics for the industry are not available. Several of the local manufacturers supplement their production programme with imported finished goods which are either sold directly as imported, or after bulkbreaking and repacking. The import statistics include imports of

finished insecticides and of some major raw materials for the production of insecticides under one heading. Also, the exports to Uganda and Tanzania as shown in the Annual Trade Reports are possibly somewhat inflated since they include products which are usually described as "pharmaceuticals". According to these statistics, Kenya exported to its neighbouring countries insecticides worth £350,000 to £500,000 per annum after 1961, in 1967 even passing the £500,000 mark. Net imports fluctuated between £550,000 and £1.1 million between 1961 and 1967.
If one assumes that the trade figures include 20 per cent (by value) non-insecticides, that about 50 per cent of the value of net imports during the past few years consisted of raw materials for the local insecticide industry which were further processed in Kenya; and that these materials constituted about 60 per cent in the value of final sales, one arrives at the following values (table 19):

Table 19. *Estimated Value of Local Production, Trade and Consumption of Insecticides, 1962–1967*
(in £1,000)

Year	Net Imports of Finished Insecticides	Local Production	Exports		Local Consumption
			Interterritorial	Domestic	
1962	293	488	351	21	409
1963	323	539	394	19	449
1964	389	649	338	81	619
1965	457	762	246	34	939
1966	436	727	349	53	761
1967	340	566	363	55	488

Source: Annual Trade Reports. Figures adjusted.

Among the locally produced insecticides, chemicals for the control of ectoparasites on lifestock take the first place, with over 50 per cent of the value of total sales. They are mostly based on toxiphine. The largest part of these products are sold in Kenya through the Kenya Farmers Association (KFA) acting as distributors. Second in importance are agricultural chemicals, especially for the coffee crop in Kenya and Tanzania and for the cotton crop in Uganda. The consumption of DDT for cotton in Uganda is subsidized by the Uganda Government at 50 per cent of the price (1966–67). Another major item are disinfectants which are sold mainly to the Government on contracts. All other products are not very important in terms of their share in total sales. Aerosols the local production of which has increased considerably as a result of quantitative import restrictions since mid 1965 (practically a ban on imports from outside East Africa) reached a value of about £30,000 per annum in 1966–67 a great portion of which is exported, particularly to Tanzania.

The future outlook for the insecticides industry in Kenya is mainly determined by the development of local consumption. Exports to the Partner States of the Common Market, which in the past have taken up a considerable portion of total output, are likely to decrease as a result of the vigorous import-substitution policy followed by the Tanzania Government. Several firms operating in Kenya were adjusting their expansion programme to this effect during 1966–67 or had by then already constructed new factories at Dar es Salaam. In addition to the Tanzania market, factories at Dar es Salaam have a favourable location to supply markets of neighbouring countries like Zambia and Burundi. Similarly the Uganda market will most likely also become more difficult for Kenya producers in the long run, although to a lesser extent.

Thus, local consumption will be the main determinant of the development of the insecticides industry in Kenya. It is very difficult to make forecasts in this respect. Much will depend on the readiness of the small African farmers to apply more insecticides, a question connected with the speed with which the smallholders will increase the share of cash crops on their farms. The consumption of insecticides has, to be sure, spread at a rapid pace until 1965; in 1966 and 1967 it dropped again considerably however. Since all factors (in particular those of a psychological nature) which determine the employment of insecticides are not known, it is not easy to make any reliable forecasts. It should be mentioned that on the basis of the performance during the first half of the sixties the ECA assumes a rate of growth of 15 per cent p.a.[70] which would give a total consumption of roughly £1.8 million in 1970.

d) The Match Industry

The history of the match industry in Kenya goes back to the year 1954 when a factory was built on the Kinangop north of Nairobi. After several years of operation this plant discontinued production. The majority of the shares of the company (the East African Match Co. Ltd.) changed from European into Asian ownership, and, in 1960, a new factory was built about 8 miles outside Mombasa, off the main highway to Nairobi. This location was chosen since most of the raw materials are imported, and also with the intention to sell a large portion of the production to Tanzania. The Company produces safety matches of standard size and in standard packing. Since 1965, two more factories have started production — the Associated Match Company Limited at Jinja in Uganda, which is an associated company of the Madhvani Group of Companies; and the Kibo Match Corporation Ltd. at Moshi in the Kilimanjaro Region of Tanzania, which, like the Kenya plant, is owned and managed by a local Asian group.

70 ECA: *Recherche sur l'industrie chimique,* p. 87.

The production process of the Kenya match factory is modern and highly mechanized. Only a small part of the machinery has been taken over from the old factory on the Kinangop. Most of the machines are new. The factory does not produce its own splints but imports them from overseas.

The East African Customs and Excise Department publishes figures of stockroom receipts of excisable commodities which can be taken to be approximately equal to production figures. According to this source, production of the Kenya match factory in recent years was as follows:

	in 1,000 gross boxes
1961	90
1962	185
1963	299
1964	424
1965	497
1966	734
1967	450 (approx.)

The expansion of production of the factory has been rather steady and came about partly as a result of the increased experience which workers and management gained over the years. With an output of about 500,000 gross boxes in 1965, the factory worked at about two thirds of its capacity of about 750,000 gross boxes.

The development of consumption of matches is shown in table 20.

Table 20. *Trade and Consumption of Matches, 1962–1967*
(in 1,000 gross boxes)

Year	Imports		Local Production [b]	Exports			Consumption
	Interterr.	Domestic [a]		Uganda	Tanzania	Other	
1962	1,4	321.7	195.2	22.6	56.8	–	438.9
1963	0.2	207.4	325.3	60.9	113.4	2.8	355.8
1964	–	330.9	379.1	67.8	122.7	0.1	519.4
1965	39.9	79.2 [c]	545.8	111.3	111.5	0.1	441.9
1966	63.2	97.8	645.3	188.5	33.9	11.1	572.8
1967	26.4	70.1	499.0	101.8	35.1	0.2	458.4

[a] Net imports for home consumption after warehousing; in units of containers with up to 50 matches.
[b] Deliveries from stockroom.
[c] Most of this was imported during the previous year and released from warehouses in 1965. New imports in 1965 amounted to only about 15,000 gross boxes.

Source: EACSO: *Annual Trade Reports.*

The figures for imports and also for consumption show rather violent fluctuations from year to year which are supposed to be due to stock changes on the part of the dealers. Still, several trends are clearly visible:

- Imports from outside East Africa have been decreasing as a result of increased local production.
- Exports to Uganda increased until 1966. Exports to Tanzania which made up about a third of total production of the Kenya factory until 1965 first showed a decline in that year. In mid-1965 the importation of matches into Tanzania from Kenya and Uganda had become subject to licensing. Subsequently, with the increase in production of the Moshi plant, exports to Tanzania dropped and had virtually ceased by 1967.
- The industry is exporting a decreasing share of its production.
- The development of local consumption is not clearly distinguishable.

The ex-factory price per gross boxes of matches (including distribution cost and excise tax) was Shs 14/50 in 1966–67. In 1966, the excise tax was raised from Shs 3/- to Shs 5/- per gross boxes. Imports are subject to a Shs 10/- duty and to licensing. There is no additional excise tax on imports so that the effective price protection for the local match industry is now Shs 5/- per gross boxes of matches.

Imports of matches come mainly from Sweden and retail for at least 20 cts. per box, while the retail price for the local product is 15 cts. per box. This price is uniform all over East Africa.

The average ex-factory price for sales to Uganda and Tanzania can be calculated on the basis of the interterritorial trade statistics. Prices for sales to Uganda and Tanzania showed decreases until 1965 when they were Shs 8/20 (per gross box) and Shs 8/16 respectively. In 1967 they were Shs 10/07 and Shs 8/83.

When analysing the consumption of matches in Kenya a definite increase between 1962 and 1967 is noticeable inspite of the irregular way in which consumption developed during this period. Although it is difficult to suggest a growth rate which would allow precise forecasts, it is estimated that the consumption of matches in Kenya will have reached about 600,000 gross boxes by 1970.

The new match factory in Uganda has a capacity of about 450,000 gross boxes p.a. sufficient to satisfy local Ugandan demand. In addition the Tanzania factory has plans for expansion, and will in the near future be able to cope with the local Tanzanian market. Export possibilities to other African countries seem remote.

If we allow for a 5 per cent share of imports in home consumption, there is, therefore, little chance that by 1970 the Mombasa plant will find markets for more than 600,000 gross boxes in Kenya or in the neighbouring countries, so that it is likely that about 20 per cent of the productive capacity will still be unutilised by that time.

e) The Oil Refinery

Since December 1963, Kenya has an oil refinery at Mombasa. The East African Oil Refineries Limited is owned by four international oil companies, each of which is holding about 25 per cent of the share capital. These companies are British Petroleum, California Texas, Esso Standard Eastern, and Shell Petroleum.

The refinery processes crude oil on behalf of its four share holders and three other companies. The buying of the crude oil, its delivery to the refinery, the conversion of the basic oil products into the respective branded products by adding certain components and the marketing of the finished products is done by these companies. The refinery distills the crude oil into nine different basic products, namely LPG (liquid petroleum gas for cooking), motor spirit, jet fuel, lighting kerosene, power kerosene, automotive gas oil, marine and industrial diesel oil, fuel oil, and bitumen. All of the crude petroleum has to be imported. Prospecting for oil in the Coastal and the North Eastern Region of Kenya has so far been unsuccessful. The crude oil is pumped from the oil jetty to the refinery via a pipeline.

The production of the Refinery until 1967 is shown in table 21. The throughput of crude oil reached 504 million gallons or 1.95 million tons in 1967, which is 97 per cent of the rated capacity of 2 million tons p.a.

As soon as 1964, most of the local consumption of refinery products was supplied by the Mombasa Refinery. In 1965, the overall share of imports

Table 21. *Throughput and Output of Refinery Products at the Mombasa Refinery, 1963–1967*
(in 1,000 Imp. Galls.)

Subject	1963	1964	1965	1966	1967
Throughput of Crude Petroleum	34,619.3	392,577.5	466,393.5	468,500.0	504,400.0
Output					
LPG	35.6	1,794.5	2,804.1	3,311.0	..
Motor spirit	6,031.5	64,866,0	78,568.7	76,138.9	..
Kerosene	2,647.1	31,713.7	49,675.8	47,373.9	..
Gas oil	4,739.3	38,609.4	49,360.1	57,055.9	..
Diesel	711.0	20,463.6	25,498.7	22,961.1	..
Fuel oil	9,974.1	147,907.0	158,987.1	149,554.9	..
Bitumen	–	2,353.6	6,021.8	7,911.3	..
Export residue	7,610.5	62,357.0	73,358.0	68,286.7	..
Total output	31,749.1	370,064.8	444,274.3	432,593.7	..

Source: Republic of Kenya: *Statistical Abstract*, 1967, p. 75; same publisher: *Economic Survey, 1968*, p. 77.

in local consumption was less than 1 per cent. Table 22 shows the consumption of refinery products in Kenya and also interterritorial and domestic exports.

In 1965, the geographic distribution of the refinery's sales (which totalled £15.8 million in that year) was as follows:

	%
Kenya	*38*
Uganda	*14*
Tanzania	*18*
outside East Africa	*30*

In the middle of 1966, a second refinery started operating in East Africa, the TIPER[71], at Dar es Salaam. The TIPER is managed by the Italian ENI-Group of Companies and has a rated capacity of 600,000 tons throughput of crude oil p.a. There are plans to double this capacity in the near future. The Dar es Salaam refinery will take up the production of bitumen later on. Except for bitumen it has roughly the same production programme as the Mombasa Refinery. It is now serving the Tanzanian market with large exports to Zambia through a white products pipeline.

The value of total sales of finished products by marketing companies (£15.8 million in 1965) excludes duty paid and distribution cost. The exise duties on products of the refineries are equal to rates of duty on imported products. In 1965, these rates were as follows:

motor spirit	Shs 1/40 per gallon[72]
kerosene	Shs –/60 per gallon
light amber fuel	Shs 1/40 per gallon
liquid petroleum gas	Shs –/08 per gallon
other products	free

The duty receipts to the Kenya Government from sales of petroleum products were £4,189,000 in 1965, £4,817,000 in 1966; and £5,483,000 in 1967[73].

In terms of gross output, the refinery is by far the largest commercial business in Kenya. With domestic exports of £4,773,000 in 1965, and as high as £7,406,000 in 1967, petroleum products took third place in the Kenyan export statistics after coffee and tea (second place after coffee in 1967) and contributed over 10 per cent to the value of domestic exports. Most of the domestic exports of petroleum products consisted of low-value residual oils, jet fuel, heavy black fuel, and light amber diesel oil (see table 22).

---

71 Tanganyikan and Italian Petroleum Refining Co. Ltd.

72 The duty on motor spirit has been increased to Shs 1/50 p.g. in 1966.

73 EACSO: *Annual Trade Report, 1965.*

Table 22. *Consumption and Exports of Refinery Products, 1964–1967* [a]
(in million Imp. gallons unless otherwise stated)

SITC Number	Product	Kenya Consumption [b]				Exports: Interterritorial: Uganda			Exports: Interterritorial: Tanzania			Exports: Domestic			Total Sales of Refinery Products		
		1964	1965	1966	1967	1965	1966	1967	1965	1966	1967	1965	1966	1967	1965	1966	1967
332 1 2	Motor spirit (other than aviation spirit)	35.6	35.6	37.4	39.4	23.0	24.3	25.4	23.4	18.0	14.2	1.6	8.4	8.7	83.6	88.1	87.7
332 2 1	Jet fuel	18.5	23.1	33.9	33.8	6.1	6.5	8.9	0.5	0.9	0.9	22.8	25.3	23.3	50.5	66.6	66.9
332 2 2	Illuminating kerosene	8.9	9.6	9.9	11.7	6.4	8.0	7.4	7.9	5.6	5.4	1.0	2.1	2.2	24.9	25.6	26.7
332 2 3	Power kerosene	1.0	0.9	0.8	0.7	–	–	–	–	–	–	–	–	–	0.9	0.8	0.7
332 3 1	Heavy black fuel for low speed marine & stat. eng.	5.9	6.4	7.1	7.2	1.7	2.1	2.3	10.2	5.8	2.9	6.0	7.9	18.4	24.3	22.9	30.8
332 3 2	Light amber fuel for high speed engines	25.1	26.1	29.6	32.6	12.6	14.8	15.3	14.2	15.5	16.0	4.6	7.1	11.8	57.5	67.6	75.7
332 4 0	Residual fuel oils (marine, furnace, etc.)	91.8	92.1	96.5	60.8	3.5	3.3	3.8	29.7	14.9	71.0	109.7	120.6	161.5	235.6	235.3	267.1
332 9 1	Asphalt & bitumen (tons)	12,545	23,376	29,552	41,110	3,498	2,235	2,433	3,135	5,854	8,431	10,048	16,107	17,074	40,057	53,748	69,038
341 1 1	Liquid petroleum gas (tons)	1,746	1,878	2,472	3,243	492	764	1,037	1,144	1,283	502	3,478	3,938	1,346	6,992	8,417	6,128

[a] Figures for exports and total sales are given only for 1965 to 1967. Total sales as sum of Kenya consumption and exports thus disregard stock changes and the remaining imports.
[b] Figures from the E.A. Statistical Department quoted in *Kenya Statistical Digest*, Vol. IV, No. 4 (Dec. 1966), p. 23, except for items 332 9 1 and 341 1 1 which are from the Annual Trade Reports.

Source: EACSO: *Annual Trade Reports.*

The prospects of the Mombasa Refinery will be influenced in the near future by the increase in production of the new refinery at Dar es Salaam. After 1967, the reduction in sales to Tanzania which, in 1965, took 18 per cent of total sales will make itself felt. The Dar es Salaam refinery may also take some of the Mombasa Refinery's domestic exports especially those to ships calling at both harbours. Both factors will probably reduce the overall sales of the refinery or at least prevent a further rapid expansion in the near future. Later on, the growing markets in Kenya and Uganda as well as in some adjacent territories will more than compensate for the losses incurred by the operations of the TIPER at Dar es Salaam. The Revised Development Plan does not expect a full utilization of the existing capacity before 1972[74].

II. Locational Problems

The source of the raw materials is the most important determining factor for the choice of location of the chemical and allied industries in Kenya. If the raw materials originate mainly from local sources, the factory tends to be located close to the source of the main raw material and will have a strong export orientation. It has been shown above in chapter I, para. 2 of part C that industries, which import most of their raw materials, produce intermediate and final consumer goods mainly for the domestic markets in Kenya and East Africa. They are located in the main market centres. In general, these industries are protected against competition from outside East Africa by tariffs and quantitative restrictions.

The distinction between either local or imported raw materials is neither rigid nor eterna. It is conceivable that at a certain point in time a factory will be able to substitute a previously imported raw material by one which becomes locally available. Those substitutions have happened in a rare number of cases in some of the enterprises investigated but were never significant enough to justify reconsideration of the original choice of location. On the other hand, switches from a local raw material supply to imports have also happened in cases where the local supply could not keep pace in quality, quantity or price with the requirements of the manufacturer or with foreign competitors. These changes in supply would have locational consequences if the raw material which was originally purchased locally had an important influence on the siting of the manufacturing process, and if the location of the local raw material was different from either the main markets for the final product or the port of importation for the imported

74 Republic of Kenya: *Revised Development Plan*, p. 265.

raw material used subsequently. In none of the industries investigated was this the case, so that changes in the source of supply had no significant locational relevance. Most significant was — as the investigations proved — the closeness to the main markets as the major locational determinant for those industries serving predominantly the local markets which gave Nairobi — among other more historical factors — its eminent importance as industrial centre in Kenya.
Among the industries which are processing predominantly local raw materials the soda ash industry, the diatomite industry, the pyrethrum industry, and the wattle extract industry can be regarded as industries with a strictly supply-oriented location. The processing plants in these branches are located close to the place of the mineral, agricultural or forestal resources. The choice between alternative locations is in those cases rather limited. If the natural resources are found in climatically unfavourable or, with respect to communications, isolated areas this may result in increased capital and operational cost of projects. A point in case is the example of the Magadi Soda Works which has — due to the remoteness of the area from the next large town — to maintain a heavy burden of overheads for ancilliary services.

The infrastructural investments of the Magadi Soda Works Company include a water supply by pipeline and a company-owned electricity plant, a 60-mile road to the outskirts of Nairobi and a 90-mile railway line, company-housing for its entire labour force, schools, clubs, shops, medical and other services. A few years before the sales cut in 1963, when the labour force was nearly twice as high as by the end of 1965, the Company had finished an investment programme into ancilliary social services which involved a total capital outlay of about £800,000. Shortly before, a new water pipeline had to be built at a cost of about £250,000. In 1961, the "investment in housing, including water supply, sewage and electricity" ... represented "approximately £1,000 per African employed" [75].
The labour force at Magadi has continuously been reduced during the post-war period while output first increased. This means at the same time that output per worker increased quite considerably.

In Kenya's cement industry special locational problems arise in the case of the Athi River factory.

The governing factor for the location of cement industries is the supply of raw materials and especially of limestone which contributes about 80 per cent in weight to the total raw material inputs. Most cement factories are, therefore, located in close neighbourhood to the lime quarries. This is the case of the Bamburi factory which is located in the middle of large deposits of limestone, the gypsum being also found in the surroundings. The Athi River factory, on the other hand, has to transport its lime stone over a distance of 64 miles by rail from Sultan Hamid. It is estimated that the railage makes the production of Athi River cement about 8 per cent more expensive than the cement of a factory located in the immediate vicinity

75 M. F. Hill: *op. cit.*, p. 142.

of its limestone quarries. It seems, therefore, that real or expected advantages in the form of closeness to the main market, more favourable climatic conditions, cheaper power through connection to the public net, more sufficient supply of water, nearby deposits of calcrete and closer location to the gypsum quarries around Garissa (the gypsum still has to be transported over a distance of about 220 miles by road) have made the Athi River cement works one of the rare cases where a location for a cement plant has been chosen away from the limestone deposits.

The fertilizer industry in East Africa will have to solve particular locational problems in the future when it will be necessary to establish the new productive capacities required to satisfy the increasing demand for fertilizers. Local production of fertilizers in East Africa is presently limited to the TICAF factory at Tororo in Uganda and Windmill Fertilizers at Nakuru, Kenya. TICAF produces simple super phosphates utilizing the large deposits of phosphate bearing soil of the Sukulu Hills near Tororo. The sulphuric acid for the fertilizer production is also produced at Tororo by TICAF on the basis of imported sulphur. Some surplus production of sulphuric acid is sold to outside customers, mainly the textile industry at Jinja, Uganda.
The decision to locate the phosphatic fertilizer factory at Tororo was straight forward. The phosphate bearing soil loses so much weight during the production process that a processing plant away from the deposits would have been uneconomic. As has been shown in a preceding chapter the main market for fertilizers in East Africa is in Kenya, in particular in the former "White Highlands" around Nakuru, Nyeri and Kitale, for which the Tororo factory is favourably located. In spite of its favourable location the factory has been experiencing sales difficulties since 1967. The main reason for this is a shift in the structure of the Kenya fertilizer market away from "straight" fertilizers — either phosphate or nitrogen or potassium — to fertilizer mixtures, a blend of two or three of the main nutrients. For fertilizer mixtures it is more convenient to use triple super phosphate which has an active phosphate content per ton of product of more than double of the single supers, resulting in savings of transport costs.
The changing structure of the fertilizer market was recognized and encouraged by the second existing fertilizer factory, Windmill Fertilizers at Nakuru. The location of this factory is purely market-oriented. It is producing mixed fertilizers on the basis of imported nitrogenous, phosphatic and postassium ingredients. The phosphate ingredients are imported from overseas in the form of triple supers.
It can generally be said that new fertilizer capacities in East Africa will follow the same locational forces as the two already existing plants with factories for "straight" fertilizers close to the source of supply of the raw materials and for mixed and compound fertilizers close to the market. Raw materials for "straights" are found as phosphates near Tororo in Uganda and near Lake Manyara in Tanzania. Due to better means of communication

with the main market, the Tororo deposits have better prospects in the future.
As far as nitrogenous fertilizers are concerned possible raw materials are an ample and inexpensive power supply, which Uganda could offer, or oil refinery products, which Mombasa or Dar es Salaam could offer. Mombasa or Dar es Salaam would be favourably located to process imported ammonia in a first phase. In this case, Mombasa would have an additional advantage over Dar es Salaam since it has a better access to the present main markets in the Kenya Highlands. At present and in the near future the demand in East Africa is not large enough to warrant the establishment of a fully integrated nitrogenous fertilizer plant. Given the need for such a factory to supply the whole of the East African market an agreement on an East African basis is a precondition for the success of any nitrogenous fertilizer project.
For those branches of the chemical and allied industries which cover their raw material requirements mainly by imports — examples are the soap, paint, insecticide and match industries — the choice of location is predominantly market-oriented. A second determinant is the relation between the cost of the imported raw materials and the value of the finished products. Finally, the third major determinant for the choice of location is — in the case of the chemical and allied industries, as well as for manufacturing units of other sectors — the pull exerted by more favourable conditions of production in the big cities, particularly at Nairobi. These favourable conditions include a better and cheaper availability of electricity and water, a wider and more differentiated supply of technical and administrative services — like specialized repair shops, garages, banks and insurance companies — and a better supply of a qualified local and expatriate labour force. These favourable conditions and services are in general not available in smaller towns and outweigh disadvantages connected with a location in big cities like higher cost for unskilled labour and higher rents. Of the industries mentioned above the soap, paint and insecticide industries are clearly market-oriented. Soap factories exist in all the larger East African towns, the two biggest producers — and one medium-sized plant — at Nairobi and medium and small factories in other towns all over East Africa. This market-orientation of the soap industry exists even though the smaller producers also import most of their raw material requirements.

The apparent market orientation of the soap industry in East Africa can be explained by the high incidence of distribution cost in relation to the cost of transport of the raw materials from the coast to the factories. There are three main reasons that tend to increase distribution cost:

- the raw materials lose very little weight in the production process;
- water is a major material which is ubiquitous in all sales markets;
- and the distribution of the finished product to the dealer generally takes place in

small quantities and by road transport, whereas the raw materials are bought in rather large quantities by rail [76].

This explains why soap factories at Kampala can compete with factories at Nairobi which have lower production costs but higher distribution costs for sales on the Uganda market.

Similar reasons for the market orientation are valid for the paint industry which is concentrated at Nairobi.

During the production process (virtually all of the raw materials have to be imported) the raw materials do not lose weight, i.e. the transport cost for the ingredients is lower than for the finished product because of smaller quantities sold and the use of more expensive road transport for distribution. Secondly, the product sold has a fairly complicated nature and requires, therefore, technical advice to the customers as to the optimal paint to be used for a particular purpose. To give this advice is the job of the manufacturer because the technical know-how of the dealer is limited in East Africa.

From the point of view of unit cost of production, a location close to the coast is clearly more favourable to a factory with a high import content of materials. Under such conditions a factory at Mombasa or Nairobi will always have lower production costs than a factory, say, at Kampala. For the production of oil refinery products and to a lesser degree of matches, Mombasa is therefore a favourable location.

A number of industries in Kenya which are operating mainly on the basis of imported raw materials encountered locational problems when the two Partner States imposed restrictions on the free flow of trade into their territories in order to foster their own industrialization. This affected those industries which had conceptually been established to supply the total area of the East African market, e.g. the paint, the insecticides and the match industries.

When the paint industry established itself in East Africa most firms chose Nairobi as location. This took place in the late 1950's when Kenya's construction business experienced a boom period. A few years later, in the beginning of the sixties Kenya's economy slumped into a general depression while in Uganda and Tanzania the economies developed at a brisk pace and the consumption of paint in these two countries increased rapidly Uganda even overtaking Kenya in 1963/64. At this time the factories at Nairobi were firmly established with a combined capacity several times as big as the market in the whole of East Africa. It was, therefore, not economically justifiable for anyone of the companies to construct an additional plant either at Kampala or at Dar es Salaam because the fixed cost for running a new plant at Kampala or Dar (including not only the capital cost but also the largest part of the labour cost, namely for the technical and supervisory personnel) would in general be higher than the advantage gained through savings in transport cost and closer contact to the customers in the other two countries. The pull towards the market was strong only at the moment when the first investment decision was taken.

The following construction of blending plants in Uganda and Tanzania was under-

---

76 The quantities purchased are large relative to the quantities of the finished products sold. They are small if one compares them with European conditions. It can be estimated that the raw materials in East Africa are about 10–15 per cent more expensive because of the smaller quantities purchased.

taken to improve the general market position in Uganda and Tanzania but was probably also the result of some pressure by the Governments of these two countries on the paint companies to establish industrial plants there. The blending plants at Kampala operate efficiently on a very small scale and establish the necessary close contact between paint manufacturer and customer without giving up the advantages of centralized production. In the case of Dar es Salaam the situation is different. Here a major market coincides with a place of importation so that transport cost for the imported raw materials are practically non-existent once the goods are landed in East Africa. Dar es Salaam offers, therefore, a good location to paint manufacturers for a supply of the coast area and the Tanzania hinterland. There are three paint factories at Dar now supplying most of the requirements of paints in Tanzania.
Some of the manufacturers of insecticides in Kenya responded to the partial loss of the Tanzania market by establishing manufacturing units at Dar es Salaam. They did not expect separate plants supplying the Tanzanian market to have appreciably higher cost of production as the processes used are simple and the minimum economic size of the plant is small. A location at Dar es Salaam may even be more favourable than at Nairobi with the savings in transport cost for the raw materials. Difficulties are expected only in providing the staff for the top management and technical jobs. But even if this means higher labour cost the increase in total unit cost will probably be very small. Dar es Salaam as a location could be favourable also from the point of view of export possibilities into neighbouring countries outside East Africa.
For the match industry, with the loss of the Tanzania market, Mombasa has lost its locational advantage. Although most raw materials continue to be imported, Nairobi and the area north west of Nairobi is now by far the most important market and a location at Nairobi would appreciably decrease distribution cost. Also, part of the packing materials are bought at Nairobi which again favours a place at or near Nairobi as a location. The present location is not ideal for another reason. If the Company intends to take up a local production of splints sometime in the future there is no adequate wood supply near Mombasa suitable for the production of splints. An alternative to imports of splints from overseas could, for the time being, be purchases from the new plant at Moshi were there is a considerable surplus capacity in splint production. Later on, a local production of splints and a relocation of the factory near the main market and the supply area of wood for splints should be considered.

III. Comparison of the Structures of the Chemical and Allied Industries

In analysing the chemical and allied sector certain structural characteristics may be pointed out which shall be summarized in this chapter.

1. Cost Structures

In table 23 the cost structures of the chemical and allied industries have been summarized.

Table 23. *Cost Structure of the Chemical and Allied Industries, 1965–1966*
(in % of total cost)

Industries	Raw Materials total	Raw Materials local	Packing Materials	Labour	Capital	Water, Fuel, Electr.	Other Cost
Soda Ash	..	high	..	..	..	..	..
Diatomite	*18*	*17*	*9*	*33*	*14*	*14*	*13*
Cement	..	high	..	*14–18*	*9–13* [a]	*25–35*	*37–49*
Glass	*20*	*13*	*6*	*27*	*24*	*16*	*6*
Pyrethrum Extract	*83*	*80*	..	*6*	*5*	*1*	*5*
Wattle Extract	..	high	..	high	..	..	..
Phosphate Fertilizer	*41*	*11*	*7*	*19*	*15*	*13*	*5*
Soap	*80–90*	*10–15*	*2.5–5*	*5*	*2*	*2*	*3*
Paints	*50*	*3*	*12*	*17*	*8*	*13*	
Insecticides	*63*	*0*	*12*	*13*	*5*	*7*	
Matches	*65*	*0*	*5*	*18*	minor	minor	
Oil Refinery Products	*60*	*0*	..	*3*	high	..	..

[a] Depreciation only. Other capital cost, in particular interest, are included under "other cost". Other capital cost take about 10 per cent of total cost.

The 12 industries examined show a very wide range in their cost structure. In most industries, raw material is the major cost item[77]. In general, the value added by the production process is small compared with the value of the material inputs taking as an indication of this the share of labour costs in the overall cost structure. This is especially the case with pyrethrum, soap, paint, insecticides, the match industry, and the oil refinery.

The fertilizer, soap, paint, insecticide, and match industries and the oil refinery import most of their raw materials. Their backward linkage effects are small. The soda ash, diatomite, cement, glass, pyrethrum extract, and the wattle extract industries process mainly local raw materials, often for export, but in the case of the cement, glass and fertilizer industries, also for local consumption. These industries have strong backward linkages. In most cases these backward linkages are created not only by processing mineral and agricultural raw materials, like soda, phosphate bearing soil, diatomite, sand,

77 The cost structure of the pyrethrum industry disregards the differences in ownership of processing plants and treats the whole processing as an integrated economic unit. The value of the raw materials corresponds to the pay-out to the farmers for their deliveries of dried flowers.
With regard to the fertilizer industry, the sulphuric acid plant is considered as an integrated part of the fertilizer factory so that the relatively small part of sulphuric acid which is sold to outside customers is disregarded.
With respect of the soap industry, the figures of table 23 are estimates for factories in East Africa with a production programme representing the typical demand structure, i.e. producing mainly laundry soaps and only to a small degree toilet soap. The two expatriate factories at Nairobi, E.A.I. (Unilever) and Colgate-Palmolive, have specialized in more expensive grades of laundry soap and toilet soap. Their cost structure, therefore, will differ from that of table 23.

or pyrethrum flowers and wattle bark respectively, but also by purchase of energy, water, services, and to a certain degree already of manufactured products, like packing material.

The forward linkages of the industries of the chemical and allied sector are generally not very pronounced. They exist in the glass and cement industry, but also in the oil refinery, the insecticides and paint industry. The products of these industries are not intermediate products in the strict sense but rather auxiliary materials which are needed for the production of certain other goods. A potential for further forward linkages exists in the case of the oil refinery, and to a lesser extent, in the case of the soda ash, diatomite and wattle extract industries, but only in the long run. The possibilities for backward linkages are more obvious, particularly of the paint industry, the insecticides industry (DDT), the soap industry (coconut oil) and the match industry (wood).

In many of the industries analysed, packing materials constitute a sizable portion of total cost (in the paint and insecticide industries over 10 per cent). Virtually all packing materials used in Kenya are produced locally. There are several factories manufacturing cardboard boxes, one manufacturer of multiwall paper sacks (E.A. Packaging Industries Ltd. at Mombasa, a Canadian subsidiary) and two producers of metal containers (The Metal Box Company Ltd. at Thika, a subsidiary of a large British concern, is specialized in small boxes; Metal Containers of East Africa Ltd., a subsidiary of the Dutch Van Leer Group, manufactures the larger sizes of over 2 gallons up to 46-gallon drums). Paper sacks are used in the soda ash, fertilizer, diatomite and cement industries and metal boxes are the main packing materials in the paint and insecticide industries and are used by the oil refinery.

Also the share of labour cost in total cost varies considerably between the different industries. In the oil refinery only about 3 per cent of total cost is accounted for by payments to the labour force, while in the glass industry the share of labour cost is close to 30 per cent and in the diatomite industry over 30 per cent.

A high share of capital cost relative to labour cost is a good indication that a certain activity is particularly capital intensive. Of the industries examined, this could be observed in the case of the oil refinery, although no exact figures for the capital cost were available. High values of capital relative to labour cost, with labour cost still exceeding capital cost, were observed in the glass, cement, fertilizer, and pyrethrum extract industries.

In the chemical and allied industries energy costs are often important because of high temperatures necessary to bring about chemical reactions. In the cement industry energy costs, including water, occupy one fourth to one third of total costs. Similarly, the soda ash, phosphate fertilizer, diatomite, and glass industries need relatively large amounts of fuel.

2. Capital, Labour and Output

Among the other structural relationships which were examined, are estimates on the capacity utilization, the capital investment per member of the labour force and average capital/output ratios. All of these series show wide differentials between the individual industries (see table 24).

Most of the industries investigated underutilized their capacity. The diatomite, the soap and the paint industries had particularly low rates of capacity utilization. The danger of major unutilized capacities also exists in future years for those industries which in 1965–66 were able to produce at or close to the capacity limit, like the oil refinery, the cement industry and the wattle extract industry, mainly because of expected decreasing exports. Most industries can considerably increase their output without further major investments. In several industries the "normal" number of shifts could, from a technical point of view, easily be increased. Apart from sales considerations there is generally a hesitancy to do this because it would be difficult to find

Table 24. *Internal Ratios in the Chemical and Allied Industries, 1965–1966*

Industries	Capacity Utilization [a] (%)	Fixed Capital (at cost) per member of the labour force (in £)	Average Capital/Output Ratio		Share of Europeans and Asians in Tot. Lab. Force (%)
			Present Output	Capacity Output	
Soda Ash	*13*	about 5,000	about 3	about 1.2	*35*
Diatomite	*40*	(350) [b]	(0.2) [b]	(0.2) [b]	*5*
Cement	*90*	5–12,000	1.5–2.4	1.5–2.0	*15–20*
Glass	*80*	2,000	0.6	0.5	*10*
Pyrethrum Extract	*68*	3,400	0.3	0.2	..
Wattle Extract	*90*	low	..	..	..
Phosphate Fertilizer	*100*	1,625	1.3	1.3	*8*
Soap	*60*	1,000–1,500	0.3	0.1–0.2	*10–15*
Paints	*60*	1,500	0.4	0.3	*20–25*
Insecticides	*80*	2,000	0.3–0.4	0.3	*10–25*
Matches	*70*	800– 900	0.65	0.5	*10*
Oil Refinery Products	*95*	over 20,000	0.3	0.3	*20*

[a] On the basis of a "normal" number of shifts.
[b] The cost value of the fixed capital assets is much lower than the original purchase value.

the additional skilled and highly skilled personnel, and an appreciably lower productivity of unskilled and semi-skilled workers on the night shift would have to be expected.

The investment in fixed capital assets per member of the labour force is another possible measure of the degree of capital intensiveness of an industry. Relative to the number of workers employed, the capital invested in fixed assets in the chemical and allied sector is higher than in most other manufacturing industries[78]. Among the chemical and allied industries the oil refinery has the highest capital investment per employee (over £20,000). The cement industry, with over £5,000 per worker, is also very capital intensive. The middle range of investment per worker in the industries analysed is between £1,000 and £2,000, the lowest being £800 to £ 900 in the match industry.

It would be wrong to consider these figures as the average capital cost of providing one job. This is much higher because one would have to include investments in stocks and other working capital which the figures above do not take into account.

In planning economic development the marginal or incremental capital/output ratio is of particular importance to calculate the investment requirements for a projected increase in output. The historical average capital/output ratio can help to calculate the marginal ratio and is often of a similar magnitude to the marginal ratio.

There may be major differences between both ratios if the industry concerned experiences – with increases in output – considerable economies or diseconomies of scale. The average ratio, therefore, can be only an indication, and for planning purposes it would have to be adjusted. For macro-economic planning, investments in infrastructures, which are supplementary to directly productive investments in plant and machinery would also have to be included. From the gross output figures, purchases from sources outside the firm would have to be excluded. With these limitations in mind, the average capital/output ratios have been estimated for the industries analysed.

As most industries were working below capacity the capital/output ratios at the capacity limit are in these cases lower than the actual ratios. Most industries showed average capital/output ratios of under 1 and even under 0.5, particularly if the capital invested (at cost) was related to the value of the capacity output. The highest capital/output ratios are found in the cement and fertilizer industries, the lowest in the soap and the pyrethrum extract industries where the value of the raw materials and of the finished product is very high and the value added correspondingly low.

In the last column of table 24 the share of Europeans and Asians in the total labour force has been listed. These values give an indication of the share of highly skilled employees in the total labour force, assuming that Africans are still the exception among highly skilled personnel. This assumption has been verified in interviews with the business community. A high percentage of Europeans and Asians in general coincides with a high degree of capital intensiveness which shows that capital and high skills are complementary in the chemical and allied industries. The paint industry

78 In 1966 the national average of investment per employee was about £2,500. This figure did, however, not limit itself to investments in fixed assets. Republic of Kenya: *Revised Development Plan,* p. 257.

seems to be an exception with an about average investment per employee (or capital intensiveness) and a high porportion of highly skilled personnel. The high overall number of Europeans and Asians here is explained by the fact that this industry (similarly also the insecticide industry) requires highly skilled and experienced persons in the sales force.

3. Comparison of Costs and Productivity with those of Plants in Developed Countries

The analysis of the cost structures of the individual industries shows in some branches marked differentials compared with cost structures of similar plants and industries in developed countries. In other branches no particular deviations are noticed. In both cases (also in the latter one) differentials in productivity may exist which are due to higher prices for inputs (for raw materials, labour etc.) or due to reasons which result from the capacities of the plants as well as from the size and structure of the market. The various factors determining the cost and productivity differentials in the chemical and allied sector in East Africa are, of course, of different weight in the individual industries examined although they work very often in the same direction and produce similar results. The reasons for the cost and productivity differentials in the paint, soap and glass industry are to a certain extent also valid for the other chemical and allied industries, and are therefore included in the following discussion.

The Paint Industry

The most important cost difference per unit of output between paint factories in East Africa and in, for example, Europe is in the material cost. The cost for the raw material in East Africa is about 25 per cent higher than in Europe. This is for two main reasons which are interrelated, namely differences in stage of development of the economy and differences in the size of the market. In a developed country with a balanced economy, a paint factory usually has the suppliers of its major raw materials close by or at least in the same country. The transport cost of the raw material to the factory door is low because of shorter distances and the possiblity of supplying from door to door without reloading. Regarding the second reason, paint factories in Europe are many times as large as the East African factories, due to a much larger size of the market available.
By using bigger production units they are able to not only reduce the labour and capital cost (the "fixed" or partly fixed cost items) per unit of output but also the material cost. This is because the material can be purchased in large quantities which reduces the purchase price per unit and the transport cost per unit of the factory frequently, these paint factories are vertically integrated into chemical complexes where the raw materials for the paints are produced in the same complex. The higher material cost in East Africa increases the total unit cost of the final products by over 10 per cent.

What has been said for the raw material is similarly true for the packing material. The boxes and tins are made locally but again on a small scale (and therefore at higher cost) and of mainly imported raw materials which are more expensive here than they are in Europe.

In discussing differences in labour cost one has to distinguish between differences in wage rates and in total labour cost per unit of output. Wage rates in East Africa are normally considered to be much lower than in industrialized countries. This is true only for unskilled labour for which wages in East Africa are about 30 per cent of what they are in Europe. In the case of semi-skilled workers, i.e. those who need a certain amount of formal and on-the-job training before they can be utilized, wage differentials are smaller, the East African workers getting about one half of the wage of their European colleagues. For skilled workers there exist little differences in wage rates and for highly and management jobs wages in East Africa are about twice as high as in Europe if we take into account that expatriates have to be used for these jobs.

In addition to their basic salary, expatriates receive a long leave of usually three months at home every two years with transport paid for themselves and their families, together with other extras, like housing allowances, etc. which are usually not granted at home. As the expatriates constitute a sizable portion in total employees in the paint industry, this probably just about compensates for the cost advantage in the semi-skilled and unskilled grades.

The second factor influencing labour cost are differences in productivity. These differences are very marked indeed in the paint industry. One can assume that the output per worker in the East African paint industry is only about 20 per cent of that in the paint industry of a developed country. This is only partly due to the lower skills and the shorter experience of the majority of the East African workers. The skilled and highly skilled personnel also have a lower efficiency here. While the first is easily understandable the lower efficiency of the upper echelons of the labour force is the result again of the smaller production units in East Africa. A highly skilled employee is underemployed in his particular skill because of the smallness of the firms here; on the other hand he is supposed to also do other jobs which are below his qualifications but for which the employment of an additional person is not economic. In addition, each firm in the East African paint industry needs a number of highly skilled specialists even though through the connection to companies overseas some highly specialized jobs, like in research and development or sometimes also in purchasing raw materials, are done by the parent company for the East African subsidiary.

The lower productivity of labour in East Africa is much more important than possible wage rate differentials in determining the high labour cost per unit of output. Empirical investigations suggest that labour cost per unit of output in paint factories of developed countries are in the region of a tenth for factory labour and at the most a third for highly specialized and management jobs of comparable cost in the East African paint factories.

All the factories in East Africa are trying to improve their productivity of labour, i.e. increase output per man employed or per man-hour. This can be done either by increasing output with the same labour force or by reducing the labour force while still producing the same output. Various combinations of these possibilities have been used. Output has been expanded with a constant labour force by organizational improvements, by using larger batches or by more mechanized production methods, the latter being probably the least important device and the first the most important. But as sales only increased slowly the overall labour force was decreased as a result of increased productivity in the industry. Increased productivity should only be

regarded as one possible method in lowering cost of production. In an industry where labour takes only 17 per cent of total cost a concentration on increases in the productivity of labour may well fail to bring about the hoped for reduction in unit cost if it entails an increase in other cost items particularly capital cost. The most effective method to bring down all cost items per unit of output at the same time seems to be to go to a larger scale of production.
With the present size of the market this is only possible through a closer coordination of the existing paint factories, i.e. by each specializing on a few products. Unfortunately, the Governments concerned missed the opportunity of including the paint industry in the list of licensed industries, thereby limiting the number of paint companies in East Africa from the beginning. There is no doubt that only the tight protection granted to them attracted as many as there are now. A loosening up on this protection might very well force the paint factories to coordinate their production programmes in order to enable them to reduce their cost of production and to make their prices more competitive with those of imported products.
A voluntary cooperation among the paint producers to coordinate their production programme would be most advantageous if it worked on an East African basis. The new Treaty for East African Cooperation provides for tariffs in interterritorial trade, particularly on goods produced in Kenya. Tariffs on paints from Kenya would certainly induce the manufacturers to produce all kinds of paints also in Uganda and Tanzania. This would restrict the possibility for cooperation among the paint producers to their production in Kenya. The Paint Industry has a forum of discussion in the East African Paint Industries Association which could be a valuable organization to look for a solution of the question of the necessary coordination of the production programmes of its members.

The Soap Industry

Major differences in cost of production between the East African producers and soap manufacturers in developed countries are due especially to the higher cost of the raw materials in East Africa. The reason for this is that, as in the paint industry, small markets and a small scale of production result in small orders for raw materials. This makes the purchase of oils particularly more expensive. Thus the materials at the factory gate in East Africa are more expensive by 10 to 15 per cent than in Europe, and as about 90 per cent of the total cost of production is material cost, total production also becomes more expensive by roughly 10 to 15 per cent. Wage and productivity differentials are, therefore, of little importance in the total cost of production in the soap industry.
To achieve sizable reductions in cost, the cost of the raw material has to be reduced. This can be done either by pooling purchases of several producers or by intensifying or starting the production of some of the raw materials locally, thus saving on transport costs. The first possibility seems hardly viable, as the business policies of the two overseas firms are decided in Europe, and also because much of the purchasing in done by the parent companies. Still, pooling of purchases of some of the medium-size firms could reduce the cost of the raw materials for them. A better method seems to be to encourage and develop the supply of local raw materials, mainly of tallow and coconut oil.

The Glass Industry

Labour, material and capital cost, in this order, are also the most important cost items in similar plants in Europe. Considerable differences exist, in particular, within labour cost. In Europe, wages are far more important than salaries while in the glass industry in Kenya the share of wages in total cost is smaller than that of salaries. The reason for this divergency may be a difference in definition, i.e. the remuneration for identical jobs may in Kenya be called salaries whereas, for example, the German labourer for the same job may be paid on a weekly basis und receive a wage. It is more likely, however, that differences in wage (or salary) rates are more important. In 1966, the wage scale at the Kenya Glass Works Ltd. after a dispute with the Kenya Chemical Workers' Union was fixed by the Industrial Court as follows[79]:

Grade 1	Shs 575/–	per month
Grade 2	Shs 390/–	per month
Grade 3	Shs 303/50	per month
Grade 4	Shs 258/50	per month
Grade 5	Shs 255/–	per month

The wages in the glass industry of the Federal Republic of Germany are about three and a half to four times higher. Salaries, on the other hand, are in general higher in East Africa, in the glass industry on average by about 20 per cent. Both factors together explain why, in total labour cost, salaries in Kenya take a larger share than wages while the share of wages in Europe is much higher than that of salaries.

If one compares the productivity of labour in the Kenya glass industry viz-a-viz European conditions one finds that in Kenya about 22 employees are needed to produce 1,000 tons of output per annum, while in Europe only about 13 employees are required to produce the same annual output in factories with a similar production programme and scale of operation. The productivity of labour would, therefore, in Europe be about 1.5 times of that in Kenya and this difference would be due mainly to differences in the skill of the labour force and to a lesser degree to variations in production techniques (although in Kenya more labour is generally applied for auxiliary services like packing and handling). With overall labour cost per employee in Kenya much lower than in Europe – wages and salaries together are at most about 40 per cent of the European level – one can conclude that labour cost per unit of output in the Kenya glass industry is about 60 per cent of that prevailing in Europe, again assuming about equal size of plant, and a similar production programme.

Of course, this assumption is not quite realistic. European glass factories are usually bigger in terms of total capacity and their production programme is narrower. While in Kenya the forms are changed two to three times a week the large markets in Europe allow much longer runs which results in a higher productivity so that there remains possibly no advantage at all in terms of labour cost per unit of output for the Kenya glass manufacturers.

An appreciable difference in relative as well as in absolute terms between Kenya and Europe exists in capital cost. Capital cost in Kenya take up about 25 per cent of total cost, in Germany, about 20 per cent of gross output including profit. As most of the plant and equipment has to be imported and also as the cost of installation of the equipment is higher in East Africa, this increases proportionately the annual cost of depreciation as well as interest.

A reduction in cost of production in the glass industry in Kenya is possible mainly by a specialization of the factories. As all factories in East Africa belong to the same concern there are no diverging business interests which could prevent this. Obstacles might be encountered if the Governments prevent a further specialization by intensifying their autarchic policies. With glass factories now in each of the three

79 The Kenya Gazette, 1st February 1966, p. 109, Notice No. 374, Cause No. 51 of 1965.

countries, an agreement in this sector seems easier to achieve than in other industries where plants exist only in one country – in general this country is Kenya – and where the other two countries are net importers of the respective products.

Even though in most cases no figures could be obtained, it seemed that in 1966–67 all industries of the chemical and allied sector operated profitably with the diatomite industry and possibly the match industry as exceptions. It is important to remember that these profits could be made although most firms were working below the capacity limit. The small size of the market in Kenya and mounting difficulties in exports especially to Tanzania are the main reasons for this unsatisfactory utilization of capacities. The manufacturers of finished products particularly depend on extensive protection in the form of tariffs and quantitative restrictions, so that competition through imports from overseas is virtually excluded. As a result, local products are in general more expensive than imported goods would be if they could be sold on the market without restrictions, even — for some products — after the imposition of the present rates of tariffs.

As has been mentioned in the discussion of the individual industries, the small size of the market is not the only and perhaps not even the most important reason for the high cost of production in some of the industries analysed. In some branches, several firms are sharing the market between them, and it is only as a consequence of this that the local market has become too small for the individual firms to operate efficiently at a reasonably large scale. It seems that the Kenya Government missed the opportunity to limit the number of firms in time. A relaxation of the import restrictions should now force these firms to increase their efficiency. One way of improving efficiency could be through closer cooperation; for example, by specialization of the production programmes and by centralized purchasing to take advantage of low-cost bulk supplies of materials.

IV. Contribution of the Chemical and Allied Industries to the Overall Development of the Economy

In this concluding paragraph, the contribution which the chemical and allied industries make to the overall economic development of the country will be briefly examined. There are a number of criteria which may be applied, among which there are, as most commonly used criteria, the value added, the effects on employment, on government revenue and on the balance of payments. Since figures for the chemical and allied sector are only available to a limited extent, the discussion on the value added and the effects on government revenue will be excluded in the following.

1. Effects on Employment

The Kenya economy is suffering from an undesirable degree of unemployment of unskilled workers. Industrial development has failed so far to remedy this state of affairs. Among the manufacturing industries, the chemical and allied sector is particularly capital intensive. In 1964, it contributed about one fourth to the net output of the manufacturing sector but employed only one tenth of its labour force. The capital investment per employee of £1,000 to £2,000 (in some industries £5,000 to £10,000 or more) is far above the average. This is partly due to technical reasons. Most chemical industries apply capital intensive techniques of production and if a given product is to be manufactured there is often no alternative technique available. Only in ancilliary services (packing, transport within the factory, etc.) are alternative methods applicable, but also here labour saving devices are sometimes used to economize on the abundant unskilled labour.
One reason for this is the high price of unskilled labour in relation to its relative scarcity in the economy. The price of unskilled labour per time unit, the wage rate, is much lower in the East African manufacturing sector than it is in industrialized countries, on the average about 25 to 30 per cent of the European level. The productivity of labour measured in terms of physical output per member of the labour force is much lower in East Africa — between 25 and 50 per cent of the European level, depending on the industry. The cost of unskilled labour per unit of output in Kenyan industrial enterprises is, therefore, in many cases not much different from that in Europe, in spite of the low wage rates. The low productivity of unskilled workers in East Africa can probably be largely attributed to the environment from which they originate. As a result of their non-industrial sociological background, unskilled workers frequently lack a sense of time and efficiency which is the basis of any organised industrial activity. In addition they are generally lacking a minimum of general technical experience, which in industrialized countries is considered almost natural and part of the modern way of life.
The same applies to the more skilled African workers, e.g. to those who work as machine operators. They have attained their skills mainly by in-service training through which they were taught how to handle for example, a certain machine, but they are lacking even a superficial knowledge about the way in which the machine works. This means that they are not able to repair the slightest mechanical fault, and that incorrect handling of machines with high cost for breakdowns, is very frequent. The wage rates for these semi-skilled workers are relatively high because they have already a certain scarcity value, but their productivity is much lower than in Europe so that their cost per unit of output is in general higher than it would be in Europe.

According to the opportunity cost concept, the prices paid to the factors of production should be equal to their opportunity value, i.e. equal to the wage which would be paid on an alternative job. As there is a high rate of unemployment, and alternative jobs in the manufacturing sector are not available the opportunity cost of unskilled labour is the wage attainable in traditional agriculture, which is extremely low. Social considerations and pressures by the trade unions have pushed wages up during the recent years and further wage increases are expected. The lowest wages for male general labour in the chemical industry were about Shs 200/- per month in 1966. However, the declared target of the Kenya Chemical Workers Union is to push this level up to Shs 350/- per month[80].

The prevalence of high wages has induced many firms to substitute capital for unskilled labour, a rational decision from the point of view of the entrepreneur, but undesirable for the economy as a whole. The result is not only a high degree of unemployment, but also the acceleration of the growth of a dual economy with a wide economic and social gap between the modern and the traditional sectors.

Until now the Kenyan Government has not done very much to induce private industries to use more labour intensive devices in their factories. On the contrary, the investment allowance to write off 120 per cent on new investments[81] is an incentive for the firm to invest capital rather than to employ more labour even when more labour intensive methods are available.

There are several possible ways decreasing this inequality between existing wage rates and opportunity wages of unskilled workers and of improving the present unemployment situation:

- No further wage increase for unskilled workers should be granted for a determined period of time. This period should cover several years in order to facilitate long-term planning by private firms.
- The Government should consider tax concessions or outright subsidies calculated on the basis of the number of unskilled workers employed.
- It is doubtful whether the investment allowance for income tax purposes has attracted any additional capital to Kenya in the past. An abolition of this concession should be considered. This would have to be done on an East African basis.

While unskilled labour is abundant in Kenya there is a great shortage of skilled and highly skilled personnel, including personnel with high technical and managerial abilities. These qualifications have until now been almost entirely absent among Africans. Most of the middle and all upper levels of the labour force in the manufacturing sector are therefore filled either by

80 The Kenya Gazette, 22nd February 1966, p. 190, Notice No. 639, The Industrial Court, Course No. 63 of 1965.

81 See p. 132.

Asians or by Europeans. The wage differentials between jobs requiring high qualifications and unskilled jobs are very large. In general, for the top jobs which have to be filled with expatriates, higher salaries have to be paid than for comparable employment in Europe. In the chemical and allied industries the requirements for highly skilled personnel are usually greater than in many other industries. At the present time this is a factor increasing the cost of production for this industry. A number of firms are endeavouring to prepare more local employees for the more highly skilled jobs through systematic in-service training and through scholarships to technical and other educational institutions. By this policy these firms reduce their own labour costs and at the same time help to diminish the serious bottlenecks in the field of skilled manpower.
It is often argued that underdeveloped countries suffer from a high degree of scarcity of capital and that, therefore, the price of capital should be high, thereby automatically favouring labour intensive methods of production. In the chemical and allied industries in Kenya this has not been found to be a consistent argument.

For a commercially profitable project, long-term capital is in general not difficult to find. This is true at least for loan capital to supplement available equity capital. Sources for loan capital are banks, other financial institutions like the C.D.C., the D.F.C.K. or the I.C.D.C. or the parent companies overseas. The rates of interest for loan capital are not much higher than in Europe. The same can be said of shortterm capital.

2. Effects on the Balance of Payments

Most developing countries have difficulties in finding the foreign exchange to finance the imports of investment goods which are necessary for economic development. Furthermore, more and more exports are necessary to finance the servicing of the foreign aid which the country has received in the form of credits. It is, therefore, vital to find goods suitable for export. With respect to export earnings in Kenya the chemical and allied industries play a very important role since over 50 per cent of all exports of manufactured products are chemical and allied goods [82].
In the following paragraph the net contribution of the chemical and allied industries to the overall balance of payments of the country is analysed. The estimates do not include all factors emanating from the industries and influencing the balance of payments, and the following quantifications can only be regarded as estimates. Indirect effects, (e.g. linkage effects to other industries) which in turn influence the balance of payments are not included.

---

82 See table 2, p. 129.

Among the positive effects of new industries on the balance of payments one has to distinguish between effects resulting from exports and those resulting from import substitution (local production minus exports). Negative effects are made up of imports of raw materials and of capital outflows for various purposes. They may be relatively important where expensive raw materials have to be imported for processing, where a large portion of the profits paid out as dividends are transferred abroad because most or all shares of the company belong to foreigners, where most capital goods have been imported and the capital output ratio is high, and where a large number of expatriates are employed who spend a considerable part of their earnings on imported goods and transfer part of their salaries abroad. Since the industries of the chemical and allied sector are based mainly on local raw materials and since exports form a substantial part of their production (the positive and negative factors are working in the same direction here) this group of industries sometimes has a high net favourable balance of payments impact which, as will be shown, is much less significant in industries based on imported raw materials.

Industries Based Mainly on Local Raw Materials

Of the industries which are based on local raw materials the soda ash, diatomite, pyrethrum and wattle extract industries export 90 per cent or more of their production, mainly to overseas countries. The positive impact on the balance of payments of these industries is confined to the value of their exports. It can be estimated that all of the negative factors together claim about 40 per cent of the export earnings in this group of industries so that about 60 per cent of the original export earnings remain as a positive net impact on the balance of payments in the case of the soda ash and wattle extract industries and somewhat more in the pyrethrum extract and diatomite industries.

The second group of industries based mainly on local raw materials are the cement, glass, and the phosphate fertilizer industries[83]. As to the cement and glass industries, both were originally intended as import substituting industries. In addition, they have, later on, become important export industries. The net favourable impact on the balance of payments of both of these industries is considerable, and relative to their exports or production, higher than in any other industry. An approximate indication about both industries' influence on the balance of payments is given in table 25.

83 The phosphate fertilizer industry at Tororo is only mentioned here in passing because among its raw materials imported sulphur is dominant in terms of value and it is, therefore, not typical for this group, and also because it is not a Kenyan industry.

Table 25. *Estimation of the Balance of Payments Impact of the Cement and Glass Industries, 1965–1966*
(in £1,000)

	Cement	Glass
I. *Positive Factors*		
Import substitution	1,200	290
Exports	1,887	280
II. *Negative Factors*		
Imports of raw materials	600	50
Transfer of profits and interest	270	–
Depreciation on imported capital goods	200	30
Transfers of salaries of expatriates and consumption of imported goods by employees and their families	200	80
III. *Net Positive Impact (I–II)*	1,847	410
in per cent of exports	*98*	*147*

Source: Own calculations and estimates.

Table 26. *Estimation of the Balance of Payments Impact of Certain Chemical Industries based Mainly on Imported Raw Materials, 1965–1966*
(in £1,000)

	Soap	Paint	Insecticides	Match	Oil Refinery
I. *Positive Factors*					
Import substitution	1,600	420	480	150	8,000
Exports	1,100	580	280	100	10,000
II. *Negative Factors*					
Imported materials	1,850	450	400	175	9,600 [a]
Profits and interest transferred	200	80	80	–	1,000
Depreciation on imported capital goods	50	50	20	10	1,000
Additional imports of consumer goods and transfers of salaries of expatriates and consumption of imported goods by employees	50	100	50	15	400
III. *Net Positive Impact (I–II)*	550	320	210	50	6,000
in per cent of exports	*50*	*55*	*75*	*50*	*60*

[a] of which about £9.1 million are crude oil.

Source: Own calculations and estimates.

Industries Based on Imported Raw Materials

Within the group of industries based on imported raw materials the soap, paints, insecticides, and match industries have been established exclusively to substitute imports on an East African basis. All four industries have sizable interterritorial exports of 30 to 50 per cent of their production and virtually no domestic exports. The market orientation of the oil refinery at Mombasa is different. The oil refinery which has to import its entire demand of crude oil is the main export industry of Kenya which contributes over 25 per cent to total manufacturing exports and about half of all exports of the chemical and allied industries.

The net positive impact on the balance of payments of the industries based on imported raw materials (the oil refinery included) relative to their exports is about the same as of the pure export industries (see table 26).

Before the refinery started operation, Kenya spent about £8 million annually on imports of refinery products. In 1965, imports of refinery products, including crude oil for refining, totalled about £9.6 million, £9.1 million of which were spent on crude oil for further processing in the refinery. In the same year, the value of total exports of refinery products was about £10 million so that "Kenya's own petroleum and oil requirements were met with no cost to the balance of payments, except in so far as profits earned by the refinery were paid abroad"[84]. This, however, takes into account only the current and direct effects of the refinery on the balance of payments. The overall impact of the refinery on the balance of payments has to consider direct and indirect effects. Even though the indirect influences on the balance of payments can be estimated only roughly we can notice quite clearly that the net impact is still positive although considerably smaller than visible at first sight.

Bibliography

Dyson, W. H.: The Superphosphate Industry in Uganda, in: *Chemistry in Britain,* Vol. 1, No. 11 (Nov. 1965).

East African Common Services Organization: *Treaty for East African Co-operation.* Nairobi, Government Printer, 1967.

—: East African Customs and Excise Department: *Annual Trade Reports of Kenya, Tanganyika and Uganda,* 1962–1967. Mombasa.

Hardy, N.: Pyrethrum in Kenya, The Board and its Functions, in: *The Times Review of Industry,* April 1962.

Hill, M. F.: *The Story of the Magadi Soda Company.* Birmingham 1964.

84 Republic of Kenya: *Economic Survey, 1966,* p. 19.

Jones, G. D. Glynne: Pyrethrum in Kenya, The Story of a Natural Insecticide, in: *The Times Review of Industry,* April 1962.
Kenya, Republic of: *African Socialism and its Application to Planning in Kenya,* Sessional Paper No. 10. Nairobi, Government Printer, 1965.
—: Statistics Division of the Ministry of Economic Planning and Development: *Census of Industrial Production, 1963.* Nairobi 1965.
—: *Development Plan for the Period 1965–66 to 1969–70.* Nairobi 1966.
The Madhvani Group of Companies (ed.): *Enterprise in East Africa.* Published in about 1966.
Paint – A £1 Million Industry in East Africa, in: *East African Trade and Industry,* Vol. X, No. 132 (Febr. 1965).
Paul, Rana Satya and Batt, Janardan T. (eds.): *Industry in East Africa 1964–65.* Nairobi 1965.
Reichelt, Hans: *The Chemical and Allied Industries in Kenya* (Preliminary Report). African Studies Centre of the Ifo Institute for Economic Research, München 1967 (mimeo.).
The Revolution of a Local Industry, in: *East African Trade and Industry,* Vol. XI, No. 141 (Nov. 1965).
Stedman, A. H. and Irvine, B.: Pyrethrum in Kenya, Flower to Concentrate, in: *The Times Review of Industry,* April 1962.
Tanganyika and Zanzibar, The United Republic of: *Tanganyika Five-Year Plan for Economic and Social Development, 1st July, 1964–30th June, 1969,* Vol. I. Dar es Salaam, Government Printer, 1964.
Uganda Government: *Work for Progress, Uganda's Second Five-Year Plan, 1966–1971.* Entebbe, Government Printer, 1966.
United Nations, Economic and Social Council, Economic Commission for Africa: *Recherche sur l'industrie chimique et sur celle des engrais en Afrique de l'Est, élaboration de données concernant la planification,* Report submitted to the Conference on the Harmonization of Industrial Development Programmes in East Africa, Lusaka, 27. 9.–5. 10. 1965, document E/CN. 14/INR/83. July 1965 (mimeo.).
—: *L'industrie du ciment et des industries connexes en Afrique de l'Est,* Report submitted to the Conference on the Harmonization of Industrial Development Programmes in East Africa, Lusaka, 27. 9.–5. 10. 1965, document E/CN. 14/INR/84. July 1965 (mimeo.).
—: Economic Commission for Africa and Centre for Industrial Development: *Prospects for the Development of the Chemical Industry in Africa,* Paper submitted to the Symposium on Industrial Development in Africa, Cairo, 27th January–10th February 1966, document E/CN. 14/AS/III/22 (10th December 1965) (mimeo.).

Government Periodicals

Kenya, Republic of: *Economic Survey, 1966* and *1968,* Prepared by the Statistics Division of the Ministry of Economic Planning and Development. Nairobi, 1966 and 1968 resp.
—: *The Kenya Gazette,* 1st and 22nd February 1966.
—: Statistics Division of the Ministry of Economic Planning and Development: *Kenya Statistical Digest,* Vol. I, No. 3 (Sept. 1963) and Vol. IV, No. 4 (Dec. 1966).
—: Statistics Division of the Ministry of Economic Planning and Development: *Statistical Abstract, 1965* and *1967.* Nairobi, 1965 and 1967 resp.

DEVELOPMENT AND STRUCTURE OF INDUSTRY IN UGANDA

by

Thomas Oursin

Contents

List of Tables

Within the framework of the technical assistance program of the Federal Republic of Germany, the Ifo-Institut für Wirtschaftsforschung was requested in 1964 to send advisers to Uganda to establish a system of industrial statistics. In order to carry out this mission, Thomas OURSIN worked in the Statistics Division of the Ministry of Planning and Community Development in Entebbe, Uganda, from 1964 to 1965. This work war carried on up to the end of 1966 by Lübbe SCHNITTGER. The material procured in this period and published by the Government of Uganda forms the statistical basis of the following report.
Thomas OURSIN, member of the research staff of the Ifo-Institut since 1957 and of the African Studies Department since 1961, carried out studies of development aid problems in tropical Africa, worked on behalf of the European Economic Community, Brussels, on transport planning in Togo, and took part in investigations of possibilities for industrialization in equatorial Africa. Since 1967 he has been working in the Transportation Projects Department of the International Bank for Reconstruction and Development, Washington, D.C.
We are indebted to Mr. John FOSBERRY of Munich for translating this treatise into English.

A. THE DEVELOPMENT AND STATUS OF INDUSTRY IN THE ECONOMY OF UGANDA

Uganda, formerly a part of the large colonial area of British East Africa, was an early target of British colonial policy in East Africa. The sources of the Nile and the kingdoms on the northern banks of Lake Victoria were the objectives of the first expeditions of explorers, missionaries and businessmen. The history of the opening up of East Africa, which is closely linked with the construction of the railway from Mombasa on the Indian Ocean to the highlands around Lake Victoria, resulted in an important shift of emphasis. Kenya, in the beginning only a transit area on the way to Uganda, developed into the gravicenter of the entire region: its central location, its favorable conditions for the development of a modern, European-style agriculture, and the large proportion of British inhabitants that had settled here in conjunction with the priorities of British colonial policy made Kenya the dominant element in the East African economic area. This development also became clearly apparent in the industrial sector. As far back as between the two world wars, in Kenya the foundations were laid for industrial development, and consciously promoted by the introduction of protective tariffs, including the two neighbouring countries, Uganda and Tanganyika, as markets.
In contrast, up to the early fifties Uganda's industry remained virtually confined to the processing of agricultural products for export: primarily cotton ginning, coffee curing and tea processing. Apart from this, at that time there was only a modest consumer goods industry for the supply of the domestic market[1]. Only in the course of the fifties was a start made on the more intensive expansion of industrial production in Uganda. Two events characterize government economic policy in this epoch: the remarkable development of the infrastructure and the foundation of the Uganda Development Corporation (UDC), which is hitherto probably the most successful government development corporation in tropical Africa.
This policy was made possible by a favourable development of government finances[2]. Like most raw-material-producing countries, in the first decade following the end of the war Uganda did good business on the world

1 Mainly two sugar factories, saw mills and wood-based industries, grain mills, oil-seed mills and soap manufacture.
2 Cf. L. Schnittger: *Besteuerung und wirtschaftliche Entwicklung in Ostafrika.* Berlin – Heidelberg – New York, Springer-Verlag, 1966, p. 163 et seq.

markets. Coffee and cotton, the country's most important export goods, brought high prices. More than most other raw-material-producing countries, Uganda utilized this development to procure public revenue. Two methods were adopted: the levying of export taxes and the siphoning off part of the export receipts through the Marketing Boards, which have a marketing monopoly for coffee and cotton. The accumulated reserves were not only used to stabilize purchase prices in periods of declining prices on the world markets, but also to a considerable extent to finance general development projects[3].

It is to this strengthening of the country's financial position that Uganda owes her good infrastructure: an extensive highway network, a high level of health and education facilities, a sufficient supply with electricity of the important centres of the country from the Owen Falls hydroelectric station, and the expansion of the railway network in the west and north of the country. It is difficult to judge the extent to which improvement of the infrastructure promoted development of the productive sectors of the country. Sometimes the view is expressed that Uganda's infrastructure is overdimensioned and that the positive effects on the economy have not come up to expectations[4]. Nevertheless it cannot be denied that utilization of the energy potential of the Nile and the building up of transport routes were an important precondition for building up industry.

A considerably more direct influence on the development of industry was exerted by the Uganda Development Corporation (UDC), which was founded in early 1952[5]. It commenced operations by taking over the Government's interests in the country's industry (Uganda Cement Industries, Lake Victoria Hotel and Uganda Fish Marketing Corporation), and in the course of about fifteen years it developed from these modest beginnings a position of substantial economic power with numerous subsidiaries and interests in almost all sectors of Uganda's economy. The capital stock of the corporation, which amounts to US$8 mill. of which US$6.4 mill. has been paid in, is held exclusively by the Government. The position of UDC in Uganda's industry is described in more detail in the following section.

---

3 In the period from 1945–1960, 26 per cent of the total receipts for coffee and cotton were transferred to the public treasury; 7 per cent derived from surpluses of the Boards and 5 per cent from export taxes went into various development funds; 14 per cent derived from export taxes were taken over directly into the current budgets.

4 Cf. D. Walker: Marketing Boards, in: *Problems of Economic Development,* edited by E. A. G. Robinson. London – New York, Mac Millan & Company Ltd. and St. Martin's Press Inc., 1965, p. 575.

5 Cf. in this connection International Bank for Reconstruction and Development (IBRD): *The Economic Development of Uganda.* Baltimore 1962, p. 273 et seq and E. J. Pauw: *Das Geld- und Bankwesen in Ostafrika.* München, Weltforum-Verlag, 1969.

The development and position of industry in Uganda is difficult to assess in statistical terms[6]. According to the available data, in the first half of the sixties the industrial sector contributed one-tenth of the gross domestic product. Related to the monetary sector only, i.e. excluding the subsistence economy, industry's share increased to about one-seventh. More than one-fifth of all registered wage-earners and salaried employees in 1964 were employed in industry[7].

It is interesting to note that from 1956 to 1964 industry has not increased its share in the gross domestic product, but has grown at the same pace as the entire economy (see table 1). Manufacturing alone, i.e., excluding cotton ginning, coffee processing, the sugar industry, mining and quarrying and the generation of electricity, even developed at a rate below average. In 1964 it contributed roughly 3.5 per cent to the gross domestic product as against 4.5 per cent in 1955 and 5.3 per cent in 1956.

The already mentioned Survey of Industrial Production has shown that the former national product calculations for various branches of industry gave too low values, and that industry's share in the aggregate gross domestic product for 1963 and 1964 must be set at a minimum of 11 per cent. Moreover, in 1965 and 1966 numerous industrial plants reached the production stage and have substantially increased the value of Uganda's industrial output. Nevertheless, considered against the background of the figures in Table 1, the planned objectives of the second development plan (1966–1971) must be described as rather ambitious[8]. The industrial sector in Uganda, excluding mining and electricity generation, is intended to grow 61 per cent during the period of the plan, which is equivalent of an annual growth rate of 10 per cent. The manufacturing industry alone, i.e., excluding cotton

6 It was only within the framework of the "World Census 1963" supported by the United Nations that the collection of data on industrial production was initiated in Uganda. For this reason, comprehensive information broken down into branches of industry is available for the first time for 1963 and 1964 only. (See Uganda Government, Statistical Division, Ministry of Planning and Community [Economic] Development: *Survey of Industrial Production, 1963 and 1964*, Entebbe 1965 and 1966. Hereafter quoted as Uganda Government, *Survey 1963 and 1964.*) Comparable data over a longer period of time are available only from the computations of the Gross Domestic Product, but its sectoral breakdown does not provide a satisfactory insight into the structural changes of Uganda's industry.

7 Cf. Uganda Government, Statistics Division, Ministry of Planning and Community Development: *1965 Statistical Abstract.* Entebbe, Government Printer, 1965, p. 89 (hereafter quoted as: Uganda Government: *1965 Statistical Abstract).* However, the share of one-fifth is exaggerated in that the number of wage-earners and salaried employees have hitherto been covered only incompletely by the statistics, and various occupational groups, e.g. household servants, are completely lacking in the employment statistics.

8 Uganda Government: *Work for Progress. Uganda's Second Five-Year Plan 1966–1971.* Entebbe, Government Printer, 1966, p. 77 et seq.

Table 1. *Contribution of Industry to Uganda's Gross Domestic Product at Factor Costs, 1955–1964*
(at 1960 prices)

Industry	Unit	1955	1956	1957	1958	1959	1960	1961	1962	1963	1964 [a]
1. Cotton ginning Coffee processing Sugar industry	1,000 £	4,584	4,750	5,341	4,826	4,127	3,880	4,517	4,465	6,419	6,760
2. Mining and quarrying	1,000 £	1,197	1,321	1,661	1,980	2,145	2,232	2,469	2,776	2,892	3,180
3. Food industry	1,000 £	1,087	1,126	1,291	1,363	1,233	1,235	1,200	1,107	1,069	1,323
4. Other industries	1,000 £	4,700	5,986	5,275	5,080	4,706	4,810	4,839	4,612	4,584	4,664
5. Electricity generation	1,000 £	899	1,098	1,387	1,864	1,788	1,939	2,031	2,140	2,399	2,557
6. Industry (excl. building industry)	1,000 £	12,467	14,281	14,955	14,913	13,999	14,096	15,056	15,100	17,363	18,484
7. Change as against previous year	%		*+14.6*	*+4.7*	*—0.3*	*—6.1*	*+0.7*	*+6.8*	*+0.3*	*+15.0*	*+6.5*
8. Gross domestic product	1,000 £	126,589	133,614	139,255	140,240	147,376	152,125	149,146	150,244	164,734	173,160
9. Change as against previous year	%		*+5.5*	*+4.2*	*+0.7*	*+5.1*	*+3.2*	*—2.0*	*+0.7*	*+9.6*	*+5.1*
10. Industry's share (6. as % of 8.)	%	*9.8*	*10.7*	*10.7*	*10.6*	*9.5*	*9.3*	*10.1*	*10.1*	*10.5*	*10.7*

[a] provisional

Sources: Uganda Government, Ministry of Planning and Economic Development, Statistics Division: *The Real Growth of Uganda 1954–1962.* Entebbe 1964; and Uganda Government: *1965 Statistical Abstract.*

ginning, coffee processing and the sugar industry, is planned to expand as much as 12 per cent per year.
According to the formulations of the plan, the planned increase of industrial output requires annual gross capital investments of £9 mill. No reliable figures are available for industrial investment in the past. Only in 1963 to 1965, which brought a substantial increase in investment in connection with the erection of numerous new industrial enterprises, it is probable that an investment volume of £9 mill. per year was approximately attained. The objectives laid down in the plan will therefore be attainable only if the lively investment in the years from 1963 to 1965 can be maintained over the entire planning period.

B. THE PROMOTION OF INDUSTRIAL DEVELOPMENT

Industrial development in Uganda is being promoted at the present time by:

- the government,
- foreign, primarily British, private capital, and
- the minority of Asian origin.

Until now, domestic entrepreneurs and domestic private capital have been without notable influence in Uganda's industry. The government and the UDC have been endeavoring for some years, with the help of the Small Industry Development Reserve formed in 1963 by UDC, to give domestic forces access to modern trade and industry. It is, however, still too early to appraise the success of this difficult undertaking[9].

I. The Uganda Industrial Charter[10]

Like almost all less-developed African countries, Uganda has also promulgated a series of regulations for the promotion and protection of private investments. The basic principles of the government's policy with regard

9 In 1963, this task was entrusted to African Business Promotion Ltd., whose assets were taken over by the newly founded National Trading Corporation (NTC). The NTC started operations on January 1st, 1967.

10 Cf. also Th. Oursin: *Uganda als Wirtschaftspartner.* Köln, Bundesstelle für Außenhandelsinformation, 1965, p. 52 et seq.

to new investments in industry were laid down in the Uganda Industrial Charter in 1964. It applies to all enterprises which contribute to the development of industrial projects and "... to whom the Government of Uganda has granted Approved Status by the conclusion of an Agreement based on this Charter" (Article 2). The industrial Charter confirms Article 22 of the constitution of Uganda, which provides far-reaching protection against nationalization. In turn, the government expects domestic capital and domestic labour to be permitted a fair share in the enterprise. It is expected that as many domestic employees will be engaged as the progress of the production process permits. Special emphasis must be placed on the training of domestic personnel. The government on its part undertakes to facilitate the import of all machines, raw materials and semi-fabricated goods required to attain the production objective. However, domestic raw materials must be used to the greatest possible extent.
Undertakings which operate within the framework of the Industrial Charter are subject to the general tax laws of Uganda. It is possible, however, to obtain approval for higher depreciation allowances and to apply for reimbursement of duties paid on imports of raw materials for industrial processing in Uganda. For the import of certain products complete freedom from customs duties can be obtained, both for raw and semi-fabricated materials and for capital goods.
The industrial Charter formulates the general framework within which private enterprises can operate in Uganda. All particulars are laid down in the Agreements, which are the basis for the issue of a "Certificate of an External Approved Enterprise". As a notable extension of the provisions of Industrial Charter, the Foreign Investment Protection Act also regulates the transfer of profits. The holder of a "Certificate" is guaranted the free transfer of profits, the proceeds from the sale of the enterprise, principal and interest of loans and compensation paid for any expropriation of the enterprise.

II. The Uganda Development Corporation

As indicated, the government, represented by UDC, has taken over a leading role in industrial development. The UDC can be regarded as one the most successful examples of development corporations in Tropical Africa. Ever since its foundation it has (regularly) operated at a profit, even though not all of its subsidiary and associated companies were always able to achieve a surplus. The profits were regularly ploughed back into the corporation and made it possible to start many new undertakings. At the end of 1965, the

consolidated balance sheet of UDC and its subsidiaries closed with assets in the amount of $9.7 mill. The net profit before taxes reached the record figure of £1.7 mill. in 1965 [11].
The statutory instruments [12] of UDC read: "to facilitate the industrial and economic development of the Protectorate, promote and assist in the financing, management, or establishment of:

- new undertakings,
- schemes for the better organization and modernization of any undertaking,
- the conduct of research into the industrial and mineral potentialities of the protectorate".

UDC may acquire participations, extend loans and guarantees and take over managements. It is subject to supervision by a Board of Directors, the members of which are appointed by the government. Under certain conditions the government may issue instructions to UDC in matters involving the interests of the public. Government approval is required for capital increases, the foundation of new enterprises, and the acquisition of new or increase of already existing participations. In the colonial epoch the influence of the government on UDC's current business was slight [13]. UDC is subject to the provisions of company law and in comparison to the private business sector enjoys no substantial privileges, especially not in respect of taxation.
UDC's interests are subdivided into four main spheres: finance, agriculture and food industry, mining and manufacturing, and tourism and hotels.
The UDC group has a bank of its own (UGADEV Bank Ltd.), the functions of which are essentially limited to serving the group. The real estate of UDC is concentrated in a special company, as are the investments in foreign countries. In order to afford the investing public at home and abroad the opportunity of acquiring interests in the UDC sphere, shares of five profitable firms were placed in an investment company (Uganda Crane Industries, Ltd.), the shares of which were placed in Uganda and on the London capital market. Finally, in 1965 a new financing company, the Development Finance Company of Uganda (DFCU), was founded, in which, in addition to UDC, the Commonwealth Development Corporation, the Deutsche Entwicklungsgesellschaft (DEG) and the Netherlands Overseas Finance Co. Ltd. hold equal interests. The DFCU has made credits and equity capital available to new enterprises and in some cases taken over shares of already existing firms that were formerly held by UDC. This provided UDC with new funds. The

11 East African £ (EA £) = 20 shillings (shs) = 11.20 DM. The official unit of currency is now the Uganda Shilling (1 sh = 0.56 DM).
12 Uganda Protectorate: *The Uganda Development Corporation Ordinance 1952 (no. 1 of 1952) as amended by the Uganda Development Corporation (Amendment) Ordin. 1955*. Entebbe, Government Printer, 1961.
13 Cf. Columbia University School of Law: *Public International Development Financing in East Africa*. New York 1962, p. 38.

main reason for the choice of this construction was that the right to hold a direct interest in UDC is reserved for the government of Uganda.

UDC's agricultural interests are concentrated in Agricultural Enterprises Ltd. The main effort of Agricultural Enterprises Ltd. is directed towards the expansion of tea plantations and tea factories, and the establishment of large cattle farms. In the food industry field, in 1967 a factory for soluble tea and a plant for manufacturing starch from cassava were under construction. Plants for the production of potable alcohol and for meat processing are already in operation. Finally, UDC has interests in firms in the fish and milling industry.

UDC subsidiaries are the sole producers in Uganda of cement and cement-asbestos articles, superphosphate, enamelled household goods, knitwear and hosiery, etc. 1966 UDC's share in the total output of cotton fabrics in Uganda was over 80 per cent. Through participations UDC also exerts an influence on the mining and smelting of copper, and on the production of matches, paper sacks, fishing nets, structural steel, and agricultural implements. Furthermore, UDC is the biggest hotel owner in Uganda. In 1967 it was operating eight hotels in all parts of the country and three safari lodges in the two major national parts. A new luxury hotel in Kampala was almost completed.

The distribution of UDC's net assets among the most important sectors of the economy is shown in Table 2, which clearly demonstrates the dominant position of industry. In 1965 its share was 50 per cent, the textile industry alone accounting for 25 per cent of the corporation's net assets. UDC's share in the whole of Uganda's industry cannot be established with certainty from the available data. Including the subsidiary and associated companies, UDC's share in the output of the whole industry (excluding the building

Table 2. *Breakdown of UDC's Net Assets (consolidated balance sheet) by Economic Sectors at the End of 1965*

Sector		Share in %
Agriculture		*25.9*
Mining		*3.2*
Industry		*49.8*
thereof Textile industry	*25.4*	
Cement & building materials industry	*9.3*	
Food & beverage industry	*6.0*	
Hotels and tourism		*8.0*
Finance		*5.2*
Investments		*7.9*
Total		*100.0*

Source: Calculations based on *Annual Report 1965.*

industry) is estimated at about 15 per cent in 1963; in the same year its share in the manufacturing industry alone reached an estimated 30 per cent. These figures have probably grown in recent years.
Uganda's second five-year plan clearly spells out the key role of industrial development for the attainment of the set targets. However, the government's scope of action to achieve those objectives is limited. Despite the important position of the Uganda Development Corporation, particularly in in the field of industry, industrial progress in Uganda is dependent to a great extent on the co-operation of foreign capital and expatriate entrepreneurs, and on the willingness of the Asiatic minority to invest. In this respect government development policy can create the necessary preconditions, smooth the way and offer incentives; the action itself must come from other quarters. It would be inaccurate, however, to regard this constellation as a specific difficulty of Uganda. On the contrary — the experience and large capital resources of UDC provide government industrialization policy with an instrument which many African states do not have at their disposal. UDC's joint ventures with domestic and foreign private capital, which have been formed ever more frequently in recent years, have created a feeling of security in Uganda's industry, have mobilized private capital without the fear of expropriation on the one hand, the fear of excessive foreign influence on the other hand being allowed to become too strong.

III. Foreign Private Capital

Next to the UDC, foreign — especially British — capital is an important source of risk capital in Uganda's industry. Many enterprises are financed by foreign private capital, among others the copper mine at Kilembe, the cigarette industry, parts of the beverage industry, a factory for agricultural implements and the newly constructed works for the production of bicycle tires. In addition, in some UDC enterprises, foreign companies have been appointed managing agents. This form of cooperation ensures Uganda's industry the experience and know-how of European engineers and managers.

IV. The Role of the Asian Minority

The minority of Asian origin is the third big group participating in the production process. In 1963 about 82,000 persons of Asian origin were living in Uganda, that is about 1 per cent of the total population[14]. In the colonial epoch, this population group acquired a substantial share in the wholesale and retail trade, in the repair and minor trades, in medium-level administration jobs, in salaried and skilled occupations and in the professions. In Uganda Asians own a number of coffee and tea plantations and all the sugar factories. At a very early date they also became active in certain spheres of industry, especially in cotton ginning and coffee processing, in the saw mill, soap and oil mill industry, and in the small scale manufacturing of wearing apparel.

Since Uganda attained independence in 1962, several remarkable changes can be observed in the role of the Asian population group in industry and allied spheres[15]. In the processing of farm produce the share of Asian enterprise is declining. Numerous coffee processing establishments and cotton ginneries have been taken over by African cooperatives. On the other hand, several Indian entrepreneurs have gone into completely new sectors of modern industry. The leaders in this movement are the two "Madhvani" and "Metha" groups, which have achieved considerable economic power in Uganda and, over and beyond that, in the whole of East Africa on the basis of their big sugar factories. Madhvani, in particular, has succeeded in building up a remarkable group in the manufacturing industry. Among other things, it now embraces, in addition to the traditional fields of processing agricultural products and closely related activities (sugar refining and confectionery, cotton ginning, oil milling and thus production of edible fats), a cotton spinning and weaving mill, a match factory, a paper sack factory, and an electric steel work. "Madhvani" and UDC work together in all these enterprises. "Metha" has begun to build up several metalworking plants, including a large iron foundry and a plant for the manufacture of agricultural implements and vehicles. Finally, a plant for the assembly of tractors was set up a short time ago. In this connection, the Industrial Promotion Service of the Aga Khan Group has to be mentioned, which has participated in recent years in a few industrial projects.

It is probably correct to assume that this sally into an industrial terra nova is not solely attributable to economic considerations, but also to the endeavours of Indian economic leaders to take the new political constellation into account. The government is making an effort to transfer not only agricultural production, but also the processing and marketing of farm produce to African hands. Asian entrepreneurs have reasons to fear they will lose ever more ground in these spheres. On the other hand, political pressure in

---

14 Uganda Government: *1965 Statistical Abstract,* p. 5. Cf. in this connection I. Rothermund: *Die politische und wirtschaftliche Rolle der asiatischen Minderheit in Ostafrika.* Berlin – Heidelberg – New York, Springer Verlag, 1965.

15 The developments in 1967 and 1968 cannot be covered in this study.

the direction of "Africanization" in the manufacturing industry may be expected only at a later phase, all the more so because Indian groups are increasingly entering into participations with UDC.

C. STRUCTURAL FEATURES

I. The Main Sectors of Industry

According to the results of the Surveys of Industrial Production, in Uganda at the present time, distinction can be made among the following industrial sectors:[16]

- processing of agricultural products
- mining and quarrying
- manufacturing
- electricity generation and distribution

The most important data on the structure of these four branches of industry are contained in table 3.

Table 3. *Uganda's Industry*[a] *by Main Industrial Groups in 1964*
(establishments with 10 and more employees)

Industry	Establishments	Employees on Dec. 31, 1964		Turnover		Value Added	
	No.	No.	%	Mill. Shs	%	Mill. Shs	%
Processing of agricultural products	282	18,672	*38.8*	768.7	*46.5*	78.2	*18.2*
Mining and quarrying	117	6,971	*14.5*	57.5	*3.5*	35.0	*8.2*
Manufacturing	322	20,838	*43.3*	768.3	*46.5*	263.3	*61.4*
Electricity	1	1,621	*3.4*	58.8	*3.5*	52.6	*12.2*
Total	722	48,102	*100.0*	1,653.3	*100.0*	429.1	*100.0*

[a] excluding building industry

Source: Uganda Government: *Survey 1964.*

16 The building industry will be excluded from the following presentation, since the statistics available for it, especially for earlier years, are still incomplete. The calculations in the national accounts relate, as far as can be established, not so much to the institutional sector "building industry", but primarily to overall construction activity.

1. Processing of Agricultural Products

The sector "Processing of Agricultural products" embraces coffee processing establishments, cotton ginneries and tea factories. The chief function of these establishments is to transform the country's most important agricultural export commodities — cotton, coffee and tea — into an exportable condition. The processing operation is relatively brief and simple. Only the tea factories produce a final product; coffee and especially cotton undergo decisive further processing in other enterprises, generally abroad. Coffee processing and cotton ginning constitute the oldest branches of industry in Uganda. New establishments are opened only to a limited extent. On the other hand, Uganda's tea industry is still relatively young; in 1964 it comprised 29 establishments. Their number will increase further in the coming years with the planned expansion of acreage for tea plantations.

The sector "Processing of Agricultural Products" hardly ranks lower than the manufacturing industry as far as employees and turnover are concerned; nearly half of the total industrial turnover is accounted for by this sector. On the other hand, its contribution to the aggregate value added by industry is comparatively small. The share of value added in relation to the gross output (VA/GO quotient) in 1964 was 0.10 for "Processing of Agricultural Products" as against 0.35 for the manufacturing industry.

The further development of the sector "Processing of Agricultural Products" is dependent on the capacity of world markets for coffee, cotton and tea. The consumption of domestically produced coffee and tea in Uganda is not known, but up to now it has probably been extraordinarily low. Only in the case of cotton is a notable proportion processed domestically and then sold on the East African markets. After the opening of a second textile factory, domestic sales of ginned cotton rose from 9 per cent in 1963 to nearly 12 per cent of the total output in 1966.

The great dependence on the world markets leaves the branches of industry discussed here little room for an autonomous development policy and an appreciable expansion of production. At best there are genuine growth chances for tea. In the case of this latter product Uganda's role is that of a small supplier who can step up output and exports to a certain extent without immediately modifying supply and demand relationships on the world market. The contribution of the tea factories to Uganda's industrial output is nevertheless still modest: in 1964, 1,500 persons were employed in 29 factories, i.e., about 3 per cent of the total industrial labour force. This group's share in the industrial value added amounted to 2.6 per cent.

2. Mining and Quarrying

Very heterogeneous elements are combined in this group. Since the Kilembe copper mine on Uganda's western border commenced operations in 1954, the data for this enterprise have assumed predominant importance in the whole sector. 96 per cent of Uganda's total mining exports in 1964 were copper. The favourable trend of copper prices in the recent past has probably increased this figure further. In 1964 exports rose to about 18,000 tons of blister copper. In addition to copper, small quantities of tin, tungsten, beryllium and lead are also mined in Uganda. Moreover, large phosphate deposits have now been exploited for some years in the south-east of Uganda. Statistically, however, this activity is included under the chemical industry (fertilizers) and is not contained in the figures for mining.
The copper concentrate obtained at Kilembe is transported over 400 km (250 miles) by rail to Jinja, where it is transformed into blister copper in a copper smelter. Unfortunately the limited deposits of the copper mine make the production of electrolytic copper in Uganda unprofitable. The copper wire factory recently established in Kenya therefore has to obtain its raw material elsewhere. Statistically the copper smelter at Jinja belongs to the metal industry. The turnover shown for mining in Table 3 — as far as copper is concerned — is based on the internal accounting price for the copper concentrate and cannot be compared with the export receipts for blister copper. A turnover of 57.5 mill. shs. for the sector "Mining and Quarrying" in 1964 compares with export receipts of 136 mill. shs. for blister copper alone in the same year[17]. This unusual relation is not only indicative of the high value added by the copper smelter, but above all is explained by the marked rise in copper prices in recent years. The resulting increase in receipts was assigned to the metal industry alone, and not to mining.

3. Manufacturing

Even before the end of the second World War, a modest consumer goods industry had grown up in Uganda. It supplied primarily the home market, but to a certain extent also the neighbouring countries of Kenya and Tanzania. Of the 264 establishments of the manufacturing industry covered by the industrial statistics for 1963, 47 had already started production prior to 1945. The share of these establishments in the turnover of the manufacturing industry in 1963 was a good quarter. Almost all the establishments of this first stage of development are based on domestic raw materials and agri-

17 Uganda Government, Statistics Division of the Ministry of Finance: *Background to the Budget 1966–67*. Entebbe, Government Printer, 1966, p. 17 (herafter quoted as Uganda Government: *Background).*

cultural products: sugar industry, tobacco processing, sawmills and woodworking, oil mills processing cotton seed, and soap factories. The only notable exception is the printing industry, which was already highly developed even before the second World War.
Under the economic policy of the fifties, which was described at the beginning, and the influence exerted by the UDC after its establishment, in the period from 1955–1959 activity in the founding of industrial enterprises reached a certain climax. In this period, 82 new enterprises of the manufacturing industry went into production; in 1963 they accounted for one-third of the output of the manufacturing industry. They embraced the food, beverage, furniture, textile, and structural clay products industries, typical examples of a medium stage of industrial development, as can also be observed in other less developed countries. In the ensuing years the growth of industry slowed down very appreciably, in which connection political factors — Uganda became independent in 1962 — also probably played a part. Only in recent years, especially in 1965 and 1966, did the number of newly founded firms rise again.

4. Electricity Generation and Distribution

Uganda is rich in hydroelectric power reserves. The potential of the Nile alone, which on its way through Uganda drops half of the total difference in levels between Lake Victoria and the Mediterranean, is estimated at 2–3 mill. kW. Since 1954, the Owen Falls Hydroelectric Station has been in operation at Jinja, where the Nile flows out of Lake Victoria. The installed capacity is currently 135,000 kW; a capacity increase to 150,000 kW is planned, which will bring the power station up to the limit of its capacity.
From Jinja the important areas of Uganda are supplied with electricity. One main transmission line connects Kasese in the west and Tororo in the east with Jinja. In the north, Soroti, Lira and Gulu, and in the west, Masaka, Mityana, Hoima, and Masindi are connected to the network. Hence, together with several smaller hydroelectric and thermal power stations, electricity is available to nearly every possible industrial location in Uganda. Electricity generation and distribution is the responsibility of the Uganda Electricity Board. The figures given for a electricity generation in table 3 relate solely to this enterprise. Owing to its special structure, this particular field will be largely excluded from the following considerations.

II. Industrial Locations

The northern bank of Lake Victoria has been known for some time as a zone of above-average population density and lively economic activity. For this reason colonial policy aimed its first efforts in the East African interior at this area. At present about half of Uganda's population lives in the zone covered by the administrative districts of Masaka, Mengo, Busoga, Bukedi, and Bugisu, which extend to a depth of 100–120 km (60–75 miles) north of Lake Victoria and from the Tanzanian border to the Kenyan border (see table 4). This zone makes up only about one-quarter of the country's total area. Due to the construction of the Uganda railway, which reached Lake Victoria at Kisumu shortly after the turn of the century, this area was linked up with the world economy at an early date. The railway was extended in stages to Jinja and Kampala, and has now reached the western frontier of the country. A northern line leads from Tororo via Mbale to the Nile at Pakwach. The trunk road coming from Nairobi is asphalted from Tororo to beyond Mbarara and together with numerous major and minor roads, the majority of which are well-built, ensures a degree of penetration of the rural areas of this particular zone that is extraordinarily good for African conditions. Kampala, Jinja, Mbale, and Entebbe, the four biggest towns in Uganda,

Table 4. *The Lake Zone of Uganda* [a]

1. Population (1959)	Number	3,180,000
Percentage of total population	%	*49*
2. Land area	sq. km.	50,400
Percentage of total area	%	*25*
3. Population density (1959)	No./sq. km.	63
4. Share of Lake Zone in total output of		
a) Sugar	%	*100*
b) Coffee [b] (estimated) (1964)	%	*90*
c) Cotton [c] (average for period 1956–1961)	%	*62*
d) Tea [c] (1963)	%	*50*
5. Share of Lake Zone in		
a) Railway network (estimated) (1965)	%	*45*
b) Asphalt roads (estimated) (1964)	%	*75*
6. Share of Lake Zone in Uganda's urban population [d]	%	*75*

[a] Administrative districts of Masaka, Mengo, Busoga, Bukedi, and Bugisu (including Mbale).

[b] Based on cultivated area.

[c] Based on output.

[d] Towns with more than 3,000 inhabitants.

Sources: Uganda Government: *1965 Statistical Abstract;* Uganda Government: *Survey 1963;* Uganda Government, Department of Lands and Surveys: *Atlas of Uganda.* Entebbe 1962; East African Railways and Harbours: *Annual Report 1964.* Nairobi 1965.

and also such important centres as Masaka and Tororo are united in this lake zone within a relatively small area.

From this regions comes the greater part of Uganda's agricultural export products. The entire sugar output, about nine-tenths of the coffee, roughly half of the tea and nearly two-thirds of the cotton are produced here. Without any exact data being available, it can be concluded with a high degree of certainty that in the Lake Zone there is a concentration of national income that is far above average and, above all, a concentration of monetary purchasing power that is decisive for the sale of industrial products. In the light of these facts it seems almost "self-evident" that Uganda's industry is also concentrated in this zone.

Unfortunately the regional breakdown of the data does not provide complete information on the locations of industry in Uganda. The statistics conceal the fact that the manufacturing industry is concentrated in a few towns, especially Tororo, Iganga, Kakira, Jinja, Lugazi, and Kampala. Of the 322 establishments of the manufacturing industry, 294 are concentrated in the south of the country (in the Buganda region and the eastern region); they employ more than 90 per cent of the labour force of this sector (see table 5).

Mining and quarrying and the establishments for the processing of agricultural products are limited in their choice of location to a great extent by natural location factors. These branches of industry constitute the major part

Table 5. *Regional Breakdown of Uganda's Industry in 1964* [a]

Industry	Buganda [b]	Eastern region [c]	Western region	Northern region	Total
		I. Number of Establishments			
Processing of agricultural products	178	63	22	19	282
Mining and quarrying	10	3	104	–	117
Manufacturing	193	101	20	8	322
Total	381	167	146	27	721
		II. Labour force			
Processing of agricultural products	..	..	..	..	..
Mining and quarrying	345	284	6,342	–	6,971
Manufacturing	11,817	7,384	1,478	159	20,838
Total	..	..	..	..	..

[a] Excluding electricity and building industry.
[b] Mengo, Masaka and Mubende.
[c] Busoga, Bukedi, Bugisu, Teso and Sebei.

Source: Uganda Government: *Survey 1964.*

of the enterprises established in the other parts of the country. In the western region alone there are more than 100 mines in operation, although these, with but a few exception, are minor or very small enterprises. Then, outside the Lake Zone, there is a certain number of saw mills, structural clay and repair establishments. On the other hand, the majority of the coffee processing establishments, cotton ginneries and tea factories are in the Lake Zone, though far more evenly distributed over the entire area than the enterprises of the manufacturing industry.

The current Five-Year Plan gives no indication of any steps towards influencing the regional distribution of Uganda's industry. On the contrary, a progressive concentration process is expected in the areas of Kampala, Jinja and Tororo. Although other parts of the country are also supplied with electricity and are connected up to the transport network, almost all new undertakings prefer to settle in the south of the country. In these parts higher wages and land prices have to be paid, but these disadvantages are more than offset by proximity to the market and to the administration in Kampala, the better schooling of the labour force and other factors. Finally, a factor that is not without importance in the choice of location is the fact that expert European personnel, who are indispensable to the industrial production process for some time to come, can only be induced with great difficulty and at extra cost to work in more remote parts of the country for any length of time.

III. Firm Size

On the basis of the available data, relevant statements on firm size can be made only for the sector "Manufacturing Industry". Relative to the number of establishments, small and medium-sized firms dominate in Uganda's manufacturing industry. In 1964, of 322 establishments only 44 had more than 100 employees (cf. table 6). However, most of the results are influenced

Table 6. *Size Structure of the Manufacturing Industry in 1964*
(establishments with 10 and more employees)

Size Category of Employees	Establishments Number	%	Labour Force Number	%	Turnover Mill. Shs	%
10–19	119	*37*	1,699	*8*	50.2	*7*
20–49	110	*34*	3,350	*16*	72.3	*9*
50–99	49	*15*	3,204	*15*	77.2	*10*
100 and more	44	*14*	12,585	*61*	568.6	*74*
Total	322	*100*	20,838	*100*	768.3	*100*

Source: Uganda Government: *Survey 1964.*

to a substantial extent by the establishments of this size. In 1964 this group accounted for 60 per cent of all employees and 74 per cent of the aggregate turnover of the manufacturing industry. Only four firms had more than 500 employees in 1963. They contributed nearly one-fourth of the turnover of the manufacturing industry. This relation is typical of many developing economies; it characterizes the great weight of a few enterprises in what is on the whole a very small industrial sector. The big enterprises in Uganda concentrate on a few branches of industry, especially the sugar and beverage industry, saw mills and plywood industry, oil mills, chemical industry, textile and metal industry. These enterprises are comparatively modernly equipped and capital-intensive. The annual turnover per employee in this size class is correspondingly high. Whereas in 1964 the average turnover per employee in the manufacturing industry was about 37,000 Shs, in the top size class it reached more than 45,000 Shs, while the turnover of firms with less than 50 employees was only about 24,000 Shs per employee. The decisive factor for the capital intensity and turnover per employee is not so much the firm size, however, but primarily the branch of industry to which an enterprise belongs, which in turn affects the size of the firm.

IV. Employment and Wages

At the end of 1964, 48,100 persons were employed in Uganda's industry (excluding the building industry), which is more than one-fifth of all persons working for wages and salaries. As shown in table 3, roughly 39 per cent of all industrial employees are engaged in the "Processing of Agricultural Products" and 43 per cent work in the manufacturing industry. These figures, which give the position at the end of the year, conceal considerable seasonal fluctuations in the labour force of the sector "Processing of Agricultural Products", which are attributable mainly to the cotton ginning establishments. Table 7 is a compilation of the employment status over the course of 1964 for selected industries. Greater fluctuations in employment during the year are observed only in a few sectors of the manufacturing industry, e.g., in the oil and fats industry, which is dependent on the cotton harvest.
These seasonal fluctuations contrast with the movements of individual workers, called labour turnover. In developed economies this term is used for changes from one job to another, in the majority of cases within a branch of industry. In Africa these inter-firm changes are overlaid with a repeated movement of numerous employees between the modern sector of the economy and the traditional agricultural sector. The statistical data for Uganda's industry offer no proof of the frequently asserted extraordinary labour turn-

Table 7. *Fluctuations in Employment in Selected Industries*

Industry	Number of Employees on 31. 3. 1964	30. 6. 1964	30. 9. 1964	31. 12. 1964	Average
Processing of agricultural products	21,199	10,746	9,241	18,672	14,959
thereof					
Cotton ginning	14,842	4,688	3,221	12,296	8,762
Coffee processing	5,054	4,670	4,586	4,888	4,794
Manufacturing	19,981	19,752	20,120	20,838	20,157
thereof					
Grain milling	311	273	318	391	323
Beverage industry	903	916	916	879	904
Textiles and garments	3,089	3,083	3,126	3,191	3,122
Oil and fats industry	1,357	1,164	1,072	1,121	1,179
Soap industry	330	346	337	377	348
Metal industry and engineering	1,730	1,732	1,784	1,895	1,785

Source: Uganda Government: *Survey 1964.*

Table 8. *Labour Turnover in the Manufacturing Industry of Uganda* (in %)

Industry	Labour Turnover Rate 1963	1964
Manufacturing Industry	*12*	*10*
thereof		
Meat and fish industry	*22*	*21*
Grain milling	*2*	*2*
Sugar and tobacco industry	*24*	*12*
Beverage industry	*7*	*5*
Textile and garments industry	*8*	*11*
Sawmilling and plywood industry	*8*	*8*
Furniture industry	*9*	*3*
Printing industry	*9*	*4*
Chemical industry	*44*	*33*
Oil and fats industry	*4*	*4*
Soap industry	*8*	*10*
Glass and cement industry	*18*	*19*
Metal industry and engineering	*12*	*14*

Source: Uganda Government: *Survey 1963* and *1964.*

over in African industry. On average, in 1963 and 1964 a labour turnover rate[18] of 10–12 per cent was recorded for the manufacturing industry (see table 8). Only in a few branches of industry, for instance in fish and meat processing, the food industry, chemical industry, cement and metal industries,

18 No. of workers replaced: total labour force.

was this average figure exceeded to any notable extent. The available data, however, afford no possibility of interpreting the deviations from the mean, some of which are substantial. The generally small fluctuations from year to year suggest that peculiarities specific to the various branches of industry have a significant effect on labour turnover. Furthermore — as established by several individual studies — young industrial enterprises have a higher labour turnover than older ones, since the training of a cadre of qualified personnel is a time-consuming process under African conditions[19].

1. Origin of Workers

In the East African common market comprising Kenya, Tanzania and Uganda, workers could move freely from one country to another during the colonial period. Even today this freedom is still largely ensured, but recently efforts have been made to increase the proportion of Uganda nationals in the country's industry. To a certain extent this policy affects workers from Tanzania and from the neighbouring western countries of Rwanda, Burundi and Congo, but most particularly workers from Kenya (see also table 9). Good traffic connections, an always present pressure of unemployment and Kenya's clear lead in industrial development have resulted for a long time now in people from Kenya accepting employment in Uganda. 12 per cent of all industrial employees in Uganda at the end of 1963 came from Kenya. Their share rises to over 20 per cent in the manufacturing industry, and in individual branches of industry it lies far above that figure. In many enterprises the skilled jobs are held mainly by Indians and Kenyans. Asians make up

19 The general experience that the labour turnover declines with the age of the enterprise and the training of a cadre of experienced personnel is confirmed by a number of case studies carried out in 1965 in selected industrial establishments in Uganda. In a large establishment which is under European management and has been working in Uganda for decades the following breakdown of employees by length of service was determined:

Length of service (years)	Percentage of total labour force
0– 5	*8.4*
6–10	*46.4*
11–15	*32.1*
16–20	*9.7*
21 and more	*3.3*

According to this table, at that time over 90 per cent of all employees had been with the firm for five years or more, and almost half more than 10 years. These results could probably be classified as good even under European conditions. See East African Institute of Social Research: Economic Development Research Project Papers No. 69, 73, 75, 88 and 100. Kampala 1965 and 1966, respectively.

nearly a tenth of all employees in the manufacturing industry, a figure which is in clear contrast to the one per cent share of the Asian population in Uganda's total population. The Asians work predominantly in skilled and foremen's jobs, and in occupations requiring tradesmen's qualifications. One per cent of all employees are Europeans; they are almost exclusively in leading positions.

Table 9. *Labour Force by Regions of Origin in 1963*
(in % of labour force)

Industry	Region of origin				
	Uganda	Kenya	other parts of Africa	Asia	Europe
Processing of agricultural products	*80.0*	*6.1*	*9.0*	*4.8*	*0.1*
thereof Tea industry	*58.4*	*7.8*	*29.2*	*3.3*	*1.3*
Mining and Quarrying	*74.8*	*7.3*	*11.2*	*3.9*	*2.8*
Manufacturing	*60.8*	*20.2*	*8.4*	*9.3*	*1.3*
thereof					
Sugar and tobacco industry	*49.3*	*20.7*	*19.5*	*10.2*	*0.3*
Beverage industry	*50.8*	*27.7*	*8.6*	*10.6*	*2.3*
Textile and garments industry	*71.6*	*12.1*	*12.5*	*2.1*	*1.7*
Sawmilling and plywood industry	*78.4*	*11.2*	*5.6*	*4.6*	*0.2*
Furniture industry	*48.9*	*34.1*	*6.7*	*9.5*	*0.8*
Printing industry	*59.3*	*21.8*	*1.6*	*13.8*	*3.5*
Oil and fats industry	*56.3*	*30.3*	*2.0*	*11.4*	–
Metals industry, engineering	*47.0*	*26.9*	*8.7*	*15.8*	*1.6*

Source: Uganda Government: *Survey 1963.*

2. Wages

Table 10 gives important data on labour costs in Uganda's industry. The share of labour costs in the total costs (column 2)[20] reveals relationships which were already observed in the discussion of the VA/GO quotient. Mining and quarrying, as primary production activities, have the highest labour costs in the whole of industry. Also the sawmilling industry and the glass and cement industry, which win their own raw materials for processing, have high wage shares. On the other hand, wages play only a subordinate role in the sector "Processing of Agricultural Products" and in the oil mill and soap industry.

The fact that the wage share depends above all on a sector's capital intensity, on the production depth and also on the value of the raw materials to be

20 Hereafter called "wage share".

Table 10. *Labour Costs in Uganda's Industry in 1964*

Industry	Wages and salaries (incl. payments in kind)	Share of total costs	Gross hourly wage	Gross annual wage per employee
	1,000 Shs	%	Shs	Shs
Processing of agricultural products	29,168	*4.0*	.	1,950
thereof				
Cotton ginning	14,607	*5.1*	.	1,667
Tea industry	3,589	*8.0*	1.07	2,558
Mining and quarrying	25,147	*56.2*	1.58	3,674
Manufacturing	87,950	*15.0*	1.92	4,363
thereof				
Sugar and tobacco industry	17,630	*13.6*	2.80	6,065
Beverage industry	5,978	*20.4*	2.72	6,613
Textile and garments industry	15,665	*24.5*	2.14	5,018
Sawmilling and plywood industry	5,503	*30.5*	0.96	2,076
Printing industry	5,610	*32.7*	2.75	5,778
Oil and fats industry	3,313	*4.4*	1.13	2,810
Soap industry	1,013	*4.6*	1.21	2,911
Metals industry and engineering	8,475	*9.6*	2.07	4,748
Glass and cement industry	4,751	*27.4*	1.68	3,935

Source: Uganda Government: *Survey 1964.*

processed becomes clear when a comparison is made with the mean wage rates and the wage shares. Despite above-average wage rates in the sugar and tobacco industry and in the metals industry, the wage share of these branches of industry lie below the mean for the manufacturing industry. On the other hand the sawmilling industry pays on average the lowest wages in Uganda, but its wage share lies far above the average of the manufacturing industry. The wage share demonstrates clearly the sensitivity of various sectors to wage-policy measures. Since the attainment of independence, wages in many African countries, and also in Uganda, have risen sharply. Labour-intensive sectors such as the printing industry, the sawmills, the cement industry, to say nothing of mining, are greatly affected by this development.

The wage rates shown in Table 10 are the mean of a wage scale with very broad limits. The differential between the lower, middle and upper salary groups, which to a large extent is synonymous with the differential between African, Asian and European employees, is considerably greater in Africa than under European conditions. As table 11 shows, the average wages of African employees have risen substantially faster in recent years than those of Asian and European employees. Nevertheless, in 1965 an Asian employee earned almost six times as much, and an European even eighteen times as much as an African employee. These figures apply to the entire private sector. As industrial wages are usually at the top of the wage scale for African

Table 11. *Average Wages of Male Employees in the Private Sector* [a] *by Population Groups*
(Shs per year)

Year	Europeans [b]	Asians	Africans
1962	34,960	11,240	.
1963	37,160	11,340	1,720
1964	37,940	12,100	1,860
1965	39,580	12,680	2,240

[a] Agriculture, industry, commerce, and services.
[b] Without additional payments in kind such as free housing, free air passages, etc.
Source: Uganda Government: *Background,* p. 31.

employees, it can be assumed that the relations within industry are a little less crass.
The same limitation applies to table 12, from which it can be seen that in 1965 not even a quarter of all African wage-earners in the private sector earned more than 200 Shs per month or 2,400 Shs per year.

Table 12. *Distribution of Male African Wage Earners in the Private Sector* [a] *by Wage Groups*

Wage group (Shs per month)	1962 %	1963 %	1964 %	1965 %
Up to 99	*64*	*41*	*37*	*27*
100–199	*22*	*43*	*49*	*50*
200–499	*12*	*13*	*11*	*19*
500 and more	*2*	*3*	*3*	*4*
Total	*100*	*100*	*100*	*100*

[a] Agriculture, industry, commerce, and services.
Source: Uganda Government: *Background,* p. 33.

The salaries of the European and Asian executives, who cannot be dispensed with for some time to come, are no small burden on the payroll accounts of industry. However, these general remarks should not be taken as grounds to conclude that every European costs the enterprise fifteen to twenty times as much as an African. The wage and salary structure presented in table 11 expresses, though in an exaggerated form, the different situations of the various groups of persons in the industrial enterprise. As Africans are promoted to higher positions, their emoluments rise substantially. A realistic presentation of the wage and salary structure of the African personnel of modern, large industrial establishments is given in table 13. It shows that trained personnel earn 400 to 500 Shs, plant foremen and supervisors 900 to 1,400 Shs monthly.

These labour costs are undoubtedly considerably lower than in Europe, but measured by the productivity of African workers they must be ascribed a substantial weight. Therefore in Uganda, too, ever more labour-saving rationalization investments are being made, not the least of the reasons being the expansive trade union and government wage policy. As a rule new establishments are equipped with machines incorporating the latest engineering advances. In this respect, therefore, we are again confronted with the frequently discussed question of whether the consequent negative effects on the demand for labour is consistent with the country's overall economic situation. It is worth considering whether a less aggressive wage policy combined with measures to influence the import of machines and equipment might be employed to bring about a factor combination in industrial production which, by greater utilization of the factor labour, is more in line with the development status of a country like Uganda.

Table 13. *Wage Structure of African Personnel in Selected Industrial Establishments in Uganda in 1964*

Wage group (Shs per month)	Employees per wage group expressed as a percentage of the total labour force (excl. European and Asian executives)		
	Establishment A	Establishment B	Establishment C
Up to 150	*3*	*0*	*0*
150–199	*25*	*52*	*0*
200–299	*20*	*22*	*29*
300–399	*19*	*12*	*26*
400–499	*26*	*5*	*12*
500–999	*4*	*6*	*27*
1,000 and over	*3*	*3*	*6*

Source: East African Institute of Social Research: Economic Development Research Project, Papers No. 69, 73 and 75. Kampala 1965.

V. Sectoral Structure

A general survey of the most important data for Uganda's industry is given in table 14. The object of the presentation in the following section is to provide indications of important magnitudes and indicators for selected industries. As can be seen from table 14, more than two-thirds of the value added of the manufacturing industry is concentrated in four branches of industry: the sugar, tobacco, textiles, and metals industries. Hence less than ten large establishments determine to a high degree the statistical picture of Uganda's industry. All these sectors have in common that they attain a high VA/GO quotient, i.e., a high share of value added in the gross output.

Neglecting the profit situation of the individual sectors and enterprises, the VA/GO quotient is an expression of the production depth of the various branches of industry. This connection becomes clearly evident on comparing the VA/GO quotients for Mining and Quarrying, and Processing of Agricultural Products. The mining industry produces raw materials, buys only few inputs from other sectors of the economy and as a result, attains a high

Table 14. *Turnover, Value Added, and VA/GO Quotient in Selected Industries in 1964*

Industry	Turnover		Value added		VA/GO Quotient [a]	Turnover per employee	Value added per employee
	Mill. Shs	%	Mill. Shs	%		Shs	Shs
Processing of Agricultural Products	768.7	.	78.2	.	0.10	51,390	5,230
Mining and Quarrying	57.5	.	35.0	.	0.63	8,410	5,110
Manufacturing	768.3	*100*	263.3	*100*	0.35	38,120	13,060
thereof							
Sugar and tobacco industry	188.9	*24*	77.1	*29*	0.41	64,980	26,520
Beverage industry	38.4	*5*	14.9	*6*	0.39	42,520	16,450
Textile and garments industry	86.7	*11*	37.7	*14*	0.44	27,760	12,080
Sawmilling and plywood industry	21.7	*3*	9.1	*3*	0.42	8,170	3,420
Oil mills	82.1	*11*	6.6	*3*	0.08	69,600	5,630
Soap industry	22.7	*3*	1.3	*0.5*	0.06	65,330	3,630
Glass and cement industry	29.9	*4*	15.5	*6*	0.55	25,280	13,070
Metals industry and engineering	146.9	*19*	62.2	*24*	0.45	82,290	36,530
Printing industry	19.1	*2*	7.7	*3*	0.40	19,720	7,970

[a] VA/GO quotient $= \frac{\text{Value added}}{\text{Gross output}}$

Source: Uganda Government: *Survey 1964.*

added value in comparison with the gross output. The situation is entirely different, for instance, in the case of the coffee processing establishments and the cotton ginning plants. They buy the raw materials from agriculture and subject them to brief processing, which especially in the case of cotton ginning is highly mechanized. Accordingly, the VA/GO quotient of the sector "Processing of Agricultural Products" is only 0.10 as against 0.63 for the sector "Mining and Quarrying".

Corresponding relations, though with the opposite sign, are found in the case of the indicator "Turnover per employee". In the sector "Processing of Agricultural Products" it is about six times as high as in the mining industry.

Apart from the sector-specific factors of the production depth, of course, the capital intensity of the production methods and the combination of the factors of production capital and labour also have an effect on turnover and value added per employee. Since no data are available on the capital intensity and capital-output ratio of Uganda's industry, the indicator "value added per employee" is not conclusive. For instance, the above-average figures for the sugar and tobacco industry, the beverage industry and the metals industry permit the conclusion that they have a relatively high capital intensity, but also a relatively favourable position as regards earnings.
The figures for the oil mills and soap industry show a striking deviation from the mean. In both sectors an above-average turnover per employee is coupled with an extraordinarily low value added per employee. The VA/GO quotient is correspondingly low and, in fact, lies below that for the sector "Processing of Agricultural Products". This relation is probably not due solely to technological factors, but also to the competitive situation in these sectors. The oil milling and soap factories are relatively old industries in Uganda. The production installations have in many cases not kept pace with modern technological development. In both sectors a large number of enterprises compete with each other. The profits, a substantial component of the value added, are correspondingly low. Finally, as was shown in the previous section, wages in both sectors lie considerably below the average for the manufacturing industry.
Similar relationships are also responsible for the low value added per employee in the sawmilling and plywood industry. The fact that this sector nevertheless attains a high VA/GO quotient is attributable to the timber being felled by the sawmill enterprises themselves. Hence, as in the case of mining, the sawmills are in part primary production units which are listed together with the sawmilling and plywood industry for statistical purposes.
The highest turnover per employee in 1964 was achieved by the metals industry. This result is very much influenced by the copper smelter at Jinja. The high world market prices for copper ensured this enterprise extraordinary good earnings in recent years.

VI. Destination of Sales

As shown by table 15, in 1964 almost half of the total output of Uganda's manufacturing industry was sold abroad. This result is decisively influenced by a few enterprises in a small number of sectors. More than 70 per cent of the total exports came from five enterprises, i.e. two sugar factories, a cigarette and tobacco factory, a textile factory, and a copper smelter. However, blister copper with export earnings in 1964 that made up over a third of total exports, can hardly be classified as a product of the manufacturing industry in the true economic sense of the word. Like coffee and cotton, it is the product of a primary production activity, which is merely converted into an exportable state. Finally the oil and fats industry is very export-intensive; in 1964 it exported nearly two-thirds of its total output, mainly in the form of oil cake, an important livestock feed.

For African conditions the integration of the three countries Kenya, Tanzania and Uganda is fairly advanced. One fifth of the volume of the three countrys' foreign trade in 1964 was transacted within the common market. Kenya managed to secure the lion's share of this East African trade. In 1964 it accounted for almost two-thirds of aggregate deliveries, but only for a good quarter of the aggregate purchases. But also for Uganda's industry, Kenya and Tanzania have become important markets. The sugar and tobacco industry, the oil and fats industry, the textile industry, and the soap industry sell large proportions of their output to the two neighbouring countries. The latest agreement reached by the three governments under the Treaty for East

Table 15. *Destination of Sales of the Manufacturing Industry in 1964*

Industry	Uganda	Kenya	Tanzania	Other African Countries	Rest of the world	Total	Exports as % of total sales
	in 1,000 Shs						
Meat and fish industry	5,296	2,058	1,174	1,200	329	10,057	*47*
Grain milling	28,041	–	86	–	574	28,701	*2*
Sugar and tobacco industry	110,522	64,268	11,783	62	2,260	188,894	*41*
Beverage industry	36,575	606	1,242	–	16	38,438	*5*
Textile and garments industry	41,419	25,903	19,329	–	–	86,651	*52*
Sawmilling and plywood industry	16,920	994	7	2,634	1,098	21,654	*22*
Printing industry	18,010	805	18	28	288	19,149	*6*
Oil and fats industry	31,099	29,294	2,544	189	18,930	82,056	*62*
Soap industry	15,862	4,327	2,547	–	–	22,736	*30*
Glass and cement industry	25,311	1,412	2,075	1,081	–	29,879	*15*
Metals industry & engineering	21,984	5,957	2,712	132	116,106	146,889	*85*
Miscellaneous industries	79,919	6,819	3,966	–	2,535	93,239	*14*
Total	430,958	142,443	47,483	5,326	142,136	768,342	*44*
Share in %	*56*	*19*	*6*	*1*	*18*	*100*	.
Comparative figures, 1963 (Share in %)	*60*	*19*	*6*	*1*	*14*	*100*	.

Source: Uganda Government: *Survey 1964.*

African Co-operation with a view to preserving and expanding the common market, though in a greatly modified form, are therefore of vital importance for several large sectors of Uganda's industry.
Uganda's strong ties to the East African common market, the traditions of a common colonial past and political difficulties in the neighbouring countries to the east and north, have hitherto induced Uganda's industry to refrain from opening up extensive markets for its products in the southern Sudan, the eastern Congo and in Rwanda and Burundi. Yet the geographical conditions are not unfavourable; since the construction of the railway lines to northern and western Uganda and the improvement of the highways to Rwanda, the neighbouring countries can be supplied from Uganda's industry without any difficulty. In 1964, mainly the following products were supplied to the neighbouring countries in the north and west: fresh and frozen meat, plywood cases for the export of tea, and cement. Especially the eastern provinces of the Congo should provide worthwhile potential outlets for many other products of Uganda's industry. However, the marked encapsulation of the individual economic regions, which can be observed everywhere in Africa, cannot be overcome overnight.

VII. Patterns of Industrial Development

Hirschman and other authors[21] have inquired into the interdependence of the various branches of industry and developed the concept of "backward and forward linkages" to describe typical patterns of industrial development. Linkages occur when the activities of a production firm induce the establishment of new undertakings for the commercial exploitation of its outputs or for the local production of its inputs. In addition to the scope of the possible linkages, in investigating the linkage-inducing value of new industrial establishments the main issue is the stringency of such linkages, i.e., the probability with which a new industrial plant will result in the foundation of further establishments on the input and output sides.
Intensive interindustrial input and output relations are the hallmark of a developed industrial economy. The complicated production methods of modern industry and the increasing differentiation of demand result in the splitting up of the industrial production process into a growing number of

21 A. O. Hirschman: *The Strategy of Economic Development.* New Haven, Yale University Press, 1960; H. B. Chenery and T. Watanabe: International Comparisons of the Structure of Production, in: *Econometrica,* Vol. 26 (1958), p. 487 et seq.; G. B. Baldwin: Industrialization. A Standard Pattern, in: *Finance and Development,* Vol. III (1966), No. 4, p. 274 et seq.

separate production stages. The figures for the West German industry clearly demonstrate this pattern. Less than a third of the industrial gross output sold on the home market in 1961 comprised consumer durables and consumer goods, more than two thirds were supplied in the form of industrial intermediate products and capital goods to the productive sectors of the economy, primarily to industry.

In Uganda, on the other hand, there is a marked deviation in these relations: in 1963 more than half of the industrial output sold on the home market went to the consumption sector; only 44 per cent was passed on for further industry, the sawmilling and plywood industry, the textile industry, and the manufacturing field, there is a clear predominance of those branches of industry which produce for the ultimate consumer: the branches of the food industry, the sugar, tobacco and beverage industries, the textile and garments industry, and the soap industry. Capital goods are manufactured only to a very small extent.

Intermediate products are made by the glass and cement industry, the metals industry, the sawmilling and plywood industry, the textile industry and the oil mills. A large, though not accurately determinable proportion of the gross output of the motor vehicle repair establishments likewise goes into industry, mainly the transport industry. The great majority of intermediate products, however, come from the cotton ginning and mining industries. The local textile industry and the oil mills take practically all domestic sales of the cotton ginneries; the copper ore is transformed in the copper smelter to blister copper. Finally, only about a third of the electricity output goes to private households and other ultimate consumers; two thirds go to trade and industry.

The manner and direction in which manufacturing processes were gradually built up in Uganda's industry can be demonstrated by a series of cases. The cotton industry, in the broadest sense of the word, belongs to the sectors of the economy that are acknowledged to have a high linkage-inducing potential. Considering the flow of goods the chain of linkages extends from cotton growing via the cotton ginneries to the textile industry and the oil mills. However, the decisive linkage inducing effect emanated not from cotton ginning, as the first industrial process in the chain, but from cotton growing. It is practically impossible to export unginned cotton from an inland country like Uganda. In other words: the setting up of cotton ginneries is not a decision "induced" by cotton growing. The decision to grow cotton must coincide with the decision to set up ginneries. However, the setting up of further processing stages is not a matter of course.

In Uganda at the present time[22], two fully integrated cotton spinning and weaving mills with ancillary textile finishing departments are in operation.

22 Cf. in this connection H. Helmschrott: *Struktur und Wachstum der Textil- und Bekleidungsindustrie in Ostafrika.* München, Weltforum-Verlag, 1969.

Table 16. *Breakdown of Domestic Sales of Uganda's Industry by Type of Utilization in 1963*
(in 1,000 Shs)

Industry	Type of utilization: Intermediate demand (semi-finished and intermediate industrial products)	Type of utilization: Final consumption (durable and non-durable consumer goods)	Total domestic sales
Processing of Agricultural Products	72,000[a]	–	72,000
thereof			
Cotton ginning	72,000	–	72,000
Mining and Quarrying	42,000	–	42,000
Manufacturing	92,156	288,714	380,870
thereof			
Meat and fish industry	–	6,265	6,265
Grain milling	–	21,795	21,795
Bakery products & confectionery	–	12,033	12,033
Misc. food industries	–	11,626	11,626
Sugar & tobacco industry	3,520	85,334	88,854
Beverage industry	–	33,551	33,551
Textile, footwear, and garments	8,000[a]	38,446	46,446
Sawmilling and plywood	12,742	148	12,890
Misc. wood products	916	1,043	1,959
Furniture industry	1,000	4,150	5,150
Printing industry	4,000[a]	12,777	16,777
Rubber industry	2,000[a]	4,195	6,195
Chemical industry	3,264	–	3,264
Oil and fats industry	8,100	22,229	30,329
Soap industry	14	15,046	15,060
Structural clay products	2,490	–	2,490
Glass and cement industry	18,039	150	18,189
Metal industry and engineering	14,081	6,520	20,601
Motor vehicle repairs	13,990[a]	13,000	26,990
Motor-cycle and bicycle industry	–	406	406
Electricity generation	30,040	16,062	46,102
Total industry (excl. building industry)	236,196	304,776	540,972
Share in %	*44*	*56*	*100*
In comparison: Industry of German Federal Republic 1961 (%)	*69*	*31*	*100*

[a] Estimated and calculated by author on the basis of direct investigations. The intermediate demand could not be determined in full in every case. For instance, a small proportion of the tea and coffee output is consumed domestically.

Sources: Uganda Government: *Survey 1963;* IFO-Institut für Wirtschaftsforschung: *Input-Output Tables for the West German Economy with provisional results for 1961.* München 1964, Table X.0.

The cotton fabric is worked into garments predominantly in small trades establishments and private households. The garments industry in Uganda, which is still at the beginning of its development, uses chiefly imported semi-finished goods, fine cotton poplins and synthetic fibre products. The existence of a shirt factory, which originally worked solely with imported fine fabrics, induced the local cotton weaving mills also to include fine fabrics in their production programme. In this way the forward linkage "cotton ginning — spinning mill — weaving mill — textile finishing" was supplemented by the backward linkage "shirt factory — fine fabric manufacture".
Cotton ginning likewise served as the point of departure for the development of a notable oil and fats industry in Uganda. This is another clear case of forward linkage. The oil and fats industry then provided the impetus for the establishment of a factory for small cans and for the local production of caustic soda. This chain does not include the soap industry, which operates mainly on the basis of imported oils and fats.
The extent to which potential backward linkages actually result in the setting up of establishments at preceding production stages depends essentially on whether, with a given technological and economic minimum capacity of the production installations, the local production costs for the planned output are lower than the prices of competitive imported goods. For instance, in Uganda there has been for some time a cement factory which imported substantial quantities of paper sacks, and an important sugar industry. But not until 1966 was it possible to realize plans for setting up a paper sack factory, the chief reason being that until then there was not an adequate market to permit utilization of the minimum capacity of a paper sack factory. Hirschman[23] calls such production plants satellite industries, because the product they manufacture is purchased only by one or a few industries. In the case of backward linkage — according to Hirschman — it is often a characteristic feature of a satellite industry that its minimum capacity lies above the demand of the principal industry. A typical example of forward linkage emanating from the cement industry is found in Uganda in the form of numerous small production plants for the manufacture of prefabricated cement elements and a plant of the asbestos cement industry.
Marked linkage effects are also attributed to the iron and steel industry. With the setting up of a small electric steel plant which uses mainly scrap as raw material, Uganda has made a modest start in this field. The main product is reinforcing steel for the building industry, but the production programme is to be expanded considerably during the current Five-Year Plan. Existing factories for the manufacture of steel door and window frames and of simple agricultural implements are to be supplied with semi-finished products of the required dimensions and qualities; a wire-drawing plant is intended to provide the basic material for a nail factory which is

23 Hirschman: *op. cit.*, p. 96.

already in operation; finally, band steel is to be produced for packing raw cotton.

As a final example of backward linkage, mention should be made of the plywood industry in Uganda. In this case the decisive impetus came from the great increase in tea output in East Africa. Prefabricated tea chests which only need to be assembled by the tea factories are the chief item in the production programme of the plywood factory.

Hence the linkage theory makes an interesting contribution to the understanding of the latest industrial development in Uganda, although no attempt has been made here to quantify the effects. Even though the degree of industrial interdependence is still much lower than in an industrial country, especially in very recent times the foundation of numerous new industrial undertakings has been induced by already established enterprises. So in Uganda, the linkage-inducing mechanisms which HIRSCHMAN considers so important for the economic progress of less developed countries are already discernible, although only to a modest extent.

D. INDUSTRIALIZATION IN THE EAST AFRICAN COMMON MARKET

Up to the end of the colonial epoch, East Africa was a largely integrated common market. Especially the industrial sector of the three countries was oriented to a great extent to the East African area as a market and source of supplies. Kenya's industry has drawn the greatest benefit from this development, but in 1964 about a quarter of Uganda's industrial output also went to the two neighbouring countries.

The common market of colonial days was liberal in character. There were no concepts and instruments for the implementation of an industrial policy aiming at a balanced regional development. Therefore economic co-operation in East Africa was necessarily confronted with difficulties when three sovereign states replaced the economic unit "East Africa". The visible sign of this disintegrating movement was the dissolution of the East African currency union and the introduction of three independent currencies in Kenya, Uganda and Tanzania.

There has been no lack of attempts in past years to develop an East African concept of industrial development. Great hopes were placed in the "Kampala Agreement" concluded by the three governments in 1964. The nucleus of this agreement was the allocation of exclusive production rights for certain products among the three countries. In the light of her substantial lead in industrial development, Kenya was prepared to concede her two partners an above-average share in the industries that were to be newly established. In addition to these agreements affecting location policy, the three governments resolved, under certain conditions, to permit quantitative restrictions on trade in locally produced industrial products within East Africa.

The Kampala Agreement never came into force, not the least of the reasons being that no agreement was reached among the three governments in many other spheres of economic policy, and that an overall conception of economic co-operation in East Africa was practically non-existent. The parties came to the conviction that interstate relations ought to be regulated anew in their entirety by a comprehensive treaty. After about two years preparation, based on the recommendations of the "Philips Commission" and including several ideas taken over from the Kampala Agreement, this treaty was signed by the three heads of government in Kampala on June 6, 1967. It bears the title "Treaty for East African Co-operation"[24]. The points of the treaty that are relevant for this study are as follows:

- The idea of allocating individual countries exclusive production rights in the industrial sphere was dropped. The old licensing system under which the production of certain goods can be taken up only with a license from the East African Industrial Council will be limited to the small number of branches of industry hitherto subject to these licensing requirements, and will expire in the mid-seventies. However, a new and essentially similar law valid for the Common Market is to replace the varying statutory regulations of the three countries.
- The principle of duty-free trade in East Africa has been retained. This principle, however, is perceptibly restricted by the introduction of a transfer tax on industrial products. Under this arrangement, a member country which has a trade deficit vis-a-vis any other member country in the field of industrial production, may levy a transfer tax on transactions with that other member country. The volume of trade on which the tax is imposed must not exceed the trading deficit. The tax can be levied only if products of the same nature are manufactured in the deficit country, or if their manufacture can be anticipated within a period of three months. The transfer tax may not exceed 50 per cent of the applicable external tariff rate for the product concerned.
- Finally, it was resolved to establish an East African Development Bank as an important instrument for the promotion of industrial development in the Partner States and in the Community as a whole. Under its charter (Art. 1), among other things the object of the Bank is[25]:

24 East African Common Services Organization: *Treaty for East African Co-operation.* Nairobi, Government Printer, 1967.

25 D. Rothschild (ed.): *Politics of Integration. An East African Documentary.* Nairobi, East African Publishing House, 1968, p. 330.

Table 17. *Uganda's Industry in 1964*

Industry	Establishments Number	Employees on 31. 12. 64 Number	Turnover 1,000 Shs	Value added 1,000 Shs	VA/GO Quotient [a]	Turnover per employee Shs	Value added per employee Shs	Wages and salaries [b] 1,000 Shs
A. *Processing of Agricultural Products*	282	18,672	768,719	78,237	0.10	51,388	5,230	29,168
Cotton ginning	133	12,296	311,000	36,753	0.12	35,494	4,195	14,607
Coffee processing	120	4,888	408,380	30,394	0.07	85,186	6,340	10,972
Tea processing	29	1,488	49,339	11,090	0.21	35,167	7,904	3,589
B. *Mining and Quarrying*	117	6,971	57,528	34,964	0.63	8,406	5,109	25,147
Metal mining	110	6,526	54,970	33,865	0.64	8,557	5,272	24,388
Stone quarrying	7	445	2,558	1,099	0.43	6,090	2,617	759
C. *Manufacturing*	322	20,838	768,342	263,251	0.35	38,118	13,060	87,950
Meat and fish industry	3	299	10,057	868	0.09	35,790	3,089	1,166
Grain milling	14	391	28,701	2,091	0.07	88,858	6,474	938
Bakery products and confectionery	14	696	18,692	3,575	0.19	27,208	5,204	2,323
Miscellaneous food preparations	7	208	13,292	1,258	0.09	66,129	6,259	523
Sugar and tobacco industry	21	2,947	188,894	77,089	0.41	64,979	26,518	17,630
Beverage industry	8	879	38,438	14,866	0.39	42,520	16,445	5,978
Textile and garments	21	3,191	86,651	37,705	0.44	27,755	12,077	15,665
Cordage, rope and twine	3	286	4,285	1,289	0.28	17,707	5,326	535
Footwear	5	142	1,865	346	0.18	15,542	2,883	400
Sawmilling and plywood	25	2,691	21,654	9,074	0.42	8,168	3,423	5,503
Miscellaneous wood products	7	129	2,659	906	0.35	20,298	6,916	469
Furniture	24	703	6,136	1,997	0.33	10,227	3,328	1,735

Table 17, continued

Industry	Establish-ments Number	Employees on 31. 12. 64 Number	Turnover 1,000 Shs	Value added 1,000 Shs	VA/GO Quotient [a]	Turnover per employee Shs	Value added per employee Shs	Wages and salaries [b] 1,000 Shs
Printing and publishing	25	1,013	19,149	7,740	0.40	19,721	7,971	5,610
Rubber products	7	189	6,677	2,122	0.31	36,288	11,533	1,158
Chemical industry	6	421	7,074	1,618	0.24	17,467	3,995	1,595
Oil and fats industry	16	1,121	82,056	6,637	0.08	69,598	5,629	3,313
Soap Industry	6	377	22,736	1,264	0.06	65,333	3,632	1,013
Structural clay products	5	452	3,459	2,005	0.60	8,779	5,089	1,064
Glass, cement und concrete products	14	1,224	29,879	15,452	0.55	25,278	13,073	4,751
Metal industries and engineering	30	1,895	146,889	65,208	0.45	82,291	36,531	8,475
Electrical machinery	3	62	841	557	0.66	15,868	10,509	236
Motor vehicle repairs	55	1,493	27,859	9,463	0.35	18,773	6,377	7,829
Motor cycles and bicycles	3	29	399	120	0.30	19,950	6,000	41
D. *Electricity Generation and Distribution*	1	1,621	58,779	52,606	0.89	37,273	33,358	5,700
E. *Building and Construction*	72	8,941	99,371	30,586	0.31	13,310	4,097	21,409
Total Industry [c]	794	57,043	1,653,368	459,644	0.26	32,417	9,012	169,374

[a] Value added: Gross output.
[b] Including social expenditures and payments in kind.
[c] Differences in totals are due to rounding off.

Source: Uganda Government: *Survey 1964.*

"• to provide financial and technical assistance to promote the industrial development of the Partner States;
• to give priority, in accordance with the operating principles contained in this Charter, to industrial development in the relatively less industrially developed Partner States, thereby endeavouring to reduce the substantial imbalances between them;
• to further the aims of the East African Community by financing, wherever possible, projects designed to make the economies of the Partner States increasingly complementary in the industrial field."

Under its charter (Art. 13) the bank will place $38^3/_4$ per cent of its loans, etc. in each of Uganda and Tanzania and $22^1/_3$ per cent in Kenya.
These brief indications of the industrial policy aspects of the new treaty on East African co-operation will suffice for our present purposes. Under the terms of the treaty Uganda, and naturally also Tanzania, will enjoy more favourable conditions than previously for the further development of her industry within the East African framework. In the forseeable future she need have no fear of burdens impairing her exports to Kenya, but is herself nevertheless in a position to give new branches of industry a certain degree of customs protection in the form of the transfer tax. Furthermore, she will enjoy substantial benefits deriving from the capital to be mobilized with the help of the Development Bank.
The Treaty came into force in December 1967. At the present time it is impossible to say what effects it will have on Uganda's industrial development. Much will depend on the good will of the governments to co-operate in a spirit of mutual trust especially in the sphere of industrial policy. The limited potential markets and the scarcity of investment capital make agreements particularly in this field urgently necessary. The industrial licensing system has yet to be worked out. The system employed hitherto operates without any location policy concept at East African level. Here a gap must be closed in order to ensure also for the less favourable locations in the common market — and this of special importance for Uganda — an appropriate share in industrial development.

Bibliography

BALDWIN, G. B.: Industrialization: A Standard Pattern, in: *Finance and Development*, Vol. III (1966), No. 4, p. 274 et seq.

CHENERY, H. B. and WATANABE, T.: International Comparisons of the Structure of Production, in: *Econometrica*, Vol. 26 (1958), p. 487 et seq.

Columbia University School of Law: *International Development Financing in East Africa.* New York 1962.

East African Common Services Organization (Edit.): *Treaty for East African Co-operation.* Nairobi, Government Printer, 1967.

East African Institute of Social Research: Economic Development Research Project Papers No. 69, 73, 75, 88, 89, and 100. Kampala 1965 and 1966 respectively.

East African Railways and Harbours: *Annual Report 1964.* Nairobi 1965.

HELMSCHROTT, H.: *Struktur und Wachstum der Textil- und Bekleidungsindustrie in Ostafrika.* München, Weltforum-Verlags-GmbH., 1969.

HIRSCHMAN, A. O.: *The Strategy of Economic Development.* New Haven, Yale University Press, 1960.

International Bank for Reconstruction and Development: *The Economic Development of Uganda.* Baltimore, The Johns Hopkins Press, 1962.

NIXON, F. I. and STOUTJESDIJK, A. J.: Industrial Development in the Kenya and Uganda Development Plans, in: *East African Economic Review,* Vol. II (1967), No. 2, pp. 65–78.

OURSIN, Th.: *Uganda als Wirtschaftspartner.* Köln, Bundesstelle für Außenhandelsinformation, 1965.

ROTHERMUND, I.: *Die politische und wirtschaftliche Rolle der asiatischen Minderheiten in Ostafrika.* Berlin – Heidelberg – New York, Springer-Verlag, 1965.

SCHNITTGER, L.: *Besteuerung und wirtschaftliche Entwicklung in Ostafrika.* Berlin – Heidelberg – New York, Springer-Verlag, 1966.

Uganda Development Corporation: *Annual Reports.* Kampala.

UGANDA Government: *Work for Progress. Uganda's Second Five-Year Plan, 1966–1971.* Entebbe, Government Printer, 1966.

UGANDA Government, Department of Lands and Surveys: *Atlas of Uganda.* Entebbe 1962.

UGANDA Government, Statistics Division of the Ministry of Finance: *Background to the Budget 1966–67.* Entebbe, Government Printer, 1966.

UGANDA Government, Statistics Division of the Ministry of Planning and Community Development: *1965 Statistical Abstract,* Entebbe, Government Printer, 1965.

—: *Survey of Industrial Production 1963.* Entebbe 1965.

UGANDA Government, Statistics Division of the Ministry of Planning and Economic Development: *Survey of Industrial Production 1964.* Entebbe 1966.

—: *The Real Growth of the Economy of Uganda 1954–1962.* Entebbe 1964.

UGANDA Protectorate: *The Uganda Development Corporation Ordinance 1952 (No. 1 of 1952) as amended by the Uganda Development Corporation (Amendment) Ordin, 1955.* Entebbe, Government Printer, 1961.

WALKER, D.: Marketing Boards, in: *Problems of Economic Development,* edited by E. A. G. ROBINSON. London–New York, McMillan & Company Ltd. and St. Martin's Press Inc., 1965, pp. 574–598.

CRAFTS AND SMALL-SCALE INDUSTRIES IN TANZANIA

by

Karl SCHÄDLER

Contents

List of Tables

The following contribution by Karl SCHÄDLER is mainly based on an inquiry into the economic and social situation, as well as into the opportunities for development of crafts and small-scale industry, in Tanzania. The author undertook this inquiry with the support of the Fritz Thyssen Foundation, at Cologne. The work included addressing a questionnaire to firms in all the larger towns of Tanzania; it was carried out, with interruptions, between the autumn of 1965 and that of 1967. The questionnaire comprised altogether nineteen sets of questions about ownership, structure of capital assets and financial resources, employment situation and working hours, production and marketing, income and business situation, expansion plans, union membership of employees, and trade organization. It will be possible in the following article to set out only a few of the conclusions reached. The full study, entitled "Crafts, Small-scale Industries and Industrial Education in Tanzania", was published as No. 34 of the "Afrika-Studien".
K. SCHÄDLER has worked since 1962 at the Ifo Institute for Economic Research, at Munich, and since 1963 has been on the staff of its African Studies Centre. He has hitherto applied himself to various tasks in the field of industrial research; he also worked for the European Economic Community, at Brussels, on a preparatory study of communications in the Ivory Coast, and on the First Development Plan for Togo. He further prepared studies covering Guinea, Malawi, Tanzania and Zambia, and was commissioned by the International Labour Office (ILO) to produce studies of crafts in Peru and Chile.

A. THE ROLE OF CRAFTS AND SMALL-SCALE INDUSTRIES IN THE ECONOMIC DEVELOPMENT OF TANZANIA[1]

Introduction

There is no single term embracing both kinds of economic activity — crafts and small-scale industries. Crafts are tentatively defined here as manufacturing and technical servicing (installation, maintenance and repair) executed by craftsmen, working alone or with employed craftsmen, helpers or apprentices and without extensive division of labour. Considerable skill but little, if any, specialization is needed in the performance of labour and management functions, and articles are mainly produced one at a time, with individual variations, often to the requirements of a particular customer.
Small-scale industries on the other hand denote certain types of small processing and manufacturing enterprises — activities in the production sector of an economy which differ from each other only slightly in magnitude, applied techniques, scale of operation, nature of entrepreneurship, social organization or localization. As opposed to crafts, however, manufactured articles produced and services rendered by small-scale industries do not demand special skills from the labour force involved. Command of a limited scale of manipulations suffices to operate the enterprise. In various social respects small-scale industries are closely related to "crafts", but in technical respects they are nearer to large-scale industries. While crafts are largely oriented towards the local market, it often happens that small-scale industries work for a larger market, inside or outside the country. Certain criteria, however, are considered to be implicitly common to both crafts and small-scale industries. Among these are:

- a closer, personal or face-to-face relationship between the owner/manager and the operating personnel;
- lack of capital;
- relatively little specialization in management;
- smallness; the "economic compass" of industrial establishments in the same industry and in the same country.

---

1 This only refers to the mainland of Tanzania.

Since there is no general agreement as to the best way of defining crafts and small-scale industries, statistical, administrative, and analytical definitions applied have to conform to the immediate purpose of the study undertaken. Among the statistical definitions most commonly employed, namely the number of employees, the amount of capital invested, the use of machinery, the amount of horsepower installed or the value added by manufacture as size classification criteria, the first criterion seemed to be the most adequate for use in the survey. As to the dividing line between crafts and small-scale industries, on the one hand, and large-scale industries on the other, where the scale chosen varies considerably, the number of 100 employees was taken as the dividing line. The same figure was likewise employed in recent studies of the International Labour Organization (ILO) and of the Economic Commission for Africa (ECA).

I. Arguments for and against Promotion

In discussions about the role which crafts and small-scale industries may play in the process of economic development certain arguments of an economic, social and political nature are brought forward for and against measures of promotion.

Arguments in Favour of Promotion

Among the economic arguments in favour of promotion of crafts and small-scale industries it is often stated that the returns from heavily capitalized industries, on account of their more complicated organization and longer development period, are generally much more slowly realized than those of crafts and small-scale industries, and the likelihood of quick returns is obviously an important consideration in determining the order of priority in countries where the rate of capital formation is low. Another argument usually makes the assumption that production in small firms is more labour-intensive (in terms of the capital-labour ratio) and that the economies in developing countries are characterized by a structural disequilibrium at the factor level, involving scarce capital and redundant labour. Here, favouring small enterprises rather than large would help to correct this disequilibrium, because more workers could be employed with a given amount of capital. Further it is stated that an important role of crafts and small-scale industries is that of ancillary suppliers to large industries, and that often large units are only able to operate economically because of the services and supplies

which they receive from the small-scale business sector[2]. Some further points are: small enterprises have special adaptability to varying production and market conditions, elasticity in technical and economic organization; they provide ideal training grounds for entrepreneurship and management, and finally mobilise hidden or idle financial resources.
Apart from these economic reasons, which favour crafts and small-scale industries, these are said to confer a number of social advantages. Here, the main argument — assuming that crafts and small-scale units are widely dispersed in the country and need no concentration — is the adverse effect of large-scale industries in big towns, and their attendant evils. Moreover, it is argued, the spread of crafts and small-scale industries in town and country will assist the whole population to grow accustomed to conditions of life in a more industrialized community, without causing any sudden break with their traditions or previous way of life.
Among the political arguments in favour of promotion one fact stressed is that the establishment of large industries in the capital city, and perhaps in one or two other urban centers, must aggravate, in the popular conception, the differences in status between the rural areas and the large towns; an even distribution of small enterprise nuclei throughout the country may show the population that the Government's concern is for the welfare of all, and is not merely confined to urban dwellers. In countries with non-indigenous but economically dominant minorities the case for promotion of crafts and small-scale industries also poses the problem in racial terms: only through small enterprises are indigenous entrepreneurs likely to emerge.

Arguments against Promotion

The labour-absorption argument is the principal object of criticism by economists, who feel that this approach is in fact a "better-distribution" argument[3]. Hence new components are introduced which make the labour-absorption argument subject to certain premises, or only when considered in another light. As to the capital-saving argument, one of the strongest arguments brought forward against it is that the effect is to reduce savings by increasing labour's share of income. But even a higher capital-output ratio may in the long run imply slower growth and higher unemployment because of the lower propensity to save, if it be supposed that under these circumstances the secular rate of capital formation lags behind the increase in the labour supply.
In evaluation of the contribution made by crafts and small-scale industries

2 In Tanzania only about 10% of the craftsmen supply other firms with their products; another 7% sell to the Government, and the rest supply individuals.
3 A. N. AGARWALA: *Some Aspects of Economic Advancement of Underdeveloped Economies.* Allahabad–Bombay–Delhi, Kitab Mahal, 1958, p. 33.

towards social development it is claimed that, on the average, workers in large-scale industries are better off than those in small enterprises, and are less "exploited". They usually receive better wages, have shorter working hours and better social security facilities. The arguments of "decentralisation" brought forward in favour of small enterprises (as opposed to the over-population effect caused by large-scale industrialization) is countered by the argument that most of these enterprises are settled in any case in urban centres, and that any generally applied promotion would produce only a negligible effect by way of halting the drift from the land to the towns.
Since crafts and small-scale industries constitute a high percentage of "self-employment" it is argued that, on the whole, there is probably less political stability in countries where this "self-employment" is prevalent than in those where the bulk of industry is organized in large-scale enterprises. In addition — and this refers to the "equality" argument — the total volume of savings and taxes which is generated by a large number of small incomes is almost inevitably smaller than the volume generated by an equal total income in the hands of a smaller number of people. Also, since small firms are generally not as technically progressive as large firms, the choice of greater present equality may hinder the rapid growth of the economy, and hence postpone the attainment of a higher standard of living for the whole population in the future.

II. Importance of Promotion in Tanzania

From these pros and cons quite different conclusions may be drawn as to the applicability of arguments in the case of Tanzania. It will probably not be possible to make a clear-cut decision in favour of either small- or large-scale industries based on both economic and social considerations, because it is difficult to assess the importance of economic and non-economic objectives as well as because of the dearth of factual information on which to base an economic analysis. The decision taken would depend, to a large extent, on the individual point of view of the observer.
Yet even if special efforts to assist the development of Tanzania's crafts and small-scale industry may be justified on economic or social grounds, these pale into insignificance when compared to the case for such promotion on political grounds. To a very considerable degree it is true that Tanzania's future industrial entrepreneurs can only emerge from the nuclei of small enterprises, be they workshops of craftsmen, or small-scale industries or retail and wholesale enterprises. Needless to say, this refers mainly to the African Tanzanian, since most established industrial ventures, particularly

the larger ones, are the result of overseas initiative, and even the smaller establishments are almost entirely owned by non-Africans. But a situation where the industrialist's functions are confined to the non-African population is quite untenable for political reasons, especially if the future economic development of Tanzania is to take place within the framework of the newly conceived policy of "self-reliance".

"Self-reliance" as understood here means self-knowledge, i.e. the ability to assess one's own situation objectively. Tanzania's economic situation is far from glittering, considering the country's great dependence on foreign assistance, not so much in monetary terms but in terms of manpower. This includes manpower in all skilled categories, not excluding craftsmen. Many artisans' positions in the larger industrial firms are still occupied by expatriates. The rest are held by Asian craftsmen, who can claim to represent a long tradition in Tanzania. These Asian craftsmen constitute the bulk of skilled craftsmen in Tanzania; only in recent years have they given way to some "Africanization", if one may apply the term in this context. But they have been the object of some misgiving concerning their attitude towards complete integration, although to a lesser extent than wholesalers and retailers.

There can be no doubt that large-scale industries also contribute a considerable share to Tanzania's economic development, and stressing the role of small-scale entrepreneurship is not intended to deny the importance of large enterprises. The point is that one of the most important means to create future African industrialists — who are at present non-existent in Tanzania — will be to foster the small entrepreneurs. Aside from small businessmen, the craftsmen must make up the core from which future Tanzanian industrialists can emerge, and to this end they must be trained and supported adequately. It certainly is true that "each and every major occupational group has contributed entrepreneurial talents and carriers of economic development", as REDLICH[4] has stated; and it seems natural that craftsmen, who often contribute an immense store of know-how and technical ingenuity, may also provide future industrialists in Tanzania — as they did, for example, in Nigeria[5].

---

4 F. REDLICH: Entrepreneurship in the Initial Stages of Industrialization, in: *Weltwirtschaftliches Archiv,* Vol. 75 (1955), p. 65.

5 Out of 300 firms, for instance, covered in a multi-industry survey in Nigeria, 68 per cent were established by former journeymen (P. KILBY: *African Enterprise: The Nigerian Bread Industry.* Stanford, Hoover Institution, 1965, p. 93, footnote 7). The first occupation held was craftsman as stated by 31 per cent of Nigerian sawmilling entrepreneurs; next come, 22.4 per cent who indicated clerical positions (J. R. HARRIS and M. P. ROWE: *Entrepreneurial Patterns in the Nigerian Sawmilling Industry.* N.I.S.E.R. Reprint Series No. 24. Ibadan, 1966, p. 85).

B. THE PRESENT SITUATION OF CRAFTS AND SMALL-SCALE INDUSTRIES

I. Main Structural Characteristics

There are roughly 100 entrepreneurs engaged in small-scale industries and 1,600 independent craftsmen (1966–1967) (see table 1)[6]. As to the structure of crafts and small-scale industries the main characteristics are:

- In terms of number of establishments, tailoring and woodworking represent the two most important trades, each trade representing about 300 establishments. Motor vehicle repair, and shoe making and repairing follow with about 200 establishments each. The remaining trades are inferior in number: 29 out of 35 activities covered in the survey represent less than one third of the total number of establishments. Such traditional crafts[7] as matweaving and pottery making, as well as such modern crafts as typewriter or air conditioner repair, are included in this group.
  Among the small-scale industries soap manufacturers (35), laundries (18), dry cleaning (16), and producers of chemical products (8) are already quite numerous. There are also firms producing pre-cast concrete articles, plastic goods, paints, fez caps and aluminium wares.
- Almost 85 per cent of all establishments are concentrated in the ten major townships of the country, and almost one third have settled in the capital. Dar es Salaam has also attracted the greatest variety of trades and about 40 per cent of small-scale industries. Here again, tailors and woodworkers

6 According to the survey the total number of independent craftsmen in Tanzania is 1,583, the number of small-scale industrial firms being 93. Since the craftsmen interviewed total 708, and the small industry entrepreneurs interviewed 24, the coverage ist 45 per cent and 25 per cent respectively, the overall coverage being 44 per cent.

7 In the following no particular distinction, however, is made between "traditional" and "modern" crafts unless special reference seems to be advisable. The term "traditional" crafts as opposed to "modern" crafts is understood to comprise all fields of craft activities typical of "African" Tanzania, i.e. crafts which are exercised usually by Africans and encountered throughout the country (not only in coastal areas where foreign influences were active) like weaving, blacksmithing, pottery, woodworking etc., and the techniques of which are learnt by tradition. Though the term relates to traditional techniques rather than to the crafts as such, it inherently engenders associations of backwardness and stability which are very often misleading; "traditional" crafts experienced a constant and dynamic evolution.
The term "modern" crafts is employed to denote crafts and craft techniques which were not typical of Tanzania, and were adapted only through influences from foreigners — though it is of course recognized that no exact border line can be drawn between "traditional" and "modern" crafts.

Table 1. *Number and Activities of Establishments in Tanzania in 1966–1967 by Major Townships*

Trade or Industry	Arusha	Bukoba	Dar es Salaam	Dodoma	Mbeya	Morogoro	Moshi	Mwanza	Tabora	Tanga	Other towns	Total
Crafts												
Agricultural plant repairers	1	–	1	1	–	1	–	1	8	2	9	24
Bakers	5	5	11	6	5	3	4	10	8	8	18	83
Barbers	4	9	37	5	3	10	9	9	11	–	9	106
Bicycle repairers	–	–	6	–	2	2	2	7	1	3	9	32
Butchers	–	–	14	4	2	3	4	–	–	–	4	31
Electricians	1	2	13	–	2	–	4	4	–	4	5	35
Shoemakers, cobblers	12	11	50	8	8	13	18	13	9	7	40	189
Gold and silversmiths	–	1	16	–	–	2	–	3	1	6	1	30
Letterpress printers	1	1	14	–	–	1	3	8	2	2	6	38
Motor mechanics	13	–	38	18	8	6	17	26	12	30	31	199
Photo technicians	–	–	6	–	4	2	3	5	–	2	5	27
Sheet metal workers, tinsmiths	2	–	25	1	–	2	8	2	2	–	4	46
Tailors	8	14	115	12	12	20	14	53	10	15	25	298
Watch repairers	–	9	5	5	10	7	1	–	–	6	16	59
Woodworkers, carpenters	16	6	82	17	11	8	20	30	24	26	65	305
Other crafts	5	7	39	1	9	–	2	1	–	1	12	77
Sub-total for Crafts	68	65	472	78	76	80	109	172	88	112	259	1,579
Small-scale Industries	4	–	38	4	4	2	7	8	2	9	15	93
Total	72	65	510	82	80	82	116	180	90	121	274	1,672

Source: Own survey.

constitute the most important trades with 115 and 82 establishments, followed at some distance by shoemakers (50), motor vehicle repairers (38) and barbers (37). Other towns in which a nucleus of small-scale industries exists are Tanga, Mwanza, and Moshi.

- With the exception of Mwanza, where non-Africans constitute two thirds of the craftsmen and entrepreneurs, in most of the major townships the number of Africans about equals that of non-Africans, who are mostly Asians[8]. However, there are considerable differences as to the trades preferred by the two groups: there are almost twice as many non-Africans engaged in motor vehicle repair enterprises as Africans, but less than half as many in sheet metal work. Other fields of African dominance are woodworking (172:106), watch repair (37:22), barber shops (71:33) and butchery (18:13). Non-Africans on the contrary prefer such trades as letterpress printing (35:2), baking (41:32) and goldsmithing (30:2).
- Workshops of independent craftsmen have on the average three employees, and small-scale industries ten[9]. Taking the estimated total number of craftsmen (1,600) into account, the extrapolated total of employees amounts to between 5,000 and 6,000. The average employment per firm varies of course considerably from trade to trade: among the top are motor mechanics (10), letterpress printers (10) and bakers (9), followed by electricians and goldsmiths, each trade employing 5 persons on the average. In all of these trades non-Africans — mostly Asians — predominate.

II. Social Status

Craftsmanship in Tanzania is identical to a great extent with Asian activities in this sector: though on a much smaller scale, Asian craftsmen who came

8 "Asian" is the generic term for descendants of the Indian subcontinent in East Africa, and was introduced after the separation of India into Pakistan and India in 1947, when it proved necessary to find a common designation for settlers of Indian, Pakistan and Goan background. (See I. Rothermund: *Die politische und wirtschaftliche Rolle der asiatischen Minderheit in Ostafrika.* Berlin–Heidelberg–New York, Springer-Verlag, 1965, p. 1 f. and A. Bharati, A Social Survey, in: *Portrait of a Minority. Asians in East Africa,* edited by D. P. Ghai, London–New York–Nairobi, Oxford University Press, 1965, p. 18 et seq.)
Besides the rather numerous group of Asians only 27 Europeans are engaged in crafts and small-scale industries in Tanzania, mainly in motor vehicle repair (16), bakeries (4), letterpress printing (3) and electrical engineering (2); there is also one barber and one carpenter. The number of Arabs in this sector is negligible — there are probably less than ten, mostly working as butchers.

9 Since only 24 small industrial firms were covered by the survey (out of about 100), this figure may be subject to some deviation. However, given the relatively small number of small-scale industries in comparison to the total of firms, the overall average will probably not be biased.

from the subcontinent continued to play (and taught their children to play) their specific role, which was imposed on them by the tradition of their ethnic or religious descent[10], only, however, within the Asian community or even only within the different respective groups.
The African craftsman's role is much harder to assess. Apart from the blacksmith's position in the traditional society, African craftsmen in Tanzania do not possess any fixed status of social significance because of their capacity as craftsmen in general or as craftsmen of a specific trade. The reason is simply that in East Africa a peculiarly African craftsmanship is non-existent because several external influences hindered any development of such a class. The different immigrant groups (Asians and Europeans) which came to Tanzania during the last hundred years were made up in part of skilled artisans, which had an adverse effect on the development of African craftsmanship. Government training of African craftsmen was shortlived; beginnings were made during the period of German occupation. British efforts in this area were half-hearted and insufficient owing to uncertainty about the future of the territory, and later to the second world war. After independence, policy discontinuity hindered effective action in this field. Private training for Africans was offered in negligible amounts by the mission schools, and private industry's offering of such training has been — quantitatively and qualitatively — limited.
African craftsmen as such are not identified as a specific group in society, but are considered to belong to the general blue collar labour force in the country, and hence occupy a social status sometimes inferior to that of clerks. The situation is, however, considerably different if specific trades are under review instead of the often only vaguely conceived notion of "crafts". This was revealed by a job preference test executed in the Mwanza Region[11], and was also found to be true in other parts of Africa, particularly in Kenya[12] and the Congo[13]. Thus, preference for a trade such as motor

---

10 See in this context M. SINGER: Changing Craft Traditions in India, in: *Labour Commitment and Social Change in Developing Areas,* edited by W. E. MOORE and A. S. FELDMAN. New York, Social Science Research Council, 1960, pp. 258–276.

11 J. D. HEIJNEN: *Results of a Job Preference Test Administered to Pupils in Standard VIII,* Paper presented at the Conference on Education, Employment and Rural Development sponsored by the University College, Nairobi, Kericho, 1966 (mimeo), (following quotations of papers presented to this conference will — after author and title — appear abbreviated as Kericho Papers, 1966).

12 In Kenya three different tests were executed during the last few years: E. ANDERSON: *Primary School Leavers in Rural Areas,* University of East Africa, Social Science Conference, Nairobi, December 1966 (mimeo); O. NEULOH (Ed.): *Der ostafrikanische Industriearbeiter zwischen Shamba und Maschine.* München, Weltforum-Verlag, 1969; D. KOFF: *Education and Employment, Perspectives of Kenya Primary Pupils,* Kericho Papers, 1966.

13 N. XYDIAS: Labour: Conditions, Aptitudes, Training, in: *Social Implications of*

mechanics can far exceed that for a clerk or other "white collar" occupation — a fact which seems to negate "the opinion held by many commentators that the school leavers refuse to work with their hands[14].

The findings of the test in the Mwanza Region, executed in four Upper Primary Schools of Mwanza town and three Upper Primary Schools of the Rural Area, show that the pupils under review ranked "Garage Mechanic"[15] second out of twenty-four possible choices after "Medical Assistant" in the Rural Area, and in Mwanza town even gave this trade the same number of points as "Medical Assistant", thus putting both in the first place.
However, the next craft, "Carpenter", ranks only seventh and tenth respectively, while "Bricklayer" and "Tailor" fell back in the Rural Area to the third and in Mwanza town even to the fourth quarter of the scores (15th/17th and 17th/18th places respectively).

These results, together with the similar findings of the other tests mentioned in Kenya, suggest that the trade of "Garage Mechanic" (or "Motor Vehicle Repairer", "Motor Mechanic") plays a somewhat exclusive role in terms of reputation and preference — an assumption which is supported by the overwhelming number of applicants for classes teaching the subject in Trade Schools. The fact that other trades which "dirty one's hands" usually fall back considerably in preferences in these tests makes the generally accepted opinion that "white collar jobs" are preferred to "blue collar jobs" not completely invalid — the job of a "Motor Mechanic" may simply be considered to be an exception. Moreover, it should be borne in mind that, given the reasons for the preference of a particular job stated in these tests — in this case "Motor Mechanic" — the choice of vocational status is supposedly more oriented towards wages paid than to the question whether these wages are received by dirty or clean hands. It has also been shown elsewhere that "the school leaver will make his strongest bid for the class of jobs with the most appealing net advantages, of which money income and its regularity are the principal ingredients"[16].

III. Skills and Aptitudes

In Tanzania, as well as in the whole of East Africa, skills and aptitudes of to-day's craftsmen have their roots in the ethnological history of the country.

Industrialization and Urbanization in Africa South of the Sahara, Paris, United Nations Educational, Scientific and Cultural Organization, 1956, p. 357 ff.

14 J. D. Heijnen, *op. cit.*, p. 2.

15 Almost 50 per cent of the boys stated as reasons for this choice "good wages, much profit". *Ibid.*, p. 14.

16 A. Callaway: School Leavers and the Developing Economy of Nigeria (from the Dec. 1960 Conference Proceedings published by N.I.S.E.R., Ibadan. Reprinted in: *West Africa,* issues of March 25, April 1, 8, 15, 1961), p. 8.

Arabian, Asian and finally European needs and necessities together with traditional African demands made craftsmen acquire or preserve a variety of skills and aptitudes ranging from pottery through silversmithing to photograph developing or motor vehicle repairing. In the past some crafts were — and to some extent still are — preferred or shunned by one or another ethnic or religious group. Preferences for trades are found especially within the Asian community, and are a relic of the indigenous caste system. As a result of this tradition, and the tradition of Asian craftsmen in East Africa generally, it is this community which carries on Tanzanian craftsmanship.
Asians provide most of the skilled manual personnel such as mechanics, electricians, tailors, carpenters, etc.[17 18]. This adherence to traditional patterns, of course, also tends to exclude skills and aptitudes from outsiders, who — if there are no other means of training — remain at a somewhat inferior level.
Since Africans in East Africa do not enjoy a tradition of craftsmanship as is the case, for instance, in West Africa, these vocational outsiders are very often Africans. However, their role as only second-grade craftsmen is sometimes superficially interpreted as being due to innate characteristics of Africans in general.
If skill may be defined as the product of talent, training and experience, some clues as to the last two components, namely as to the "skill index", are provided by the results based on the survey undertaken. Here, questions were introduced as to the "years of experience in the profession actually performed, including trade school" (entrepreneurs only) (see table 2) and to the "type of professional training received" (both entrepreneurs and employees). Possible answers to the latter question were "Trade school — missionary school — father/relative — other workshops" [19].
Responses of the craftsmen numbering about 500 — roughly one third of the Tanzanian total — show that, on the average, craftsmen had 16 years' experience in their trade. At the top are the goldsmiths, an exclusively Asian domain, followed by the shoemakers and the sheet metal workers. Carpenters,

17 See D. P. GHAI and Y. GHAI: Asians in East Africa: Problems and Prospects, in: *The Journal of Modern African Studies*, Vol. 3, No. 1, 1965, p. 38. It is estimated that about 25 per cent of Asian workers are engaged in "skilled manual" jobs, i.e. are craftsmen, and a further 15 per cent perform professional and technical occupations part of which may also be included in the craftsman category. See D. P. GHAI: An Economic Survey, in: *Portrait of a Minority*, edited by D. P. GHAI. London–New York–Nairobi, Oxford University Press, 1965, p. 96.

18 The building trade is a special domain of Asian craftsmen, and DELF says in this respect: "Like the other East African capitals, Dar es Salaam is not only built largely by Asian contractors, masons, and carpenters, but also looks in many respects like a prosperous Indian town." See D. DELF: *Asians in East Africa*. London–New York–Nairobi, Oxford University Press, 1963, p. 52 f.

19 Some of those interviewed, however, were not satisfied with these alternatives, and chose to give the somewhat enigmatic answer "own initiative".

Table 2. *Average Years of Experience of Craftsmen in Selected Trades*

Trade	Years									Average	Total of responses
	0—5	6—10	11—15	16—20	21—25	26—30	31—35	36—40	Over 41		
Bakers	2	3	4	1	–	1	–	–	–	11	11
Barbers	16	9	5	3	7	2	4	2	2	15	50
Electricians	2	2	5	2	–	–	–	–	2	16	13
Shoemakers, cobblers	13	13	10	7	8	8	9	6	6	20	80
Gold and silversmiths	2	2	3	1	5	2	–	2	5	25	22
Motor mechanics	5	3	4	4	1	1	2	–	1	15	21
Sheet metal workers, tinsmiths	5	2	2	1	2	1	2	1	2	19	18
Tailors	47	31	18	16	12	9	8	4	6	14	151
Watch repairers	5	5	5	2	1	–	–	1	1	13	20
Woodworkers, carpenters	31	25	24	12	13	2	1	6	4	12	118
Total										16	504

Source: Own survey.

watch repairers and bakers have relatively little experience, whereas the electrical repairers, with an average of 16 years' work experience, represent exactly the average for all trade groups.

It must be borne in mind that the average number of years' experience in a particular trade is also a function of the extent to which the skills thus attained or improved are in demand. A comparison of the average number of years' experience of the workers in various trades would be meaningful only in a static economy in which no expansion or contraction of the one or the other trade occurred. Thus the older trades would show an average of more years' experience, i.e. skills and experience collected but in decreasing demand, while the "younger" trades would show an average of fewer years' experience, which, however, represent skills that are increasingly demanded by employers.
Although the figures obtained are of but limited value when applied to a specific trade, they do suggest some conclusions about the relative growth or decline of different trades. The presence of many newcomers in a trade will depress the average, and similarly their absence will raise the average for that trade. In this sense a low average number of years' experience among those practising a trade may be taken as an indication that the trade is dynamic, while a high average may indicate that a trade is static or declining.
In the Tanzanian case these figures may also allow an additional interpretation. Trades with small averages — with the exception of bakers — are an African domain, suggesting that the newcomers during the last years were mainly recruited from the African community.

The second component of the "skill index", the training received, is reflected by the answers in table 3 [20]. The results show that 45 per cent of the total of 549 independent craftsmen received their training in other workshops, and 39 per cent were able to get industrial instruction from their own father or a relative. Less than 10 per cent attended Government trade schools, about 5 per cent claimed their skill to be the result of their "own initiative" and only about 3 per cent went through mission trade schools. The picture, however, changes considerably if the training of employed craftsmen is analysed. Here, out of a total of 702 employees about one fifth had had the chance to be instructed by a relative, the majority of 457 having depended on other workshops for their training. Some 8 per cent showed "own initiative" with respect to training, 5 per cent went through trade schools and 3 per cent through mission schools.
If the interpretation of these findings is correct they would seem to suggest that, other things being equal, "home training" provides skills enabling craftsmen to set up and keep a workshop of their own more easily than if the skills had been acquired in another workshop. Out of the craftsmen who received "home training" there are now roughly twice as many independent craftsmen as there are out of those who received instruction in other workshops. It may be supposed that in other workshops the learner is able to acquire only such manipulations and skills as are necessary to perform certain parts of the

20 Trades with less than 10 responses to these questions were excluded.

Table 3. *Type of Industrial Training Received in Selected Trades*

Trade	Independent craftsmen						Employed craftsmen					
	Trade school	Mission school	Father/ Relative	Other work-shops	Own initiative	Total respond-ing	Trade school	Mission school	Father/ Relative	Other work-shops	Own initiative	Total respond-ing
Bakers	1	–	3	6	–	10	–	–	12	57	–	69
Barbers	4	2	12	25	6	49	2	–	16	11	–	29
Electricians	4	2	2	5	–	13	2	6	–	1	1	10
Shoemakers, cobblers	4	1	31	23	1	60	2	4	14	24	–	44
Gold and silversmiths	1	–	17	4	2	24	1	–	12	27	–	40
Motor mechanics	3	–	6	12	3	24	2	–	–	169	–	171
Sheet metal workers, tinsmiths	2	–	16	32	3	53	–	1	9	3	–	13
Tailors	11	6	79	61	8	165	17	4	29	61	48	159
Watch repairers	–	–	8	10	1	19	–	–	8	7	–	15
Woodworkers, carpenters	14	8	43	60	7	132	10	5	34	97	6	152
Total	44	19	217	238	31	549	36	20	134	457	55	702

Source: Own survey.

trade determined by the employer. The learner thus has not the chance to obtain a general and intensive training; training with a relative, however, does provide this chance.

It may be argued that one of the most important factors which enable a young craftsman to become established is not skill but capital, and most of the above-recorded craftsmen receiving their training in the workshop of a relative might very well either have taken over the enterprise of their kin, or might have got the initial financial support to open a workshop of their own. Yet figures obtained in another inquiry during the same survey show that this is true in only a small number of cases: less than 8 per cent out of a total of 505 independent craftsmen who responded to the question how they came into possession of their enterprise, had taken over the enterprise from their father or a relative, and less than 15 per cent out of a total of 531 craftsmen were able to get funds for the establishment of their own workshop from relatives — the majority namely, 413, claimed their own savings to be the source of their workshop's initial financing.
It may be assumed that most of these "own savings" could only be accumulated by transforming skill into money income and that, therefore, the statement made above is verified, i.e. that in Tanzania industrial training received from relatives is more conducive to ownership of an establishment and hence is probably more sound.

As to the different trades under review, the figures show that in trades where Asians predominate, such as goldsmithing, tailoring and footwear, "home-trained" craftsmen outnumber those with "other workshop training" — in the case of goldsmiths by 4 to 1. The impact which missionary industrial instruction has had on the advancement of craftsmen, if the establishment of one's own workshop may be taken as a measure of advancement, is surprisingly small. Independent craftsmen who received missionary training make up 3.5 per cent of all independent craftsmen questioned, while employed craftsmen with this background make up 3.0 per cent of all employed craftsmen interviewed. The picture is somewhat better for governmental trade schools, the corresponding figures being less than 10 per cent in the case of independent craftsmen and about 5 per cent in the case of employed craftsmen.

IV. Financial Aspects

It is a well-known fact that small enterprises in developing countries are particularly hampered in their development by the lack of capital and credit facilities — obstacles which need not be further discussed here. The situation in Tanzania does not seem to differ from that in other developing countries.
According to the survey Tanzanian craftsmen have on the average about TShs 35,000/- invested in their workshops. Bakeries are the most heavily capitalized, with TShs 130,000/-, followed by motor mechanics with TShs 107,000/- and goldsmiths with TShs 80,000/-, while barbers are the least capitalized trade with TShs 600/-.

The main source of funds for the initial financing, i.e. the capital needed for the opening of the workshop, was provided by almost 80 per cent of craftsmen out of their own savings. Less than 15 per cent were able to get funds for the establishment from their relatives, the remaining 5 per cent being financed by "other" sources and Government loans.
As sources of credit, Tanzanian craftsmen prefer relatives to all other sources. Almost half of 134 entrepreneurs covering ten trades would rather take money from their relatives than go to "other" sources, mainly private money lenders or firms (29 per cent), to banks (18 per cent) or to the Government (3 per cent). Only in one trade, motor vehicle repair, are banks the chief source of credit. Tailors and bakeries often enjoy credit from "other" sources, whereas the barbers stick exclusively to their family when they are in financial trouble. With regard to the interest to be paid on loans information is available only for some trades. Thus for electrical repairs it is 9 per cent, for shoemakers 11 per cent, for barbers 20 per cent and for tailors 25–30 per cent per year.
A new source of credit is claimed to have been provided by privately started "Savings and Credit Societies" (Shirika la Akiba) since the middle of the sixties. Created as self-help co-operative financial organizations, they are groups of people united by a "common bond" of association[21]. The aim of organization is to accumulate capital mainly by saving, and to make low-cost loans to members for worth-while purposes at low rates of interest. There are no capital profits paid to outsiders from the operation of the society, and all the latter's earnings, after legitimate expenses and allocation to reserves, are returned to the members in the form of dividends on their shares. Some societies also refund to borrowers part of the interest they paid on loans during the past year.

The societies already comprised a total membership of over 18,000 in 1967, distributed among 141 organizations which saved and borrowed about TShs 2 million within one year. Since most of the societies are for the time being situated in rural areas, craftsmen have so far taken little advantage of these facilities. They are, however, apparently very much interested in this way of meeting financial problems[22].

---

21 The "common bond" concept means that the members of a Savings and Credit Society also belong to a clearly defined group such as employees of the same company, members of the same church, fraternal, business co-operative society or other organization, or reside in the same community or village. All participation, including the accumulation of savings and the making of loans, is confined to the membership group within the "common bond". The "common bond" is considered to be one of the "key factors in making a savings and credit society successful. It fosters a feeling of obligation within the membership, and borrowers are inclined to take this responsibility seriously." See *Savings and Credit Societies in Tanzania.* Dar es Salaam, 1967 (mimeo.), p. 1.

22 See below, p. 265.

Until recently craftsmen and small entrepreneurs have been somewhat neglected by the Government in regard to credit facilities. Apart from the "African Loan Funds" and the "Local Development and African Productivity Loan Funds", which existed even before independence, and which under point 12 also envisaged loans for the "Purchase of tools, equipment and implements necessary for running home industries"[23], official credit sources were available almost exclusively for agricultural or industrial enterprises on a larger scale. A new supply of credit from a semi-official source was, however, provided from the National Small Industries Corporation (NSIC), which since 1967 has offered machinery on hire-purchase to small-scale industrial entrepreneurs and craftsmen, and thus smoothes the way to entrepreneurial independence, especially for the African craftsman, who is mostly the one to suffer from financial shortcomings, the Asian craftsmen being able largely to rely on kinsmen belonging to the extended family.

According to a scheme, which was still in the preparatory stage in 1967, additional possibilities of receiving initial loans for the establishment of their own workshop are to be created for Tanzanians who served in the National Service and there took craft courses. The necessary funds will be accumulated through the monthly payments made by industrial firms to the National Service as remuneration for the work of the servicemen under apprenticeship contracts in these firms[24]. Loans which will be confined to buying machinery are intended to run for long terms and at low interest rates; they will be granted by preference to those craftsmen who are heading for up-country settlements where artisans are needed.

V. Income and Wages

Naturally, one of the questions in the survey which the interviewees were most reluctant to answer was the one pertaining to their income. Nevertheless both the number of responses and the apparent veracity of the responses were considerably above expectations. Aggregate data for some trades seemed not to be excessively unrealistic, and are accordingly given below.

As to income and wages a distinction must, of course, be made between the income of independent craftsmen and entrepreneurs in small-scale industries and the wages earned by craftsmen who are employees. According to the survey independent bakers rank highest with TShs 5,700/-, and sheet metal workers lowest, the average income being TShs 2,100/-. The relatively high incomes of goldsmiths, motor mechanics and bakers reflect the high investments involved in these trades, be it in machinery (bakers, motor vehicle

23 Tanganyika: *Report on the African Loan Funds together with the 1955 and 1956 Accounts for the Local Development and African Productivity Loan Fund.* Dar es Salaam, 1958, p. 2.

24 See also below, p. 271.

repairers) or stocks (goldsmiths). Together with electricians, these trades, moreover, are predominantly filled by Asians — these being considered to count more highly skilled craftsmen among their ranks than Africans.

The overall average wage is about TShs 250/-. The overall average, however, is much less interesting than the averages differentiated according to origin of wage earners. In the field of wages similar trends with respect to professional and racial differences are found, although Asians comprise only a small minority among craftsmen; of a total of 1,887 craftsmen employed in 431 firms, 1,681 were listed as Africans and 206 as Asians. Only 7 per cent of the African employees earned TShs 400/- or more per month, but 75 per cent of the Asian employees of the total under review fell under this category. On the average, Asian craftsmen earn more than two and a half times as much as their African counterparts. The difference between the two groups is least in sheet metal working and greatest in watch repairs — however, the coverage in the survey is very small in the latter case and therefore has only limited significance. On the other hand, the three trades of tailoring, woodworking and shoemaking may provide some significant data, as they include more than a third of employed craftsmen in Tanzania. Tailors average TShs 365/- per month and woodworkers TShs 505/- per month, yet Asian tailors earn more than twice as much as their African fellow craftsmen, while Asian carpenters earn nearly four times as much. Asian shoemakers receive more than three times the pay of their African counterparts.

African craftsmen earn most if they choose to be goldsmiths (TShs 300/- per month), or motor mechanics (TShs 290/-), but are also relatively well paid if they happen to be letterpress printers (TShs 270/-) or electricians (TShs 260/-).

Amongst Asian craftsmen, carpenters take home the highest wages (TShs 800/-), followed by watch repairers (whose African counterparts are last on the scale) and motor mechanics. Poorest paid are sheet metal workers, with TShs 230/-, almost reaching the average for all African craftsmen.

VI. Co-operative Organizations

The extension of the co-operative idea into the industrial sector in Tanzania fitted perfectly into the new political pattern of the Government after independence[25]. It was felt that institutionalized co-operatives were a

25 In the agricultural field the Tanzanian co-operative movement already has a long tradition and records considerable achievements. As early as in 1925 the Wachagga, shortly after having started to grow coffee on the slopes of Mount Kilimanjaro, formed the first African co-operative, the "Kilimanjaro Native

continuation of the traditional way of life, with its extended family system, and thus much more congenial to African feelings and attitudes than, for example, a purely capitalistic or communist approach: co-operatives embody much better the idea of the so-called African Socialism, with its concept of "self-help" and "Ujamaa"[26], than any other form of economic activity does. In addition the co-operative form was seen as a means well suited to realize the achievements of independence and to obtain control of the economy by the indigenous people rather than by expatriates and others, non-African in origin. Thus it was decided to embark on a crash programme for the organization of co-operatives in vast sections of the country which until then were largely untouched by the movement, namely the central and coastal parts, Mtwara and Ruvuma in the South and the Western areas. The expansion took place not only in the agricultural sector but also in the industrial field, where co-operatives had hardly existed at all.

Producer Co-operatives[27]

Up to 1966, 27 industrial producer societies (crafts) were fully registered and another two were on probation. Although in the case of agricultural co-operatives the political pressures were considerable and societies were organized from "on top", without genuine local demand or even understanding, this was probably true to only a lesser degree in the case of industrial co-operatives. Here, in many cases the organizers were under the mistaken impression that the public would automatically favour them, despite higher prices or

---

Planters Association". To-day there are about 1,600 agricultural co-operatives in the country. See M. Paulus: *Das Genossenschaftswesen in Tanganyika und Uganda – Möglichkeiten und Aufgaben.* Afrika-Studien No. 15, Berlin–Heidelberg–New York, Springer-Verlag, 1967, p. 6; The United Republic of Tanzania: *Report of the Presidential Special Committee of Enquiry into Co-operative Movement and Marketing Boards.* Dar es Salaam, Government Printer, 1966, p. 5, and I. O. W. Scheel: *Tanganyika and Sansibar.* Bonn, Kurt Schroeder Verlag, 1959, p. 84 f.

26 Kiswahili, denoting common weal, mainly achieved by working and living together as a family, etc.

27 Generally speaking two types of co-operatives may be differentiated, namely the "joint enterprise" and the "common facility" co-operatives. The former type is denoted as one in which members amalgamate their individual production processes and business operations in one unit, thus ceasing to function as individual enterprises (e.g. producer societies), whereas members of the latter type maintain the separate identity of their operations, the society providing one or more specific facilities or services which they all need (e.g. purchasing and supply societies, credit societies, processing societies, marketing societies etc.). See International Labour Organization: *Services for Small-scale Industry.* Geneva, ILO, 1961, pp. 3 et seq. and *Co-operative Information.* Geneva, ILO, 1964, pp. 2 et seq.

poor quality of their products, merely because they were co-operatives[28]. Also it was probably often felt that after registration — which had become a relatively uncomplicated process — co-operatives would be further helped by the supervisory services of the Co-operative Development Division in the management of their affairs, the keeping of accounts, etc.; obviously there was also a general belief that co-operatives have "special status", and that therefore immediate and substantial loans are available to finance operations as soon as the registration is completed.

Most of the industrial and craft co-operatives (usually 10–15 members) were founded with varying contributions from the members, a fact which led to different positions of members within the society and hence to internal troubles, or even — since the anticipated Government loans were not granted — to mere registrations followed by a winding up of business[29]. Thus in 1967 only 15 industrial or craft societies were counted, and most of these were doing poorly and did not seem to have good prospects[30]. The reason for most failures was lack of capital and lack of knowledge about the effective demand for products, shortcomings which are still problems for the remaining co-operatives.

Purchasing, Marketing and Credit[31] Co-operatives

This "common facility" type of co-operatives, functioning only in some sections of business, make members dependent on one another and yet leave ample room for individual entrepreneurial activity, which in any case is not willingly abandoned by craftsmen. In 1967 neither purchasing nor marketing co-operatives were known to exist among crafts and small-scale industries in Tanzania. Since they do not alter the social status of an enterprise, i.e. do not deprive it of its capitalistic character, they were, politically, not interesting and hence have not been promoted at all.

However, Tanzanian craftsmen for their part seem not uninterested — at least in purchasing co-operatives. Out of a total of 532 craftsmen interviewed from ten different trades, about 60 per cent would favour the formation of such a society. With respect to marketing societies the feeling was divided, about half on either side being for and against such a co-operative, whereas credit societies were able to concentrate the highest percentage (about 70 per cent) in favour of their introduction.

28 The United Republic of Tanzania, *op. cit.*

29 See also M. Paulus, *op. cit.*, p. 64.

30 There were nine tailoring societies (Dar es Salaam, Bukoba, Iringa, Moshi, Morogoro, Kilosa, Masasi, Musoma and Mtwara), three building or contractor societies (Arusha, Morogoro and Masasi), two carpenter societies (Dar es Salaam and Lindi) and one women's handicraft co-operative society (Dar es Salaam). See also Geiger and Armstrong: *The Development of African Private Enterprise.* Planning Pamphlet No. 120, of the National Planning Association. Washington 1964, p. 34 f.

31 As to credit societies see above, p. 261 f.

VII. Racial Relations

When racial issues are under review in East Africa, only relations between Africans and Asians seem worth mentioning; after independence the racial tensions between Africans and Europeans or Asians and Europeans, even before "Uhuru" only to a limited extent prevalent, diminished to a negligible size. And except for Zanzibar, which in 1964 was the scene of a revolution with racial overtones, racial differences between Arabs and the other groups are practically non-existent in Tanzania — they could hardly arise, given the small numbers and the limited influence of Arabs on the mainland.
Racial conflicts, however, do exist between Africans and Asians. Whereas the European's position is still too elevated and remote — he is the object of hostility but his position is unchallenged[32] — the Asians occupy positions which are objects of immediate African aspiration. Although the African resentment is particularly concentrated on the Asian control of retail trade, it is also felt that the dominating role of Asian craftsmen could easily be played by Africans. Another reason why the Asian minority has been specially marked out for friction lies in its social structure: the Asian social organization is closed to outsiders. Whereas Africans can easily observe the European way of life, the Asian way of life remains a mystery[33]. And especially after "Uhuru" it was held against the Asians that their identification with the fate of East Africa was mere lip-service, since they would not integrate with the Africans either socially or economically. At another level, Asians are often accused of holding back the progress and participation of Africans in the economy of the country. It is further alleged that Asian business firms have not consciously aided Africanization, being for the most part solely concerned with their own economic salvation, and that in the past they have spared relatively little energy for the economic advancement of Africans[34].
Since the close family ties among the Asian community extend strongly into the business sphere, it was only natural that Asians recruited their labour supply for skilled manual and managerial positions from their own kinship, at least from their own caste. To train an African for such a post would not only have meant the loss of this job for a member of the family; it would also be more expensive than training a relative, who usually receives less pay and, because of the educational background within the family, is easier to train. Thus a relative could fill the position in question more quickly. And finally, of course, it may seem unwise to Asians to give an African, who

32 Y. P. Ghai: The Asian Dilemma in East Africa, in: *East Africa Journal,* March 1965, p. 10, and I. Rothermund, *op. cit.,* p. 34.
33 Y. P. Ghai, *op. cit.,* p. 11.
34 D. P. Ghai, *op. cit.,* p. 104.

might be a future competitor, a sound all-round training. But this is only one motive among many others.
One might expect that for these reasons in Asian firms a large proportion of Asians and relatives of the proprietor would be employed, but that this would be the case to a more limited extent in African firms. However, the findings of the survey show that the picture is almost the reverse.

Of 222 African firms employing African craftsmen, 41 per cent employ relatives of the proprietor, while of 201 Asian firms employing Asian craftsmen, only 22 per cent have relatives working with their enterprise.
These figures are, however, more meaningful if the number of employees is given: the 222 African firms have 243 relative employees (out of a total of 596 African employees) whereas the 201 Asian firms employ only 96 (out of a total of 217 Asian employees).

It may be further argued that if such close family ties within the Asian business world exist, a considerable number of craftsmen would have taken over the enterprise from the father or a relative. But, as has already been demonstrated, only a small fraction of the craftsmen questioned had taken over the workshop from their kinsmen; the majority claimed to have started the business on their own[35].
These findings, however, should not necessarily be interpreted as providing contradictions to the above-described extended family system. For it might very well be argued that, in the first case, the relatively small number of kindred employees of Asian craftsmen in comparison to those of African employers affords evidence that to some extent Asian craftsmen, once they are established and have a workshop of their own, earn enough money to have their offspring become "something better", given the fact that caste limitations or preferences in respect of profession are no longer coercive or ubiquitously prevalent. As to the second phenomenon, the equally small number of "inherited" workshops, the conclusion may be drawn that in certain trades there has been expansion which made the establishment of new enterprises necessary, i.e. there simply were not enough enterprises to be "inherited". This assumption may be supported by the relationship, assumed above[36], between expanding trades and the owner's years of experience. Precisely those trades which were denoted as "declining" (or at least not expanding, as the others were), show the highest percentage of craftsmen who have taken over the enterprise from their father or a relative.
Given these limitations, the alleged Asian "closed shop" attitude may be looked upon from a somewhat different angle, and be absolved from part of the generalizing criticism of which it has been the object.
Unlike other states which are not interested in minorities applying for citizenship (e.g. Indonesia with its Chinese minority, and Ceylon with its Indian

---

35 See above, p. 260.
36 See p. 258.

minority), the East African countries had no objection to this, and Asians were advised by African authorities, as well as by several of their own leaders who have retained political power or influence, to take out Kenyan, Ugandan, or Tanzanian citizenship according to their place of residence. The official deadlines for application for local citizenship were two years after independence. But only part of the Asians chose this alternative; the rest did not change their citizenship (British Commonwealth, Indian, or British proper), and hence must face, sooner or later, difficulties with regard to their presence in Tanzania. Between the different groups the proportions of those who have taken citizenship vary considerably. Following the recommendations of the Aga Khan, the Ismailis[37] constitute the greatest percentage of new citizens, whereas among the various Gujarati-speaking Hindu communities the applicants for citizenship were in the minority[38].

Those Asians in civil service positions who refused to accept local citizenship state that it may not help them much in the long run, since the mere fact of East African citizenship will not prevent the authorities from replacing Asians of whatever citizenship by Africans the very moment such personnel is trained, with or without equal qualifications. This peculiar apprehension is, however, not relevant to the Asian craftsmen, who are — with the exception of the Sikhs — mainly Gujarati-speaking Hindus, and of whom only a relatively small proportion have taken citizenship. The possibility that their permits will not be indefinitely extended seems much more likely. But it is they who would suffer most if their presence is no longer welcome in Tanzania, for they do not know where to turn. Since they belong to the lower and middle income class they were not able to transfer substantial amounts of capital like the rich, who are thus internationally mobile; nor do they want to return to Pakistan or India, where they would face only poverty and perhaps even hunger.

37 The Shi'a Khoja Ismailis (Ishmailis), as their correct designation goes, are the most thoroughly modernized group in East Africa's Asian community, and have the least connections with their home country. Usually, the older members of this group and those men who are heads of family have acquired citizenship. (See I. ROTHERMUND, *op. cit.*, p. 13; BHARATI, *op. cit.*, p. 197, and G. DELF, *op. cit.*, p. 53.)

38 The Gujarati-speaking Hindus form roughly 70 per cent of the total Asian population, with the Patels and Lohanas numerically and economically the dominating castes — economically, however, on a par with the less numerous Shahs and the Banya, the latter belonging to the merchant caste by tradition (BHARATI, *op. cit.*, p. 17).

C. POLICY OF PROMOTION OF CRAFTS AND SMALL-SCALE INDUSTRIES

When evaluating various measures which contributed toward the promotion of crafts and small-scale industries in Tanzania in the past one may distinguish between direct and indirect measures. The history of direct assistance to the small entrepreneur and craftsman is extremely short — in fact, it dates back only to the beginning of the sixties. Although industrial education and training, which have a much longer tradition in Tanzania, had the rather general aim of favouring overall economic development, they also favoured the development of crafts and small-scale industries. This having been recognized, specific measures of education and training are considered to be of particular importance in drawing up programmes for promotion of crafts and small-scale industries.

I. Industrial Education and Training[39]

Before the second world war craft classes at Government schools were found everywhere in the country, the main centres being at Dar es Salaam and Tanga.

An elaborated system of industrial education and training did not, however, as yet exist. After the war it was felt that craft training should be centralized in one school. The assumption was that industrial training, once separated completely from ordinary education, would prove to be much more efficient and at the same time more economical. Facilities became available in Ifunda, and in 1951 the school was opened with 273 students; about half were high-school graduates (ex-Standard VIII), and half ex-Askaris who came over from Mgulani, an ex-Askari training centre established after the war. Stu-

39 A systematic survey of industrial education and training in Tanzania, which in the past has been threefold, namely at Government schools, where craft classes were attached to Upper Primary and Secondary Schools and — from 1950 onwards — to the two Trade Schools in Moshi and Ifunda, in missionary schools and in private and governmental workshops on a more or less irregular basis, is not possible in the scope of this study. The reader is referred to the author's extensive and detailed discussion of this matter in "Crafts, Small-scale Industries and Industrial Education in Tanzania" (Munich: Ifo Institute). In the present study this is discussed only in relation to public industrial training in the context of the development of industrial training and its adaption to the needs of the economy.

dents, who were later required to have Standard VIII as a condition for entry, attended courses in school for three years, and were supposed to end their course with two years in an employer's establishment. At that time it was felt that the first Trade School supplied Tanzania's slowly expanding industry, on a regular basis, with skilled craftsmen who had some technical background and knowledge, and who had reached certain qualification standards which were generally accepted. In 1954, therefore, it was considered necessary to go ahead with a second training centre, which was established in Moshi. In the opening year, 1957, over 200 students were enrolled in this second Trade School.

The capital outlay for both schools was about £500,000, but the returns from this relatively high investment proved to be below expectations. Many of the graduates of Moshi or Ifunda did not get jobs at once, or not in the lines for which they were trained, because the training offered by the schools was too theoretical and not applicable to working life. The serious deficiencies of the schools' syllabus were not detected until almost a decade had elapsed.

Partly on the recommendation of the Manpower Planning Unit, set up in 1959 with the help of the Ford Foundation, it was decided in 1964 to convert the Ifunda Trade School into a Secondary Technical School, and two years later the Moshi Trade School followed the same pattern. Students in these institutions now receive a basic, full-year secondary education, with a technical bias, which enables them to enter the Dar es Salaam Technical College. If they do not qualify for entrance, students may seek further training at the City and Guilds of London courses at the same institution, provided that they are sponsored.

Government craft training at schools in Tanzania would have ended with the last trade pupils from Moshi, who were left over from both schools after conversion, and who completed their instruction in 1967, had it not been for last-minute plans. These foresee a renaissance of the old and almost buried Trade Schools, albeit with a new look. After two years of basic training the new system selects the inferior half of the 80 students admitted at Ifunda, and these then receive two years of craft training, ending in the City and Guilds of London Certificate; this training is offered at Moshi. The superior half receive further instruction at Ifunda, also for two years, and finish with the Cambridge School Certificate.

On the assumption that the new craft syllabus in Moshi has been purged of the deficiencies contained in the old syllabus, it is still open to question whether Trade Schools such as Moshi or Ifunda will not continue to produce "sophisticated", swelled-headed alumni, who do not meet the demands of industrial life and who have no notion of work discipline. Again and again it was apparent that the main difficulty in educating and training craftsmen, for the particular function they have to fulfil within the framework of the new Policy of Self-Reliance, is to get them to return to work again upon completion of training. It is not surprising that it has proved extremely difficult to convince trade school boys that they first have to take up work as craftsmen, and only later on may occupy positions as supervisors, when their abilities have grown.

With regard to the training provided at Moshi and Ifunda it is to be expected that the apter pupils will constitute the majority of new students at the Dar es Salaam Technical College, and will thus provide Tanzania with technicians, who are also badly needed. The less talented pupils will continue to swell the ranks of the army of clerks, which is so often the object of comment and criticism.

The new scheme introduced in the Tanzania National Service may eventually produce the additional craftsmen so urgently needed by Tanzania. In this scheme, volunteer Service men, all having at least an upper primary level of schooling, will receive a three months' basic craft training during their service. They are then sorted out according to their abilities and assigned to various industrial firms, where they serve a two-year apprenticeship, with time off to attend theoretical day courses at the camp on certain days. Upon completion of the apprenticeship they undergo an examination at the National Trade Testing Centre, and receive certificates according to their performance.

This ambitious scheme, which is to provide openings for between 400 and 500 apprentices, follows rather strictly the continental pattern of apprenticeship, which in spite of being several hundred years old has proved to be extremely efficient even in a modern industrial environment. The National Service volunteers start to do manual work from the very beginning without receiving additional education. They are not set to worshipping the golden calf of the Cambridge School Certificate or the City and Guilds of London qualifications, and thus are not spoilt for their final testing as craftsmen in the proper sense, as distinguished from foremen or supervisors. So far, many more volunteers with much higher qualifications have presented themselves than was previously anticipated. At the same time firms have shown eagerness to co-operate, and have readily signed apprenticeship contracts with the National Services. As yet, no serious complaints have been recorded from either side.

The National Service Scheme was introduced at a time when another training project already planned in 1965, the "National Industrial Training and Apprenticeship Scheme", was about to be launched with the assistance of UN and ILO. It was decided that basic responsibility for training artisans should be left with industry itself. Besides a revision of the Immigration Regulations, requiring the training of Tanzanian counterparts for each position occupied by an expatriate, the Ministry of Labour was asked by the National Standing Manpower Committee to draft the aforesaid scheme. With funds totalling almost £300,000, and the assistance of 6 ILO experts, the scheme provides for on-the-job training programmes conducted by employers in their plants under the guidance and supervision of the Ministry of Labour. The facilities at Moshi are scheduled to be offered for sandwich courses during the training period. Together with the already firmly established National Trade Testing Centre, which sets the much needed qualification standards, the new Ministry of Labour scheme seems to be another step forward in producing the needed skilled artisans.

In 1967 the two approaches — the National Service and the Ministry of Labour as assisted by the Manpower Planning Unit and UN/ILO — did not, however, yet show the necessary co-ordination of their programmes, although they were moving in the same direction. Because of unforeseen delay, for which the Ministry was not responsible, the Ministry's programme lagged behind the National Service project, the implementation of which was further advanced. Whether enough places will remain, once the National Service has begun to train boys in substantial numbers, will depend on the form of apprenticeship contracts which the Ministry offers, and which may possibly provide some sort of refund for "over-training" expenses. Which of the two large-scale apprenticeship programmes the Tanzanian Government will emphasize in future is not foreseeable, and is very likely a question of subsidiary importance, since both programmes have the appropriate orientation. However, it may be hoped that the lack of co-operation between the programmes will be overcome despite the difficulties involved.

Another agency, the National Small Industries Corporation (NSIC), which plays a role in the comprehensive development programme of the Tanzanian Government, is starting an apprenticeship scheme of its own, although on a much smaller scale. The NSIC's "Cottage Industries Training Centre", which was expected to be in operation at the end of 1967, will train 25 persons per year in a course Casting six months. It seems, however, that this project, which is obviously biased towards the "handicrafts" and related cottage industry sections of the economy, will not interfere with the other two large-scale operations. The centre will seek to devise new and improved methods of developing skills in woodworking, metalworking, basketwork and weaving.

II. Other Measures of Promotion

1. Review of Promotion Policy

Although the need for promotion has for some time been frequently stressed, effective steps in this direction were taken only recently with the assistance of the International Labour Organization[40].

40 The following is based on International Labour Organization: *Technical Expert Meeting on Development of Managerial and Entrepreneurial Resources in Africa,*

Following a brief survey carried out in mid-1961 concerning the possibilities of organising industrial co-operatives in certain trades in Tanzania, an ILO expert was assigned to the country from 1962 to 1964 to advise and assist the Government in implementing a programme for increased African participation in small-scale manufacturing activities.

Suggestions were made aiming at forming and developing small-scale industrial co-operatives under African ownership and management, e.g. co-operatives for building construction, carpentry, tailoring, pottery, basket work and mat weaving. It was recommended that wherever lack of capital and experience would constitute the main barriers to African participation in small-scale manufacturing activities, these could in many instances be surmounted through co-operative action by pooling artisans' skills and financial resources, to be supported by credit and management assistance from the Government.

As a follow-up to this industrial co-operative mission a programme for promotion and development of small-scale industries was started in 1965 by the Ministry of Industries, Mineral Resources and Power (Small-Scale Industries Section). It comprised the establishment and operation of training-cum-production and common facilities centres for metal, woodwork and fibre processing, and the setting up of training programmes for artisans with a view to improving methods and techniques of production, product design and marketing. This programme was supplemented by the National Institute of Productivity, which was created at the end of 1965 as a joint operation of the Government, the United Nations Development Programme and ILO. The scheme was to run for five years. The Institute is designed to promote and improve productivity throughout the country in both small-scale and large-scale industrial enterprises.
Apart from this a comprehensive plan for the accelerated development of small-scale industries was prepared by the Tanzanian Government. It called for an integrated policy concerning tariff protection with regard to products suitable for domestic manufacture on a small scale, and schemes for entrepreneurial development through closer co-ordination of public action in the field of small industries by various Government ministries, and in particular through establishment of the National Small Industries Corporation (NSIC) as an important promotional tool for small-scale industrialization.
The implementation of crafts and small-scale industries promotion through the NSIC, which was created as a subsidiary of the National Development Corporation and of the Workers Development Corporation, and which functions under the guidance of the Ministry of Industries, Mineral Resources and Power, was mainly envisaged by way of providing common production and training facilities through an Industrial Estate, the Cottage Industries Training Centre[41] and an Industrial Workshop.

Information Paper, MAN. DEV./Africa Meeting 12. Geneva, ILO, 1966, p. 15 et seq.

41 See above, p. 272.

In 1967 the latter was already completed in Dar es Salaam, and provided facilities for about 100 woodworkers (carpenters, woodcarvers, cabinetmakers) and 76 metal-workers (sheet metal workers, tinsmiths, charcoal stove makers) — all African craftsmen who were taken out of their previous slum quarters. Artisans pay a small rent for small but separate workshops, and are provided with raw material at wholesale prices through NSIC; there are common machine rooms for each trade, and a centre from which several instructors are operating to give advice. Other cottage industry estates are planned up-country, but no concrete steps had yet been taken to realize these plans.
The Industrial Estate is finally to provide facilities for small-scale industries, which will be of a larger size than those installed in the industrial workshop mentioned above. Rents are supposed to run higher, so as to make the estate self-supporting except for certain costs, such as power facilities, which are to be met out of public funds. The equity capital was to be TShs 2 million, and the same amount was to be sought from the National Bank of Commerce, establishing bodies being the NDC and RASSCO Ltd. of Israel; however, a number of difficulties had delayed the implementation of the projects.

Since 1967 NSIC also provides machinery for craftsmen and small entrepreneurs on hire purchase. The craftsmen will have to deposit 20 per cent of the cost of machinery, and then pay the remaining amount within a period of seven to ten years. Under the new scheme, special concessions will be given to entrepreneurs from up-country areas in order to accelerate the dispersal of industrial activities there.

2. Basic Tasks of Craft Promotion

When reviewing the economic policy pursued vis-à-vis crafts and small-scale industries in the past, one should be aware of the limitations which a policy of promotion will have in Tanzania. If programmes of promotion are to have any chance of success they must be drawn up with due regard for the political principles and objectives of that country. However, since any modern Government will have as one of its principal objectives the long-run optimizing of economic growth, the economic goals, although subsidiary to political considerations, cannot be neglected.
In Tanzania, one of the main political objectives is proper participation of Tanzanians in the economic life of the country. This goal seems easily realizable. Of course, a fair proportion of those engaging in business in Tanzania are non-citizens; but even if the problem of non-Tanzanians in Tanzania is ignored, there remains the problem of Africans and Asians — both Tanzanian citizens — who live and work side by side but who are racially, religiously and culturally distinct groups[42]. The distribution of economic and political influence between these two groups is uneven, the Asians having the

42 The European and Arab communities do not play a significant role in crafts and small-scale industries, and are therefore neglected in this context.

preponderance of economic influence whilst the Africans enjoy all the political influence.

Thus the Tanzanian Government is confronted with a dilemma in trying to achieve its objectives. The expulsion of non-citizens would cause severe economic setbacks, and have repercussions on foreign policy, and a policy of promotion of "Tanzanians" (without reference to ethnic groups) would benefit Asians as well as Africans, or perhaps even mainly Asians, which would lead to unrest among the African population, displeased at seeing its long-promised economic equality postponed to the future. A one-sided promotion of Africans alone, however, if openly proclaimed, would necessarily lead to reproaches of racial discrimination, which is incompatible with TANU's political platform, and to which President Nyerere has been outspokenly opposed.

The only way out of the dilemma seems to be a compromise, namely promotion for Africans under the slogan of promotion for Tanzanians. To the observer it appears that this policy was and still is pursued, although of course unofficially and unavowedly. This policy works toward achieving the objectives set, and gives no pretext for claims of racial discrimination from Asians or from abroad. In any case, the Asian community does not, in fact, expect equal treatment, realizing that equality in this respect would mean only a one-sided promotion in their favour.

But what are the requirements for a programme of promotion which speeds up African participation in this sector without doing direct harm to the Asian community? General measures such as tax relief or tariff protection are obviously not sufficient. More emphasis will have to be put on direct schemes, and particularly on schemes intended to make African craftsmen more competitive vis-à-vis Asian craftsmen, for example by

- raising the level of quality of African craftsmanship and work performance, and by
- bringing about a natural selection, thus diminishing the supply of unqualified craftsmen.

As a supplement to the programmes which have been launched in pursuance of this aim the realization of these objectives can be achieved by improving industrial education and by promoting co-operatives offering common facilities.

III. Suggestions

1. Improvement of Industrial Education

This promotion measure seems to be the most important, since it is felt that in the long run a decisive advancement of African craftsmen can be achieved only through effective training schemes.

Standardization

Given the fact that a number of institutions are already engaged in craft or industrial training, each following its own pattern and very often with little co-operation between them, some standardization in this field seems highly desirable. Given the other fact that the origin and background of these institutions are varied (Ministry of Labour, National Service, Ministry of Education, missions of different belief, etc.), a general agreement from each side on common standards for industrial education and training may be achieved only step by step. The initiative in such endeavours will certainly rest with the Government, but the crafts and small-scale industries directly concerned should also have a say, possibly through some kind of federation which might be set up to represent their interests.

Trade Schools

In view of the relatively inconclusive experiences gained by the Trade Schools in Moshi and Ifunda, it is only with some hesitation that special efforts by the Government can be advocated in this direction. The new syllabus designed in 1967 does seem, however, to have eliminated some of the deficiencies in the old programme; and the new programme, which divides the students, reserving Ifunda for the more promising, has the advantage of giving those students who most need practical training a chance to obtain it. The initial training at Moshi only lasts two years and is followed by sandwich courses, as conceived by the Ministry of Labour for its apprenticeship programmes, which open the way potentially to an intensification of craft training for ongoing artisans. At the same time the students at Ifunda are trained for more advanced work, need less practical instruction, and usually attend the Technical College at Dar es Salaam once they have passed their school examinations.

It is felt that these sandwich courses provide an especially important means for instruction and ancillary theoretical education, and that Moshi — and perhaps even Ifunda — should eventually be reserved exclusively for such courses, thus making training facilities available to a much larger number of apprentices than would be possible with full-time schooling. In comparison with apprenticeship-cum-supplementary training, full-time schooling has the disadvantage that it is not oriented towards actual business practice and conditions, and may thus be considered of doubtful value in any case.

Apprenticeship Schemes

Together with the sandwich courses in Moshi provided by the Ministry of Labour (if the scheme is finally implemented), and the day release courses of the National Service, the apprenticeship schemes of both institutions seem to be the most important tool for fostering industrial education in Tanzania. It is self-evident that between these two institutions, the Ministry of Labour and the National Service, there needs to be close co-ordination of both schemes as well as common standards in regard to the length of apprenticeship, to the remuneration given, to the qualification prerequisites and so forth. The newly established Cottage Training Centre of NSIC may also provide a considerable contribution in this field.
Schemes to grant compensation and/or approval payments for taking apprentices under contract, and for successfully accomplished trade testing of apprentices, may be considered as means to provide incentives for entrepreneurs.

Trade Testing

If the suggestion is accepted that the promotion of craftsmen — and especially African craftsmen — must be based on sound industrial education and training, it follows that this education must have generally acknowledged and accepted standards, which serve by their very nature as an incentive, in order to be both attractive to the learner and esteemed by the employer.
Until recently, however, one of the main deficiencies in Tanzanian industrial education was the lack of generally accepted qualification standards[43]. With the introduction of the National Trade Testing Centre in Dec. 1966 an important institution has been established to meet these demands.
Trade testing could moreover make an important contribution towards raising the level of craftsmen who intend to open their own shops. This procedure would prevent unqualified craftsmen from becoming independent entrepreneurs. That would have several favourable results; the economic loss associated with the entry into the market and eventual bankruptcy of unqualified competitors would be minimized.
In addition, trade testing should be applied in connection with the programme of industrial estates for craftsmen. Although it is too early to asses

43 Except for the certificates of the Trade Schools, which, however, were too small in number to be relevant.

the value of the estate established by NSIC at Dar es Salaam, the scheme seems to be working well and no adverse effects have been reported. While it is urged here as an appropriate programme for further extension, it involves relatively heavy capital expenditure. It is indeed quite a costly promotion measure, and should be managed with great care as regards the selection of craftsmen who are to benefit from it. It would of course be senseless to promote any craftsman irrespective of his qualification, a policy which would in practice amount to discrimination against capable craftsmen and a waste of resources.

2. Common Facility Co-operatives

Producer or industrial co-operatives have not been a panacea for the development of crafts in Tanzania; common facility societies, however, may prove to be a factor for promotion in this field. More particularly the purchasing co-operatives, but also the credit societies which have been under consideration are expected to attract widespread interest among Tanzanian craftsmen, as was learned in the survey. Both kinds of institution can confer considerable advantage by increasing profits and facilitating investment, whereas marketing societies still seem to be at the moment of lesser importance, except for woodcarvers, some of whom are included in the NSIC programme.

Bibliography

AGARWALA, A. N.: *Some Aspects of Economic Advancement of Underdeveloped Economies.* Allahabad–Bombay–Delhi 1958.

ANDERSON, E.: *Primary School Leavers in Rural Areas.* University of East Africa, Social Science Conference, December 1966, Nairobi.

BHARATI, A.: A Social Survey, in: *Portrait of a Minority. Asians in East Africa,* edited by D. P. GHAI. London–New York–Nairobi, Oxford University Press, 1965.

CALLAWAY, A.: *School Leavers and the Developing Economy of Nigeria* (from the Dec. 1960 Conference Proceedings published by N.I.S.E.R., Ibadan. Reprinted in *West Africa,* issues of March 25, April 1, 8, 15, 1961).

DELF, D.: *Asians in East Africa.* London–New York–Nairobi, Oxford University Press, 1963.

GEIGER and ARMSTRONG: *The Development of Private Enterprise.* Planning Pamphlet No. 120 of the National Planning Association. Washington 1964.

GHAI, D. P.: An Economic Survey, in: *Portrait of a Minority,* edited by D. P. GHAI. London–New York–Nairobi 1965.

— and GHAI, Y.: Asians in East Africa: Problems and Prospects, in: *The Journal of Modern African Studies,* Vol. 3, No. 1, 1965.

GHAI, Y. P.: The Asian Dilemma in East Africa, in: *East Africa Journal,* March 1965.

HARRIS, J. R. and ROWE, M. P.: *Entrepreneurial Patterns in the Nigerian Sawmilling Industry.* N.I.S.E.R. Reprint Series No. 24. Ibadan 1966.

HEIJNEN, J. D.: Results of a Job Preference Test Administered to Pupils in Std. VIII, in: *Kericho Papers,* 1966.

International Labour Organization: *Services for Small-scale Industry.* Geneva, ILO, 1961.

—: *Co-operative Information.* Geneva, ILO, 1964.

—: *Technical Export Meeting on Development of Managerial and Entrepreneurial Resources in Africa,* Information Paper, MAN. DEV./Africa Meeting 12. Geneva, ILO, 1966.

KILBY, P.: *African Enterprise: The Nigerian Bread Industry.* Stanford, Hoover Institution, 1965.

KOFF, D.: Education and Employment, Perspectives of Kenya Primary Pupils, in: *Kericho Papers,* 1966.

NEULOH, O. (Ed.): *Der ostafrikanische Industriearbeiter zwischen Shamba und Maschine.* Afrika-Studien No. 43, München, Weltforum Verlag, 1969.

PAULUS, M.: *Das Genossenschaftswesen in Tanganyika und Uganda — Möglichkeiten und Aufgaben.* Afrika-Studien No. 15, Berlin–Heidelberg–New York, Springer-Verlag, 1967.

REDLICH, F.: Entrepreneurship in the Initial Stages of Industrialization, in: *Weltwirtschaftliches Archiv,* Vol. 75 (1955).

ROTHERMUND, I.: *Die politische und wirtschaftliche Rolle der asiatischen Minderheit in Ostafrika.* Berlin–Heidelberg–New York, Springer-Verlag, 1965.

Savings and Credit Societies in Tanzania. Dar es Salaam 1967 (mimeo.).

SCHELL, I. O. W.: *Tanganyika und Sansibar.* Bonn, Kurt Schroeder Verlag, 1959.

SINGER, M.: Changing Craft Traditions in India, in: *Labour Commitment and Social Change in Developing Areas,* edited by W. E. MOORE and A. S. FELDMAN. New York, Social Science Research Council, 1960, pp. 258–276.

Tanganyika: *Report on the African Loan Funds together with the 1955 and 1956 Accounts for the Local Development and African Productivity Loand Fund.* Dar es Salaam 1958.

Tanzania, The United Republic of: *Report of the Presidential Committee of Enquiry into Co-operative Movement and Marketing Boards.* Dar es Salaam, Government Printer, 1966.

XYDIAS, N.: Labour: Conditions, Aptitudes, Training, in: *Social Implications of Industrialization and Urbanization in Africa South of the Sahara.* Paris, United Nations Educational, Scientific and Cultural Organization, 1956.

POLICIES OF MARKETING BOARDS IN EAST AFRICA

by

Werner LAMADE

Contents

List of Tables

The study on Policies of Marketing Boards in East Africa by Werner LAMADE is the outcome of a field investigation sponsored by the Fritz-Thyssen Foundation, Cologne, which the author conducted in respect of the marketing system for agricultural products from January 1966 until February 1967 in Kenya, Uganda and Tanzania[1]. Special attention was focused on the structure, functions, methods of operation and the problems of the marketing boards as well as on measures of rationalization or streamlining of the marketing boards and their policies. In the following, however, only some of the findings of this investigation will be elucidated.

Upon graduation from university, LAMADE specialized in problems of agricultural development in developing countries. From 1962–63 he was a fellow of the "Seminar für Landwirtschaftliche Entwicklung am Institut für Ausländische Landwirtschaft, Berlin-Dahlem" (Seminar on Agricultural Development at the Institute for Foreign Agriculture, Berlin-Dahlem); from July 1964 to July 1965 he was working for the Food and Agriculture Organization (FAO) in the Research Department of the Ghana Food Marketing Board to assist in the preparation of a price stabilization programme. Since spring of 1967 LAMADE has been working in the FAO Commodities and Trade Division in Rome.

---

1 The research on which this study is based came to a close at the end of 1966. The nationalization of key positions of the Tanzanian economy at the beginning of 1967 shortly after the "Arusha Declaration", which contained the aims of Tanzania's future socialist policy, did not leave unaffected the agricultural sector including the marketing of agricultural products. The final changes in the organization of the marketing system, and its channels and agencies through the steps taken had then not yet been determined when this study was concluded. However, it was already visible then that Government influence on the whole marketing system, including the boards, would increase. The entire marketing chain of some industries was brought under closer control by the take-over of links in the chain hitherto controlled by private firms. The nationalization of flour mills, the pyrethrum processing company, sisal export firms, etc., strengthened Government control over these industries by extending its influence over the flow of agricultural products (including the processing) from the producer to the ultimate local consumer or to the export agency respectively. The reader should be aware of these new developments which took place during the first months of 1967 and which could not be taken into consideration in this study any more.

A. INTRODUCTION: HISTORICAL DEVELOPMENT OF MARKET CONTROL AND MARKET ORGANIZATION OF AGRICULTURAL PRODUCTS NOW UNDER MARKETING BOARDS

Although the three East African countries experienced a common colonial history which very often resulted in similar patterns of political, economic, and social structure, the economic policy pursued in the three countries with regard to market controls and the organization of agricultural crops showed distinct differences between Tanganyika on the one hand and Kenya on the other, the development in Uganda being of lesser importance in this instance. The various steps and the diversified motives which gave birth to the existing patterns of today's regulatory means of production and marketing of agricultural products, will be outlined in brief to explain the system of marketing boards in East Africa, its functioning, its problems as well as the tendencies and future prospects of development.

Development of Market Controls and Market Organization of Crops in Tanzania

Before the Second World War (the initial attempts to organize the marketing of agricultural products go back to the early twenties) market controls of various kinds were imposed on some crops produced for the domestic as well as for the export market. Such regulatory means included, for instance, compulsory sales on Native Authority Markets, compulsory grading, fixing of minimum prices, licensing of traders, etc. Generally speaking, there existed no uniform pattern during this period; the degree of market control for various crops differed widely.

One attempt, however, was made in the late thirties to devise a more uniform system of marketing control, at least for crops grown by African farmers. Originally, an ordinance was introduced, the Native Produce (Control and Marketing) Ordinance, which was to authorize Government to establish Control Boards for any African produce where it was considered expedient. Strong protests from the Indian trading Community, however, compelled the Government to confine the scope of this bill to the "Native Coffee Industry" [2].

2 With regard to marketing before the Second World War see Ch. Leubuscher: Marketing Schemes for Native-grown Produce in African Territories, in: *Africa*, Vol. XII, No. 2 (April 1939), p. 163–188.

As a result, two coffee boards in the Moshi and the Kilimanjaro region were established, i.e. the Moshi Native Coffee Board and the Bukoba Native Coffee Board. These boards were given powers of control over cultivation, preparation and marketing of African grown coffee in the respective areas.
During the war the marketing and prices of almost all export commodities were controlled under Defence Regulations. Prices for scheduled crops were fixed and the Government appointed agents to purchase and export these products.

Post-war Years up to 1962

The war-time control system was more or less maintained until the end of the forties and for some crops until the early fifties. In 1949 a second attempt was made to streamline the marketing structure for African grown produce. The African Agricultural Products (Control and Marketing) Ordinance which was enacted for this purpose provided "for the declaration of areas in which the production and purchase of specified produce may be controlled and regulated by Boards which may be given power with the consent of the Legislative Council to make orders for the compulsory marketing of produce through an agent appointed by the Board" [3]. As at the end of the thirties, the intention was to create area or provincial boards to determine the marketing pattern for specific crops in a certain limited geographical area. In actual fact, this Ordinance only replaced the old individual schemes by a comprehensive new one. Apart, however, from the existing area boards, i.e. the Moshi Native Coffee Board, the Bukoba Native Coffee Board, the Nyamirembe Native Tobacco Board, and Songea Native District Tobacco Board (the two latter were established after the war and during the war respectively), which were now reconstituted, only one Board was newly established under this Ordinance, namely the Lake Region Hedge Sisal Board.
As far as export crops are concerned the first nation-wide marketing board, however, came into existence under a separate Act. A one-channel marketing scheme was established for cotton in 1952 with the foundation of the Lint and Seed Marketing Board. By contrast, minor export crops grown by African farmers, such as oilseeds, were freed from control and purchased through private traders as agents and exported by big export-import firms. The regulations according to which these crops were to pass through Native Authority Markets were seldom obeyed. The exclusively or mainly European grown crops, such as sisal, tea and pyrethrum were decontrolled in the late forties and early fifties, starting with sisal in 1949. Growers were permitted to sell by private contracts or, in the case of sisal, through a new marketing organization formed in this year, the Tanganyika Sisal Marketing Association (TASMA).

3 Tanganyika, Department of Agriculture: *Annual Report 1949*. Dar es Salaam, Government Printer, 1949, p. 43.

Coffee, a crop grown by African and European farmers alike, was sold through co-operative organizations from 1952 onwards (in respect of the African grown coffee) and from 1954 on (in respect of the European grown coffee). This system had already existed prior to the war with regard to African grown mild coffees.

The first statutory marketing organization for certain food crops with monopoly powers was already established in 1949. The sale of a number of crops, of which the most important one was maize, to the Grain Storage Department was made compulsory[4]. The functions and aims of this body were essentially the same as those of its successor, the NAPB. After its dissolution in 1956 a 2-year transition period followed when controls were gradually relaxed. Thereafter commenced a period of virtually free marketing without almost any restrictions, which came to an end when Tanzania achieved independence.

The Period from 1962 up to the Present Day

In 1962 a period of great diversity ended. When in that year the new legislation known as the Agricultural Products (Control and Marketing) Act 1962, came into force, repealing the African Agricultural Products (Control and Marketing) Ordinance of 1949, the initial intention again was not the creation of national boards covering the whole country, but the establishment of regional or district boards, some of which were to deal with a number of crops. In 1962–63, some fifteen boards were established along the lines of this ordinance[5]. These boards, some of them multi-commodity, some single-commodity boards, were not meant to handle crops themselves, but to issue compulsory marketing directives prescribing the outlets through which the commodity had to pass. In general, these outlets were cooperative unions. Since there was no clear definition of the marketing policy, the following years, however, represented a period of confusion. Some of these boards issued regulations at a time when national boards were already in existence covering the whole country and establishing their own channels. At the end of 1966 several of these area boards were still in existence although only on paper. The major break-through to the present system, which was by no means consistent but more uniform than ever before, occurred between

4 Some notes on the operations of the Grain Storage Department can be found on p. 333.

5 These were the Tabora Region and Kahama District Agricultural Products Board, Central Region Agricultural Products Board, Morogoro Region Agricultural Products Board, East Lake Region Agricultural Products Board, Southern Region Agricultural Products Board, Southern Region Cashew Board, Rungwe Coffee Board, Rungwe Rice Board, Kilimanjaro Coffee Board, Pare Rice Board, Lushoto Wattle Board, Mara Dairy Board, Arusha Dairy Board, and the Kilimanjaro Dairy Board.

1962 and 1964 when the idea was conceived to introducing new boards on a country-wide level, and abolishing boards operating on a regional or area basis. By the end of 1966 twelve boards were in existence which influenced marketing in one or the other way. Thus, the period commencing in 1962 and bringing an end to the more or less free marketing of most of the crops by the introduction of marketing boards must be considered a period of transition which was expected to terminate in 1967–68 when a more systematic programme was scheduled to come into force [6].

Development of Market Controls and Market Organization of Crops in Kenya and Uganda

In reviewing the development of market controls and market organization of crops in Kenya, it should always be kept in mind that the marketing boards in Kenya originated during a period when European farmers — with the exception of the cotton-growers — were the only large-scale producers for the market. Most of the Kenyan Boards were founded not on the initiative of Government, but under the pressure of European producers. They were "producer boards" in the sense that the emphasis was placed rather on the production or general regulatory side of an agricultural industry than on marketing [7]. These boards aimed mainly at the safeguard of European farmers in Kenya — as one Government official in an unpublished report of 1963 put it: "Historically the formation of several commodity boards is not unconnected with European agriculture. High cost production by European farmers of products such as cereals and dairy products needed not only tariff protection from imports but also subsidizing by consumers. This was particularly essential in the case of commodities of which there were exportable surpluses which had to be sold at a 'loss', i.e. at world market prices which were below cost of production." The connection of large-scale European farming with some highly specialised agricultural industries (maize, dairy, cattle, pigs) offers an explanation for the large number of boards in Kenya covering crops and other agricultural produce which in Tanzania and Uganda were produced by African peasants mainly for subsistence consumption or only to a rather minor extent for the market.
The progress of the development of market controls of agricultural products in Uganda was much less rapid and there were always fewer marketing boards in Uganda than in Tanzania and Kenya. The first marketing board (for cotton) was established in 1949, and another one (for coffee) in 1953. At the beginning of 1967 the Uganda Government planned to set up a

6 See below, p. 342 et seq.
7 Their discussion is included here because they affect one or the other marketing aspekt and the dividing line between a mere production board and a marketing board is hard to draw.

marketing board which was to bring the marketing of a number of important food crops and minor export crops under statutory control. At that time the Uganda Government also intended to establish a Dairy Board dealing with problems of milk marketing and distribution[8].

African Socialism and Marketing Policy

Beside the specific reasons and motives resulting from the economic and political situation in the individual countries which determined the system of production and market controls, the marketing policy in East Africa was shaped by a factor which all three East African countries had in common, although to a varying degree. Most reasons for bringing all the major export and food crops under the control of marketing boards in one way or another, are found in the adopted post-colonial political philosophy of African Socialism. African Socialism is nowhere universally defined and therefore is interpreted differently in all African countries which claim Socialism as the ultimate objective in regard to the structure of their respective societies.
Marketing boards were originally set up not to exchange a capitalist agricultural structure for a socialist one but to overcome deficiencies in the capitalist system and to make it acceptable again for the agricultural producer. With this idea in mind, marketing boards had been introduced earlier in West and East Africa by the colonial governments. After independence, African governments recognised the possibility of marketing boards being used as tools for attaining goals related to an agricultural and general economic policy within their development plans, no matter whether such plans embodied a socialistic outlook.

It was recently maintained that next to "Marxism other Western values, especially those obtained from colonial economic practices have influenced the African interpretation of Socialism. Although the colonialists may have espoused a laissez-faire ideology, in practice they preferred order and regulation to a competitive market economy ... The colonial bureaucracy set up marketing boards, price controls, price supports, sales quotas, compulsory savings, and the general regulation of trade and industry ... Although these colonial economic practices may not have been socialistic, the extensive governmental regulations and bureaucratic passion for economic order have carried over into a good deal of contemporary African socialist thinking."[9]

What, however, is the relationship between African Socialism and marketing boards in East Africa?
In a sessional paper the Kenyan Government, which at least theoretically bases its version of African Socialism on the same principles as Tanzania,

8 *Uganda Argus,* May 7th, 1966.
9 Ch. F. Andrain: Patterns of African Socialist Thought, in: *African Forum,* Vol. I, No. 3, 1965, p. 45.

namely the "mutual social responsibility" as a whole[10], states that "the marketing boards will be used to promote a socialist organisation of the country's economy"[11].

Unfortunately, there exists no statement presenting a clear official definition of the relationship between marketing boards and African Socialism in the other two East African countries. This may be due to the fact that African Socialism itself has not been defined clearly enough: much less has the position of marketing boards within this political concept been stated.

In Tanzania the relationship between African Socialism and the role of marketing boards was brought to light by the political and economic development which has been taking place in recent years. Firstly, Tanzania's version of African Socialism is based on "Ujamaa". President Nyerere translates "Ujamaa" by "familyhood" but wants to see the traditional concept and spirit of brotherhood extended from kinship or tribal groups to the whole nation, or an even greater entity. African Socialism "is opposed to capitalism which seeks to build a happy society on the basis of the Exploitation of Man by Man; and it is equally opposed to doctrinal Socialism which seeks to build its happy society on a philosophy of Inevitable Conflict between Man and Man"[12].

An immediate outcome of this philosophy was the tremendous promotion of the co-operative movement in Tanzania, resulting in the establishment of a great number of new co-operative societies after independence as the next greater unit to be ruled by the extended-family spirit[13].

In order to make these new co-operative units viable, it was, however, crucial to protect them from the keen competition of the extremely experienced Asian traders and to guarantee them an outlet and a price for the produce marketed on behalf of their members. The agricultural co-operatives, therefore, were established to act under the protecting umbrella of marketing boards which were to appoint them as their sole buying agent. Thus, the promotion of the marketing boards after Independence was an indirect outflow of the need to guard the primary pillars on which African Socialism was to be built[14].

---

10 Republic of Kenya: *African Socialism and its Application to Planning in Kenya,* Sessional Paper No. 10. Nairobi, Government Printer, 1965, p. 4 (Quoted in the following as Republic of Kenya: *African Socialism*).

11 Ibid., p. 39.

12 J. K. Nyerere: *Ujamaa, the Basis of African Socialism.* Dar es Salaam, Government Printer, 1962.

13 The aim of establishing co-operatives in many sectors of the economic life as a means of introducing African Socialism coincided favourably with another goal, namely, to break the predominance of the Asian trading community, and to Africanize trade, particularly the trade in primary products.

14 In this context it should be mentioned that the Tanganyika African National Union (TANU), the ruling party which "is entrusted first of all with building

Secondly, in many developing countries planning of economic development in order to husband the limited resources frequently extended to the control of marketing not only of the one or two major export commodities but also of the less important export crops and the main local food crops. In Tanzania a tendency had become more and more apparent in 1966–67, towards using the marketing boards as tools for the implementation of a rationalized agricultural policy designed by Government, comprising production, marketing and eventual processing of all agricultural crops produced for export as well as for the domestic market. This implies necessarily that decision-making is taken away from the boards and delegated to Government[15]. Principally, marketing boards as institutions fit into a capitalist as well as into a socialist economic system. Yet it seems that the stronger the tendency of a country toward socialism, the greater becomes Government influence on the activities of marketing boards.

B. STRUCTURE OF THE SYSTEM AND TYPES OF MARKETING BOARDS

At the end of 1966 there were twelve marketing boards in existence in Tanzania operating on a national scale[16]. There were fifteen boards in Kenya which thus had the highest number of boards, while Uganda had only two boards.
The marketing boards in the three East African countries were the following:

In Tanzania

the National Agricultural Products Board (NAPB),
Lint and Seed Marketing Board (LSMB),
Tanganyika Coffee Board (TCB),
Tanganyika Tobacco Board (TTB),
National Wheat Board (NWB),
National Sugar Board (NSB),
Tanganyika Pyrethrum Board,
Tanganyika Sisal Marketing Board (TSMB),

up of the Tanganyika nation founded on the precepts of Ujamaa" claims to be the initiator of the idea to create the National Agricultural Products Board.

15 See below p. 342 et seq.

16 See also W. Lamade: Marketing Boards in Tanzania, in: *Zeitschrift für Ausländische Landwirtschaft,* Jahrgang 7, Heft 4, Oktober 1968, pp. 334–348.

Tanganyika Tea Board,
Tanganyika Papain Board,
Tanganyika Seeds Board,
Tanganyika Dairy Board.

In Kenya

the Coffee Marketing Board,
Cotton Lint and Seed Marketing Board,
Pyrethrum Marketing Board,
Maize and Produce Board,
Kenya Meat Commission (KMC),
Kenya Tea Development Authority (KTDA),
Wheat Board,
Upland Bacon Factory Board,
Kenya Dairy Board (KDB),
Pig Industry Board,
Coffee Board,
Tea Board,
Pyrethrum Board of Kenya,
Canning Crops Board,
Interim Horticultural Development Council.

In Uganda

the Coffee Marketing Board,
Lint Marketing Board.

In respect of their organizational set-up, their functions, and their regulatory powers considerable differences prevail between the existing boards not only of Tanzania and Kenya and/or Uganda, but also between the boards in the individual countries. In an attempt to classify the marketing boards in existence at the end of 1966 by applying criteria regarding the physical involvement and actual market power exerted by these boards, one may distinguish between [17]:

17 The FAO has developed a different system of categories classifying marketing boards in (1) Advisory and promotional boards (not handling commodities), (2) Regulatory boards (not handling commodities), (3) Boards stabilizing prices without trading, (4) Boards stabilizing prices on domestic markets by trading alongside other enterprises, (5) Export monopoly trading and price stabilization boards, and (6) Domestic monopoly trading and price stabilization boards. This system was, however, not applied here for two reasons, firstly because of the great emphasis which is laid upon price stabilization (with four out of six types), secondly because it would be difficult to fit into this system boards which have

- Self-trading two-sided monopoly boards for the export and/or domestic market, — Type I
- Non-self-trading two-sided monopoly boards for the export and/or the domestic market, which appoint a sales agency to which the monopoly is conferred, — Type II
- Non-self-trading two-sided monopoly boards for the export and/or domestic market, which do not physically handle products either by trading themselves or through an agent, but direct a specific crop through a one-channel marketing system, — Type III
- Boards vested only with statutory powers confined to regulatory activities such as licensing exporters and fixing minimum export prices. These boards may moreover promote the specific industry including marketing and advise the government on these matters. — Type IV

In applying these criteria one arrives at a classification which is shown in table 1. The marketing boards do not constitute a coherent system in any of the three countries as they have mostly been established according to specific needs at specific times. Although they may be categorized in four types, their operation methods are by no means consistent. There often exist, however, strong similarities between the marketing boards of the same type from one country to the other as will be briefly discussed in the following.

In Tanzania the National Agricultural Products Board, the Tanganyika Coffee Board, and the Lint and Seed Marketing Board perform virtually the same functions in much the same way as their equivalent boards in Kenya (Maize and Produce Board, Coffee Marketing Board, Cotton, Lint and Seed Marketing Board), and in Uganda (Coffee Marketing Board and Lint Marketing Board), although one or the other aspect of operation method, particularly with regard to price policy, may differ.

In Kenya two Boards share the responsibility of regulating the pyrethrum industry and marketing pyrethrum and its products. The Pyrethrum Marketing Board in Kenya determines the annual quota to be produced, accepts, grades and makes payment and markets the pyrethrum products, after having appointed a contractor to produce the extract[18]. The Pyrethrum Marketing Board in Kenya moreover conducts research into pyrethrum processing and marketing. Left to the Pyrethrum Board was only the licensing of growers in accordance with the total annual quota decided by the Pyrethrum Marketing Board and the implementing of the research into the agronomic side of pyrethrum. These functions were in Tanzania also performed by the Tanganyika Pyrethrum Board. This Board controls the one-channel marke-

---

monopoly rights but do not engage in physical marketing themselves but rather delegate it to agencies.
See J. C. Abbott and H. L. Creupelandt: *Agricultural Marketing Boards — Their Establishment and Operation,* Marketing Guide No. 5. Rome, Food and Agricultural Organization, 1966, pp. 4 et seq.

18 This is the Pyrethrum Processing Company of Kenya of which the share-holding is: Pyrethrum Board 58 per cent, Mitchell Cotts Ltd. 30 per cent, and the Commonwealth Development Corporation 12 per cent.

Table 1. *Types of Marketing Boards in Tanzania, Kenya, and Uganda at the end of 1966*

Name of Board	Self-trading export and/or domestic monopoly boards	Non-self-trading export and/or monopoly boards		Regulatory, promotional and advisory boards
		Appointing sales agents with monopoly	Issuing compulsory marketing order for one-channel marketing	
	Type I	Type II	Type III	Type IV
Tanzania				
Nat. Agric. Products B.	×			
Lint & Seed Marketing B.	×			
Tang. Coffee Board	×			
Tang. Tobacco Board		×		
National Wheat Board		×		
National Sugar Board		×		
Tang. Pyrethrum Board			×	
Tang. Sisal Marketing B.				×
Tang. Tea Board				×
Tang. Papain Board [a]			×	
Tang. Seeds Board			×	
Tang. Dairy Board		×		
Kenya				
Coffee Marketing Board	×			
Cotton Lint & Seed Marketing Board	×			
Pyrethrum Market. Board	×			
Maize and Produce Board	×			
Kenya Meat Commission	×			
Kenya Tea Dev. Auth.	×			
Wheat Board		×		
Uplands Bacon Fact. Board [b]		×		
Kenya Dairy Board			×	
Pig Industry Board			×	
Coffee Board				×
Tea Board				×
Sisal Board				×
Pyrethrum Board				×
Canning Crops Board				×
Interim Horticult. Development Council				×
Uganda				
Coffee Marketing Board	×			
Lint Marketing Board	×			

[a] Not working.

[b] This board operates the Uplands Bacon Factory. It has no complete monopoly because it handles only about 95 per cent of the total production.

ting of pyrethrum in Tanzania by the Tanganyika Extract Company which buys the pyrethrum flowers, pays the producers and sells the pyrethrum extract (pyrethrin)[19].

The Kenya Meat Commission (KMC) is a statutory body which has no equivalent in Uganda or in Tanzania. It has the exclusive right to purchase, process and sell livestock, meat and byproducts on a wholesale basis. If this board exercised its power to the full extent, all livestock raised in Kenya would be processed through the slaughterhouses of the KMC and be exported or sold on the home market from there. The KMC, however, actually only buys for the supply of urban centres and for export, because operations in rural areas would appear to be too costly. Of the total offtake in Kenya of about 800,000 heads of cattle each year, the KMC handles about 200,000. The rest is purchased and sold by small butchers in the rural areas, either with the permission of the KMC or illegally.

The Kenya Tea Development Authority is not a marketing board in the strict sense; its duties cover much wider fields. The Authority founded for the promotion of tea growing of African smallholders guides the cultivation from the early stages of planting by extension services, loans, etc. up to the point of harvesting. It also processes tea and markets it. Inasmuch as it has monopoly powers to market the processed tea it is grouped under boards of type I.

The National Wheat Board in Tanzania and the Kenya Wheat Board operate very much along the same lines. In addition to performing advisory functions to the Government, they plan and control the distribution of wheat to mills. As in Tanzania where the Tanganyika Cooperative Farmers' Association is the sole appointed agent to handle the total crop, the Kenya Farmers' Association fulfills this role in Kenya, having the sole right to purchase and distribute wheat in Kenya directed by the Wheat Board's decisions.

The Kenya dairy industry and pig industry are organised along similar lines with a board controlling the industry and one major organisation handling by far the greatest proportion of the products controlled. Both industries play a minor role in Tanzania and Uganda and their organisation is in its initial stages because cattle is of much less importance in these two countries. There are, for example, approximately 350,000 high-grade dairy cattle in Kenya compared with 7,000 in Uganda and about 10,000 in Tanzania. The Kenyan Dairy Board has the power to control sales of dairy produce by producers, to control prices on wholesale and retail levels, to allocate quotas to producers, etc. Its main agent is the Kenya Co-operative Creameries, the oldest and largest co-operative society in Kenya. It handles most of the milk produced in Kenya on a large scale as well as milk produced on small peasant farms.

19 This company, in which Mitchell Cotts held majority shares, was nationalized in early 1967.

Two boards control pig breeding and marketing. The Pig Industry Board has statutory powers to license breeders, to allocate quotas to factories and butchers for slaughter and to purchase pigs from licensed breeders. The second board is the Uplands Bacon Factory Board, operating a factory which processes more than 95 per cent of the total offtake of pigs, apart from advising the Pig Industry Board on prices to be paid. The aim of both the Kenya Dairy Board and the Pig Industry Board is the stabilisation of the industries concerned by a price discrimination policy which will be discussed later.

In Kenya the Coffee, Tea, Sisal, Pyrethrum and Canning Crops Board are regulatory and/or promotional and advisory boards concerned with licensing producers and care of the general well-being of the industry, mainly the production side, by carrying out research and other means of promotion. In the case of tea and sisal they have their equivalent in Tanzania, and instead of having separate boards for coffee and pyrethrum the powers and functions of the Kenyan boards are given in Tanzania to the Tanganyika Coffee Board and the Tanganyika Pyrethrum Board respectively. The Interim Horticultural Development Council was in 1966 a purely advisory body to the Government on matters concerning production and marketing and the promotion of the industry.

The two boards in existence in Uganda in 1966–67 for coffee and cotton were both of the type of the classical export monopoly marketing boards[20] as they developed in West Africa, commissioned, apart from their marketing functions, with stabilising producer prices between seasons. The Lint Marketing Board in Uganda is exactly of the same type as the Cotton Lint and Seed Marketing Board in Kenya and the Lint and Seed Marketing Board in Tanzania. The Coffee Marketing Board of Uganda operates along slightly different lines from the boards handling coffee in Tanzania and Kenya which do not intend to stabilise producer prices.

C. RECENT TRENDS IN THE SYSTEM OF MARKETING BOARDS

I. Extension of Controlled Marketing

Viewing the history of the marketing of agricultural products in East Africa there appears to be a trend towards organised and controlled marketing of

20 The Coffee Marketing Board is not strictly a monopoly board because it does not market wet processed robusta coffee and the arabica coffee grown by the Bugisu Co-operative Union both passing through private trade channels.

an increasing number of products in all three East African countries since the end of the Second World War. More and more commodities were brought under existing or newly established boards. This tendency was not uninterrupted but showed setbacks, for instance, when the Grain Storage Department was dissolved in Tanzania in 1956 and the country returned to free marketing of staple food crops which were formally controlled by this Department. A breakthrough came in the early sixties and Tanzania reached its peak of marketing board control around 1966. In Kenya this development started in the early fifties and this country had already reached the maximum number of boards by about 1960.

It is interesting to compare this common trend with the recommendations of the World Bank Missions visiting the three countries in the early sixties. The mission to Uganda considered as undesirable any marketing controls for commodities other than those already strictly controlled by that time (cotton and coffee)[21]. Although no mention was made of the advantages and disadvantages of a more centralised marketing system under a statutory organisation which does not necessarily involve operations against the forces of a free market (e.g. a board operating by means of a buffer stock scheme alongside private trade[22]), it seems that the mission was opposed to any institutional intervention with private trade activities. The mission to Tanganyika adopted a rather careful and uncommitting attitude towards the whole issue of control. It favoured intervention in some aspects of marketing, such as compulsory grading but it even admits that one channel marketing might be feasible[23]. It did not, however, commit itself to any particular course of action, and proposed that "policy should be kept flexible"[24]. The mission to Kenya finally expressed a quite different view. It saw a strong case for government intervention with the marketing process: "Some system of organised marketing is essential; an organisation is essential; and to fulfill national objectives, government intervention is essential."[25]

Despite these different approaches towards intervention with the marketing

---

21 "The mission believes there should be greater reliance on the market and we do not recommend the setting of fixed prices for commodities that are uncontrolled at present." The International Bank for Reconstruction and Development: *The Economic Development of Uganda.* Baltimore, The Johns Hopkins Press, 1962. p. 191.

22 Such a scheme is outlined in J. C. ABBOTT and H. C. CREUPELANDT, *op. cit.*, pp. 73–111.

23 The International Bank for Reconstruction and Development: *The Economic Development of Tanganyika.* Baltimore, The Johns Hopkins Press, 1961, pp. 126–127.

24 Ibid., p. 124.

25 The International Bank for Reconstruction and Development: *The Economic Development of Kenya.* Baltimore, The Johns Hopkins Press, 1963, p. 106 (in the following quoted as IBRD: *Kenya*).

of various agricultural commodities, the tendency towards organised and controlled marketing was rather uniform in all three countries. Both the number and the volume of agricultural products, which were placed under marketing control, increased.

Thus in Tanzania crops which accounted for over 65 per cent of the monetary value of production were controlled by a monopoly one-channel-system under marketing boards in 1965. Crops constituting about 30 per cent of the monetary value of production were otherwise directed by decisions of a marketing board. Only a small share of the agricultural monetary net output (apart from livestock and livestock products) was marketed freely, the most important of these being pulses, sorghum and all sorts of fruits and vegetables.

In respect of the two former crops it could be considered only a matter of time until they would be put under the jurisdiction of the NAPB, leaving only the latter unaffected. It was recognized that it would be hardly feasible (at least for the time being) to centralise the marketing of fruits and vegetables because their perishability makes their marketing very difficult, and facilities requiring large amounts of capital such as refrigerated storage and special transport equipment would be necessary.

When this study was completed, the three Governments contemplated the establishment of a number of new boards. In Tanzania the formation of a statutory livestock organisation was expected in the near future, and in Kenya a statutory board for horticultural crops was under consideration, expanding the powers of the present Interim Horticultural Development Council. In Uganda the creation of new marketing boards was planned[26], bringing under control a number of important food crops, minor export crops, and milk. This clearly proves that the phase of expansion of controlled marketing by extending control over more and more commodities had not yet been concluded.

With the establishment of the boards planned in Tanzania and Uganda hardly any other commodity of economic importance in these countries would exist which would not be controlled in one way or another by a statutory organisation. Exceptions are only crops such as tea, sisal and the like whose marketing has been highly organised for a long time. In Tanzania even in these cases government intervention is growing, for instance for sisal, whereas in Kenya, up till now, boards for these crops have preserved the character of producer boards to a large extent.

Although the trend towards organised and controlled marketing by separate boards has not come to an end yet, another tendency discussed in the following can clearly be observed in all three countries, although not to the same extent.

---

26 See above p. 288.

II. Amalgamation of Marketing Boards

As indicated before, it is characteristic of the marketing boards existing in East Africa that they very often have widely differing functions and powers which in many cases, moreover, are not clearly defined. In order to abolish this state of uncertainty and plurality a streamlining of the marketing board system has proved necessary in all three East African countries. It is expected that with the amalgamation of a number of boards, the marketing of crops with virtually the same characteristics which was hitherto conducted by separate bodies can in future be dealt with by one.

The arguments in favour of an amalgamation of boards are

- Total staff could be reduced and overhead costs would decrease.
- Facilities now owned by every single board could be used commonly according to a properly worked out plan of operation. A multi-crop board could use transport and storage facilities more economically and at reduced costs by appropriate seasonal planning according to the various crop seasons.
- Exchange of information between headquarters of the boards (which often are not located in the capitals of the respective countries) and the Ministries represented on the boards could be facilitated and speeded up.
- Representatives of Ministries on the boards would not need to travel as much in order to attend board meetings and sessions of the executive committees.
- Market analysis and sales promotion which would have been too costly for one of the existing boards with a more limited field of operation could possibly be afforded by one board alone for a number of crops commonly [27].

There seems to be no doubt that in all three East African countries a streamlining of the present system would be advantageous and increase efficiency. The crucial question, however, appears to be which boards ought to be amalgamated and regrouped in each country in order to arrive at the most suitable and workable combination.

Tanzania

In Tanzania the Presidential Special Committee of Enquiry into Co-operative Movement and Marketing Boards proposed in 1966 the gradual amalgama-

27 The Lint Marketing Board of Uganda had, for example, to close its London sales offices in 1966 because expenses were too high compared with the volume of direct sales overseas.

tion of all "the existing Boards into two, one dealing with crops whose market is dominated by local consumption, and the other with crops raised mostly for export"[28]. It was further proposed that the Seeds Board and Papain Board be abolished so that the composition of crops under the jurisdiction of the two boards would look as follows:

Export Marketing Board	*Marketing Board for domestic crops*
Cashew nuts, oilseeds, copra and Cassava (from NAPB)	Maize, paddy and rice (from NAPB)
Coffee (from TCB)	Wheat (from NWB)
Cotton (from LSMB)	Sugar (from NSB)
Pyrethrum (from Tanganyika Pyrethrum Board)	Dairy Produce (from National Dairy Board)
Tea (from Tanganyika Tea Board)	
Tobacco (from TTB)	
Sisal (from TSMB)[29]	

This proposal is striking on account of its simplicity. Clearly, if such boards could be given a precise assignment, e.g. the same aims and functions, these two boards might be able to work more efficiently than the twelve single ones in existence at the end of 1966. However, some thought has to be given to a number of problems.

Firstly, it would be advantageous if the functions, powers and buying and sales arrangements for all commodities and crops handled by one board were similar if not the same. This, for instance, is the case, with the Regional Marketing Boards in Nigeria each handling a multitude of crops for which they have the same functions, powers, buying arrangements and other operation methods. However, not every type of board is suitable for all conditions. The suitability of a board type varies and depends on factors like policy objectives, type of commodity and the conditions under which it will have to operate.

It is certainly easier for the domestic crop board than for the export board to solve the problem of identical functions and powers. Functions, operation methods and marketing problems for crops like maize, paddy, rice, wheat and sugar are rather similar. It would, however, be more difficult to define identical functions, powers and ways of operation for an aggregated

---

28 The United Republic of Tanzania: *Report of the Presidential Special Committee of Enquiry into Co-operative Movement and Marketing Boards*. Dar es Salaam, Government Printer, 1966, p. 44 (in the following quoted as the United Republic of Tanzania: *Enquiry into Co-operative Movement and Marketing Boards*).

29 Although not mentioned in the Report, it has to be assumed that sisal would also come under such a board.

export board. In 1966, functions and operation methods for export commodities to be administered by such board varied widely.

Cotton, cashew nuts and oilseeds were marketed through a monopolistic one-channel-system and handled by the boards on their own account. Coffee was not handled physically by the TCB but sold on trust for the co-operatives. The boards for tobacco and pyrethrum had also monopoly power but did not handle these crops physically themselves. The former had delegated physical handling to co-operatives or private firms respectively, the latter did not influence physical handling at all. The Tea Board and Sisal Marketing Board were vested merely with regulatory powers to a rather differing extent.

Another problem is the question of representation on a multi-commodity board. In the case of an export board producers of each single crop, in the case of a domestic board also the consumers, and where industrial processing of a product already exists, also this sector of the economy, e.g. ginneries and mills, would have to be represented.

Again a solution to the problem of representation could probably be found easier for an amalgamated board for food crops than for export commodities giving membership (apart from the Ministries concerned) to the co-operative movement representing growers of maize and paddy, to the Tanganyika Farmers' Co-operative Association representing growers of wheat, the Sugar Growers' Association representing growers of sugar and possibly to a trade and milling representative. Such a board could take appropriate policy decisions and it would be easier for the managerial staff to cope with operational necessities because the problems of the crops covered do not differ very widely.

On an amalgamated marketing board for export crops the problem of representation would be more difficult. The different export crops require an extremely broad knowledge and an acquaintance with all problems concerned on the part of board members in order to take appropriate policy decisions and to enable the managerial staff to operate such a mammoth board for crops with widely differing technical and economical features. Problems of sisal marketing differ substantially from the marketing problems of coffee, pyrethrum or tobacco which in turn vary from these of cotton, cashew nuts etc. A specific operational set-up had been developed for each of these crops, in the course of time, enabling the respective boards composed of twelve or more representatives to acquire considerable experience in directing their particular industries.

The question of representation is rendered complicated by differences in the size of holdings of producers of agricultural products and by differences in the membership of producer organisations. In Tanzania some crops are exclusively produced by smallholders and estate growers, like coffee, others almost exclusively on estates, like sisal[30]. Their organisational set-ups also differ. Growers of some crops

30 Apart from small quantities of hedgerow sisal grown near Lake Victoria to

are organised exclusively in co-operatives, e.g. producers of cotton and of coffee, while producers of wheat and pyrethrum are grouped in co-operatives as well as growers' association, others merely in a growers' association, e.g. producers of sisal. A single Export Marketing Board would consequently be rather large if all groups are represented and, therefore, hampered in decision making. On the other hand, an Export Board with only few members can hardly cope with the whole range of different operational and economic problems for the various crops. The only way out would nevertheless consist in keeping a new amalgamated board small in membership. If such a body is not to lack knowledge about outstanding economic, agricultural and operational problems it will have to be composed mainly or exclusively from representatives of competent ministries. Far-reaching powers in deciding over specific problems would have to be assigned to the managers of the various departments who will need specialised knowledge of the crops they handle.

Finally, a problem of location will arise when marketing boards will be amalgamated. The new comprehensive marketing boards would logically have to be located in Dar es Salaam. This would certainly create difficulties for some boards, such as the Tanganyika Coffee Board at present in Moshi and the National Wheat Board with its marketing agency, the Tanganyika Farmers' Co-operative Association (TFCA) and the National Dairy Board in Arusha, all in the centre of production areas. Communication would prove extremely difficult notably in respect of the traditional auction sales for coffee in Moshi, and the necessary close daily co-operation with the coffee farmers. Further, the arrangements for pulping, fermentation, and drying, for bulking various lots, payment, etc. would probably increase costs if all the operations are directed from Dar es Salaam.
On the other hand economies in overhead and headquarters costs can be expected by an amalgamation into two boards, provided they will not become mammoth organisations beyond control. The Presidential Special Committee, in fact, does not foresee such a danger. In 1966, the three boards with considerable staffs were the NAPB, the LSMB and the TCB with a total of approximately 300 employees.
To be accurate, the staffs of the network of agencies working on behalf of a board would also have to be taken into consideration, e.g. of the TFCA and of INTRATA[31] which have taken over marketing functions on behalf of the Wheat Board and the NAPB for the marketing of wheat and cassava respectively. An amalgamation would only be sensible if the proposed two new boards with a total of not more than between 200 and 300 permanent employees would be able to handle or direct through agents approximately 500,000 tons of produce so far marketed by all the boards. The Presidential Special Committee considered this to be possible.

---

protect crops against marauding animals and apart from a small number of African settlement schemes.

31 INTRATA = International Trading & Credit Company of Tanganyika.
TFCA = Tanganyika Farmers' Co-operative Association.

Although comparisons of marketing boards in different countries usually have to be made with caution, these figures would compare quite favourably, for instance, with a marketing board in Colombia which handled a maximum of 400,000 tons and had 968 employees or in El Salvador handling a maximum of 50,000 tons with 284 employees. Both these boards have no monopoly but pursue their marketing functions in competition with private enterprises [32].

The Presidential Special Committee envisaged the best solution in dividing each of the two boards' personnel into two groups, namely, a section which would deal with administrative questions for all crops handled by the two boards and a group of technical specialists for each crop who would manage a different crop department of the two boards.
The range of arguments pro and contra will most probably not permit a solution on purely economic grounds but will require a political decision. The choice is, of course, not one of either maintaining the system of a great number of single boards as it was the case in 1966 or forming them into two boards. There exists a whole range of other possibilities in between, such as amalgamating the Wheat Board and the Sugar Board on account of their similar problems with the foodcrop section of the NAPB and leaving the other big export boards (export section of the NAPB, LSMB, TCB, TPB, TSMB and of the Tanganyika Tea Board) to function on their own.
The National Dairy Board constitutes a problem of its own. It is hardly possible to bring it under a comprehensive domestic marketing board because of its completely different problems from other agricultural commodities. It would have to remain separate with the possibility of extending its powers on the whole livestock industry if this were desired.

Uganda

Although Uganda had only two boards at the end of 1966, the tendency towards an amalgamation of marketing boards was even visible there. The Committee of Enquiry into the Cotton Industry of 1966 proposed in its report the amalgamation of the Lint Marketing Board and the Coffee Marketing Board and the attachment of the then not yet existing Agricultural Produce Marketing Board to it, so as to have only one board for all agricultural crops [33]. The proposed Dairy Board would have to work on its own as is the case in Tanzania because of its widely different problems. The reasons given for an amalgamation are similar to those put forward in Tanzania: Economies in the number of staff, common use of marketing facilities and a common sales promotion bureau overseas.

---

32 See J. C. Abbott and H. L. Creupelandt, *op. cit.*, p. 107.

33 See Uganda Government: *Report of the Committee of Enquiry into the Cotton Industry 1966.* Entebbe, Government Printer, 1966, p. 57 (quoted in the following as Uganda Government: *Inquiry into the Cotton Industry, 1966*).

Kenya

Official statements in Kenya on the development and the role of marketing boards within a socialist society underline the necessity of re-organizing the system of marketing boards: "The growth of ... (the marketing boards) ... in the past has been haphazard and in some cases intended to protect only one interest or group. There are too many boards leading to duplication of effort, waste of manpower and confusion in policy. It is therefore necessary to review and streamline the organisation and operation of all marketing boards and to use them as a positive agency for promoting our socialist policies." See Republic of Kenya: *African Socialism*, p. 39.
In 1960, already before the visit of the World Bank Mission in 1962, which considered Kenya "over-boarded" and favoured "some streamlinig of the boards, their functions, and their consultative obligations"[34], the Committee on the Organisation of Agriculture had put forward some proposals for the fusion of some of the statutory agencies. In fact, there have been some major changes in the early sixties. The multi-commodity provincial marketing boards (the Nyanza Province Marketing Board and the Central Province Marketing Board) having monopoly power over a large number of crops for exports and home use and acting as agents for the former Maize Marketing Board and for the Kenya Farmers' Association were merged into the Kenya Agricultural Produce Marketing Board in 1964, which extended its activities to crops grown in other provinces (Coast, Rift Valley, etc.) as well. Political pressure by the Luos in Nyanza warranted the division of this body into two boards, the West Kenya Marketing Board for Nyanza and the Kenya Agricultural Produce Marketing Board for all other provinces which performed also agency functions for the Maize Marketing Board.
In turn, these three boards were amalgamated in early 1966 to form the Maize and Produce Marketing Board. As a result, a type of board came into existence (for maize as main crop and a number of minor crops internally consumed and exported) which had almost its exact equivalent in Tanzania. Furthermore, with the granting of more power to the Wheat Board, the Cereal Producers (Scheduled Areas) Board had become superfluous and was abolished. Moreover, a number of boards originally designed to serve the purpose of marketing produce grown by Africans disappeared or were merged with their respective boards which until then had served European farmers (two provincial tea marketing boards, the African Nyanza Province Sugar Marketing Board and the African Livestock Marketing Organisation). For 1967 it was intended to merge the Kenya Dairy Board and Kenya Co-operative Creameries into a Kenya Dairy Commission.

---

34 IBRD: *Kenya*, p. 111.

In 1966, a motion in Parliament by members of the Kenya People's Union (KPU), the opposition party to the ruling Kenya African National Union (KANU), urged the abolishion of all existing marketing boards and their replacement by a single body. The Kenyan Government rejected this proposal, conceded, however, that there was need for a greater streamlining of the board system[35]. In fact, in 1966–67 there was scope for further amalgamations, e.g. coffee and pyrethrum could be governed by a single board for each crop, the Pig Industry Board could be amalgamated with the Upland Bacon Factory Board or even transferred to the Kenyan Meat Commission to have one body responsible for all kinds of meat as already proposed by the World Bank Mission to Kenya[36].
There may also have been scope for the fusion of the wheat board with the Maize and Produce Marketing Board and the Canning Crops Board with the Interim Horticultural Development Council. To sum up, although the trend towards streamlining is seen also in Kenya, the envisaged changes are not as incisive and not so clearly expressed as in the two other East African countries.

III. The New Role of Co-operatives

Another trend noticeable already for years in East Africa is the increasing importance of co-operatives in the role of buying agents of the marketing board. Although the concept of a "Socialist Society" differs widely in respect of all three East African countries, the co-operative movement is considered to be its basic element. In Tanzania, where co-operatives have a long and successful history in some sectors of the economy, co-operatives were very often simply superceded by marketing boards, which thus neatly integrated them into the marketing boards system. By contrast, the functional and organisational links between co-operatives and marketing boards were distinctly less close in Uganda and Kenya as will be shown later. The role of co-operatives as buying agents has, however, been considerably strengthened in the last decade also there.

Tanzania

As mentioned before, after the achievement of Independence it was believed that a rapid expansion of the co-operative movement and the replacement of all private produce trade by co-operative societies was the "deus ex

35 *East African Standard,* July 30th, 1966.
36 IBRD: *Kenya,* p. 111.

machina" to solve economical, social, and political problems simultaneously and to lay the foundation stone for a new "African Socialist" society.

This spirit persuaded the government to put heavy political pressure on the creation of numerous co-operative societies and unions. The number of co-operative societies almost doubled after Independence; it rose from 857 in 1961 to 1,533 at the end of April 1966. The position of these co-operatives in the buying system in 1966 was as follows: Where crops under one or the other type of a monopoly board were grown exclusively or mainly by smallholders, the latter were mostly organised in co-operative societies which did the primary buying from growers (covering crops such as maize, paddy, cashew, oil seeds, wheat, as well as cotton lint and seed, coffee, tobacco and pyrethrum). The co-operative unions were made the main buying agents of the board taking over produce from the primary societies. Estate growers or their organisations could sell their products directly to the boards or its appointed sales agency, e.g. sisal growers. Sugar was an exception since the cane production and its transformation into the final product were integrated in the same companies[37]. This meant that the two marketing boards in Tanzania handling produce physically on their own account (NAPB and LSMB) and three of the four boards using marketing agencies (TCB, Tanganyika Tobacco Board and the National Wheat Board) employed co-operative societies and unions as their sole buying agents[38].

This expansion could not continue indefinitely without causing serious weaknesses and soon revealing the lack of the two main pillars on which successful co-operatives are built, namely the co-operative spirit as well as sound economic management. The rapidity of expansion did not allow a simultaneous instruction of the members of the co-operatives in co-operative principles and the training of the great number of qualified managers required. This state of affairs did not remain without impact on the role of co-operatives as the boards' marketing agents. Many new co-operative societies — in general not the long established ones — rendered marketing services less efficient than private traders formerly. In many cases prices paid to producers were lower, payments to growers delayed, the number of trading posts decreased, co-operative buying stations were opened too late and further away than formerly, etc. Since the delivery of the farmers' produce to the co-operatives was made compulsory, competition from other traders

---

37 Only the Kilombero Sugar Company, one of the five sugar producers in 1966, had a scheme for outgrowers under which it purchased about 15 per cent of its requirements.

38 A distinction must be made between buying and selling agents which are not necessarily the same institutions. The Tanganyika Tobacco Board, for instance, uses exclusively co-operatives for buying tobacco (apart from the British American Tobacco Company [Tanzania] Ltd.), but uses private firms as selling agents.

exerting a pressure to reduce costs and render improved services was normally excluded. One remedy to force efficiency upon the societies would therefore be to put them under competitive pressure, the argument against this measure being in general that most of the societies are still too young to survive under such pressure. Competition would certainly mean a deadly blow for many new co-operatives. Given sufficient time, however, they could improve their performance and increase efficiency as many longer established societies have proved.

The Report of the Presidential Special Committee puts forward a broad catalogue of measures for strengthening the co-operative movement and improving efficiency, covering all aspects from the creation of a Unified Co-operative Service to incentive payments, the education and training of co-operative personnel, and the re-organisation of the top level institutions[39].

The report expected that the co-operative movement would be "growing into the functions now assigned to it in the whole marketing system"[40]. "Defending the legitimate claim" that the marketing boards operate for the benefit of the farmers, thus stressing the genuine interests of co-operatives vis-à-vis the boards and the government, the Committee proposes "that the position of the boards be changed so that in their marketing and other operations they be the agents of the co-operatives"[41]. As a practical consequence it further proposes "That the functions performed by the boards, except as to food crops locally consumed, should be gradually shifted to the co-operatives as the capacities of the latter grow"[42]. If this should materialize the trend towards a strengthening of the role of co-operatives in the buying sphere will not be reversed but rather be accentuated in future.

Uganda and Kenya

The role of the co-operatives in Kenya and Uganda as agents of marketing boards is by far less important. It has, however, shown a growing significance in recent years. In Uganda the percentage of seed cotton, for instance, passing through co-operatives before it reaches the Lint Marketing Board has risen considerably although deliveries to co-operatives were not compulsory. The percentage of seed cotton handled by co-operative societies, unions and co-operatively owned ginneries increased from 13.7 during the

39 A description of the weaknesses of the co-operative movement and a catalogue of measures to overcome these is given on pp. 9 through 38 of this Report.

40 The United Republic of Tanzania, Report of the Presidential Committee of: *Enquiry into Co-operative Movement and Marketing Boards,* p. 55.

41 *Ibid,* p. 56.

42 *Ibid,* p. 56.

season 1957–58 to 31.1 per cent in 1960–61 and to well over 50 per cent of the total production in 1965–66[43]. A similar trend can be observed in the collection of coffee crops in Uganda. Beyond the rising importance of co-operatives as buying agents there seemed to be a tendency towards increasing representation of co-operatives in the marketing of crops by the boards as it is seen from the proposed bill for the Agricultural Produce Marketing Board which was under consideration during 1966–67. This bill provided for a close link of the planned marketing board with the co-operative movement: "It is the intention of Government that the co-operative movement should participate fully in this scheme. This will be done through ... representation on the board of directors of the Board, and in the actual buying operations of the Board by the appointment of representatives of co-operatives where this is considered to be both in the interest of the co-operative movement and for the effective benefit of the Board." [44]

In Kenya a similar development can be observed with boards handling the export crops of smallholders. The share of production of coffee and pyrethrum passing through co-aperative channels increased considerably during the last ten years. While the coffee production of Kenya doubled from 23,900 tons in 1955–56 to 50,300 tons in 1965–66, the percentage of coffee bought by co-operatives increased from 0.8 per cent to 50.0 per cent during the same period. The development for pyrethrum is similar. The total pyrethrum production doubled from 3,100 tons to 6,100 tons between 1956 and 1965. The percentage of co-operatives in the total production marketed rose from 10 per cent to 69 per cent[45].

In cotton marketing, too, the role of co-operatives as buying agents of the board is becoming more and more important. In 1962 a pilot scheme was started in the Nyanza and Western Provinces giving co-operatives a monopoly in buying seed cotton from the farmers. In view of the fact that since then the buying allowance paid to co-operatives has risen from shs 1/- per 100 lbs to an average of shs 2,50[46], the Kenya Government announced that it will try to strengthen the co-operative movement by a new legislation introduced in November 1966 and to increase its efficiency by various training programmes[47]. The importance of co-operatives as buying agents for

---

43 Uganda Government: *Enquiry into the Cotton Industry, 1966.*

44 Unpublished draft of an Act providing for the establishment of a marketing board for food and minor export crops.

45 See Republic of Kenya, Statistics Division — Ministry of Economic Planning and Development: *Statistical Abstract, 1965.* Nairobi, Government Printer, 1965; *Annual Reports of the Coffee Board, the Pyrethrum Board of Kenya, and the Pyrethrum Marketing Board.*

46 Republic of Kenya: *Development Plan for the Period 1965–66 to 1969–70.* Nairobi, 1966, p. 199.

47 *Ibid.*, p. 200 et seq.

marketing boards will undoubtedly grow further. This is not only true for the primary marketing of export crops but also for food crops. The Maize Commission of Enquiry, for instance, urges Government to "encourage co-operative societies in maize producing areas to organise for the purpose of collecting maize from small producers" [48].

D. PRINCIPLES, ACHIEVEMENTS AND PROSPECTS OF PRICE POLICY OF MARKETING BOARDS

Discussions as to future policies of the marketing boards center around the price stabilization policy which constitutes a traditional function of marketing boards. Other regulating powers and functions of the boards such as the licensing of producers, exporters, advising of governments research etc., are considered to be of secondary importance and will not be discussed in the following. For Tanzania the discussion has to be extended to cover a comprehensive nationalized agricultural price and taxation policy which has been under consideration in this country.

I. Price Stabilization Policy

1. The Theoretical Framework

a) Possible Aims of the Price Policy of Marketing Boards

In general there are a number of objectives which the price policy of a marketing board can aim at by virtue of the statutory powers delegated to it. Boards in many countries have had a great autonomy and have not been interfered with. In these cases they were relatively free to determine the price level each year within the limits of its legally fixed aims. Prices worked out

48 Republic of Kenya: *Report of the Maize Commission of Enquiry, 1966.* Nairobi, Government Printer, 1966, p. 24 (in the following quoted as Republic of Kenya: *Maize Commission of Enquiry*).

by the board had in general to be approved by the Minister in charge. Unless a government had a special interest in fixing a certain price on political grounds the approval was only nominal. Often, however, governments intervened to achieve political rather than economic aims by a price policy implemented by the marketing boards. Their policy became strongly influenced or wholly determined by the government. A different ministry (usually the Ministry of Finance) decided independently upon taxes to be imposed on sales or exports which the boards had to collect on behalf of the government. In this case more objectives have to be added to the following catalogue which would not be limited to the agricultural industry or sector for which a board was established but which would affect the whole economy. Possible aims for a price policy of marketing boards may be the following:

- Securing maximum sales prices by means of the board's market power and passing the total proceeds (less marketing costs and taxes) on to producers, thus aiming at achieving higher producer incomes from sales of agricultural products than before the existence of the board.
- Securing lower consumer prices of foodstuffs than before, thus reducing the part of income which consumers have to spend on essential foodstuffs.
- Stabilizing producer and/or consumer prices by reducing price fluctuations interseasonally and/or intraseasonally.
- Stabilizing producer incomes over seasons (which is not necessarily the same as raising or stabilising producer prices).
- Equalizing geographical price differences for food crops.
- Equalizing returns from sales to markets or outlets with differing prices.
- Obtaining funds for sales promotion, research and for the extension and improvement of conditions conducive to more efficient marketing (e.g. building of feeder roads, marketing training institutions, etc.).

A marketing board can pursue a single aim out of this catalogue or a whole bundle simultaneously. However, some of the aims are incompatible with each other, as will be seen later. A marketing board then faces the choice between alternatives and must determine the policy best suited to meet the requirement of specific groups of producers or consumers, of industries or of the whole economy. Political decisions from outside the board as to priorities will then be indispensible.
A rather controversial issue as to the future agricultural price policy in East Africa, in particular in Tanzania, centers around the question whether producer prices of agricultural products should be permitted to fluctuate according to world or home market conditions or whether they should be stabilised over the seasons. The advocates of a stabilisation policy as well as the protagonists of non-interference with fluctuating prices in general each

claim for their method (1) that the highest agricultural output can be achieved, (2) that highest producer incomes are guaranteed and stabilized and (3) that benefits for agriculture and the general economy are maximized. This will have to be discussed in more detail.

b) Interseasonal Price Stabilization of Export Crops vs. Non-Stabilization

When discussing a policy of price stabilization by boards handling crops themselves or through agents a distinction has to be made between produce destined for export and foodcrops locally consumed[49]. A justification of such a policy for the latter does not necessarily mean a justification for the former and vice versa.

What in fact is the meaning of stabilizing producer prices between season? Two explanations can be excluded from the outset. Price stabilization cannot be assumed to involve payment of the same price to growers over a number of seasons, or producer prices to be above the level of export prices over a long time. Price stabilization can only mean that prices paid to producers have to follow the trend of world market prices but short-term fluctuations around the trend are to be smoothed out and that producers have to be sheltered against their excesses. The imponderabilities of forecasting the trend and distinguishing it from only temporary fluctuations and adjusting the producer price policy accordingly, naturally puts a heavy responsibility on a marketing board entrusted with such a task[50].

A policy of cushioning producers against interseasonal price fluctuations on the world market is usually backed by the argument that a higher degree of stability in producer prices would constitute an incentive to growers to increase output. Such a policy, however, has more than one effect, namely "the effect on production and incomes in the export sector itself" and "the effect on the rest of the economy"[51]. To arrive at suitable conclusions as to whether a price stabilization policy should be advocated for or disqualified outright for crops grown in East Africa, the main arguments against a price

49 In Tanzania, for instance, the Presidential Special Committee did not make this distinction in its report. It proposed categorically that all price assistance funds should be abolished. See The United Republic of Tanzania: *Enquiry into Co-operative Movement and Marketing Boards*, p. 40.

50 See P. T. Bauer and B. S. Yamey: *The Economics of Under-developed Countries.* Welwyn, Herts and Cambridge, James Nisbet & Co. Ltd. and the University Press, 1959 (Reprint), p. 232.

51 United Nations Economic and Social Council, ECA Standing Committee on Trade: *National Stabilization Measures. National Marketing Boards and Price Stabilization Funds in Africa,* Meeting on Commodity Price Stabilization, Lagos, Nigeria, 15 May, 1962.
Document No. E/CN 14/STC/CS/1.

stabilization policy will be briefly discussed in the light of the above mentioned two possible effects[52]. These arguments are:

- If anything is to be stabilized, it is the incomes of producers that should be stabilized and not the prices of the products. Taking for granted that the output of these products varies from season to season due to weather conditions, pests, and other reasons, the stabilization of prices will often destabilize the income of farmers. Moreover, depending on the level on which prices are stabilized, actual incomes of farmers may be lower than potential incomes[53].
- Curtailing producer prices for a particular crop of which export prices are booming results in a lower production of this crop than would happen if the total price were paid to growers, provided that growers act in a "normal" way. On the other hand, if prices of a commodity on the world market are depressed and higher prices would be paid to producers than justified by the market price, a higher production is stimulated with a possibly further depressing effect on world market prices, depending on the share of the specific product of a country in total world supply. Without interference the market provides an incentive to produce more when export prices are high, and discourages production when export prices are low. A stabilization policy which can only curtail producer prices when market prices are high and support them when world market prices are low appears to have precisely the contrary effect.

This result being detrimental in itself by destabilizing the international market for primary commodities is said to have other corollaries. Apart from the effects on production and incomes of farmers, the attempt to stabilize price fluctuations may affect the economy in the following way:

- By not paying the prices possible to producers in boom times and reducing thereby the possible maximum output, total possible sales to the world market are reduced. This accounts for a cut in potential export earnings and thereby in the domestic product. A price stabilization policy either cutting down or expanding production for export at the wrong times makes for a lower real national income compared with normal supply reactions to external price movements.

As the first point has considerable effects on producer incomes in the export sector, the third point on the rest of the economy, while point two affects both producer returns and the whole economy, the validity of these arguments has to be scrutinized.

---

52 The following discussion concerns only exports crops. Crops produced for the home market are dealt with separately. See below, p. 321 et seq.

53 See for example P. T. BAUER: *West African Trade.* London, Routledge & Kegan Paul Ltd., 1963, table 24, p. 301.

What are the effects of stabilized prices on producer incomes? Supply variations due to climatological factors or the ravaging effects of plant diseases are a common feature in agriculture. In general, price fluctuations caused by fluctuations in supply bear to some extent a built-in stabilizing effect on producer incomes in the export sector. A higher supply is associated with lower prices and a lower supply with higher prices.
Thus, a stabilized price combined with a heavily fluctuating supply may in fact result in widely destabilized incomes. This, however, depends on the proportion of the country's share of the commodity in the total world supply, and therefore on its ability to influence the world market price by withholding supplies from the market. In other words it depends on the elasticity of demand which the commodity in question faces — and to what extent other producing countries are affected by the policy of this country. This means that "when the output of a given area forms a large proportion of the total supply available to a particular market, or to the world as a whole, or where the output of competitive areas is similarly affected"[54] i.e. when the demand is inelastic, the tendency towards *stability* of producer incomes under fluctuating supplies is greater in the case of a stable than a fluctuating producer price. By contrast, if a country's supply of a commodity does not affect the world market price, this is to say when the demand curve faced is elastic and the supply of other producing countries does not fluctuate in the same way and influence the world price the tendency towards *destabilization* of producer incomes will be greater under a stable than under a fluctuating producer price. The critical value of elasticity is 0.5. In summing up it can be said that depending on the particular circumstances of supply and demand a stabilization policy for producer prices may have favourable, neutral, or unfavourable effects on total producer receipts. Producer receipts may or may not fluctuate more with than without stabilized prices, depending on the various factors mentioned[55].
The relationship between producer prices and producer income is shown in the following graph:

---

54 P. T. Bauer and F. W. Paish: The Reduction of Fluctuations in the Incomes of Primary Producers, in: *The Economic Journal,* Vol. LXII, No. 248 (Dec. 1952), p. 750.

55 For a more detailed discussion see R. H. Snape and B. S. Yamey: A Diagrammatic Analysis of Some Effects of Buffer Fund Price Stabilization, in: *Oxford Economic Papers* (New Series), Vol. XV, No. 2 (July 1963), pp. 95–106.

	Fluctuating Producer prices	Stabilized Producer prices
Elastic Demand curve	Stabilization of Producer Income	Destabilization of Producer Income
Inelastic Demand curve	Destabilization of Producer Income	Stabilization of Producer Income

A tentative conclusion can be drawn from the above consideration. Most of East Africa's export crops for which producer price stabilization may be considered to face a rather elastic demand curve (an exception may be cashew nuts). This means supply variations have only a slight or no effect on sales prices. Thus stabilization of producer prices appears to contribute to a greater destabilization of producer incomes than a policy of non-stabilization of producer prices.

With regard to the second aspect, the effect of a price stabilization policy on the economy as a whole much depends on the kind of response of farmers to changes in prices of a product or, in other words, to the supply elasticity of the specific commodity. Countries whose share of the total world demand of a commodity is not large enough to influence sales prices by withholding stocks face an elastic world demand. Given an elastic demand curve, and other things being equal, a positive price elasticity of supply, i.e. a positive response vis-à-vis a rise of producer prices or a negative response as a result of a decline in prices, will have the effect that with declining producer prices total production also declines and as a consequence earnings and domestic income decrease too. The question then arises as to which crop supply is flexible and on which freely fluctuating prices would have a detrimental effect on foreign exchange earnings and domestic product.

The extent to which the total supply responds to price changes seems to depend on many factors and varies greatly from commodity to commodity. The study of those problems in developing countries has been greatly neglected so far. It was only recently that more research was conducted on these aspects. The following considerations are therefore inevitably highly theoretical. Perennial crops such as coffee, cashew nuts, etc., will probably respond more slowly to price increases than annual crops, not only because they have a longer ripening period but mainly because producers probably want to be sure that a higher price will prevail for some time before they expand production. Similarly, in the event of prices dropping it will take some time until the refusal to replant trees brings about a remarkable decline in production. A quicker response to price changes can be expected from producers of annual field crops such as cotton. However, these are generalisations which may or may not hold for a particular country since other factors affect the response of producers to price changes, such as the type of land tenure, the organisation of production, the cost-price constellation, the system of economic and social values, whether the crop is mainly a subsistence or cash crop, price changes of other crops, and the actual opportunity to shift to those, etc. These factors differ from commodity to commodity. There can hardly be a common conclusion for all crops on how and to what extent export earnings and thus the whole economy are affected by interfering with the potential price which the world market would allow for a particular crop.

c) Instruments of the Price Stabilization Policy: Payment Systems and Price Assistance Funds

Apart from the decision whether to attempt to stabilize producer prices or not, there is another issue which is closely connected with an appropriate price policy viz payment and announcement of prices. Excluding a policy of non-interference with producer prices there are three principal price announcement and payment systems practised by marketing boards handling crops themselves or through agents:

- *One-payment system*
  with fixed producer prices announced *at the beginning of the buying season* (and changed or not changed during the season) and full payment to producers on delivery to the board's agent.
- *One-payment system*
  with fixed producer prices announced *before the planting of the crop commences* and full payment to producers on delivery to the board's agent.
- *Two-payment system*
  without fixed producer prices. *A major share of the expected sales price* is paid to producers on delivery to the board's agent. The *balance* would be paid according to actual proceeds *after* sale, after deduction of taxes, levies and costs.

The first system is the most simple one to handle administratively, and in fact has long been in use in East Africa, e.g. in Tanzania by the LSMB. However, with this system there is a risk involved. As there exists a time lag between the board's purchases and sales, the board may find itself with a surplus or loss at the end of the season owing to price movements which may occur during this period. A price stabilization fund[56] is necessary for this type

56 A fund for reducing interseasonal price fluctuations is generally called price stabilization fund or buffer stock fund. In order not to confuse the terminology

of operation which guarantees a single producer price for one season without necessarily implying interseasonal price stabilization[57].

The second system of pre-announcing producer prices seems, at first glance, to offer more advantages than the first system. This system is equally simple to handle administratively. Moreover, it relieves the farmer of all uncertainty as to the price he will receive. Thus he can "allocate his land and labour in the most efficient manner ... It has been the universal experience that the grower prefers to have pre-established prices"[58]. This method is used by the Kenya Maize and Produce Board.

In view of the risk of heavily fluctuating world market prices, marketing boards operating according to a one-payment system with pre-announced prices before planting are confronted with a problem already encountered before[59]. With pre-announced prices before planting, the period between the announcement and the actual sale may extend up to a year and more. This period is long enough to experience drastic price changes possible in the meantime[60]. The risk of a deficit is naturally greater in the case of a payment system with a price announced before planting than in the case of a system with a price announced at the opening of the buying season, because the period until the actual sales take place is longer and the possibility of price changes higher. The risk of misjudgment is diminished, however, by the magnitude of forward sales made at a date closer to the date of price announcement and at a price closer to the announced price than that prevailing at the end of the season. The risk involved is aggravated if the

---

the terms of the Report of the Presidential Special Committee will be used here. A *price stabilization fund* "is to permit a price to be announced before the buying season starts and thus before the sale on the world market occurs, so that the farmer can be paid virtually the full price on delivery of the produce to the society without concern that the world price was overestimated." *Price assistance funds are* "to accumulate money when world prices are rising by paying the farmer less than the full proceeds, and then when world prices are falling, paying the farmers more than the value of the crop by drawing on the fund". For both quotations see the United Republic of Tanzania: *Enquiry into Co-operative Movement and Marketing Boards,* pp. 53 et seq. Finally, a *price equalization fund* (for crops which are sold on the local and on the export market at different prices) serves the purpose of equalizing sales prices in such a way that all growers receive the same price no matter whether their produce is sold on the internal or external market.

57 Alternatively, another less widely used possibility to be employed would be to cover deficits or to absorb surplusses by general Government revenue.

58 G. Helleiner: *Some Comments upon the Report of the Presidential Special Committee of Enquiry into Co-operative Movement and Marketing Boards.* Dar es Salaam, University College, p. 2 (mimeo.).

59 See above, pp. 315–316.

60 For instance, the cotton price on Dar es Salaam auctions fluctuated from January to December 1965 between 218 and 176 cents per lb lint grade A. Similarly, the average fob price for all sisal dropped from £115 per ton to £79 per ton between January and December 1964.

marketing agency did not pre-announce a very conservative price but an optimistic one.

Moreover, although for annual crops the possible reallocation of resources is not unlimited because weather and soil conditions often restrict the number of crops between which a farmer may choose according to price prospects, the claim for the most appropriate allocation of production factors under this price and payment system nevertheless holds rather for annual crops than for perennial crops. For the latter this system has two shortcomings. Firstly, if it is not intended to stabilize producer prices over seasons, the price paid to the producer of perennial crops, although pre-announced, will to some extent impose an uncertainty upon him, because it will have to be changed from season to season according to world market movements. It may be assumed that producers' proper allocation or reallocation of resources depends not only on pre-announcement but also on the period of time for which he can rely on a certain price[61].
Secondly, the grower can influence the production of the year for which the price is pre-announced only "downwards" not upwards. This is to say, if he considers the announced price to be too low he simply does not harvest part of his crop. If a high price is announced, however, there exists – unlike with annual crops – no possibility of raising production since the maximum output possible is already determined. Hence, the announcement of a price which proves to be too low at the end of the season compared with the development of the world market price might be harmful to that particular industry. If producers were uncertain about their eventual remuneration – the case of the two-payments system – they still may make an effort on maintenance and harvesting. If, however, the pre-announced price is known for certain to be low, many producers may refuse to pay sufficient attention to these activities.

The third possibility indicated, the two-payment system, is at present applied in East Africa by a number of marketing boards, for instance, by the Tanganyika Coffee Board and the Tanganyika Tobacco Board. It was the standard system in the marketing of coffee when this commodity was still marketed by the four co-operative agencies in the early fifties and was not changed after the TCB took over. It was not intended to be the standard system of the TTB, but had to be adopted because the TTB had no funds to cover a possible deficit arising from prices announced at the opening of the buying season.
In Tanzania the two-payment system was strongly advocated by the Presidential Special Committee as an overall price and payment system for the

61 "In practice, the real issue is not how much greater the long-run supply elasticity is (than short-run elasticity on price changes), but how long high (or low) prices must prevail (or must be expected to prevail) ... to induce producers to change fixed factor inputs ... The production of tree crops ... is likely to be delayed until the producers are convinced that the favourable cost-price constellation will prevail for an appreciable time." See J. H. ADLER: Comments on Professor Nurkse's Paper on "The Quest for a Stabilization Policy in Primary Producing Countries, A Symposium, in *Kyklos,* Vol. XI, 1958, pp. 157–158. The same is probably true also for the improvement of quality. Only if the grower is confindet that a price for a better quality of a product will prevail for a longer period will he take the pains to improve it.

two Marketing Boards then planned and it was proposed to adapt it gradually for all crops. Compared with other payment systems the two-payment system was considered to have several advantages[62]:

- "... the second payment system permits payment of a relatively safe amount to the farmer on delivery of the produce to the society, and the amount of the second payment will depend primarily on the vagaries of the world market."
- The second payment is only made to members of co-operative societies, thus being "an incentive for farmers to join their local societies".
- "... a second payment system has the virtue, when the amount of the payment is a fair proportion of the first and second payments combined, of providing the farmer with a means of accumulating capital to finance larger purchases."
- The magnitude of the second payment depends to some extent on the efficiency and, therefore, on deductions made by the co-operative society. Hence "... members have an incentive to pay attention to the efficiency of the co-operatives".

This reasoning is subject to criticism.

It is hard to understand why only the two-payment system would allow the payment of a "relatively safe amount". Apart from a system by which an agency sells the farmers' produce and remits the returns after sale (a system which is not applied at the moment and is impractical and unlikely to be adopted), all other methods imply the payment of a "relatively safe amount" on delivery too. If it is the total amount in a system of one-payment on delivery, independent of the time of price announcement, this amount will usually be higher than the initial payment in a two-payment system.
The second argument, namely, that farmers look at the two-payment system as an incentive to join co-operatives is not conclusive. The Presidential Special Committee itself states that in Tanzania farmers in many cases have become suspicious toward a second payment because it was promised to them but never paid[63]. Farmers with little or no education who usually do not understand the rules of the world market and probably believe, therefore, that they are deprived of part of their income if they do not get the second payment will hardly be too enthusiastic to join a co-operative.
Further, there is no specific reason why a farmer should accumulate more capital to finance larger purchases of production inputs by receiving a second payment unless this second payment is transferred into a compulsory savings fund destined for the purchase of production goods. The second payment may be spent on consumer goods, too. The statement of the Presidential Committee seems to be based on the assumption that farmers make their annual expenditure plans on the basis of the initial payment and the second payment will be saved because of the uncertainty of its amount. In practice, however, there is no evidence supporting this assumption.

62 For all quotations see The United Republic of Tanzania: *Enquiry into Co-operative Movement and Marketing Boards*, p. 28.

63 See The United Republic of Tanzania: *Enquiry into Co-operative Movement and Marketing Boards*, p. 3.

The last statement is the only one in favour of a two-payment system which is convincing to some extent, provided the second payment actually depends on the efficiency of the co-operative, that is, only if the levy of the co-operatives is not pre-fixed. A single payment at the beginning of the buying season cannot make allowance for a payment according to efficiency. If the second payment actually depends on the efficiency of the managing staff the members of the co-operative may actually urge management to maximise efficiency. This possibility should, however, not be regarded as too bright.

It need not be particularly stressed that the double-payment system puts an additional burden on the staff of a marketing board and on the staff of co-operative societies and unions which suffer already from a severe shortage of skilled manpower, one of the main weaknesses of the whole co-operative movement. Moreover, a divided payment is hardly possible for low priced crops[64]. The system has, however, worked quite well with the marketing of coffee because coffee is a relatively high priced crop. The main argument in favour is that the marketing agency does, in fact, not run any risk of a sudden drop of world market price involved in a system with announcement of prices before planting or at the opening of the buying season. The case of the final sales price dropping so drastically that it is lower than the first payment is very rare. If a marketing agency cannot or does not want to bear the risk of price changes a two-payment system may be the most appropriate one despite its complications in accounting and other shortcomings.

Price Stabilization in Combination with Payment and Announcement Systems

It has already evolved from the foregoing discussion that a stabilization policy for producer prices over seasons can be combined with a one-payment system, either with prices announced at the beginning of the buying season or before planting starts. This requires no further explanation.
Theoretically also the double-payment system may be modified in such a way that export price fluctuations may be mitigated, in particular short-term price fluctuations. This modified payment system may work as follows: By the time the second payment is to be made, i.e. after the crop is sold by the marketing board, the future short-term trend of the world market price is much better known than before the crop is planted or at the time the buying season is opened. Thus, the magnitude of the second payment could

64 See also The United Republic of Tanzania: *Proposals of the Tanzania Government on the Recommendations of the Special Presidential Committee of Enquiry into the Co-operative Movement and Marketing Boards,* Government Paper No. 3. Dar es Salaam, Government Printer, 1966, p. 7 (quoted in the following as The United Republic of Tanzania: *Proposals on the Recommendations of the Special Presidential Committee*).

be adjusted to the expected export prices of the coming season. It could be higher than the actual proceeds in the current season if sales prices have risen and are likely to continue to do so; it could be lower than the potential proceeds if sales prices declined during the current season and prospects for the near future are gloomy. If the second payment is made shortly before the planting for the subsequent season commences, this may have the encouraging or discouraging effect — whichever may be desired — on production in case of annual and/or on harvested or not harvested quantities in case of perennial crops. Extreme fluctuations normally adherent to the two-payment system could thus to some extent be reduced for growers [65].
A price stabilization fund would be necessary when a payment system of this type is adopted unless general government revenue is involved. It could, however, be of a smaller size than for the other systems. The risks of incurring deficits would be less grave than with a system in which prices are announced early and total payment is made before the sales price is known. On the other hand, this method does not allow farmers to allocate resources properly, an advantage adherent to some extent in pre-announced prices.

The Question of Price Assistance Funds

Apart from the type of double-payment system which does not attempt to stabilize producer prices all other systems involve the risk that sales proceeds will not cover the announced and paid producer price plus costs of the marketing board. This risk is involved in either intra- or interseasonal price stabilization. This gives rise to the question of who shall cover deficits and who shall benefit from possible surpluses. One possibility is that deficits are covered or surpluses absorbed by general government revenue. There is, however, the danger that neither surpluses of this kind nor deficits (which may be considerable if prices of a great number of crops to be stabilized fall simultaneously) may be planned ahead and be provided for in the budget. In view of the general lack of capital in developing countries there will always be projects on which to spend surpluses but hardly enough money to cover deficits.
If, therefore, this risk is to be borne by the marketing boards funds have to be established into which surpluses are paid and from which deficits are covered. It was mentioned already that in connection with its proposal for the introduction of the two-payment system which would exclude any price-announcement and price-stabilization, the Presidential Special Committee advocated the abolition of all price stabilization and price assistance funds in Tanzania [66].

65 To the author's best knowledge the above system is applied nowhere in the world and it has never been developed in the literature before.
66 See The United Republic of Tanzania: *Enquiry into Co-operative Movement and Marketing Boards*, p. 55.

d) Price Stabilization for Food Crops

The objectives concerning a price policy for domestic foodcrops are less controversial than those concerning export commodities. It is evidenced again and again that a virtually free market for basic staples causes wide fluctuations of producer and consumer prices both during a season and from season to season. This is mainly a result of irregular supply conditions due to factors like weather and diseases, and to producer prices themselves, while demand is generally rather constant. In many cases the situation is aggravated by an insufficient marketing system, unsatisfactory storage and transport, speculation by private traders etc.

The necessity of a policy of stabilization of seasonal price fluctuations of food crops is out of the question. It was held that "the impact of such fluctuation on both producers and consumers is indisputably negative. The first run the danger of being penalized for overproduction (through rock bottom prices for bumper crops) and the second being faced with uncertitude as to regular supplies and purchase capacity; this causes stagnation of production, mass discontent and even social and political upheavals".[67]

Governments or boards may, however, find themselves in a dilemma if they are expected to stabilize producer and consumer prices alike. Economies of developing countries show a tendency towards rising prices. Farmers, therefore, want prices stabilized at a reasonably high level in order to be able to buy the relatively expensive manufactured goods and the necessary equipment for agricultural inputs. On the other hand, fluctuating and rising consumer prices of the major staple commodities contributing to a great extent to the daily food intake of the large majority of the population are a heavy burden on the budget, in particular of the urban population.

In East Africa, as in other developing countries, the food item virtually determines the total retail price index because of the importance of food in consumption expenditure[68]. Thus, strongly fluctuating and rising prices of staple commodities as a basis of wage claims brought forward by trade unions constitute an element of social unrest and, because of possibly similar fluctuations in money wages, contribute to uncertainty in the economy, thus having a strong impact on the general inflationary trend of prices.

When a price stabilization policy is to be introduced a question which will be raised is the method by which it shall be carried out. Both in the past and to date in Tanzania, Kenya and Uganda once it was decided that a marketing

67 H. L. Creupelandt in an unpublished paper on marketing boards for staple food crops prepared for a FAO-Seminar on "The Operation and Management of Marketing Boards in Africa", in Ibadan, in July 1966.

68 In Tanzania the food item had a weight of 77 per cent of the retail price index in 1966.

agency would control prices of foodstuff and handle them physically, this automatically implied that it was given a monopoly over them[69]. It seems that another possibility was not given sufficient consideration. It is worth mentioning that in order to stabilize prices it is not necessary for a board to have monopoly buying and selling power but it can operate alongside and in competition with private enterprises by means of a buffer stock. Such schemes are, for instance, quite common in Latin American countries and are also gaining more and more ground in Africa.

The basic principles of operations are that the marketing board trading in competition with private trade offers a guaranteed floor price after harvest when prices are generally low which is higher than the free market price would be. The marketing board keeps a buffer stock and resells its stocks when prices tend to exceed a ceiling price during out-of-season periods. Producers are free to sell either to the board or to private traders depending on where they get the higher price[70].

The main advantages of this scheme are that under certain circumstances it may achieve the same objectives of stabilization policy without making it compulsory for the board to buy the total marketed quantities for which storage and other facilities have to be provided, and it does not remove the pressure of competition from the board and its agencies.

In Tanzania this seemed to be undesirable politically in 1966–67 because it would to some extent expose co-operative societies to competitive pressure by the private trade. It could, however, be expected that at a later stage a certain pressure would make co-operative societies economically sounder and more efficient, and thus more viable.

A crucial and particularly difficult problem for marketing boards handling foodcrops no matter whether they have a monopoly or not, is the time of announcement of producer or buying prices respectively. Although staple foodcrops constitute perhaps the strongest case for a producer price announced before planting, provided that it is not too low to be an incentive, a serious problem may arise for the marketing board if it carries the responsibility alone. In many cases supply and prices of staple commodities fluctuate even more heavily between seasons than supply and prices of export commodities. If farmers act, therefore, as expected and expand production as a result of a pre-announced price and if an expansion of acreage coincides with an unstorable and internally unsaleable surplus, this will have to be exported normally at heavy losses. An example of this kind is provided by

69 Examples in East Africa are the Kenya Maize Marketing Board, in Tanzania the Grain Storage Department and the NAPB, and in Uganda the Grain Conditioning Plant of the early Fifties.

70 See also Food and Agriculture Organization: *The Marketing of Staple Food Crops in Africa*, Report of a Seminar held in Nairobi, August 1964. Rome, Food and Agriculture Organization, 1965, p. 50.

the Grain Conditioning Plant of Uganda in the middle fifties which found itself hopelessly in the red at the end of a season with a rich harvest. The reverse situation may occur if too low prices coincide with bad weather conditions leading to severe shortages necessitating heavy imports with resulting losses to the board. From a marketing board's commercial point of view it would probably be advantageous, at least during its first years of operation, i.e. until it has gained enough experience, to announce its buying prices only shortly before the harvest, when the supply situation and the prospective height of the market prices can roughly be estimated and buying prices fixed accordingly. The lack of incentive caused by not announcing producer prices in advance may in part be matched by a price stabilization policy designed for eliminating extreme fluctuations between seasons. If a farmer knows that the price he will receive the next year for a particular food crop will not differ very much from the one obtained during last season, a sufficient incentive is given provided that such a price is not completely unattractive.
A marketing board which also carries the responsibility for consumers does not have to think only in commercial but rather in welfare terms for the nation. Particularly in view of the latter then, a pre-announced price is highly desirable provided it constitutes a real incentive to ensure adequate supplies. This implies, however, that the government is prepared to cover possible deficits for the sake of a regular and sufficient supply of the population with basic foodstuffs unless the board is allocated a price assistance fund[71].

2. Achievements of the Price Stabilization Policies

Policy measures by which the various East African Marketing Boards influence prices of agricultural products differ widely. Many boards fix prices on different levels of the marketing chain at the beginning of the marketing season and do not change them subsequently during this season. As to food crops the price policy of the boards has aimed until now at procuring a sufficient supply of foodstuffs, in particular of maize, for the domestic market guaranteeing both adequate and, to a certain extent, stabilized producer and consumer prices. With regard to export crops only a few marketing boards handling a selected number of commodities have so far pursued a price stabilization policy. There was a large number of crops in respect of which no measures of price stabilization had been developed at all by the end of 1966. In the following price policies in the 3 countries for export crops, other than cotton, will be discussed in brief. Policies for cotton and food crops will be reviewed later separately.

71 In Tanzania this was, for example, done in 1963 when the Treasury covered a deficit in the NAPB's maize trading account.

In Tanzania stabilization of producer prices of export crops in order to reduce price fluctuations was undertaken only in the case of cashew nuts, oilseeds (both under the NAPB) and particularly cotton. Prices of these crops were initially fixed on all levels down to the producer price. Subsequently a more flexible approach was adopted. As to the two first products mentioned, the results of the stabilization policy were at the time of writing not very conclusive, since prices for cashew nuts and oilseeds were rising in the middle of the sixties when the marketing of these crops was taken over by the NAPB so that higher prices could be paid to producers than before. The price of tobacco (the whole production was absorbed by the local tobacco industry until 1964) was only fixed at the level of the buying agent. As domestic tobacco manufacturing companies had to pay a higher price than was obtained on the world market, the price policy aimed at equalizing returns to farmers, no matter whether they produced for the home or the foreign market. The producer price of pyrethrum was fixed in relation to the export price. Thus the producer price was still able to fluctuate following the movements of the world market price. For coffee and sisal no price stabilization policy existed in 1966–67.
In Uganda price stabilization policies were pursued for cotton and coffee. Prices of coffee were constantly subsidized in recent years from a fund which was accumulated in the early fifties. Nevertheless, in order to avoid even larger annual withdrawals from the fund producer prices had to be adjusted downwards in some years in the middle of the season. In other words, the producer prices announced at the beginning of the season were not always adhered to and thus they could not always be stabilized even within the same season.
In Kenya, with the exception of cotton, producer prices for no other crop merely destined for export were stabilized at the end of 1966. Boards for those crops, such as the Coffee Marketing Board, the Pyrethrum Marketing Board, etc. pursued a straight-forward price policy: growers were paid proceeds from their crop less marketing costs, duties and other charges. Only boards controlling produce for both export and home consumption aimed at a particular price policy. For instance, the Kenya Dairy Board together with the Kenya Co-operative Creameries and the Pig Industry Board operated Cess Funds for a so-called price discrimination policy. Sales prices on the internal market were artificially kept higher than they would be on a free market in order to make up losses incurred by selling these products on the world market at lower prices. In order to be able to compete on the world market and to keep considerable quantities away from the local market which would flood it and cause a drastic price fall, home consumers of milk and pig products were charged prices above export parity.

In 1966–67 cotton was the only export commodity for which in all three East African countries the stabilization of producer prices was attempted by a marketing board. Because of this reason the price policies for cotton shall be discussed in more detail.

a) Price Stabilization of Export Crops: The Cotton Example

Tanzania

In Tanzania cotton is placed under the regulatory power of the Lint and Seed Marketing Board (LSMB). Apart from an orderly marketing of cotton the board's foremost function is to stabilize producer prices within and between seasons.

The price announced at the beginning of the season was always valid for a whole year although sales prices of cotton lint fluctuated often violently from auction to auction. In 1963, for instance, the difference between the highest and lowest price per lb of AR lint[72] was 42 cents (fluctuating between 218 cents and 176 cents per lb) or almost 25 per cent of the lowest price. The average purchase price of the board was 202 cents per lb baled AR lint ex ginneries and the producer price 48 cents per lb of seed cotton throughout the year. Intraseasonal stabilization of producer prices was thus achieved.

Table 2. *Producer Prices, Sales Prices and Subsidies of Cotton in Tanzania 1957–58 to 1966–67*

Year	Produce Price of A-Seed Cotton (Lake Region) (cents/lb)	Equivalent in Cotton Lint [a] (cents/lb)	Price of AR Lint [b] (Lake Region) f.o.r. (cents/lb)	Annual Deficit (./.) or Surplus (+) of the Price Assistance Fund [c] (£1,000)	Subsidy (./.) Paid to or Deduction (+) made (cents/lb of Seed cotton)
1957–58	54	163.6	216.3	+ 114.3	+ 1.1
1958–59	54	163.6	193.6	./. 863.2	./. 8.5
1959–60	52	157.6	186.6	./. 176.3	./. 1.4
1960–61	54	163.6	200.0	./. 74.5	./. 0.6
1961–62	59	178.8	198.1	./. 775.1	./. 7.7
1962–63	55	166.6	187.9	./.1411.1	./.11.0
1963–64	50	151.5	193.7	./. 290.7	./. 1.8
1964–65	50	151.5	190.9	./. 133.4	./. 0.8
1965–66	48	145.4	171.4	..	..
1966–67	46	135.2	..	..	..

[a] Based on an outturn rate of 33 per cent except for 1966–67 figures for which a rate of 34 per cent is taken.

[b] The average price fetched for lint is taken for the Lake Region crop which usually made up more than 90 per cent of the total production for the period in question.

[c] Deficit/surplus figures do not solely reflect movements of the trading account but include other items such as income from assets held by the Price Assistance Fund.

Source: Lint and Seed Marketing Board: *Annual Report and Accounts.* Dar es Salaam.

72 The cotton lint of AR quality has a higher degree of purity than lint of BR quality. Its volume harvested is usually less than that of lint of BR quality. AR and BR cotton lint are extracted from grade A and C raw cotton (seed cotton) respectively by the ginning process. What remains is cotton seed of grade A and B respectively which can either be planted or used for oil extraction.

Since the beginning of the sixties the trend of cotton prices on the world market has been declining (see table 2). From 1964–65 to 1965–66 the sales price for the board's cotton lint dropped drastically from 191 cents per lb to 171 cents. This was about the price also expected for the 1966–67 season. The producer price for seed cotton grade A which was subsidised since 1958–59 declined as well from 1961–62 onward owing to a policy of gradually adjusting producer prices to the world market price. During one season the subsidy was as high as 11 cents per lb of seed cotton or almost 20 per cent of the producer price, not including indirect subsidies such as seed distributed free. The subsidies were paid from the Price Assistance Fund accumulated in the late forties and early fifties and transferred to the LSMB when it was established in 1952. With the reserves of the Price Assistance Fund gradually decreasing (they dropped from £5,245 million in 1958 to £3,873 million in 1965) the LSMB's price policy became more realistic.

The aim for the 1966–67 season was to pay farmers an unsubsidised price. Because of the drastic slump of sales prices from 191 cents to 171 cents the adjustment was not made in one season, namely in 1965–66, but distributed over two seasons. But even then such a reduction in producer prices would have been difficult unless other cost factors be reduced simultaneously. The whole price structure of cotton was, therefore, reviewed by the LSMB and the government for the 1966–67 season. As a result of this review a number of cost factors were reduced[73]. The reductions sufficed so that despite the considerable fall in the sales price of lint, the producer price had only to be reduced from 50 to 46 cents per lb for raw cotton. The latter did not only make a subsidy from the Price Assistance Fund unnecessary, but it rather seemed that the LSMB would make a surplus for the year 1966–67, the first one since 1958.

Two other factors contributed to this development. First, sales prices for cotton seed showed a reverse trend to that of cotton lint since cotton seed grade A fetched Shs 335/– per ton in 1964–65 and Shs 545/– in 1965–66. Secondly, the calculation of costs of the LMSB was based on an assumed further decline of prices to 160 cents per lb AR cotton lint. During auctions held in the second half of the year 1966 it turned out that this assumption was too pessimistic. In fact, the auction price per lb AR lint moved around 170 cents per lb.

The future development of cotton prices on the world market depends to a large extent on the stock pile policy of the United States who held

73 All co-operative levies were cut, among which particularly the cut of the primary society levy from 5 to 3 cents per lb seed cotton was a severe reduction. The ginning fee paid by the board to private ginneries and to those owned by the co-operatives themselves was reduced from 23 cents to 18 cents per lb because investigations had shown that ginneries had made high profits at the old rate. Moreover, the ginnery outturn rate was raised. No cost reduction could, however, be made on the board's expenses without cutting in services rendered by it.

approximately half of total stocks of cotton producing countries in the mid-sixties. A high level of world stocks alone naturally has a depressing effect on the world market price of cotton. As also in future the estimated world production will probably exceed consumption, the prospects for lint prices do not look very bright and it is very possible that the price trend of cotton prices will continue to decline further[74].
Although in Tanzania the total margin between producer price and sales price was squeezed considerably and many cost factors reduced, this did not mean that the limits of efficiency in the marketing of cotton were reached and that, if the prices for cotton lint were to deteriorate further, the price paid to producers had to be reduced accordingly. In 1966, though, it was recognised in Tanzania that the phase of permanent subsidies of the cotton crop from the Price Assistance Fund was over. With a rapidly increasing crop the total sum necessary would also grow in size. The subsidizing of the producer price at the rate applied for 1964–65 would have cost the LSMB more than £600,000 for the 1965–66 crop of over 400,000 bales. Since, as mentioned, a price stabilization policy cannot mean a permanently subsidized producer price but only a cushioning against drastic price fluctuations around the trend it was time to adjust the price policy to the declining trend of cotton prices. It was feared that a further drain on resources for a few more years would deprive the LSMB of the possibility of reducing short-term fluctuations in the future, although the fund still showed a considerable size in 1966.
Provided that a future aim of the LSMB would be to reduce price fluctuations around the trend, a fund of £1.2 million would be sufficient to pursue a price stabilization policy beyond 1970[75] at the experienced fluctuation rate of the ten years since 1957–58. The size of the fund in 1966 of about £3.8 million is thus more than sufficient. In view of a rational agricultural price and marketing policy envisaged in Tanzania price stabilization would not be only policy aim and, therefore, decisions would also have to be made on the existing price assistance funds, particularly on those in apparent excess of needs. It should be noted here that unlike many marketing boards in Africa, particularly the produce boards of the English speaking West African countries, the LSMB used its price assistance fund actually to pay it back directly in the form of a subsidy or indirectly in the form of services to farmers and did not use it for general development or unproductive prestige purposes.

74 Prices for cotton seed were, on the contrary, at a rather high level in 1965–66 although a declining trend was noticeable in 1966. Export prices of cotton seed which is mostly processed into vegetable oils and cake are mainly determined by prices of other oils and fats rather than by prices of cotton lint.
75 Based on a target production of about 81,000 tons.

Uganda

The price stabilization policy of the Lint Marketing Board (LMB)[76] had been attacked on various occasions in the past[77]. Often such criticism was directed against the marketing board as such and its justification was queried. But a clear distinction should be made here between the board's autonomous and non-autonomous sphere, between its marketing performances and its price policy. For many years the level of producer prices was not a matter for the board to decide but was determined by government for political reasons. Government influence had increased after Independence when the height of prices for cotton, a crop mainly produced by smallholders, had gained political momentum. Up to 1963 it was the function of the Lint Cotton Price Committee apointed by the Governor in Council to investigate the costs at all stages of primary marketing and processing and to propose to the Minister the prices to be paid to ginners for lint and seed. This Committee was abolished in 1963 when the power of fixing prices was conferred to the Minister of Co-operatives without his being required to inquire into the cost structure. The heavy losses of the Lint Marketing Boards after 1963 were due to a price policy designed by Government on which the board itself had little or no influence.

Theoretically price stabilization was considered to be a primary goal of the LMB. About the actual implementation of this objective by the LMS (and the Coffee Marketing Board) the Economic Commission for Africa remarked already in the late fifties that "stability of producers' prices within the season and to some extent between seasons has been deliberately sought, but budgetary and fiscal considerations have exerted an important influence on policies governing producers' prices and in the financial operations of the Marketing Boards"[78]. On the other hand it cannot be claimed that the LMB having creamed off a considerable share of sales proceeds in favourable years did not allow the farming community to benefit from those funds in bad years after 1960. Whereas in the fifties significant sums were used for general development purposes after 1960 the funds of the Cotton Price Assistance Fund were to a major extent spent on subsidizing producer prices. The annual sums spent fluctuated between £1 million (in 1963–64) and £4.6 million (in 1965–66)

---

76 Besides the Lint Marketing Board (LMB) there was only one board for export crops in existance in Uganda in 1966–67, namely the Coffee Marketing Board. The policy of both marketing boards haue been similar. Thus what will be said on the LMB will, in general, also apply to the Coffee Marketing Board.

77 Most severely in an article by D. WALKER and C. EHRLICH. See D. WALKER and C. EHRLICH: Stabilization and Development Policy in Uganda: An Appraisal, in: *Kyklos,* Vol. XII (1959), pp. 341–353.

78 United Nations Economic and Social Council, Economic Commission for Africa, Standing Committee on Trade, *op. cit.,* p. 49.

(see table 3). In 1965–66 the price paid to growers was subsidised at 50 per cent of the price which would have been justified by the world market price. This was the highest subsidy paid in years. In this year producer prices were more than ever determined rather by political than by economic considerations[79]. A reasonable price stabilization policy, i.e. the reduction of short-term price fluctuations along the trend would have warranted the gradual adjustment of the producer price actually paid to the potential producer price, this is the price at which the LMB would have broken even after having paid for cost, export duty, etc. Instead, the gap between these two prices was widening after 1963–64 which led to a complete exhaustion of the Cotton Price Assistance Fund. As a result of this, cotton producers had to face a drop in price from the unrealistic 60 cents/lb for AR seed cotton in 1965–66 to 40 cents/lb for the season 1966–67, in other words a price drop of 33 per cent. There is no doubt that with a declining trend of world market prices farmer prices had to be adjusted accordingly as was done in Tanzania. From 1963–64 on it would have been possible to do so smoothly. In 1966, however, reflections were not quite unfounded that as the immediate effects of too long and too high subsidies the Cotton Price Assistance Fund was to be abolished and the price stabilization policy discontinued as was proposed by the Committee of Enquiry into the Cotton Industry 1966.

Kenya

The Cotton Lint and Seed Marketing Board was the only marketing board in Kenya operating a price stabilization scheme by means of a Price Assistance Fund in 1966[80]. This Board is virtually operating along the same lines as its two equivalent boards in Tanzania and Uganda[81]. The role of the cotton industry in Kenya is, however, much less significant for the economy than it is in Tanzania and Uganda. In Uganda it is the second, in Tanzania the third largest foreign exchange earner[82].

Although in Kenya the subsidies paid to farmers were higher in the early sixties than in Uganda, which was mainly due to heavy development expenditure for cotton, producer prices were adjusted to a more realistic level in terms of world market prices since then, although they were still subsidized

79 Without the Uganda coup in 1966 a general election should have been held that year.

80 Before the Nyanza Province Marketing Board and Central Province Marketing Board were merged into the Kenya Agricultural Produce Marketing Board in 1964 they also were running price stabilization schemes for several crops.

81 However, in 1966 the Kenya cotton crop was sold by the Uganda Lint Marketing Board.

82 In 1964 cotton exports earned almost £10 million in Tanzania, a little over £10 million in Uganda, and £650,000 in Kenya.

Table 3. *Producer Prices, Sales Prices and Subsidies of Cotton in Uganda, 1961–62 to 1966–67*

Year	Producer Price of A Seed Cotton (cents/lb)	Equivalent in Cotton Lint (cents/lb)	Price of AR Lint f.o.r. (cents/lb)	Losses to be Paid from Price Assist. Fund (£1,000)	Subsidy [a] Paid to Growers [b] (cents/lb of A Seed Cotton)	Growers' Price at which the Board would break even (cents/lb of A Seed Cotton)
1961–62	57.0	178.0	225.00	1,758	15.5	41.5
1962–63	57.0	178.0	201.53	3,172	14.2	42.8
1963–64	51.0	159.5	217.42	1,004	4.3	46.7
1964–65	57.0	178.0	208.36	2,418	8.8	48.2
1965–66	60.0	187.5	176.96	4,600	20.0	40.0
1966–67	40.0	125.0	180.00 [c]	..	–	–

[a] Export tax is included in the subsidy.
[b] The calculation is not quite correct because the total loss was allocated to each lb of seed cotton purchased irrespective of the grade. The production of BR does rarely exceed, however, 10 per cent of the total.
[c] Expected price.

Source: Lint Marketing Board: *Annual Reports,* Kampala, Uganda Government: *Inquiry into the cotton Industry, 1966.* Uganda Government, Statistics Division – Ministry of Planning and Community Development: *Statistical Abstract,* Entebbe, Government Printer.

in 1965–66. Moreover, the growers' price was kept remarkably stable for several years since the 1963–64 season. Yet, the subsidies paid decreased due to a cutting down of other expenditure. Whereas in Tanzania and Uganda producer prices were adjusted to world market conditions so as to eliminate or at least minimize the losses of the boards in charge of cotton marketing from the 1966–67 season onwards, cotton was still subsidized in Kenya during that season. The Cotton Lint and Seed Marketing Board could theoretically continue this policy at the current rate of deficits for another two to three years before the Price Assistance Fund showing assets in the amount of £550,000 would be exhausted. There were, however, plans also in Kenya to review the producer price and subsidization policy with the aim of adjusting prices to a level reflecting export prices as from 1967–68 onwards.

Interseasonal Price Stabilization of the three East African Countries in Comparison

As a measure for the degree of interseasonal price stabilization (although a rather crude one) average percentage changes from the preceding year may be used. A comparison between percentage changes of producer prices for seed cotton and of export prices for cotton lint shows that in all three East

Table 4. *Producer Prices, Sales Prices and Subsidies of Cotton in Kenya, 1961–62 to 1966–67*

Year	Producer Price (Nyanza and Western Prov.) (cents/lb)	Equivalent in Contton Lint (cents/lb)	Price of AR Lint (Nyanza and Western Province) f.o.r. (cents/lb)	Losses to be Paid from Price Assist. Fund (£1,000)	Subsidy Paid to Growers (cents/lb of A Seed Cotton)	Growers' Price at which the Board would break even (cents/lb of A Seed Cotton)
1961–62	56.0	175.0	194.68	83.0	13.0	43.0
1962–63	56.0	175.0	189.13	184.6	18.0	38.0
1963–64	50.0	156.0	212.50	198.4	18.0	32.0
1964–65	50.0	156.0	190.55	136.8	10.0	40.0
1965–66	50.0	156.0	184.00	150.0 [a]	8.0 [a]	42.0 [a]
1966–67	50.0	156.0	180.00 [a]	..	8.0 [a]	42.0 [a]

[a] Estimated.
Source: Cotton Lint and Seed Marketing Board: *Annual Report and Accounts.* Nairobi.

African countries the marketing boards succeeded in cushioning producers from export price fluctuations to a certain extent (see table 5).
Average fluctuations of producer prices during the period from 1957–58 until 1965–66 were smallest in Tanzania at 4.6 per cent and highest in Uganda at 8.3 per cent. The corresponding average percentage change of export prices for AR lint was lowest in Tanzania (5.6 per cent) and highest in Uganda (11.9 per cent). In Kenya the producer price fluctuations averaged 6.3 per cent compared with 9.5 per cent of sales prices. Taking only the five years period from 1962–63 until 1966–67, Kenya achieved a remarkable stabilization of the producer price with a low average percentage change of only 2.1 compared with Tanzania 5.0 and Uganda 12.1 during the same period. The average fluctuations of sales prices during this period could not be calculated as they were not yet known for the 1966–67 season.

b) Price Stabilization of Food Crops

A price stabilization policy for food crops, in particular maize and paddy, which are mainly produced for the local market often forms part of a policy aiming at self-sufficiency of the specific country.

Tanzania

A policy of price fixation for a number of foodstuffs, including maize, rice, oilseeds, potatoes and beans in practise during the Second World War, was continued in its basic lines also in the immediate post-war years. An important step towards achieving the objective of selfsufficiency was the

Table 5. *Stabilization of Producer Prices for Cotton in Tanzania, Uganda, and Kenya, 1957–58 to 1966–67*

Season	Tanzania				Uganda				Kenya			
	Producer Price of A Seed Cotton		Average Sales Price of AR lint		Producer Price of A Seed Cotton		Average Sales Price of AR lint		Producer Price of A Seed Cotton		Average Sales Price of AR lint	
	cents/lb	Percentage change [b]	cents/lb	Percentage change [b]	cents/lb	Percentage change [b]	cents/lb	Percentage change [b]	cents/lb	Percentage change [b]	cents/lb	Percentage change [b]
1957–58	54	–	216	–	58	–	220	–	57	–	..	–
1958–59	54	–	194	*./. 10.1*	47	*./. 18.9*	180	*./. 18.2*	46	*./. 19.3*	174	–
1959–60	52	*./. 3.7*	186	*./. 4.1*	48	*+ 2.1*	224	*+24.4*	47	*+ 2.2*	213	*+22.4*
1960–61	54	*+3.9*	200	*+ 7.5*	55	*+14.5*	206	*./. 8.0*	54	*+14.8*	220	*+ 3.2*
1961–62	59	*+9.2*	198	*./. 1.0*	57	*+ 3.3*	225	*+ 9.1*	56	*+ 3.7*	195	*./. 11.8*
1962–63	55	*./. 6.7*	188	*./. 5.1*	57	–	202	*./. 10.2*	56	–	189	*./. 2.5*
1963–64	50	*./. 9.0*	194	*+ 3.2*	51	*./. 10.5*	217	*+ 7.4*	50	*./. 10.7*	213	*+12.6*
1964–65	50	–	191	*./. 1.5*	57	*+11.7*	208	*./. 4.1*	50	–	191	*./. 10.3*
1965–66	48	*./. 4.0*	171	*./. 12.3*	60	*+ 5.2*	177	*./. 14.0*	50	–	184	*./. 3.6*
1966–67	48	*./. 4.2*	170 [c]	*./. 0.6*	40	*./. 33.3*	180 [c]	*+ 1.7*	50	–	180 [c]	*./. 2.2*
Average for 1957–58 to 1965–66	–	*4.6*	–	*5.6*	–	*8.3*	–	*11.9*	–	*6.3*	–	*9.5*
Average for 1962–63 to 1966–67	–	*5.0*	–	..	–	*12.1*	–	..	–	*2.1*	–	..

[a] Referring to the Nyanza and Western Province.
[b] Percentage change from preceding year.
[c] Expected price.

Source: Annual Reports of the Lint and Seed Marketing Board (Tanzania), the Lint Marketing Board (Uganda), and the Cotton Lint and Seed Marketing Board (Kenya).

establishment of the Grain Storage Department in 1949, the first statutory marketing organization for food crops in Tanganyika. At that time, Tanganyika had to cope with the necessity of importing maize in four out of five years and the periodical local food shortages made it necessary to control the movements of foodstuffs and to maintain supplies in the different parts of the country. The Grain Storage Department was, therefore, assigned the following responsibilities:

- To provide producers of staple commodities with an assured market for their surplus production;
- To guarantee the supply of staple food crops at reasonable prices in centres of consumption in cases of need;
- To set up storage facilities;
- To build up a reserve for seasons of shortage.

The scheduled list of products included millet, cassava, mixed beans, paddy, rice, and maize, which was by far the most important crop. The main activities of the Grain Storage Department were concentrated on the marketing of maize, rice and beans.

During its first five years of operation the Grain Storage Department did reasonably well and up to 1953–54 it had even made an overall trading profit. The adopted price policy, however, ran the Department into considerable problems after the 1953–54 season. Although price stabilization was not a prima facie objective of the Department, the intake price for paddy remained the same from 1952 onwards and for maize from 1953–54 after the produce price for the latter had been gradually raised every year from shs 21/- per bag of 200 lbs in 1949 to shs 38/- in 1953–54.

During the last two years of the existence of the Grain Storage Department, the combination of the extremely favourable producer price paid and accidentally good weather conditions induced the production of heavy surplusses which had eventually to be disposed of on the world market at a loss of nearly shs 13/- per bag, resulting in a total trading loss of nearly £1.5 million on maize and £85,000 on rice for the two seasons 1954–55 and 1955–56.

There is no doubt that growers acted in response to the rather favourable price offered. This was not so much due to the increase of estate grown maize but rather to the expansion of acreage under maize by African growers. Large quantities also came to the market in 1954–55 and 1955–56 because the high prices tempted many peasant growers to sell their share of maize which they usually would store to meet their own needs later in the season. This is also evidenced by the development of prices in the 1956–57 season when the compulsory sale of maize to the Grain Storage Department was abolished. A poor harvest combined with the lack of stocks on the part of the peasant farmers raised the prices to Shs 50/– in some parts of the country.

In summing up it may be stated that the Grain Storage Department failed to find the right level of producer prices which induced the production of the approximate quantities needed in order to make the country self-sufficient. The inflexibility of its price policy, which did not make allowance for adjustment to market conditions, contributed to a large extent to disasterous drain on public funds which discredited government interference in the marketing of local food crops for a long time to come.

These events coincided with the inquiries of the East African Royal Commission dealing with the marketing of agricultural produce. A breakthrough to free marketing came when the Commission's Report was published in 1955. In its report the Commission strongly opposed various forms of marketing restrictions and controls and favoured their removal. Subsequently, controls over purchases of all scheduled crops, the sale of which was formerly compulsory, were removed in 1956, except for wheat.

After a transition period with guaranteed minimum prices but no compulsory sales of two years ending in 1957, the development led to a system of essentially free marketing with the only exception that all the produce had to be exchanged on Native Authority Markets in order to introduce a competitive element by facing a number of producers with a number of buyers. It soon turned out, however, that the concept of free enterprise did not work as smoothly as the Royal Commission had expected. Producers were left with virtually no protection. It was proved again that under a free marketing system the bargaining power of the producer was extremely weak. A countervailing power to the demand side which formed so-called buyers' rings virtually did not exist. This state of affairs did certainly not contribute to an increase in production.

After gaining Independence the government held that the existing system of marketing for food crops and other produce was undesirable. The intention of putting the trade of indigenous products, which were almost exclusively in the hands of Asian and Arab traders, into African hands, and the pursuit of a policy of African Socialism led to a passionate promotion of the co-operative movement. The marketing boards should serve as an umbrella on top of the pyramid in order to protect the co-operatives and to make control efficient. Hence, the National Agricultural Products Board (NAPB) was established in 1963, and gradually took over the marketing of maize, paddy, oil seeds, groundnuts and cashew nuts [83].

To what extent the NAPB succeeded in stabilizing producer prices of food-crops may be seen from the development of producer prices for maize and retail prices for maize meal (see table 6) [84]. It is shown in the table that with the commencement of the operations of the NAPB in 1963 the gap between producer and retail price widened. This means, in other words, that

83 In 1967 other products were expected to follow.

84 Corresponding figures for retail prices of maize are not available but it may be expected that these would show a similar pattern.

Table 6. *Producer Prices for Maize*[a] *and Retail Prices for Maize Meal (Posho)*[b] *in Tanzania, 1958–59 to 1965–66*

Season	Maize (cents/lb)	Maize Meal (Posho) (cents/lb)
1958–59	15.0	24.5
1959–60	11.5	27.5
1960–61	10.5	28.0
1961–62	16.0	35.0
1962–63	16.5	40.0
1963–64	12.5	34.5
1964–65	12.5	34.5
1965–66	12.5	34.5

[a] From 1958 until 1960 territorial average price of the 4th quarter; from 1960 until 1965 territorial average of December price of each year.

[b] December prices in Dar es Salaam of each year.

Source: East African Quarterly Economical and Statistical Review; Monthly Statistical Bulletin; The United Republic of Tanzania: *Statistical Abstract,* Dar es Salaam, Government Printer.

on the whole marketing services were rendered at lower costs before the board existed[85].

However, both prices remained stable from the time the board took over the marketing of maize. It seems that the competition between millers and between retailers combined with the trust in a regular supply from the board resulted in fact in the stabilization of retail prices of posho. The level, however, on which this stabilization was achieved was higher than during most years of the previous decade, with the exception of the preceding years 1961 and 1962, which were drought and shortage years. The producer price dropped to well below this level after the board had started its operations, but also below the average of the last ten years. Whether the decline of the marketed production from more than 100,000 tons in 1963–64 to 80,000 tons in 1964–65 and to less than 70,000 tons in the 1965–66 season should be attributed to the low level of producer prices or to the failure of sufficient rains during both years, is not known exactly.

One fact, however, seems to support this opinion, namely the growing problem of smuggling and illegal milling. Not only were large quantities smuggled across the border in times of shortage in Kenya and Uganda; the greater problem was illegal trading within Tanzania's borders itself. The relatively low level of producer prices and the wide gap between the producer prices and ex-store retail prices for maize and posho made it relatively easy for private traders and millers to offer higher prices than the board. This was a widely used practice and might have been a reason for the declining quantities purchased by the board. Illegal trade, moreover, was encouraged by an often sluggish attitude on the part of the primary

85 A word of warning should be inserted here because of the statistical inaccuracy of price figures which is a notorious weakness in most developing countries.

co-operatives towards collecting their members' produce and by the main agents' late opening of their buying stations, forcing the farmer into other ways of obtaining cash. Up-country policemen were frequently ignorant of the marketing laws and controls of road movements were difficult and costly.

On the other hand, for the 1966–67 season a marketed production of 110,000 tons of maize was expected. This was partly due to favourable weather conditions, partly due to farmers increasing the acreage under maize.
Several explanations are possible for this behaviour of farmers:
The stability of the price paid for growers acted as a production incentive and/or the level of the price was considered sufficient despite complaints by farmers. Early in 1966 many farmers were forced to buy back maize from the NAPB at a price twice as high as they had received themselves because they ran out of stock. It is possible that farmers wanted to avoid this situation the following season and therefore planted more to be able to hold sufficient own stocks. A further explanation would be that farmers wanted to make up for the lost income caused by the lower prices by producing greater quantities. Finally, the reason for the expanded acreage might not even be sought in economical considerations but merely in the fact that there was a strong political pressure exerted on farmers to plant more food crops.
As long as so little is known about the motives of farmers' behaviour and about reactions on prices fixed on different levels, it is extremely difficult for a marketing agency, such as the NAPB, to adopt a price policy which induces the farmer to produce just about the quantities consumed internally and which makes heavy imports and exports, both generally resulting in losses, unnecessary. Roughly, the NAPB actually succeeded in doing this[86]. Moreover, it accumulated funds which could be considered a safe-guard against future deviations from the approximate production consumption equilibrium.
The performance of the NAPB is also reflected in the development of its intake and sales prices for maize and paddy[87]. The intake price for maize grade I, for instance, was increased during every season while the sales prices decreased from 1964–65 to 1966–67 (see table 7). Correspondingly, there was a steady decline of the margin between intake and sales price of maize. Since the quantities purchased declined, the risk of

86 Export of maize in 1963–64 totalled 40,000 tons. In the 1964–65 and the 1965–66 seasons 5,000 tons and 15,000 tons of maize respectively were imported. Out of the 110,000 tons of maize presumably being marketed in 1966–67, 10,000 tons were exported as a gift to Guinea in late 1966. Exports of another 10,000 to 20,000 tons were expected until the end of the 1966–67 season unless this quantity was to be kept as an emergency reserve.

87 Intake and sales price were not identical with producer and retail price in table 6 as the Board neither bought directly from farmers nor sold directly to consumers.

Table 7. *Intake and Sales Prices of the NAPB for Maize (Grade I) and Paddy (Supergrade), 1964–65 to 1966–67*
(in Shs) [a]

Produce	1964—65	1965—66	1966—67
Maize (Grade I)			
Price delivered bagged into store	32.05	35.10	36.00
Price ex-store	47.50	46.80	46.80
Paddy (Supergrade)			
Price delivered bagged into store	54.64	56.25	57.00
Price ex-store	64.12	64.50	65.25

[a] Prices refer to a bag of 200 lbs of maize and of 75 kg of paddy respectively.
Source: Compiled from documents of the NAPB.

exports becoming necessary was reduced. Thus a cut in the levy for the export/import reserve was made possible. Consequently, the import/export loss levy accounting for shs 8.92 per bag or 20 per cent of the sales price in 1964–65 was completely abolished for the subsequent seasons.

The reduced margins were, however, neither reflected in the producer price for maize nor in the retail price for posho which remained the same as shown. In the case of producer prices, this was due to the underestimation of the actual costs on the primary buyer's level, i.e. the co-operative societies, during the first year of operation when the producer price was fixed by the NAPB. Hence, the increase of the board's intake price in the following years was not passed on to producers but was swallowed up by the actual costs of primary buyers. The change of the board's resale price (wholesale) must be considered to be too small to have any noticeable effect on the consumer price of posho. By and large the development of the intake and the sales prices for paddy shows the same pattern as for maize as can be seen from Table 7.

The success of the future price policy for foodcrops depends on the correct fixation of the producer price or the NAPB's intake price at the most appropriate level, that is, to induce a production which makes the country just about self-sufficient. According to experiences in the past, this is an extremely difficult task. If the producer price is fixed too low, the quantities coming forth might not be sufficient to meet local demand and consequently imports become necessary. If it is fixed too high, the reverse situation with oversupply and necessary exports might be the result. The NAPB has to buy all quantities offered to it, if it does not want to lose the faith of producers. It is estimated that a marketed supply of approximately 80,000 to 90,000 tons over subsistence consumption just meets consumer demand in Tanzania. The quantities of maize actually handled show that the NAPB, in addition to stabilizing the producer price has succeeded up to now in achieving the objective of self-sufficiency with an accuracy possible in this sphere by setting just about the correct price. It is often suggested that prices paid to growers in Tanzania are too low. In the light of the country's policy of self-sufficiency, however, this complaint is hardly justified. A higher producer price would possibly distort the equilibrium achieved by inducing substantially higher supplies which would have to be exported. In the long run this would mean that the board would then have to subsidize producer prices and accruing deficits would have to be covered by general revenue. This, in fact, would mean that the farming sector would have to be subsidized by other sectors of the economy. To increase the NAPB's intake price which may result in an increase of the producer price could, therefore, have an effect which may be undesirable at present.

This is a rather static view. Demand for foodstuffs will increase with expanding population, urbanization, and industrialization. Stimulation of a higher production will then become crucial. This may, for instance, be achieved by raising the productivity of the farming sector or the introduction of new hybrid seeds with which Kenyan farmers have had great success. To create the additional inputs price incentives may have to be given. Moreover, it is believed that the costs of the NAPB's buying agents, the co-operatives, will be considerably reduced in the future. In particular, stock losses due mainly to theft, storage, careless handling, etc., have contributed to income reductions of farmers. With the elimination of these shortcomings the actual producer price may rise in future.

The NAPB is not only concerned with the interests of the producer but according to its functions, also with the interests of consumers. As was shown above, the NAPB's ex-store price for maize is approximately double the price which producers receive, which, in fact, was one of the major complaints of farmers who had to buy back maize when their stocks were not sufficient. With the accumulated price stabilization it would, therefore, not seem to do any harm if the NAPB were to abandon its conservative cost calculations. A somewhat lower sales price would be possible, perhaps not for paddy but in any case for maize. This would, of course, only be reasonable if it could be ensured that these price reductions would be passed on to consumers.

It seems that there was another possibility allowing a reduction in consumer prices. In Tanzania the combined milling and retail margin of 7.6 cents/lb accounted for more than 20 per cent of the retail price of posho in 1966, which was almost three times as high as in Kenya, where the milling and retail allowances were fixed by law. It is likely that in Tanzania the major share of this combined margin covered fixed costs of milling because the surplus milling capacity was estimated three times higher than actually needed. Moreover, the mills were often rather antiquated. Thus, the problem may not have been too high milling profits but uneconomic performance of the mills. Also from this side, consumer prices could be reduced. One possibility would be for the NAPB to enter the milling and/or retail field by buying up a mill in order to compete with existing mills and by opening "fair price shops" in order to compete with the retail trade.

Uganda and Kenya

Although in Uganda prices of some minor food crops were controlled, there existed no para-state or state organisation handling food crops after the Grain Conditioning Plant was dissolved in the mid-fifties. In 1966–67 the establishment of a marketing board for food (mainly maize and paddy) and minor export crops was under discussion. It was intended to confer upon this board extensive powers to control production and prices of crops which come under its jurisdiction. The intention was to announce producer prices before planting.

The nature of the Kenyan maize problem with which the Maize and Produce Marketing Board is faced is determined by the following factors similar to those the NAPB is confronted with in Tanzania:

- Maize is the staple food of the majority of the population. The possibilities of substitution are slight and the demand for maize is consequently rather price-inelastic. Due to an increase of population of about 3 per cent per year the demand for maize rises constantly.
- Highly variable climatic conditions and rainfall are the reasons for extremely wide fluctuations in supply.
- The aim of the Kenya government is to be self-sufficient in maize, i.e. to balance home supply and demand. Imports or exports of maize are only possible at losses as in Tanzania because import and export parity prices are mostly far above or below domestic sales prices respectively.

In Kenya the maize supply and price situation has been a matter of constant complaint and discussion, and so has the role of the Maize and Produce Marketing Board (formerly the Maize Marketing Board) and its price policy. This is due to the fact that from the very beginning the Maize and Produce Board's role as to prices was not clearly defined. The Maize Marketing Act of 1959 did not oblige the board to pursue a policy of price stabilization, but rather to coordinate supply and demand by buying and selling, storing, importing and exporting, and to find an approximate equilibrium between supply and demand.

It was shown above that until the 1966–67 season in Tanzania the NAPB had come rather close to the aim of finding an "equilibrium price", keeping imports or exports at a moderate level, at least for the short time it was operating. This was not the case with the Maize and Produce Board in Kenya. Figures of imports and exports of maize to and from Kenya show that during the period 1961–62 to 1966–67 imports or exports were at a low level and demand and supply about balanced only in 1964–65 (see table 8).

Table 8. *Imports and Exports of Maize to and from Kenya, 1961–62 to 1966–67* (in tons)

Season	Imports	Exports
1961–62	66,000	10,000
1962–63	–	96,000
1963–64	–	55,000
1964–65	23,000	2,500
1965–66	90,000	–
1966–67	–	100,000 [a]

[a] Estimates.

Source: Republic of Kenya: *Maize Commission of Inquiry,* pp. 198–199.

The development of supply and prices during 1965 and 1966 gives an excellent example of the sort of problem faced by the Maize and Produce Marketing Board, and in general by monopoly boards handling food crops.

The gazetted minimum price per bag of 200 lbs maize grade II without bag when delivered to a railhead store or railway loading point was fixed at Shs 32.50 for the crop planted in 1965. This price was announced before the planting started and was identical with the price for the previous year when imports and exports were at a minimum. When 1965 turned out to be a drought year with disastrous effects on the maize crop, the guaranteed minimum price of the board was revised in the middle of the season and fixed at Shs 37/– per bag. Since planting was over, this was a mere bonus for growers with their seeds already in the ground. This new higher price, however, was intended to be maintained also for the 1966 planting season. The maize shortage in 1966, caused by the crop failure in 1965, made heavy imports of maize necessary for this year. Due to various administrative errors [88] some of the imports from USA arrived in Kenya only when supplies of the new 1966 harvest had already come to the market. The comparatively high price of Shs 37 /–combined with good weather and the application of new higher yielding maize varities had caused a bumper crop, the extent of which was not yet clear at the end of 1966. The board faced the situation that it had to export not only part of the home production but also the stocks of unsold imported maize from USA which arrived too late. These unfortunate events caused heavy losses to the board. A cess of Shs 3/50 per bag for peasant growers and Shs 4/50 for estate growers was, therefore, imposed to cover part of the loss of the Kenyan government estimated at about £3 million [89], which reduced the actual producer price again to Shs 33/50 per bag and Shs 32/50 respectively.
The imposition of cesses in years following a season with heavy losses to recover part of them was a usual practice exercised by the Maize Marketing Board. Such a cess reduced the pre-announced guaranteed price sometimes considerably and aggravated the extent of interseasonal price fluctuations. Moreover, the fact that a guaranteed price announced before planting which was reduced by a cess in the middle of the season when the extent of losses of the former season became known,

88 Described dramatically in the Report of the Maize Commission of Inquiry, Ibid., pp. 52–80.

89 *East African Standard:* November 12th, 1966.

introduced an uncertainty, rendering a pre-announced price meaningless. The Maize Commission recommended, therefore, that a price stabilization fund be accumulated by which short-time price fluctuations could be minimized [90].

3. Outlook for Future Price Stabilization

It may be concluded that in the three East African countries no unique trend pattern regarding price stabilization policies for export crops existed until the end of 1966, the time of writing. In Tanzania the government had opposed the proposals of the Presidential Special Committee as to price stabilization and had made its intention clear to pursue a policy (a) of maintaining stable prices throughout the season, (b) of protecting farmers from short-term price fluctuations between seasons for crops under the NAPB and the LSMB, (c) of maintaining price assistance funds for this purpose, and (d) of maintaining a one-payment system, if possible, with prices announced before planting but in any case at the beginning of the marketing season [91]. This meant that a policy of producer price stabilization, though a more cautious one, would be continued in Tanzania for commodities for which the necessary price assistance funds were available (cotton, cashew nuts, oil seeds). Also in Kenya, where only cotton prices are stabilized it is intended to continue price stabilization by sailing close to the wind, that is to say that producer prices will be adjusted to world market level much faster than formerly. In all cases price stabilization is closely connected with already existing price assistance funds. Governments usually do not dare to link such a policy with general revenue. This is why in Uganda price stabilization of the two major export commodities will probably be discontinued and belong to the past although by 1966 no decision had yet been made.
The situation with regard to staple food crops is different in all three countries. There is a tendency to uniformity towards interseasonal price stabilization for the main staple commodities, which have to satisfy the basic nutritional needs of the population. By the end of 1966, funds to back such a policy had only been accumulated in Tanzania in respect of maize and paddy. In Kenya, the Maize Commission of Inquiry made the recommendation to urgently set up a price assistance fund for maize. In Uganda, the situation was not quite clear. However, in the proposed bill for the minor crops board provision was also made to stabilize prices. Since at that time neither in Kenya nor in Uganda had funds from recent years been available to rely on, they would either have to be accumulated rapidly

90 Republic of Kenya: *Maize Commission of Inquiry*, pp. 23 and 29.
91 See The United Republic of Tanzania: *Proposals on the Recommendations of the Special Presidential Committee*, p. 14.

from trading activities (which would be rather difficult) or governments would have to set aside capital for this purpose unless they were prepared to link trading losses or profits with their government budgets.

II. Towards a Comprehensive Rationalized Agricultural Price and Taxation Policy: Tanzania

Traditionally, in the East African countries as well as in other countries, marketing boards entrusted with the fixation of producer prices for crops under their jurisdiction were to a certain degree autonomous within the limits of legal regulations. In cases where the government interfered through the supervising ministry, decisions on producer prices and export taxes were often taken not under long-term economic aspects but rather according to momentary fiscal needs of the government. Agricultural crops and their problems were seldom seen comprehensively in relation to each other but were mostly viewed separately. Signs of a development towards a comprehensive rationalized agricultural price and taxation policy were noticeable in Tanzania in early 1966, although certain changes in the orientation of the agricultural policy had already been made earlier. By the end of 1966, this new policy was still in its initial stages and not clearly defined because extensive research on various problems of the commodities concerned was still considered to be necessary and because the introduction of the new policy was not to be pushed too vigorously in order to allow farmers to make the necessary adjustments in their production plans.
The basic lines along which in Tanzania the new policy would have to be designed and the order of steps to be taken are as follows:

- Assessment of future prices, sales prospects, production costs, yields and rates of return for all export commodities.
- Outlining the basic economic aims to be pursued, such as the maximization of government revenue, of foreign exchange earnings, of total national income, of income of a particular population group, or of a particular agricultural sector.
- Fixation of crop priorities determining the required speed of expansion of a particular agricultural industry and the fixation of producer prices in relation to each other. This automatically implies that the magnitude of the tax burden be stipulated.

In line with the basic aims of the new policy and the priorities established, decisions have to be taken on the continuation, disruption or introduction of stabilization policies which in turn also influence the magnitude of taxes and levies to be imposed or of subsidies to be paid. Within this framework foodcrops constitute a special problem. For foodcrops a regular supply, attractive prices to growers and reasonable and stable prices to consumers, are a political necessity. Consequently, prices of foodcrops in relation to prices of other crops have to be fixed in such a way that the production pattern which secures these aims will not be distorted.

A number of difficulties may impede the setting up of a rational agricultural price and taxation policy. The notorious lack of information on possible reactions of farmers as a result of changes in the current producer price pattern and the uncertainties of the world markets are examples. Further, the impact of any tax may have varying effects on different commodities. The taxable capacity of one crop may be high (in 1966 e.g. of cashew nuts), of another one it may be low (e.g. of sisal). Still another crop may even need a subsidy in one way or another in line with pre-established policy goals. A good example for the problems which a crop may face is provided by coffee.

In 1966 part of the coffee crop of Tanzania was subsidized by the economy as a whole, and, moreover, part of the coffee growers subsidized others. Considerable quantities exceeding the Tanzanian coffee export quota allocated under the International Coffee Agreement were sold at a high discount of £30 to 50 per ton to non-traditional markets. Since coffee sold to non-traditional markets was exempted from the export tax (about £22 per ton arabica until June 1966, raised to £28 as of July) such exports constituted a loss to government revenue. Up to this amount, the whole economy subsidized the coffee industry. The discount granted was, however, generally higher than the export tax. Since all coffee proceeds were pooled, coffee sold to quota-markets subsidized coffee sold to new markets at the rate of the difference between export tax and the discount granted.

Institutional Requirements

In order to be able to implement a comprehensive national price policy, two institutional changes were considered to be necessary. First, the required machinery was to be established by creating a committee for co-ordinating policies of all administrative authorities and bodies possibly affected by a comprehensive price and taxation policy. This co-ordination of policies was to be attempted by an Interministerial Committee to be organized by the Ministry of Economic Affairs and Development Planning. According to proposals made by the Presidential Special Committee this Interministerial Committee would include representatives of the Ministries of Finance, of Regional Administration, and of Agriculture and Water Development, the co-operative unions, and the marketing board. In view of the fact that a comprehensive price and taxation policy affects the whole process of development and, in particular, the balance of payments, the Central Bank, too, should be represented on the Interministerial Committee. Apart from the boards themselves, the Ministry of Commerce and Co-operatives which supervises most of the marketing boards would also have to be represented. A co-ordinating body of this type would certainly be in a better position to decide upon crop priorities and price policies, taking into consideration the magnitude of taxes, charges and levies to be imposed.

The Tanzanian government accepted these proposals of the Presidential Special Committee in late 1966 and charged the Ministry of Economic Affairs and Development Planning with taking the organizational steps for harmonizing the various taxes, duties and levies imposed on agricultural crops. Already during 1965 and 1966 this Ministry was represented on all marketing boards in operation except the LSMB, thus increasing its influence on the process of decision making of the boards. By the end of 1966 it was expected that the legal ground would soon be prepared for opening the LSMB to this ministry also. The Tanzanian government decided further that the Ministry of Economic Affairs and Development Planning should have the final decision on the total of deductions to be made and on their allocation[92].

The second prerequisite of a comprehensive price and taxation policy is the amalgamation of marketing boards, which shall be only mentioned here as it has already been referred to above[93]. That a streamlined system of marketing boards consisting of a considerably smaller number of marketing boards (possibly only two, of which the export board would have the greater importance with respect to the policy outlined) will raise less problems than a multitude of boards requires no special emphasis.

The New Role of Marketing Boards

The implementation of a rationalized agricultural price and taxation policy will result in a change of the role of marketing boards, insofar as it will minimize the marketing boards' freedom of decision-taking regarding their own price policies. Their own concept of a suitable price policy would be integrated in the comprehensive price policy suggested by the Interministerial Committee and finally decided upon by the Ministry of Economic Affairs and Development Planning. Marketing boards would remain marketing agencies, autonomous in attempting to secure the optimum sales arrangements for their produce by means of the power delegated to them. The weight of their responsibility, however, is shifting. Formerly, their main concern was the maximum benefit of producers of a certain sector, at least as far as export crops were concerned. In future optimal marketing arrangements

92 The United Republic of Tanzania: *Proposals on the Recommendations of the Special Presidential Committee*, p. 19.

93 See above, pp. 299 et seq.

will be sought rather for the benefit of the economy as a whole than for a particular producer group.
The complete withdrawal of autonomy to fix prices will make marketing boards predominantly a tool of government for the implementation of a rationally planned price policy in the agricultural sector. This offers a number of advantages. The position of marketing boards was previously somewhat obscure insofar as they were frequently blamed for losses which may have occurred. Although it was nominally their responsibility to fix prices they often had to comply with government wishes introducing political rather than economic elements. The new role of the boards would clearly restrict them to implementing a price policy decided upon by a government body. The distinction between a board's marketing function and its function to carry out a certain price policy by deducting taxes and charges imposed by government would now be clear[94]. The change of role would not be as incisive in the case of marketing boards dealing with foodcrops because, due to the importance of basic foodstuffs, the influence of the Tanzanian government on the price fixation of foodcrops has always been more extensive.
A problem closely linked with the price policy is the administration of the price assistance and price stabilization funds. By the end of 1966 it seemed that the Tanzanian government did not intend to follow the recommendations of the Presidential Special Committee which proposed the abolishion of all assistance and stabilization funds, but rather intended to continue a price stabilization policy for cotton, cashew nuts, oil seeds, maize and paddy[95]. Whatever marketing boards market these crops in future, they will administer the corresponding funds on behalf of the government and will draw upon them when ordered to do so.
The separation of the board's marketing function and its function to carry out a stipulated price policy would ease the implementation of the proposal of the Presidential Special Committee, if considered seriously, viz eventually to make the boards for export crops the sales agents of the co-operatives, which themselves have to comply with directives received from the government[96]. Although such a move would in many cases probably only be nominal because operations would continue as before, the original concept of marketing boards would change radically since they would eventually lose their autonomy completely. The actual marketing would be subject to decisions

94 A similar distinction of the marketing and price determination function is found in several of the French speaking countries in West Africa where there is a "Caisse de Stabilisation" administrating a price assistance fund and an "Office de Commercialisation" which is responsible for the marketing of the same crops subject to a stabilization policy determined by the "Caisse de Stabilisation".

95 The United Republic of Tanzania: *Proposals on the Recommendations of the Presidential Special Committee*, p. 14.

96 See above, p. 307.

of co-operative bodies and price fixation would depend on decisions taken by the Interministerial Committee or the Government respectively. With regard to foodcrops the proposal to make the boards agents of the co-operative movement would put a marketing board in a rather contradictory position, because of the dual responsibility towards producers and consumers alike. Consequently, it would hardly be feasible.

E. COORDINATION OF MARKETING POLICIES BETWEEN THE EAST AFRICAN COUNTRIES

In the past a co-operation of marketing boards and similar institutions has existed for short or lengthy periods. In view of many marketing problems for a number of commodities common to all 3 countries co-operation between the marketing boards of the three East African countries could be beneficial to all of them. The particular needs of marketing in the three countries would be better served.

I. Co-operation between Marketing Boards and other Marketing Institutions in the Past

Past co-operation between marketing boards and the marketing institutions concerned export crops as well as food crops. In the cotton industry the boards in charge of marketing cotton in the three countries (the Lint Marketing Board of Uganda, the Cotton Lint and Seed Marketing Board of Kenya and the Lint and Seed Marketing Board of Tanzania) had concluded an agreement from the year of their establishment according to which the Lint Marketing Board of Uganda, apart from selling the Uganda cotton crop, also auctioned the cotton grown in the Nyanza Province of Kenya on behalf of the Cotton Lint and Seed Marketing Board of Kenya, and the cotton grown in the former Lake Province (Mwanza) Region of Tanzania on behalf of the Lint and Seed Marketing Board of Tanganyika. This arrangement lasted for Tanganyika until 1958 when the Lint and Seed Marketing Board started auctioning all Tanganyikan cotton in Dar es

Salaam. Kenyan cotton was sold up to 1966 by the Lint Marketing Board of Uganda, when the Cotton Lint and Seed Marketing Board of Kenya attempted to set up its own export section. Together with two private companies, whose overseas contacts were to be used, the board established a trading company of its own in order to sell its cotton directly overseas in future.
Up to 1958–59, the production and marketing of pyrethrum grown in Tanganyika was controlled by the Pyrethrum Board of Kenya. From 1962 on, when the factory of the Tanganyika Extract Company Ltd. of the Mitchell Cotts Group of Companies was completed in Arusha, all Tanzanian pyrethrum flowers were sold under contract negotiated by the Tanganyika Pyrethrum Board with this company. Since Kenya and Tanzania together produce the bulk of the total pyrethrum supply of the world and Mitchell Cotts has a decisive influence on the whole East African pyrethrum industry, an Interterritorial Pyrethrum Consultative Council was established in 1963, comprising two members each from the Pyrethrum Board of Tanganyika and of Kenya and two representatives of Mitchell Cotts and Company Ltd. It may be assumed that the functions of this Consultative Council exceed the character of a consulting agency and that actual decisions are taken by it, for instance, on production targets of the two countries.

Co-operation with regard to other export crops, like sisal and coffee, was of minor importance. Although in the middle of the fifties neither the Tanganyika Sisal Board nor the Sisal Board of Kenya were engaged in the marketing of sisal, their influence on the whole sphere of marketing was substantial by introducing common standards, uniform sales contracts, the same systems of grading, etc.
For a short while a Coffee Industry Association, founded in 1957, was in existence of which the then Tanganyika Coffee Board was a member. This Association intended to group all interests of the coffee industries of the three East African countries and attempt to attain a co-ordination of policies on various problems. It never gained practical significance, however.

For important local foodcrops there was a close collaboration at times between the three countries. The East African Production and Supply Council, set up in 1942 to co-ordinate war-time production and supply policies of the East African Territories for a number of agricultural products, continued, amongst other tasks, to operate the East African Cereals Pool after the war and dealt with the distribution of other locally produced foodstuffs, their prices to producers, the importation of products such as sugar, wheat, etc. The East African Cereals Pool was responsible for ensuring grain supplies to the three mainland territories, to Zanzibar and the Seychelles Islands. Surpluses of maize, rice and wheat of each of the three countries were delivered to the pool which operated storage facilities. From there they were either distributed into shortage areas or exported to overseas countries if East Africa as a whole had a surplus. Similarly, if there was an overall shortage the pool imported grains. When in the late forties and early fifties the Kenya Maize Control, the Grain Storage Department in Tanganyika, and the Grain Conditioning Plant in Uganda brought the marketing of maize — the main staple in all three countries — under their control, it was felt that the respective organizations would be able to cope with the shortage and surplus problems of their countries themselves. Hence, the East African Cereals Pool was replaced in 1952 by an agreement regarding the interterritorial supply of staple commodities including the principle that no exports were to be made from any of the 3 countries unless the needs of East Africa as a whole were satisfied.

This system was workable only as long as maize marketing in the countries was under control by a governmental or semi-governmental body. After the dissolution of the Grain Conditioning Plant in Uganda in 1954 and the Grain Storage Department of Tanzania in 1955, the internal and export trade was freed from all restrictions and the agreement lost its practical applicability.

The supply of wheat and sugar, however, was still governed by a common policy. From 1954 on the Department of Economic Co-ordination of the East African High Commission undertook the balancing of the requirements and supplies of wheat and sugar, a task which was taken over in 1961 by the East African Common Services Organisation (EACSO) as successor of the East African High Commission. From 1963 on sugar was imported by the countries themselves. Although in 1962 an Interterritorial Sugar Advisory Committee had been founded by the three governments, which considered setting up an East African Sugar Board, no steps towards a co-ordination of sugar policies have been taken ever since.

By the end of 1966 wheat was the only crop for which a common policy and co-operation between the marketing institutions existed. EACSO imports wheat for the three countries to meet needs in excess of the domestic supply, and there is in addition an Interterritorial Agreement on Wheat and Wheat Flour Policy ruling between Kenya and Tanzania. This agreement came into existence in 1959 and governs the licensing of mills, allocations of local wheat to mills, imports, etc. In the course of time the agreement became more and more out of force and was under review at the end of 1966, with Tanzania approaching self-sufficiency in wheat production. Uganda not being a member of this agreement has come to terms with Kenya about a mutual exchange of wheat and sugar.

It was shown that co-operation in the three East African countries among the agricultural industries and the respective marketing boards and institutions did not exist only for export crops grown on estates, but also for crops grown by African farmers, such as the main locally consumed staples, in particular maize. The trend towards nationally more independent institutions and marketing policies is not a recent development but had already become visible in colonial times. By abolishing common organisations or reducing the co-operation among them, common marketing policies and even merely informative talks diminished to a minimum after the three countries had gained political independence, when different political concepts contributed to the desire for self-determination and for economic independence.

II. Possibilities of Coordination of Marketing Policies

A co-operation and co-ordination of marketing policies for export commodities would be feasible and possible in several fields from which a number of benefits for all East African countries would result. For its coffee exports, for instance, each of the three member countries of the International Coffee Organisation was allocated a certain export quota. In the mid-sixties each country produced coffee in excess of its quota. Almost the total coffee crop of Uganda and about a third of Tanzania's crop was low priced robusta coffee. Uganda is carrying over large stocks of coffee from year to year which it cannot sell. Tanzania has so far been fortunate enough to sell all its coffee including the 1965–66 crop (which was far in excess of her quota). It will, however, be faced with unsaleable surpluses sooner or later. Hence, instead of each country having her separate export quota, the three coffee marketing boards or the three governments respectively could agree to pool their coffee quotas and to sell the maximum of the high-priced arabica of Kenya and of Tanzania under the aggregated quota and to retain only the lower-valued robusta coffee if retentions are unavoidable[97].

This would increase total income and foreign exchange earnings by the difference of export price between robusta and arabica coffee for each ton of arabica substituted for robusta. On top there would be savings in transport costs because the arabica growing coffee areas in Kenya and Tanzania (mainly in the Mt. Kenya and Mt. Kilimanjaro region) are much closer to the export ports than the robusta growing areas around Lake Victoria, both in Uganda and Tanzania.

Another possibility of co-operation between marketing boards would be in the field of price policies for controlled crops. In the past divergent price policies for the same crop posed a serious problem for all countries concerned. Depending upon whether a marketing board subsidized producer prices or whether it creamed off part of the sales proceeds, there was a considerable illegal flow of the respective produce to or from this country.

97 D. G. R. Belshaw: Agricultural Production and Trade in the East African Common Market — A Survey, in: *African Economic Problems*, edited by Ph. W. Bell and K. H. Bell, Vol. IV: Growth and Change, Issues in Planning. Kampala, Makerere University College, 1965.

For example, when the coffee price was subsidized in Uganda large illegal movements of robusta coffee from the Bukoba area in Tanzania were recorded, putting additional strains on the funds of the Coffee Price Assistance Fund in Uganda. Similarly higher cotton price levels in any of the three countries had the effect of movements of cotton from the cotton growing areas of the three countries around Lake Viktoria to this country [98].

These undesirable effects could be avoided by a co-ordination of the price policies of the marketing boards. The exhaustion of price assistance funds, the resulting diminishing importance of price stabilization policies and a closer adjustment to prices justified by world market conditions would certainly facilitate a decision to be taken in this respect by the marketing boards or the governments of the three countries.

There is another field in which marketing boards could co-operate very closely. The most important export crops of East Africa are grown in all three countries or, at least, in two of them, such as cotton, coffee, sisal and tea. Instead of trying to sell one country's products on the account of another's, common sales promotion campaigns could be launched, common market research could be promoted or even direct sales could be arranged overseas in common. Overhead costs for each country in establishing or maintaining overseas promotion and sales offices are high. For this reason the Committee of Inquiry into the Cotton Industry 1966 of Uganda, for instance, recommended in its report the abandoning of the direct overseas sales policy. The share of overheads might, however, be minimized and be allocated proportionally to the three countries if an overseas office were maintained by all three boards, or if a communal sales promotion campaign were launched. Moreover, a common office, for instance in London or New York, could even represent a number of boards dealing with different crops and agricultural products, e.g. coffee, cotton and oil seeds.

Food crops

In the field of food crops, particularly as far as maize is concerned, the existence of three statutory institutions (the Uganda Board was expected to be established in early 1967) controlling the marketing of maize offers a favourable possibility for interterritorial trade. Hitherto in Kenya there was

98 A different taxation of agricultural products may have the same effects. If as proposed heavier export taxes materialized in Tanzania in order to discourage coffee expansion in excess over her quota, this would have a depressive effect on coffee prices to producers. If the other two countries did not follow with a similar policy, large movements of coffee across the borders to Uganda could be expected. Such movements of coffee would aggravate the serious surplus problem in Uganda even more. Crops such as cotton, sisal (hedge sisal from Lake Victoria) and others may face similar problems.

an official embargo on Uganda maize imports which Tanzania also followed on some occasions, and in some years the Uganda government prohibited maize exports to the two neighbour countries.
Before maize came under control in all three East African countries in the late forties or early fifties, there was a free flow of maize in East Africa according to price differences, different times of harvest and suitable communications. When free movement of maize across the borders was prohibited, illegal trade continued resulting from different levels of uncontrolled prices (in Uganda) and controlled prices (in Kenya and Tanzania). Good or bad harvests are much better reflected by free prices and accordingly seasonal and interseasonal price fluctuations were usually wider in Uganda than in Kenya and in Tanzania where prices were controlled. Depending on price differences, maize was shipped illegally from one country to another. Thus large quantities of maize crossed the border from Uganda to Kenya in 1961 and from Kenya to Uganda in 1963. In 1965 a bag of maize could fetch at a time between shs 50 and 70 in Uganda, whereas the Maize Marketing Board in Kenya paid only shs 32 to 50 per bag. This resulted in movements from Kenya to Uganda, tentatively estimated at 100,000 to 200,000 bags of maize[99] at a time when Kenya needed her maize rather badly herself.
It can be assumed that in view of the cost structure existing by the end of 1966 imports into either of the three countries from the respective two neighbouring countries were cheaper than imports from overseas at a landed cost price of about shs 57/-. Moreover, the then rather high profit/reserve margin for the stabilization or the export-import loss reserve in Tanzania and Kenya and additionally the producer cess in Kenya imposed after years of exceptionally high losses could have been suspended by a mutual agreement on quantities destined for interterritorial exchange. Such a move would considerably lower the import price for the respective importing country. A mutual aid agreement for movements of maize would have still another advantage. Imports from overseas require commitments several months ahead. By the time a consignment arrives, the whole supply position may have changed as evidenced in the "maize muddle" of Kenya in 1965–66. Supplies from neighbouring countries could be moved much faster from stocks of the marketing board of the supporting country, which could be replenished by the import consignment arriving later.
Thus, it would generally be advantageous if the three countries embarked on a common supply and price policy for maize as their major staple food crop. One single East African Board would certainly ease an undertaking of this kind. At the different times of harvest, supplies could more easily be moved from the various regional production centres. Such a policy combined with a properly planned common program for building storage facilities

99 Between 9,000 to 18,000 tons.

would minimize the necessity for the same country to export and import to and from overseas at high costs during the same year or, in another case, to export to overseas while the neighbouring country had to import from overseas, as it happened in recent years. It needs no special mention that a policy of co-operation for maize could equally be adopted for rice and for other foodstuffs since in the three countries they are under the jurisdiction of the same boards which handle maize.

As to wheat it was mentioned that by the end of 1966 the Interterritorial Wheat Agreement was still in force. Imports of wheat were executed jointly by EACSO as a handling agent for the three countries, although each country had negotiated terms of importation separately, e.g. for imports from the United States under the PL 480 law. The spirit of co-operation between the Kenyan and Tanzanian Wheat Boards was, however, very good. Nevertheless, regulations under which the National Wheat Board of Tanzania imported wheat from Kenya (the railage of which was subsidized by Kenya allowing a profit for the National Wheat Board of Tanzania) ceased to exist in the 1966–67 season.

There was ample scope for a common wheat policy of the three East African countries, especially under the aspect that it would be related with a common maize and particular sugar policy. To some extent an interterritorial trade existed already between Kenya and Uganda, the former having a wheat surplus almost regularly, part of which went to Uganda, the latter having a sugar surplus, part of which went to Kenya. Although there existed no official agreement of mutual exchange, it may be assumed that if one of the two countries had stopped importing wheat or sugar respectively, the other country would have acted the same way. Each of the three countries could, without doubt, benefit from a common sugar policy for which the institutional framework was, however, still lacking (only Tanzania had a sugar board)[100]. Considerable savings in transport, for instance, would be achieved if areas around Lake Victoria were to be supplied with sugar produced only in Uganda, and if the Southern and Central parts of Kenya including Nairobi were supplied with sugar produced in Tanzania. Once this commodity was exported outside East Africa these exports could be undertaken from the factories in Tanzania near the coast instead of from Uganda at extremely high shipping costs. As domestic prices are higher than world market prices, an equalization fund would be required into which the countries would have to pay according to estimated benefits in order to compensate for the losses which the exporting country would incur[101].

100 Sugar policies of the three East African countries were related to some extent insofar as prices paid to producers were based on the Commonwealth Sugar Agreement price and were thus approximately the same.

101 See also Ch. S. FRANK: *The Sugar Industry in East Africa,* East African Studies No. 20. Nairobi, East African Publishing House, 1967.

By the end of 1966, the political prerequisites for co-operation between marketing boards and a co-ordination of marketing policies were far from being ideal. With the breakaway of Tanzania from the East African Currency Board chances deteriorated even further. Hopes that prospects might improve rested with measures under consideration at the end of 1966, which aimed at strengthening the East African Common Market in which such policies could be integrated.

Bibliography

ABBOTT, J. C. and CREUPELANDT, H. C.: *Agricultural Marketing Boards — Their Establishment and Operation,* Marketing Guide No. 5. Rome, Food and Agriculture Organization, 1966.

ADLER, J. H.: Comments on Professor NURKSE's Paper on 'The Quest for a Stabilization Policy in Primary Producing Countries', A Symposium, in: *Kyklos,* Vol. XI (1958), pp. 155–168.

ANDRAIN, Ch.: Patterns of African Socialist Thought, in: *African Forum,* Vol. I, No. 3, 1965, pp. 41–60.

BAUER, P. T.: *West African Trade.* London, Routledge & Kegan Paul Ltd., 1963.

— and PAISH, F. W.: The Reduction of Fluctuations in the Incomes of Primary Producers, in: *The Economic Journal,* Vol. LXII, No. 248 (December 1952).

— and YAMEY, B. S.: *The Economics of Under-developed Countries.* Welwyn, Herts and Cambridge, James Nisbet & Co. Ltd. and the University Press, 1959 (Reprint).

BELSHAW, D. G. R.: Agricultural Production and Trade in the East African Common Market — A Survey, in: *African Economic Problems,* edited by Ph. W. BELL and K. H. BELL, Vol. IV: Growth and Change, Issues in Planning. Kampala, Makerere University College, 1965.

BURKE, F.: Tanganyika: The Search for Ujamaa, in: *African Socialism,* edited by W. H. FRIEDLAND and C. G. ROSBERG, Jr. Stanford, Stanford University Press, 1964, pp. 194–219.

Food and Agriculture Organization: *The Marketing of Staple Food Crops in Africa,* Report of a Seminar held in Nairobi, 1964. Rome, Food and Agriculture Organization, 1965.

FRANK, Ch. S.: *The Sugar Industry in East Africa,* East African Studies No. 20. Nairobi, East African Publishing House, 1967.

HELLEINER, G.: *Some Comments upon the Report of the Presidential Committee of Inquiry into Co-operative Movement and Marketing Boards.* Dar es Salaam, University College, 1966 (mimeo.).

The International Bank for Reconstruction and Development: *The Economic Development of Tanganyika.* Baltimore, The John Hopkins Press, 1961.

—: *The Economic Development of Uganda.* Baltimore, The John Hopkins Press, 1962.

—: *The Economic Development of Kenya.* Baltimore, The John Hopkins Press, 1963.

Kenya, Republic of: *African Socialism and its Application to Planning in Kenya,* Sessional Paper No. 10. Nairobi, Government Printer, 1965.

—: *Report of the Maize Commission of Inquiry,* 1966. Nairobi, Government Printer, 1966.

LEUBUSCHER, Ch.: Marketing Schemes for Native-grown Produce in African Territories, in: *Africa,* Vol. XII, No. 2 (April 1939), pp. 163–188.

MARTIN, A.: The Marketing of Minor Crops in Uganda, in: *Overseas Research Publications,* No. 1 (1963), pp. 1–78.

NYERERE, J. K.: *Ujamaa, The Basis of African Socialism.* Dar es Salaam, Government Printer, 1962.

SNAPE, R. H. and YAMEY, B. S.: A Diagrammatic Analysis of Some Effects of Buffer Fund Price Stabilization, in: *Oxford Economic Papers* (New Series), Vol. XV, No. 2 (July 1963), pp. 95–106.

Tanzania, The United Republic of: *Report of the Presidential Special Committee of Enquiry into Co-operative Movement and Marketing Boards,* Government Printer, Dar es Salaam 1966.

—: *Proposals of the Tanzania Government on the Recommendations of the Special Presidential Committee of Enquiry into the Co-operative Movement and Marketing Boards,* Government Paper No. 3. Dar es Salaam, Government Printer, 1966.

Uganda Government: *Report of the Committee of Inquiry into the Cotton Industry, 1966.* Entebbe, Government Printer, 1966.

United Nations Economic and Social Council, Economic Commission for Africa, Standing Committee on Trade: *National Stabilization Measures. National Marketing Boards and Price Stabilization Funds in Africa.* Addis Ababa, Economic Commission for Africa, 1962.

WALKER, D., and EHRLICH, C.: Stabilization and Development Policy in Uganda: An Appraisal, in: *Kyklos,* Vol. XII (1959), pp. 341–353.

Periodicals, Newspapers and other Publications

Annual Reports, Coffee Board (Kenya). Nairobi.
Cotton Lint and Seed Marketing Board (Kenya). Nairobi.
Pyrethrum Board of Kenya. Nairobi.
Pyrethrum Marketing Board (Kenya). Nairobi.
Lint and Seed Marketing Board (Tanzania). Dar es Salaam.
Lint Marketing Board (Uganda). Kampala.

East African Quaterly Economical and Statistical Review.

East African Standard, July 30th and November 12th, 1966.

Kenya, Republic of, Statistics Division — Ministry of Economic Planning and Development: *Statistical Abstract*, 1965. Nairobi, Government Printer, 1965.

Tanganyika, Department of Agriculture: *Annual Report 1949*. Dar es Salaam, Government Printer, 1949.

Tanzania, The United Republic of, Central Statistical Bureau: *Statistical Abstract*. Dar es Salaam, Government Printer.

Uganda Argus, May 7th, 1966.

Uganda Government, Statistics Division — Ministry of Planning and Community Development: *Statistical Abstract*. Entebbe, Government Printer.

—: *Monthly Statistical Bulletin*. Dar es Salaam, Government Printer.

CHANNELS OF DISTRIBUTION IN UGANDA

by

Helmut LAUMER

Contents

List of Tables

List of Figures

Glossary of Expressions Used

BAT British American Tobacco (Uganda), Ltd.
duka a small retail trading firm
ghee a semifluid butter made chiefly in India
matoke a crop grown in Uganda for food
NTC National Trading Corporation
Nytil trade name for certain products manufactured by Nyanza Textile Industries, Ltd.
panga a heavy knife used for cutting undergrowth and the like
sorghum a species of grass yielding fodder and syrup
waragi a spirit made from bananas

From the autumn of 1966 until the end of 1967, in connection with the Federal Republic of Germany's technical aid, Helmut LAUMER served as an Adviser in the Statistics Division of the Ministry of Planning and Economic Development at Entebbe, Uganda. His task was to prepare and carry out the first Ugandan trade census. The studies which resulted from the first part of that work — on Wholesale Trade, on Co-operative Unions, on Commission Agents and on Retailers with ten or more Employees — were published at the end of 1967 before the author left Uganda. The study resulting from the second part — that on Retailers with less than ten Employees — was published in 1969. During his stay in Uganda Mr. LAUMER was able, by numerous visits to traders, farmers and the like as well as by discussions in the Ministries concerned, to acquaint himself with the problems of Ugandan trade. The knowledge obtained in that connection forms the basis of the following study.

Helmut LAUMER has been employed since 1955 as a research economist in the Trade Department of the Ifo Institute for Economic Research at Munich. Since that year he has carried out numerous investigations of structural and cyclical trends in wholesale and retail trade, as well as in the co-operative system, both in the Federal Republic of Germany and in other European countries.

We are indebted to *Patria* Translations, Ltd. in Dochester, England for translating this treatise into English.

A. UGANDA'S GEOGRAPHICAL SITUATION AND ECONOMIC STRUCTURE AS SPECIFIC DETERMINANTS OF TRADE

Trade as a link between producers and consumers primarily results, in the forms and structures which it from time to time assumes, from exogenous influences. The country's state of industrialisation, its dependence on exports or on imports, the population's living standard, the country's geographical structure and — not least — the Government's political ideas all set their stamp on trade. Thus, for assessing the efficiency of trade in developing countries, it is in principle necessary to apply standards other than those applicable in highly industrialised states.

The specific circumstances of Uganda, in so far as they affect trade, can be outlined as follows:

Uganda is one of Africa's *landlocked* countries, with all the disadvantages resulting from that fact. Its chief port of supply is Mombasa in neighbouring Kenya, more than 800 miles from Uganda's eastern frontier. For Uganda's import and export trade this inevitably entails increased difficulties and risks of a technical, economic and political character.

Unusually great difficulties and risks of a technical nature result from the need to carry imports from the coast to Uganda, and exports from Uganda to the coast, using transport facilities which are in some cases inadequate. The one-track railway is for example overloaded, and conforms to the technical standards of the last century; the roads are only in part asphalted; and the port of Mombasa is overworked. From the economic point of view this makes it much harder for traders to time their actions — an especially serious matter in the case of agricultural products; it increases the risk of these perishing; and — the most important point — the increased cost of transport materially impairs exporters' ability to compete. Political risks arise for Uganda's exporting and importing traders because their trade depends on good relations between Uganda and Kenya. Political tensions between the two countries may lead to restrictions, or even to the cutting of communications from and to the coast.

In Uganda's case these risks are the more serious because the country *depends*, in relatively high degree, *on the world market*. Uganda as an exporter is still largely dependent on coffee and cotton. These two products account for roughly 75 per cent to 80 per cent of the country's total exports, and because of fluctuations in world market prices, as well as in the crops, which depend on the weather, the proceeds of such exports are subject to great uncertainty. On the whole, therefore, Uganda's export trade entails risks which native firms can hardly bear alone. The export trade, especially in cotton, is for that reason mainly conducted by large overseas enterprises, which have branches in Uganda, Kenya and Tanzania, and which handle their exports on an East African basis.

Although much progress has been made during the last ten years in building up national industries, Uganda is likely to remain for a long time largely dependent on imports not only of capital goods but also of consumer goods. Of all the goods offered on the home market, that is production[1] less exports but plus imports, imports account for more than two-thirds and native products for only just one-third. This means that firms trading in Uganda incline heavily to the import trade.

Uganda's consumer goods trade has to supply a *population whose purchasing power is extremely low*. The annual average income per head works out at less than Shs 600/-. There are in that connection wide regional and social differences, which means that a high proportion of the population have an income below this average. In the towns the average income per gainfully active person is about Shs 2,600/-, but in the country it is at most Shs 500/-. In the case of the rural population, who live on the production of coffee and cotton, this income also fluctuates very widely according to the time of year; outside the crop season there are few possibilities of earning, and accordingly little demand for goods. In the main coffee and cotton growing areas there are "dukas" (that is small retail shops) and also semi-wholesalers, who keep their shops open only at harvest times.

Although Uganda has one of the best road systems in tropical Africa, the *road density is low* as compared with that found in developed economies, and *some of the roads are in a bad state*. These facts make it much more difficult for traders to perform their collecting and distributing function. The proportion of transport costs in the value of goods is relatively high. On the one hand the firms which buy up agricultural products for export or for town markets from an exceptionally large number of small and ultra-small farms, which are spread throughout the country, have to carry the produce by roads on many of which there is a great deal of dust, and this impairs the quality of the products; on the other hand the low population density, especially in the remote parts of the country, makes it unprofitable for wholesalers to deliver consumer goods there.

These brief observations may serve to show the difficulties and problems which face firms trading in Uganda. The many people who criticise the sometimes inadequate efficiency of the existing trade system, as well as its high costs and wide profit margins, often overlook these facts. The Govern-

1 Excluding food produced for subsistence.

ment too should admit that the cause of the trouble lies not only in defective ability (of the African traders), and in excessive profit-seeking (by Asiatic and European business men), but also, and primarily, in conditions which are especially difficult by comparison with those in other countries.

B. DEVELOPMENT AND STRUCTURE OF THE TRADING SYSTEM

I. The Beginnings of Institutional Trade, and its Development up till 1966

Organised institutional trade began in Uganda about the turn of the century. One of the pioneers was the Indian Allidina Visram, who started to trade in Uganda about 1900. In 1916, when he died, he left 240 shops in Kenya, Uganda, Tanganyika and the Congo. About that time Kampala was already becoming the main trading centre in Uganda. The successful exporting of cotton, which was cultivated on a major scale from about 1910 onwards, strengthened Kampala's hold on that position.
During the thirties nearly the whole of Uganda's trade was still in Asiatic hands. The first European trading companies at Kampala included the "Mengo Planters", a retail trading enterprise which was managed by a former missionary, selling a wide range of simple consumer goods and foodstuffs. Even at that time, however, the Government already began trying to interest natives in trade, and making it easier for them to penetrate that sphere. The Trading Centres Ordinance, issued in 1933, imposed local limitation on the activity of non-native traders. During the subsequent period, however, only a few Africans set up retail shops.
Not until just after the second world war did the first major Africanisation of trade begin. It started because in that period of shortage the Government began to import some necessary goods under its own arrangements, selling these goods through traders on the basis of fixed prices and profits; many Africans took the opportunity to establish a footing in trade through conducting such business, which entailed no risk. At that time, moreover, many returning soldiers invested their pay or their gratuities in small retail dukas. In 1952 there were already nearly 12,000 African traders, so that almost 70 per cent of all the trading firms in Uganda were African.
In 1952 the great majority of the African traders were widely spread in the bush, or operated in rural trading centres outside the towns. Town trading,

Table 1. *Number of Traders in Uganda, Classified by Race, 1952*

Race	Number	%
Africans	11,634	*68.8*
Asians	4,809	*28.4*
Arabs	319	*1.9*
Europeans	99	*0.6*
Others	47	*0.3*
Total	16,908	*100.0*

Source: Uganda Government, Department of Commerce: *The Advancement of Africans in Trade.* Entebbe, Government Printer 1955, p. 14.

however, remained almost exclusively in the hands of Asians. There were no African wholesalers at all. The average size of African trading firms, that is the turnover per firm, was extremely small. It is estimated that in 1952 the African firms, numbering little short of 12,000, accounted for not more than between 10 per cent and 12 per cent of the total turnover.

During the next decade the African traders greatly strengthened their position. They increasingly managed to establish a footing in the larger towns. The two largest towns in Uganda are Kampala and Jinja. The number of African firms there was of course at the outset very low, but it has risen by many times as much as that of the Asiatic and European firms.

Table 2. *Number of Trading Licences, Classified According to the Licensee's Race, Issued at Kampala and Jinja, 1952 and 1966*

	Kampala			Jinja		
	1952	1966	Percentage change	1952	1966	Percentage change
Africans	27	101	*+274*	22	64	*+190*
Asians	1,014	1,127	*+ 11*	351	333	*— 5*
Europeans	50	77	*+ 54*	22	14	*— 36*

Source: Licensing statistics of the Kampala und Jinja Town Councils.

The first comprehensive investigation of Uganda's wholesale and retail trade structure was carried out, for the year 1966, by the Statistics Division in the Ministry of Planning and Economic Development. The wholesale trade and the large retail firms (with 10 or more employees) were investigated by a complete census, the much more numerous smaller retail firms by a sample check. This for the first time provided relatively reliable information about the structure and performance of trade in Uganda.

II. Retail trade

According to the Statistics Division's findings in connection with the Census of Distribution there were in Uganda, at the end of 1966, not quite 14,000 firms. Of these firms 10,500, or 75 per cent were operating in rural and just under 3,300, or 25 per cent, in urban areas. Retail sales in 1966 were found to total Shs 1,800 million. Of this amount one-third was effected in the country's two largest and most highly industrialised towns, Kampala and Jinja.

Table 3. *Number of Retail Firms, Persons Employed and Receipts, 1966*

Location	Number of firms [b]	Persons employed [b]	Total receipts in millions of shillings
Kampala	796	5,350	474.2
Jinja	505	1,685	138.2
All other towns	1,945	7,800	565.0
Rural areas [a]	(10,500)	(47,300)	(653.9)
Uganda, total	13,745	62,135	1,831.3

[a] These and all subsequent data for the rural areas are statistically less certain than the data for the urban areas.
[b] End of year.

Source: Uganda Government, Statistics Division – Ministry of Planning and Economic Development: *Census of Distribution, Part II.* Entebbe, Government Printer, 1969 (quoted hereafter as Uganda Government: *Census, Part II*).

The average firm's annual turnover in 1966 was Shs 133,000, but more than 10 per cent of all urban retailers, and 61 per cent of all rural retailers, had a turnover less than Shs 10,000. Some 20 per cent of the retail firms in the towns, with turnovers in excess of Shs 500,000, accounted for 70 per cent of the total turnovers.

Uganda's retail trade, especially in the rural areas, is still very little specialised. Of all the firms about one-half, accounting for four-fifths of all turnovers, are general trading stores which normally cover many categories such as food, textiles, household articles, tools and medicines. In each of these they carry only a few articles, which moreover are the same in all neighbouring shops. In the towns and the larger trading centres, on the other hand, specialisation has made perceptible progress during recent years.

In 1966, of the persons totalling 62,000 who were employed in retail trade (including active proprietors and assisting family members), not quite 85 per cent were Africans and 13.5 per cent Asians. The proportion of Asians is of course a good deal higher in urban retail trade than in the rural areas. The average wage or salary paid per employee in 1966 was Shs 7,020 at

Table 4. *Percentage Proportion of Firms and Turnovers in Urban and Rural Retail Trade, According to Categories, in 1966*

Category	Towns		Rural areas	
	Firms	Turnovers	Firms	Turnovers
Grocers	*26.6*	*13.2*	*30.2*	*6.0*
General Trading Stores	*22.4*	*21.8*	*49.4*	*80.4*
Clothing, textiles, footwear	*21.1*	*17.9*	*15.7*	*10.9*
All other groups	*29.9*	*47.0*	*4.7*	*2.7*
Total	*100.0*	*100.0*	*100.0*	*100.0*

Source: Uganda Government: *Census, Part II.*

Kampala, Shs 4,970 at Jinja, Shs 4,290 on the average for the other towns and Shs 1,210 at the rural trading centres. Expenditure on wages and salaries materially affects operating costs; it accounts in the towns for about 49 per cent, and in rural areas for some 43 per cent of these. In proportion to turnover the operating costs of retail trade amount, in the towns, to 10.2 per cent and in rural areas to 9.6 per cent. The costs are relatively highest in the case of the smaller firms; as the size increases, the proportion of operating costs to turnover greatly declines.

Table 5. *Urban Retailers' Purchases, Operating Costs and Stocks, Classified by Size of Turnover, in 1966*

Turnover per firm in shillings	Goods purchased in % of turnover	Operating costs in % of total operating receipts [a]	Stock of goods (at end of year)	
			in % of annual turnover	per employee (in shillings)
Less than 10,000	*87.4*	*30.6*	*29.5*	940
10,000 to less than 100,000	*77.8*	*18.4*	*24.0*	4,650
100,000 to less than 500,000	*86.5*	*12.6*	*20.4*	10,610
500,000 to less than 1 million	*89.2*	*8.2*	*14.2*	16,370
1 million or more	*92.1*	*9.0*	*12.0*	18,300
Total	*89.4*	*10.2*	*15.2*	11,900

[a] Sales ond other income.
Source: Uganda Government: *Census, Part II.*

The effective trading profit margin for retail traders is greater than the difference of 10.6 per cent between the ratio for goods purchased in per cent of turnover (89.4 per cent) and 100 per cent, because there is no doubt that stocks greatly increased between the beginning and the end of 1967; with regard to the amount of the change in stocks, however, no definite data are available. In proportion to turnover the stocks are much greater at retail firms where turnovers are low than at those where turnovers are relatively high; this means that the frequency with which the stock turns over increases as the size of the firm rises. The small firms have a good deal of dead stock, which merely burdens the cost structure.

III. Wholesale Trade

Uganda's specific economic structure, briefly described in the first chapter, necessarily favours the existence of firms which perform wholesale functions. The country's heavy dependence on imports of consumer goods, and the great fragmentation of retail trade into firms most of which are very small, make it unavoidable to interpolate traders at intermediate stages. The sole importing agents, and the large firms which act as sole agents for Ugandan producers, are mostly located at Kampala; they sell goods, as a rule, to appointed wholesale dealers in the chief towns of districts. These dealers sell either directly to the larger retail firms, or to semi-wholesalers (that is combined retailers and wholesalers), in the adjoining minor towns and trading centres. At these latter places the goods are bought by the proprietors of small dukas in the remote trading centres; such people's demand is in most cases very small, and it would therefore not be worth their while to make purchasing expeditions to the nearest district capital, still less to Kampala. Some goods pass through as many as four wholesale stages before they reach the retailer at the point of ultimate sale. At the end of 1966 the census showed in Uganda about 550 firms (with roughly 700 branches), whose main activity consisted in wholesale trade. In addition however, as already mentioned, some of the larger retailers also conduct wholesale trade as a sideline, just as some of the large wholesalers similarly conduct retail

Table 6. *Wholesale Business in Uganda, 1966*

Sector	Number of enterprises [a]	Wholesale sales Shs '000	% of all sectors
Wholesale trade	549	2,221,704	*63.1*
Marketing boards	2	914,183	*25.9*
Co-operative Unions	28	361,811	*10.3*
Retail trade combined with wholesale	186	26,024	*0.7*
Total enterprises engaged in wholesaling	765	3,523,722	*100.0*

[a] End of year.

Source: Uganda Government, Statistics Division – Ministry of Planning and Economic Development: *Census of Distribution, 1966, Part I.* Entebbe, Government Printer 1967, pp. 6–7 (quoted here after as Uganda Government: *Census, Part I*).

trade; from the functional point of view the turnovers achieved by the marketing boards, and by the agricultural marketing co-operatives, must also be reckoned as wholesale trade. The wholesale turnover of traders in all these forms reached a total of Shs 3,575 million in 1966.
A considerable proportion of the wholesale firms in Uganda are engaged, either partly or exclusively, in import business. Of all the entprises in 1966 there were 60 per cent which, besides buying locally, also procured goods from Kenya and Tanzania; nearly 50 per cent imported from overseas. Of wholesalers' total purchases 60 per cent came from domestic suppliers, while 40 per cent were direct imports. Within the country the chief suppliers of the wholesale trade, providing in terms of value almost 50 per cent of the goods procured by this latter, were Ugandan industrial producers; not quite 40 per cent of the goods procured came from other wholesalers, mostly specialised importers or sole agents of domestic producers.

Table 7. *Breakdown of Local Wholesale Purchases by Type of Supplier, 1966*
(As a Percentage of Total Local Purchases)

Receipts per enterprise (Shs)	Manu-facturers	Purchases from Wholesalers/ Importers	Farmers	Others	Total local purchases
Less than 200,000	*19*	*78*	*2*	*1*	*100*
200,000 to less than 500,000	*14*	*84*	*1*	*1*	*100*
500,000 to less than 1 million	*29*	*64*	*5*	*2*	*100*
1 million to less than 2 million	*20*	*69*	*9*	*2*	*100*
2 million to less than 10 million	*31*	*58*	*6*	*5*	*100*
10 million and over	*68*	*18*	*6*	*8*	*100*
Total	*49*	*39*	*6*	*6*	*100*

Source: Uganda Government: *Census, Part I,* p. 18.

The three most important categories of wholesale trade are described as "General wholesalers", "Groceries" and "Clothing, footwear and textiles". Their share of total wholesale turnovers in Uganda is more than 60 per cent. On the average the greatest turnovers per enterprise are achieved by oil companies as well as by wholesalers dealing in agricultural products (see table 8).
It is true that in Uganda, like all East African countries, wholesale trade remains largely a preserve for Asiatic traders. During recent years, however, a growing number of Africans have managed to gain a footing even in such trade. Most of them are grocers, cigarette agents or general wholesalers. Of the 549 wholesale firms, covered by the Census of Distribution, 448 were in the hands of Asians; 54 belonged to Africans; 44 were in European hands, while three minor enterprises were conducted by Arabs. The 44 European

Table 8. *Number of Wholesale Enterprises and of Persons Employed, with Total Receipts and Receipts per Enterprise, 1966*

Kind of business	Number of enterprises	Number of persons employed	Receipts (Shs '000)				
			Sales		Others	Total	Per enterprise
			Wholesale	Retail			
Groceries, provisions, confectionery, drinks and cigarettes	105	1,296	518,792	17,666	4,136	540,594	4,851
Agricultural products	51	1,022	384,332	5,817	6,720	396,869	7,782
Clothing, footwear and textiles	105	879	283,708	27,226	1,750	312,684	2,977
Machinery, industrial equipment and supplies	17	308	38,589	3,545	1,748	43,882	2,581
Electrical goods	12	137	16,516	4,889	493	21,898	1,825
Petroleum products	7	446	215,214	–	1,062	216,276	30,896
Timber	9	109	10,733	687	416	11,836	1,315
Building materials and hardware	27	485	79,922	11,212	987	92,121	3,412
Chemicals, oils, drugs and related products	17	135	18,265	1,963	109	20,337	1,196
Glass, china, earthenware, plasticware, cutlery and hosiery	27	136	25,482	2,324	40	27,846	1,031
Paper, stationery and books	5	246	11,410	3,186	72	14,668	2,934
Bicycles and spares	10	64	10,427	1,934	95	12,455	1,246
Metals and metal products	3	78	15,036	1,200	4	16,240	5,413
Other goods and materials	4	20	4,298	100	2	4,400	1,100
General wholesalers	150	2,226	588,980	34,680	9,151	632,811	4,219
Total	549	7,587	2,221,704	116,429	26,785	2,364,917	4,308

Source: Uganda Government: *Census, Part I*, pp. 32, 34 and 35.

firms accounted for more than 20 per cent of the wholesale market, the 54 African for only 5 per cent.
One of the largest African wholesale firms in 1966 was African Business Promotion, now called the National Trading Corporation; another was the Uganda Bookshop, Ltd., which belonged to the Catholic Church of Uganda.
Most of the European firms engage in import and export business. In the machinery trade they predominate, accounting for 80 per cent of all turnovers in that line. The importing of petrol is exclusively in the hands of European companies.

Table 9. *Wholesale Business in Uganda, Classified by Ownership, 1966*

Enterprises owned by	Number of enterprises	Percentage of total enterprises	Percentage of total receipts
Africans	54	*9.8*	*4.6*
Asians	448	*81.6*	*73.6*
Europeans	44	*8.0*	*21.5*
Arabs	3	*0.6*	*0.3*
Total	549	*100.0*	*100.0*

Source: Uganda Government: *Census, Part I,* p. 11.

The sizes of the turnovers achieved by enterprises engaged in wholesale trade diverge widely from each other. Of all wholesale trading firms in 1966 there were 45, or 8 per cent, which had a turnover of more than Shs 10 million each; this made a total of about Shs 1,246 million, that is more than half of the turnover achieved by all wholesalers. The 184 smallest firms, with gross receipts less than Shs 1 million each, accounted for only 4 per cent of total wholesale turnovers.
Table 10 shows that per capita productivity, in the sense of gross receipts per person employed, increases at an unusually rapid rate as the size of the enterprise becomes greater. In the case of the small firms, with annual turnovers less than Shs 200,000, such per capita productivity works out at only Shs 23,000; in that of the really large firms, with annual turnovers in excess of Shs 10 million, it is more than 20 times as great.
Wholesalers achieved for 1966, on trade in goods, an average profit margin of 9.1 per cent; the margin was appreciably wider in the case of the small than in that of the large enterprises. The narrowest profit margins, averaging 5.8 per cent, were found on food sales; the widest, namely 36.1 per cent, on wholesale trade in paper, stationery and books. These material differences reflect the differing cost situation, primarily due to the fact that the rates at which stocks turn over are not the same. If to the gross profit on trade in goods, namely 9.1 per cent of the turnover, there are added the wholesalers' other receipts in the form of commissions, rent, interest and the like, and if

Table 10. *Wholesale Enterprises and Their Receipts, Analysed by Size of Enterprise, 1966*

Receipts per enterprise (Shs)	Enterprises		Receipts		Average receipts	
	Number	Percentage of total	Shs '000	Percentage of total	per enterprise (Shs '000)	per employee[a] (Shs '000)
Less than 200,000	30	*5.5*	3,299	*0.1*	110	23
200,000 to less than 500,000	54	*9.8*	18,269	*0.8*	358	62
500,000 to less than 1 million	100	*18.2*	74,061	*3.1*	741	120
1 million to less than 2 million	126	*23.0*	182,315	*7.7*	1,447	167
2 million to less than 10 million	194	*35.3*	841,335	*35.6*	4,337	269
10 million and over	45	*8.2*	1,245,639	*52.7*	27,681	541
Total	549	*100.0*	2,364,918	*100.0*	4,308	312

[a] Including working proprietors.
Source: Uganda Government: *Census, Part I,* pp. 12, 13.

the operating costs amounting to 7.6 per cent of the gross receipts are deducted from the total, the result is that wholesalers in 1966 obtained a net profit at the rate of 2.5 per cent on their gross receipts. The rates of profit were well below this average at 1.0 per cent on wholesale trade in agricultural products, at 1.1 per cent on that in foodstuffs and at 1.5 per cent on wholesale trade not concentrating on any particular range of goods. Profits greater than the average were on the other hand earned in the case of glass, china and earthenware, in that of machinery and industrial equipment, and in that of paper, stationery and books.

IV. Co-operatives

1. Agricultural Marketing Co-operatives

The first attempts to establish agricultural marketing co-operatives in Uganda date from 1913. At the end of the thirties there were in existence a number of quasi-co-operative organisations. In 1946 the Co-operative Societies' Rules were issued, which created the conditions required for orderly development of the co-operative system. At the end of that year there were in existence about 50 agricultural marketing societies. Most of them were not being run on proper co-operative principles[2].

2 A comprehensive survey of the origins of the co-operative movement in Uganda is given in Uganda Government: *The Report of the Committee of Inquiry into the Affairs of all Co-operative Unions in Uganda.* Entebbe, Government Printer, 1967, p. 10 et seq.

Today Uganda's agricultural marketing co-operatives are organised in three tiers:

Fig. 1. *Structure of Marketing Co-operatives in Uganda*

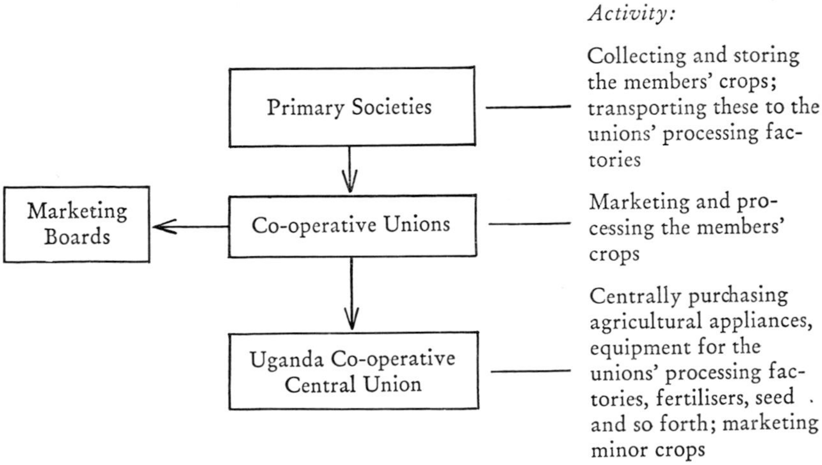

		Activity:
	Primary Societies	Collecting and storing the members' crops; transporting these to the unions' processing factories
Marketing Boards ←	Co-operative Unions	Marketing and processing the members' crops
	Uganda Co-operative Central Union	Centrally purchasing agricultural appliances, equipment for the unions' processing factories, fertilisers, seed and so forth; marketing minor crops

In 1966 there were approximately 2,000 local primary societies with about 450,000 members, organised in the 28 active co-operative unions. These unions conducted a total of 49 cotton ginneries and 16 coffee factories. Their turnover totalled Shs 365 million, of which cotton and coffee accounted for about 97 per cent.

Table 11. *Breakdown of the Co-operative Unions' Turnover, 1966*

Commodity	Shs '000	Percentage of total
Cotton	231,589	*63.4*
Coffee	122,933	*33.6*
Tobacco	4,335	*1.2*
Minor crops	2,038	*0.6*
Other commodities, etc.	4,224	*1.2*

Source: Uganda Government: *Census, Part I,* p. 22.

2. Consumer Co-operatives

The consumer co-operatives are as yet hardly significant in Uganda so far as the supply of consumer goods is concerned. It is true that the first experiments with this form of marketing were already carried out during the fifties, but they all failed with only one exception, namely that of the Lugazi Consumer Co-operative Society. Not until very recently was a new start made, with strong support from the Government and foreign experts. But by 1967, apart from the Lugazi Consumer Co-operative Society, only the Kilembe Consumer Co-operative Society (with about 1,000 members) had begun to operate. In addition three further consumer co-operatives were registered at Mbale, Masaka and Hoima, and some of these were on the point of starting operations.

The existing consumer co-operatives have formed their own wholesale purchasing company; this is named the Uganda Consumer Co-operative Wholesale Society, but up till now it has been able to operate only on a very small scale. The Ugandan consumer co-operative movement is indeed still in its first initial stage.

C. TRADE AS A MEDIUM FOR THE MARKETING OF GOODS

I. Marketing of Agricultural Products

1. Coffee

Coffee accounts for more than half of Uganda's total exports in terms of value. At least a million people are employed in producing and marketing this product. Given the consequently great importance of coffee for Uganda's economy, special importance must be attached to a smoothly efficient marketing organisation. The present system of marketing (from sale of the crop by the grower until the coffee is exported) has many weaknesses, which tend to prevent an efficient flow of goods. Here it must be borne in mind, however, that the extremely fragmented and obscure pattern of production — coffee is grown in Uganda mostly by small African farmers — makes marketing very difficult. Recently, however, a Committee of Inquiry appointed by the Government has submitted practicable proposals for improvement; these aim at streamlining the sales organisation, and at making the state of the market more clearly apparent[3].

Robusta coffee accounts for roughly 95 per cent of Uganda's coffee crop; Arabica, which is of higher quality, accounts for only about 5 per cent[4].

3 Uganda Government, Ministry of Agriculture, Forestry and Cooperatives: *Report of the Committee of Inquiry into the Coffee Industry, 1967*. Entebbe, Government Printer, 1967.

4 The following remarks refer, unless otherwise stated, to the marketing of Robusta coffee.

The majority of the African coffee growers have joined either a local primary co-operative society or an association of growers; through these they sell the dried coffee cherries — approximately 95 per cent of the entire Robusta production is sold in the dried state — to the processing factories at the minimum prices fixed by the Government. Besides these co-operatives and growers' associations there are numerous private purchasers, to whom the unorganised coffee growers sell their crop. The licensed purchasers are allowed to buy coffee only at the officially fixed marketing places; the cost of transporting the coffee to these places, often on porters' heads or by bicycle, is for account of the grower. If the grower sells his coffee to a local buyer and not directly to the factory, which is recognised in principle as being a market, the buyer will as a rule deduct a certain amount from the fixed minimum price to cover the cost of transport to the factory.

While every buyer of dried cherry is supposed to hold a licence (although in practice many illegal buyers without a licence are to be found), the less important buying of wet cherry is not controlled, nor is the number of buyers limited.

Between the primary buyers of coffee there is uncommonly keen competition, reflected in differing periods for payment and in differing prices, only the minimum price being fixed. The co-operative unions and to some extent the growers' associations conduct their own processing factories, in which they hull, clean and sort the cherries.

The coffee factories, both co-operative and private, must sell to the Coffee Marketing Board — at prices fixed by the Government — the coffee which is obtained by the dry process. Factories which employ the less widespread wet process can sell their production either on the free market or to the Coffee Marketing Board. In practice the Board buys the coffee ex factory, although the latter is responsible for bringing the coffee to the Board's storehouses at Kampala; the Board allows, in respect of transport costs, a reimbursement at fixed rates per mile on each ton of coffee.

The Coffee Marketing Board strictly verifies the quality, and declares the coffee to be in various grades. Production of the higher grades is promoted through payment of premiums; discounts are applied, in the case of poor grades, to the prices fixed.

The Board has abandoned its earlier practice of selling dry-processed Robusta coffee to exporters at auctions. Only small quantities are now offered to the local exporters; the greater part is sold direct to importers abroad through two sales offices which the Board has in New York and London. The private coffee export trade in Uganda, chiefly conducted by branches of European firms, has thus lost a good deal of its former importance.

The factories usually sell wet-processed Robusta coffee to private exporting firms, free on rail at Mombasa, without the intervention of the Coffee Marketing Board. This is done at public auctions in Mombasa.

Arabica coffee, which is not controlled by the Coffee Marketing Board either, is sold by the Bugisu Co-operative Union. Ltd., which has a monopoly in respect of such coffee. The union either sells it to exporters at Nairobi, where the auctions are held, or ships it directly overseas; the latter method has been more followed of late.

2. Cotton

Cotton is Uganda's second most important export, and therefore ranks alongside coffee as a mainstay of the country's economy. The ability of Uganda cotton to compete on the hotly contested world market essentially depends on efficient marketing, that is on provision of the quantities desired for export in the necessary quality and at the right time. For this reason the Government has largely entrusted the marketing of cotton to a central agency known as the Lint Marketing Board.

Marketing of Raw Cotton

In principle the cotton farmer has three methods available for selling his crop, thus:

- Sale to the established cotton markets, the cost of transport to the stores used by these markets being for the farmer's account.
- Sale to ginneries, which also rank as cotton markets, or to the ginneries' buying points.
- Sale through local primary co-operative societies, which collect the raw cotton in their own storehouses and ship it to the ginnery, the latter being as a rule operated by co-operative unions.

The greater part (in fact more than 60 per cent) of the cotton crop is now marketed through co-operatives, which are strongly promoted by the Government. With the co-operatives in their present state of organisation, however, this purchasing system does not work at all smoothly. An investigating committee appointed by the Government found in 1966 that many farmers, who sell their crop to the co-operatives, were paid either not at all or only with great delay[5].

Above all in the non-co-operative sector the problem of how to transport the raw cotton to the ginneries' buying points has in some cases not been satisfactorily solved. The buying points frequently lie between 70 and 80 miles apart, so that the individual farmer has to transport the cotton for very long distances, while the cost of doing so absorbs a considerable part of his sale

5 Uganda Government, Ministry of Agriculture, Forestry and Co-operatives: *Report of the Committee of Inquiry into the Cotton Industry, 1966.* Entebbe, Government Printer, 1966.

proceeds amounting to Shs -/40 per lb of raw cotton. One widespread transport system, organised by the private ginneries, is known as "Kyalo Transport". Under this system a truck (lorry) collects the farmer together with his cotton crop, conveys both to the ginnery, and afterwards brings the farmer back to his village. This system is very popular as a social institution, since the farmer can take the opportunity to buy goods in the trading centres at the place where the ginnery is located, but it is too expensive and is not economical.

For bringing the raw cotton from the buying points to the ginneries[6] the latter are responsible. After they have finished the ginning, that is separated the raw cotton into lint and seed, the cotton automatically passes into the ownership of the Lint Marketing Board.

Marketing of Lint and Cotton Seed

The Lint Marketing Board is, by law, the only buyer and seller of lint and cotton seed. In practice the ginnery is merely an agent of the Lint Marketing Board. Lint and seed are for the most part sold by the Board, at auctions in Kampala, to licensed cotton exporters[7] or to oil mills; direct exports also take place, however, for example to eastern bloc countries and to China. On lint auctions the exporter in general buys as long as six months before harvesting or ginning. The exporter weighs the bales at the ginnery. At that point the ownership passes to him on signature. Payment is made against delivery free on rail[8].

3. Minor Crops

In comparison with coffee and cotton the amount of so-called minor crops produced for the market is small. They include groundnuts, maize, beans, peas, onions, sorghum, millet and other basic foods with good keeping quali-

---

6 In the 1965–66 season there were altogether 115 working ginneries, of which between 40 and 50 were run on a co-operative basis, the rest being conducted by private operators or by growers' associations.

7 In the 1965–66 season 17 exporters had licenses. Among them the Liverpool Uganda Co. Ltd., East African Cotton Exporters Ltd. and Jamal Ramji & Co. Ltd. were the most important; these companies' total share of the market was about 50 per cent.

8 During 1967 the price of auctioned lint varied between Shs 1/90 and Shs 1/95 per lb. For every pound of raw cotton the farmer receives Shs -/40. Since it takes 3 lbs of raw cotton to make 1 lb of lint, that is equivalent to Shs 1/20 per lb of lint. The ginnery receives a processing margin of Shs -/40, out of which it has to cover all costs; a further 3 cents are payable for cost of transport to the railway station for shipment. The export duty amounts to Shs -/25 per pound of lint. The final result is a sum of Shs 1/88.

ties. One of the Uganda Government's declared aims is, however, greatly to promote the production of these crops. The object is to reduce the dangers which result from the economy's heavy dependence on coffee and cotton exports. In the light of this consideration it appears desirable to describe, in relatively full detail, the systems now in use for the marketing of minor crops.
A distinction needs to be made between two methods of marketing minor crops, the first being through private traders and the second through the co-operative system.

a) Marketing through Private Traders

Private marketing takes place as follows. The farmer sells his marketable surplus production to a primary buyer, who normally conducts a small retail shop at the nearest trading centre. Some primary buyers are African, some Asian. They sort and collect the various products, which they will generally have bought in small or ultra-small quantities. They then sell the products, as soon as they have a salable quantity, to a main buyer in the nearest large town [9]. The main buyer, in his turn, may supply the urban retail trade; otherwise he will export the products himself, or deliver them to exporters. Almost the entire business of importing minor crops is also in the main buyers' hands. Most of the main buyers are located at Kampala, Jinja, Mbale and Soroti. Altogether there are in Uganda some 70 to 80 main buyers, almost all of them Asians, who deal in minor crops. They include not only pure wholesalers, who are as a rule financially quite strong, but also operators of mills producing oil, cornflour and the like. Between the primary buyer and the main buyer there may be a number of middlemen. On the other hand the farmer may also deliver to the main buyer direct, without the primary buyer coming into the transaction; this is of course chiefly done by farmers in the neighbourhood of towns. In many cases there are produce brokers who intervene between the primary and the main buyer; they are intermediaries who neither take the goods into their own stores nor become owners of the goods. Their function is to find markets for the sellers, and goods for those wanting to buy. For doing so they charge a commission of one-quarter per cent to each party. In 1966 there were in Uganda six produce brokers, of whom four handled substantial turnovers. In the case of minor crops the marketing through private traders would present the following picture:

---

9 The primary buyer will put into store a part of the crops which he has bought cheaply at harvest time. Later, especially after the cotton season, when the farmers have cash at their disposal, he resells the produce to them (after suitably marking up the price) for their own consumption.

Fig. 2. *Marketing of Minor Crops through Private Traders in Uganda*

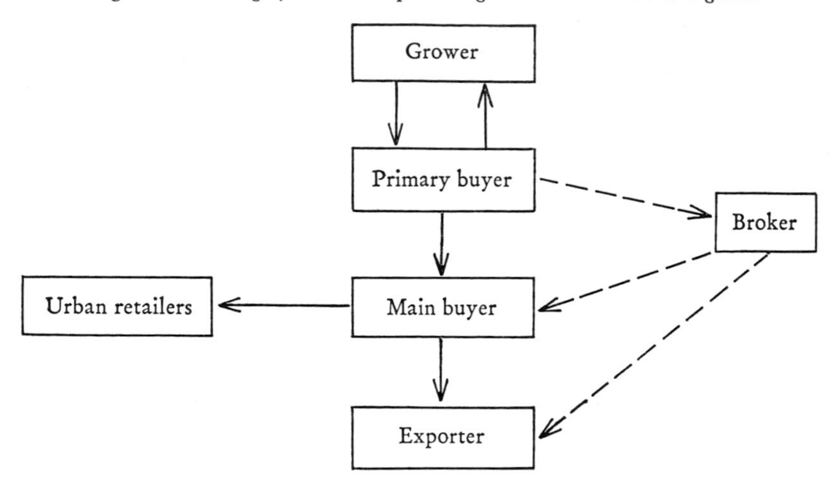

b) Marketing through Co-operatives

The cooperative marketing of minor crops had not previously been of great importance, but the co-operatives have recently been pushing it very hard. The procedure is similar to that followed in the case of cotton, but is more firmly organised. The sequence of sales runs as follows:

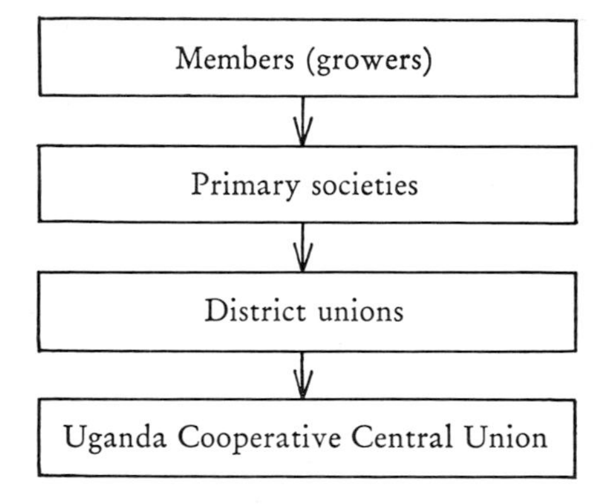

The co-operatively organised farmers sell their products to the local primary societies. These weigh and sort the products, and then pay the farmer cash. The primary societies deliver the collected minor crops at regular intervals to the co-operative district unions. These transactions too are normally handled on a cash payment basis. One function of the district unions is to advise the primary societies on all matters concerning cultivation and harvesting; others are correctly to plan and carry out the storage of the products,

to instruct the staff of the primary societies about purchasing, sorting, weighing and bookkeeping, to form a view of the market, and so forth.
The district unions, as a rule, maintain separate storehouses for minor crops; these stores enable the unions throughout the year to fulfil Government orders, for example to supply prisons, hospitals, the army and the like. At times of food shortage the stores also provide a reserve, out of which the members of the co-operatives can meet their needs. The Uganda Co-operative Central Union, Ltd. also takes part in the storage of minor crops; in addition it supports the district unions in the marketing of products, in the financing of stocks and in the creation of storage facilities. Within the framework of the Minor Crops Marketing Scheme the Government grants loans to the co-operative unions, in cash or in material form, up to a sum of shs 118,000 in each case to finance the building of storehouses for minor crops. In 1967 alone eight unions obtained such loans. These latter are repayable to the Government within eight years.

c) Government Influence

Since 1962 there has been a system of guaranteed minimum prices for minor crops; it is designed to eliminate wide fluctuations of price. Twice a year, in June and December, the Ministry of Agriculture fixes minimum prices which differ as between one region and another. In doing so it takes account of the current supply and demand situation as well as of world market prices. In addition the Government, with a view to controlling foreign trade in some important basic foodstuffs, has made it obligatory to obtain import and export licences. When there is a shortage all export licences are declared invalid, while imports are freed. At times of surplus the opposite is done.
Despite this control system it has not yet proved possible rapidly and effectively to close regional gaps in supply, that is to channel the surplus production of one district into other districts where there is a shortage of the product in question. The Government has decided therefore to remedy this state of affairs by setting up a Minor Crop Marketing Board. The strongest advocates of establishing such a board include the co-operatives, since they rightly expect that this will strengthen their own position as against private traders. As early as 1966 the Parliament of Uganda had instructed the Government to set up such a marketing board in order to achieve more systematic marketing of the minor crops, which were becoming increasingly important as an element of agricultural production, and thereby to attain greater stability supply. The promulgation of the Produce Marketing Board Act at the beginning of 1968 created the precondition for setting up the board. The latter's field of activity is defined only very broadly in the Act; its most important functions undoubtedly include the registration and licensing of

all buying agents, millers and dealers, and hence the control of selling channels. No details concerning the board's methods of working were yet known at the end of 1968. A warning should be given, however, against excessive monopolisation of the trade in minor crops, and against the eliminating of all competition at the trading stage between private traders and co-operatives. There is also a good deal of doubt about whether the co-operative system, at its present stage of development, already has enough staff and equipment to handle satisfactorily, by itself, the extremely difficult and by no means unrisky trade in minor crops.

4. Perishable Produce

The marketing of perishable produce like matoke, sweet potatoes, fruit and vegetables is less many-sided and complicated than that of non-perishable basic foodstuffs. It is almost entirely in the hands of African traders. The products are brought either directly from the producer's farm or from small local producers' markets to the weekly urban markets, of which there are usually several at the larger towns or in their neighbourhood. The produce is brought to the urban markets by trucks (lorries), buses, taxis and bicycles, with the owners of these means of transport either themselves acting as intermediate traders or simply carrying the trader and his goods.

II. Sale of Domestic Industry's Products

Most of Uganda's more important industrial firms have a tight sales organisation, which is fully comparable in its efficiency with that of corresponding firms in highly developed industrial countries. Even more than the producers in such countries, however, the manufacturers in developing countries have to allow for the fact that the density and efficiency of the distribution system is in some respects still inadequate. This compels the manufacturers to control the marketing channels, or the links in the sales chain; it also forces them to influence wholesalers and retailers through sales promotion schemes and other supporting measures. The sales organisation of the largest producers in Uganda, and the main features of their marketing policy, will now be briefly described.

British American Tobacco Company (Uganda) Ltd.

BAT is the only cigarette producer in the country. It tries to supply all retail shops not less than once a week, at fixed prices, through a chain of whole-

salers. The object is to ensure that all the retailers shall invariably have in stock a sufficiently wide selection of brands in fresh condition.
BAT pursues an extremely active sales policy. This includes not only far-reaching control but also support of the marketing system. As it stood in 1967, BAT's marketing system comprises the following links:

Fig. 3. *The Marketing System of the British American Tobacco Company (Uganda) Ltd., 1967*

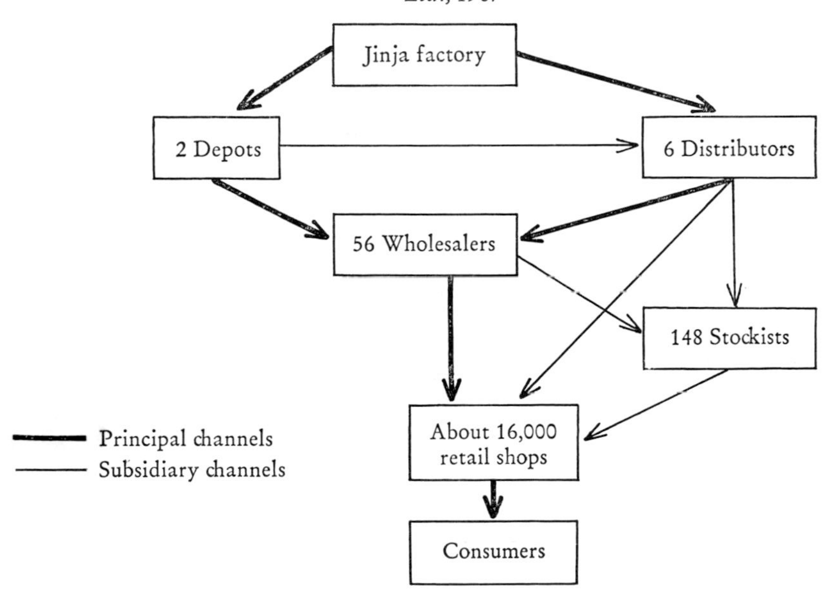

The wholesalers are in general directly supplied through the two depots at Kampala and Tororo; the wholesalers, in turn, supply the retailers in their area. Each wholesaler has the sole sales agency for a specified area, the size of which depends on the density of population, the per capita income and the traffic conditions. In thinly settled districts, where communications are poor, the individual wholesalers' sales areas are frequently so large that they find it difficult to provide regular weekly supplies for all the retailers. In such cases BAT will appoint at the remoter trading centres, on the proposal of the wholesaler, stockists whose task is to support him. Of the 56 BAT wholesalers' total sales 20 per cent reach the retailers through stockists, and 80 per cent direct.
A number of wholesalers are located in areas where traffic conditions make it uneconomical for BAT to supply them direct. In those areas the wholesalers obtain their requirements from a recognised wholesale distributor. One such is the BAT distributor at Gulu. He obtains goods from BAT by rail and

then, with his truck (lorry), supplies ten wholesalers at places like Lira, Arua, Moyo, Kitgum and so forth. These wholesalers, in turn, supply both the retailers and their own stockists [10].

African firms already predominate in BAT's wholesale network. This comprises altogether 210 firms (including distributors, wholesalers and stockists), of which 135 are in African hands; these African firms account for two-thirds of the turnover. More particularly in the case of African wholesalers BAT helps to finance the enlargement and modernisation of their enterprises. Some of the large African wholesalers began as BAT stockists. BAT, by providing financial support, enables some of its own trusted employees to build up a wholesale business. The advantage which this presents for BAT is that its products are then distributed by experienced traders, who are well acquainted both with BAT's products and with its business policy.

Virtually all transactions throughout the sales chain are effected against cash payment. Only large hotels and clubs, as well as Government institutions, are allowed six weeks' credit. The wholesalers are required in principle to pay cash on delivery of goods to them, or even in advance of that.

All transport costs which arise on conveyance of goods from the factory to the retailer are reimbursed by BAT at a fixed rate per mile. The whole of the publicity, and the campaigns to establish new brands, are moreover handled by BAT itself.

Nyanza Textile Industries Ltd.

This company is the largest textile manufacturer in Uganda. It has entrusted the whole work of selling to its own marketing firm, named Lebel (East Africa), Ltd., of Kampala. Lebel sells the Nytil products exclusively through 23 so-called main distributors, who are textile wholesalers. Only large Government consumers, like the Uganda Army and the Prisons Department, can obtain goods directly from the factory. The 23 distributors procure the Nytil products for their own account, in principle against cash payment. Steps are taken to ensure that the African traders, most of whom are relatively small, shall enjoy the same terms of competition as the larger traders, the majority of whom are Asiatic. This is ensured by the fact that no discount is allowed on the sale of Nytil products in large quantities; every trader buys at the same price, without regard to the quantity which he takes. Lebel has in principle allocated certain defined sales areas to the appointed wholesalers, but in practice has been unable to avoid cases of overlapping. No rules have been laid down about the minimum quantities to be taken, but Lebel takes constant steps to make sure that the distributors are sufficiently active.

10 Some distributors also supply retailers direct. Of their turnover 20 per cent represent such supplies, while 80 per cent of their deliveries go to wholesale traders.

Brooke Bond (Uganda) Ltd.

In principle this company, which is East Africa's largest tea producer, sells its products in Uganda directly to retailers through travelling salesmen; the retailers are visited at weekly intervals, and the goods are sold to them against cash payment. In certain areas such direct delivery is supplemented through a system of stockists; these sell Brooke Bond products from their stock to traders whom the travelling salesmen do not reach. In some areas where roads are poor and sales potential low, so that the employment of travelling salesmen would be uneconomical, Brooke Bond has appointed independent agents. Both agents and stockists sell the goods at the wholesale price laid down; both receive commission at the rate of 5 per cent. The agents also receive special allowances for their own services as transporters, and for turnovers above the average. Altogether Brooke Bond has about 20 depots of its own, besides 40 stockists and 12 agents. Approximately 11,000 retail-shops are directly supplied.

Uganda Bottlers Ltd.

This company is the most important producer of non-alcoholic drinks; for the most part it sells to retailers direct. Three agents at Masaka, Kabale and Kiskovo have been entrusted with the work of selling in more distant areas. Such agents must have the transport capacity required for fetching the goods from the factory, and for conveying them to their widely spread customers. The agents have to pay cash for the drinks as well as for the bottles and cases.

Uganda Breweries Ltd.

Ugandan Breweries sell through 30 appointed wholesalers or agents, who are distributed throughout Uganda, a particular sales area being allocated to each. At Kampala and in the surrounding area, where most of the sales are effected, direct delivery to retailers as well as to hotels and restaurants is the predominant method.

East African Distilleries Ltd.

East African Distilleries are the most important manufacturer of spirits in East Africa; their chief product is waragi, a spirit made from bananas. Sales in Uganda are effected through a network comprising approximately 25 appointed distributors, with whom the delimitation of sales areas has been agreed. In practice, however, it is often impossible to avoid overlapping between sales areas. In the Mengo district and in the capital city, Kampala,

East African Distilleries sell directly through employed salesmen to retailers and stockists. They also try, through an incentive bonus system, to make the appointed dealers exert the maximum effort for the purpose of promoting sales.

Nakasero Soap Works Ltd

The Nakasero Soap Works have no appointed sales agents in Uganda. They deliver their products by truck from their three sales offices at Kampala, Jinja and Mbale to anybody interested in buying them, whether he be a wholesaler, a retailer or a consumer. Under a system of discounts for quantity the selling prices differ, however, according to the quantity bought.
Sales in the neighbouring countries, Kenya and Tanzania, are effected through wholesalers and agents who are resident there, and on whom exclusive selling rights are conferred. These people have to guarantee a certain minimum turnover.

Uganda Millers Ltd.

Uganda Millers' marketing is organised along two lines. Large bakeries placing monthly orders for not less than 200 bags, each containing 200 lbs of flour, are supplied direct. Sales to the rest of the customers are effected through about 60 appointed wholesale distributors, who are selected in such a way that distribution throughout the country is ensured. Before firms can be considered for appointment as wholesale distributors they must, as a rule, be capable of selling at least 10 tons of flour per month; they must also have sufficient suitable storage space, as well as an adequate fleet of vehicles.

Chillington Tool Company (East Africa) Ltd.

Chillington is the country's leading producer of hoes, of which a great many are sold in Uganda; they are on sale at almost every rural duka. Up till now only two brands, the Crocodile and the Key, have been produced.
Chillington has by contract entrusted the entire marketing of its products in Uganda to two trading firms, which act as sole selling agents. The Crocodile hoes are sold by Mitchell Cotts & Co. (Uganda) Ltd., the Key hoes by Twentsche Overseas Trading Co. (E.A.) Ltd. As regards the sale of Chillington products the marketing systems employed by these two firms are very similar; the two firms, moreover, cooperate closely with each other. By way of example the system employed by Mitchell Cotts & Co. for the sale of Chillington hoes will now be described.

Mitchell Cotts are a subsidiary of a widely ramified international group. They sell not only Chillington hoes but also goods manufactured by many other producers in the most widely differing trades. Chillington hoes are sold by Mitchell Cotts for their own account, not on a commission basis.
In all Uganda's trading centres Mitchell Cotts have appointed main wholesale distributors for Crocodile hoes; in the whole of Uganda they have about 60 such distributors, of whom 13 are at Kampala alone. In each of the other towns there are, on the average, between three and four main distributors. Goods are supplied direct not only to these main distributors but also to specialised hardware shops, which are relatively few in number. The Central Co-operative Union also directly procures hoes on behalf of the co-operative unions. The whole sales system is built on the basis of cash payment.
In principle the Chillington hoes are supposed to be sold throughout Uganda at the same price. The main distributors receive from Mitchell Cotts a transport allowance (for transport from Kampala or Jinja to the main centres), which is paid out twice a year; they also receive a yearly bonus, which depends on the number of cases taken.
Mitchell Cotts have two delivery vans continuously on the road. The employees in charge buy Chillington hoes from main distributors at the normal wholesale selling price, and resell them at the same price to retailers who need them. This measure for the promotion of sales greatly increases the total turnover, since it may appreciably reduce shortfalls of turnover due to gaps in retailers' stocks. Of the total Chillington hoe sales roughly 20 per cent are effected in this way through delivery vans.

The Uganda Metal Products & Enamelling Co. Ltd. (Tumpeco)

Since 1966 this company has organised the sale of its products under its own arrangements; up till that time Lebel (E.A.) Ltd. had the sole right to sell Tumpeco products. Tumpeco sells exclusively through appointed wholesale distributors; of these there are in the whole of East Africa approximately 50, of whom 15 are in Uganda. Their areas are not delimited, but each distributor has to take goods worth at least £3,000 per annum. The appointed distributors are as a rule visited once a month by salesmen, who take orders. In the meantime, however, the distributors can also place urgent orders by post. On Tumpeco products the distributors receive an 8 per cent discount; strict cash payment is stipulated apart from a few exceptions.

Steel Corporation of East Africa Ltd.

This company too bases its marketing on independent wholesalers, who are appointed to be distributors. Three wholesale firms, trading on a large scale in household goods, act as so-called main distributors; they have to achieve certain minimum turnovers. The distributors are not limited to specified regions.

Uganda Baati Ltd.

This company entrusts the entire sale of its corrugated sheets to Galsheet Sales, Ltd. as sales agent. All the other products are sold through another independent trading organisation. This concentration, through only two trading firms, enables the company to keep its own sales department very small.

Uganda Steel Ltd.

This company is Uganda's largest producer of corrugated sheets. Like its competitor Uganda Baati, Ltd., it sells its products exclusively through Galsheet Sales, Ltd., which organises the further marketing under its own arrangements.

III. Sale of Imported Goods

A very large number of trading firms in Uganda conduct import business. On the average two out of every three wholesale firms, or retail firms with ten or more employees, maintain direct business relations with suppliers abroad; just under half of the firms procure some part of their goods directly from overseas. The big retailers buy more than half of all their incoming goods, without the intervention of specialised importers, outside Uganda and for the most part overseas. A remarkably high proportion of wholesalers' imports come from Kenya; there the large trading companies buy overseas goods from their parent company, or from associates, which are located at Nairobi or Mombasa. Other firms to which this applies include the large oil companies, which import on a substantial scale[11].
A high proportion of the purchases from abroad are handled on an exclusive basis, in the sense that numerous importing and wholesale firms in Uganda act as sole agents for manufacturing firms overseas. Some of these sole agents work for account of their principal by the direct-delivery method; that is to say, they accept orders which they pass to the foreign manufacturer, who sends the goods directly to the giver of the order. As a rule, in these cases,

11 The seven oil companies, namely Agip, BP, Caltex, Esso, Mobil Oil, Shell and Total, ship the petrol from Mombasa directly to their depots in the principal

Table 12. *Wholesale Purchases, Analysed by Country of Supplier, 1966* (as a Percentage of Total Purchases)

Receipts per enterprise (Shs)	Purchases from			Total purchases
	within Uganda	Kenya and Tanzania	Rest of world	
Less than 200,000	*74*	*11*	*15*	*100*
200,000 to less than 500,000	*71*	*15*	*14*	*100*
500,000 to less than 1 million	*70*	*19*	*11*	*100*
1 million to less than 2 million	*65*	*19*	*16*	*100*
2 million to less than 10 million	*62*	*16*	*22*	*100*
10 million and over	*58*	*29*	*13*	*100*
Total	*60*	*23*	*17*	*100*

Source: Uganda Government: *Census, Part I,* p. 18.

the agent assumes the del credere risk; for this he receives a commission on the list price. More frequently, however, the agent imports the goods on his own account, and handles the business by himself holding a stock of them. The calculation of prices for imported goods may be illustrated by two examples, based on investigations carried out by the Uganda Development Corporation's Development Division.

Brushes from the United Kingdom:	*Shs*
Price f.o.b. UK	10/-
Landed cost at Kampala (including c.i.f.[12]	14/- (list price)

towns of Uganda. The cost of rail transport from Mombasa to Kampala amounts, on the average, to between 17 per cent and 18 per cent of the wholesale price at Kampala.

Oil Companies' Filling Station Systems in Uganda, 1967

Company	Number of depots	Number of filling stations
Agip	3	30
Caltex	4	46
Esso	5	49
Mobil Oil	2	17
Shell }	5 [a]	80
BP }		20
"Total"	4	92
Total	23	334

[a] Shell and BP maintain a joint sales system.

Source: Data from the individual companies.

12 I.e. customs, railage, insurance and handling.

Shs	
Major wholesalers: list price less 20 per cent (discount based on f.o.b. price)	12/-
Small wholesalers: list price less 10 per cent (discount based on f.o.b. price)	13/-
Retail cost (list price plus 10 per cent)	15/40
Retail selling price (based on 20 per cent mark-up)	18/50

Shirts:

Net landed cost	20/-
Duty	7/30
Port handling, railage, local transport, insurance	1/10
To storage at Kampala	28/40
Wholesale mark-up (8 per cent)	30/70
Retail mark-up (15 per cent)	35/30

D. THE GOVERNMENT'S DIRECTIVES ON TRADE POLICY, AND THEIR POSSIBLE IMPLEMENTATION

The Government of Uganda has laid down its economic policy programme, and its targets for the period up till 1971, in the Second Five Year Plan[13]. While no detailed ideas about trade were worked out, the Government clearly indicated its awareness that the functions of trade will materially increase in the coming years, as the monetary sector becomes more important, and that trade in its present structure will not be equal to performance of the resulting functions. The following emerge as the Government's most important guiding principles in the matter of trade:

- To promote the efficiency of African traders;
- To increase Government influence through the transfer of trading functions to newly founded organisations;
- To build up the cooperative system.

---

13 Uganda Government: *Work for Progress, Uganda's Second Five-Year Plan, 1966–1971.* Entebbe, Government Printer, 1966.

I. Promoting the Efficiency of African Traders

Since independence was gained in 1962 the increased introduction of Africans into wholesale and retail trade, both at the outset dominated almost exclusively by Asians, has been one of the Uganda Government's declared aims. On appraisal of all the measures since executed it must be admitted that the Government, in prosecuting this aim, has acted with reason and skill. Despite many radical demands it attached prime importance less to making it harder for Asian traders (so far as they are Ugandan citizens) to pursue their calling, and more to active Government assistance towards raising the African traders' standard of performance, thereby enabling them to compete. It must be appreciated that this is a lengthy process. Although during recent years significant results have already been achieved (the number of successful African traders with flourishing wholesale businesses is clearly rising), the experience and business relations of the Asian traders, who have done so much for the economic development of the country, will remain indispensable for many years if serious difficulties of supply are not to be risked. The view is somctimes expressed that the effect of wholesale trade, especially of such trade in Asian hands, is to make goods unduly dear through excessive profit margins. After thorough study of the facts, so far as the bulk of the firms are concerned, this view cannot be confirmed. In most trades there is extremely keen competition between the individual wholesale firms, so that the danger of monopolistic price-fixing is on the whole very slight. By international standards the trading expenses and profits of wholesalers in Uganda cannot be described as excessive.

Among the Government measures for promotion of African trading firms the following are prominent:

Educating towards economic thinking, and training of traders in all matters connected with the conduct of retail and wholesale businesses.

Most African traders have a non-economic attitude, many of them still regarding conduct of the business as a part-time job; they also have little business skill. These are no doubt the chief reasons why they find it hard to compete with Asian traders. Given the traditionally established social structure of most African tribes it is, for example, hardly possible to form capital resources for financing a business. If any African's business does begin to yield a profit, all his relatives — often quite distant relatives — will feel themselves entitled to share in his prosperity. If the owner of the business refused to distribute the earnings or capital gains to his relatives, the result would be his social ostracism, or even his expulsion from the family community. On the other hand the mentality of Asian families is such that they tend to join forces in accumulating capital, even at the cost of personal privations, so as to promote the success of a business belonging to one of their members.

Opening up sources of credit, and help in capital formation.

These special difficulties, which beset the formation of capital resources for African traders, make the problem of finding capital for investment in fixed and current assets particularly urgent. Since most applicants can offer no sufficient material security, the African traders depend on help from the Government.

Creation of better facilities for supplying rural retailers through establishment of wholesale stores in remote areas

Many parts of the country are thinly settled, and communications are in some cases inadequate. These facts prevent wholesalers from regularly or frequently supplying the retailers in certain areas. The retailer is therefore forced to hold disproportionately large stocks. Apart from the fact that in most cases he is short of the capital required for this purpose, any holding of large stocks entails a correspondingly great risk of perishing. Advantage is taken of this situation by so-called travelling wholesalers; these are small intermediaries who often supply retail dukas at distant places with poor goods at a high price.

Greater concentration of rural retail trade in trading centres, and promoting of specialisation in particular trades

Nearly all rural African retailers carry an extremely mixed general-shop range of goods, among which low-profit bread-and-butter lines like sugar, kerosene, cigarettes, matches and soap predominate. Some tools and cloths eke out the range, which hardly differs as between all the traders in a wide surrounding area. Greater specialisation in particular goods would considerably increase the shops' attraction for purchasers, since they could then offer a fuller selection of cloths, tools or other goods. It is also certain that greater specialisation would favourably affect the retailer's profit. A prerequisite for specialisation is, however, even greater concentration of shops in trading centres. These centres must not be too small, and customers must be able to find in them the various specialised shops ready to hand. The trading centre should resemble a department store with various special departments, each conducted by a different shopkeeper.

The task of implementing the measures required for encouragement of African traders was first entrusted to the African Trade Development Section in the Ministry of Commerce and Industry, as well as to African Business Promotion, Ltd., a subsidiary of the Uganda Development Corporation. The two organisations have cooperated closely with each other. The emphasis in the Trade Development Section's activity was on advising

and training traders in the individual districts. African Business Promotion, besides importing goods and arranging agencies for African traders, chiefly concentrated on helping in the provision of capital; it also assumed credit guarantees, discounted bills, confirmed credits, and provided for the sale of trucks (lorries) on hire purchase terms. In the years 1962 to 1966 African Business Promotion instigated the formation of numerous buying groups for minor African traders, and supported them by providing loans. However, only a few of these organisations were successful. Internal disputes and jealousies in many cases quickly led to their collapse, and to financial losses for African Business Promotion. In 1967 only eight buying groups, comprising about 30 traders, were still functioning.
A better way to improve the terms on which the smaller African traders can procure goods has been found to be the formation of wholesale companies, in which the retailers hold a financial interest. Some of these companies, newly formed during recent years with help from African Business Promotion and from the Trade Development Department, are now operating with great success, and are fully a match for the Asian wholesalers.
On objective assessment it can be said that the work done by both organisations has been very fruitful, and has materially contributed to the advancement of African traders. With effect from 1st January, 1967 both African Business Promotion and the African Trade Development Section were merged into the newly formed National Trading Corporation. Apart from trade in goods this Corporation engages in the following activities connected with the promotion of African trading firms:

- Assuming credit guarantees;
- Discounting bills so as to enable African traders to tender for Government contracts;
- Confirming for the import trade;
- Hire purchase credit to finance procurement of trucks;
- Granting of loans;
- Auditing the books of African traders;
- Conducting courses in business organisation, accounting, financing, marketing and the like.

The National Trading Corporation establishes wholesale depots in remote areas so as to ensure a constant supply of goods to rural African traders at reasonable prices, the arrangement for such supply having previously been poor. By the end of 1968 the establishment of 12 such depots had been planned.

II. Government Influence on Trade

There is no mistaking the fact that the Government is trying to obtain greater control than hitherto of the goods flows, both from and to foreign countries, as well as inside Uganda. It believes that by doing so it can effect the distribution of goods more cheaply and more smoothly, can avert difficulties of supply, and can speed up the Africanisation of trade.

The Government's increasing activity is apparent not only in the marketing of agricultural products but also in the procurement and sale of industrially manufactured consumer goods for the home market. As regards agricultural produce marketing, attention may be drawn to the newly established Produce Marketing Board, to the marketing boards which exist for coffee and cotton, to the Dairy Board and to the Tea Authority and the Meat Marketing Board which still was in the planning stage at the end of 1968. For the sale of consumer goods on the home market the National Trading Corporation was formed with effect from 1st January, 1967. Its functions are described as follows in the National Trading Act:

- to engage in commerce and trade;
- to organise and effect exports and imports of all such goods and commodities as the Board may, with prior approval of the Minister, from time to time determine, and the purchase, sale and transport of the general trade in such goods and commodities in Uganda or elsewhere;
- to promote or aid in promotion of, subject to proper and adequate safeguards to be determined by the Board, any person being a citizen of Uganda in trade and business;
- to do all such other things as are incidental or conducive to the attainment of the above objects or any of them.

During the first six months of its existence the National Trading Corporation was already appointed to be the sole importer of onions, rice, salt and ghee. These are sold to the retail trade through a total of 36 appointed wholesale sub-distributors.

The National Trading Corporation's policy is directed to obtaining the monopoly of trade in more and more goods: "Nevertheless we shall become involved, sooner or later, in the supply of all consumer goods. We may in some cases become main distributive agents for local manufacturers, and still allow their present agents to buy through us. In the case of imported goods we shall try to secure direct appointments for the import, export and sale of the goods we need to handle. We do not wish to work through agents, although we appreciate that current contracts could be allowed to run out, except in cases where the Government has appointed or will appoint us to be the sole importer."[14] The Africanisation Committee, appointed by the Minister for Trade and Industry, also recommends considerable strengthening of the NTC's position through legal and administrative measures.

These ambitions, which aim at far-reaching or even complete elimination of private wholesale trade, and hence of all competition, appear extremely dangerous. In the light of the experience gained in other developing countries there is reason to doubt whether the effect, which results from the streamlining of distribution channels through assumption of trade functions by a state trading company, can make up for the consequent loss of the flexible effect exerted on supply and prices by competition between many private enterprises. Even with the best possible managers the conduct of a gigantic organisation, like a state trading company which holds a monopoly, is bound to be ponderous. This entails considerable risks, which may produce far-reaching effects[15].

Although the Government may prefer, for political or other reasons, to exert its influence directly in trade, it should not overlook, however, that a distribution of risks between numerous private enterprises may be of advantage; it is also cheaper, even if these enterprises earn a reasonable profit. The Government can prevent profits from rising unreasonably high by taking steps to ensure efficient competition. The National Trading Corporation ought to confine its activity in trade to categories of goods in connection with which private trade does not yet ensure proper supply of the population or smooth marketing.

---

14 See S. Y. Nyeko: Implementation of Policy, in: *National Trading Corporation*, No. 9 (September), 1967.

15 The example of Guinea may serve to make this clear:
"The state trading venture was an unmitigated disaster, afflicting the whole economy. An inexperienced Guinean management found itself in charge of what was, in effect, the largest trading firm in Africa. Despite some gallant efforts the distribution system rapidly fell victim to a massive administrative muddle ... Fundamental reappraisals were hindered by the need to maintain socialist purity, and by an unwillingness to look coolly at all alternatives. Official economic discussion, in fact, became increasingly divorced from reality ... The costs of Guinea's false starts cannot be calculated only in terms of wasted resources and forgone growth. Much of the popular enthusiasm for the regime, and for the dynamism of its leadership, has been dissipated. Cynicism and corruption have spread, and signs of disaffection appeared. The moral and political cement binding the state together has been weakened, as respect for law, and for the regime, has diminished." See Elliot J. Berg: Socialism and Economic Development in Tropical Africa, in: *The Quarterly Journal of Economics*, No. 78 (November, 1964), pp. 558–560.

III. Building up the Co-operative System

An efficient co-operative system can materially contribute towards solving the problems, some of them very difficult, which marketing in Uganda entails. The basic co-operative idea of mutual self-help is especially suited to developing countries with an agricultural production structure based on small units. The Government of Uganda is therefore much interested in building up the co-operative system, and strongly encourages that process. Even now the agricultural co-operatives already have very large shares in the marketing of the country's most important products, that is coffee and cotton; that, however, must not distract attention from the fact that the organisation of the co-operatives still leaves much to be desired. Their chief problem lies in lack of reliable and competent managers who think and act in business-like fashion. This defect has resulted during recent years in financial losses, and in muddled organisation, for numerous co-operatives. The building up of the co-operative system should therefore begin with consolidation of what already exists, above all in the shape of personnel; it should therefore start with intensive training of the staff. The co-operatives' activity should not be extended until properly trained people are available for, and capable of, meeting the requirements. Even then, however, a warning must be given against letting the co-operatives have an absolute monopoly in particular markets — a monopoly of the sort which they are already demanding[16]. The ceasing of competition with private traders would very soon torpify the co-operatives' readiness to render service. It would also seriously jeopardise the paramount aim of trade policy, which is to effect the distribution of goods as efficiently and cheaply as possible.

Bibliography

BERG, J.: Socialism and Economic Development in Tropical Africa, in: *The Quarterly Journal of Economics,* No. 78 (November 1964), pp. 558–560.

Co-op News, No. 2, May 1966.

NYEKO, S. Y.: Implementation of Policy, in: *National Trading Corporation,* No. 9 (September), 1967.

---

16 See for example *Co-op News,* No. 2, May, 1966: The Uganda Co-operative Central Union, Ltd., and the Marketing of Economic (Minor) Crops. "... Doubts that existed as to the determination of the co-operatives were cleared by the tone of 'We will not go back', and 'We want a monopoly now', which dominated all speeches at the two conferences."

Uganda Government: *Work for Progress, Uganda's Second Five-Year Plan, 1966–1971.* Entebbe, Government Printer, 1966.

—: Department of Commerce: *The Advancement of Africans in Trade.* Entebbe, Government Printer, 1955.

—: Ministry of Agriculture, Forestry and Co-operatives: *Report of the Committee of Inquiry into the Cotton Industry, 1966.* Entebbe, Government Printer, 1966.

—: *Report of the Committee of Inquiry into the Coffee Industry, 1967.* Entebbe, Government Printer, 1967.

—: Statistics Division — Ministry of Planning and Economic Development: *Census of Distribution, 1966, Part I.* Entebbe, Government Printer, 1967.

—: *Census of Distribution, Part II.* Entebbe (in preparation).

—: *The Report of the Committee of Inquiry into the Affairs of all Co-operative Unions in Uganda.* Entebbe, Government Printer, 1967.

—: *Report of the Committee on Africanisation of Commerce and Industry in Uganda.* Entebbe, Government Printer, 1968.

—: *Government Memorandum on the Report of the Committee on Africanisation of Commerce and Industry in Uganda.* Sessional Paper No. 1, Entebbe, Government Printer, 1969.

ORGANIZATION AND STRUCTURE OF TRADE IN TANZANIA WITH SPECIAL REFERENCE TO INDUSTRIAL PRODUCTS

by

Werner Kainzbauer

with a concluding chapter on Tanzania's State Trading Corporation

by

Michael J. H. Yaffey

Contents

The treatise by Werner KAINZBAUER focusses on an investigation into the structure and functions of trade with industrial products in Tanzania. The distribution trade has to fulfill a very important task in the development of less developed countries. The amelioration of economic welfare through increased production and productivity requires profound measures towards structural changes in agriculture as well as accelerated industrialisation and an expansion of the monetary system. To this end a well organized distribution system is indispensable.
The original version of this investigation published in German under the title "Der Handel in Tanzania" as Afrika-Studien No. 18 at Springer Verlag, Berlin–Heidelberg–New York 1968, presents a comprehensive picture of the distribution system in Tanzania. For editorial reasons this contribution had to be restricted to one section of the original book, namely trade with industrial products. The chapter on the activities of the State Trading Corporations (STC) has been prepared by Michael YAFFEY.
Mr. KAINZBAUER had been working as research economist in the trade department of the Ifo Institute when he was asked by the African Studies Centre to carry out the present investigation under the financial support of the Fritz Thyssen-Foundation. The field research in Tanzania was conducted in 1964/65. In the meantime Mr. KAINZBAUER has left the Ifo Institute to take on a post in private industry.
We are indebted to Hans Freiherr von REDWITZ of Munich for translating the condensed version into English.

A. INFLUENCE OF GEOGRAPHIC, SOCIAL AND ECONOMIC CONDITIONS UPON THE IMPLEMENTATION OF THE FUNCTIONS OF TRADE

The basic function of trade consists of the exchange of goods between the various branches of the economy. In the implementation of this function of exchanging goods, trade fulfills a number of partial functions showing the position of the keypoints in the achievement of trading performances. In accordance with OBERPARLEITER[1] and BUDDEBERG[2] we would like to designate these partial functions as

- Bridging of distance
- Regrouping of quantities
- Regrouping of goods
- Equalization of time
- Granting of credit
- Contact, information and consulting function.

I. Bridging of Distance

Subject of the function of such bridging is the overcoming of the distance between producer and consumer or user with the aid of self-operated or outside means of transport. Whereas in developed economies this function is losing importance more particularly through the enlargement of means of transport and the increasing safety in goods traffic, for the trade of Tanzania in wide parts of the country it represents a very important, if not the most important task of all. The main reason for it consists of the habit of the population to settle in a widely-spread fashion, the bad transport routes, the strong orientation towards export, and the little-developed transport trade.
The population of the thinly-inhabited country (57 inhabitants/sq.mile on an average) concentrates itself on the periphery. The population, however,

1 K. OBERPARLEITER: *Funktionen und Risiken des Warenhandels.* 2nd Edition, Vienna 1955.

2 H. BUDDEBERG: *Betriebslehre des Binnenhandels.* Wiesbaden 1959.

is widely dispersed in the more densely populated parts. So far, any formations of larger villages have hardly occurred; urbanization is also still in its beginnings. Tanzania is strongly geared to foreign trade. It is an export country in respect of agricultural products and an import country with regard to finished goods. The consequent result for trade is that production and consumption take place at great distance from each other. Approximately two thirds of the entire inland supply of goods are placed on the world market, more particularly to the industrial states of the northern hemisphere. In a similar way, in imports of the overall offerings of tradeable goods, ca. two thirds originate in foreign countries. Almost the entire imports and exports are handled by one of the four East African harbours. The distances to be covered in this connection amount up to 800 miles.

All areas with economic activity are connected with the coast, i.e. with one of the four East African harbours, by way of at least one means of transport: the areas in the north (Tanga-region, Kilimanjaro-Meru-territory, Sukumaland) by rail and road, the areas in the south by road only. The quality of these connections is, however, very differentiated.

Relatively reliable and independent of weather is the railway. One problem, however, arising every year is the lacking loading capacity, more particularly during the harvesting period. An over-accrual of crop to be transported, the lack of storage space, but also considerations in regard to sales policy are again and again the reasons for considerable bottlenecks in the transport of agricultural products. This more particularly applies to the Central Line (Dar es Salaam-Mwanza). Although in comparison with former times the situation has improved on account of the link-up with the railway system in the north of Tanzania as well as Kenya and Uganda (traffic peaks at different periods), the difficulties ensuing in railway transport are still as considerable now as ever before.

The long-distance highways, the other means of transport from and to the coast, are in a generally bad condition. Only about 10 per cent of the main highways are macadamized, the remaining 90 per cent are earth or sand roads, the passability of which is in part greatly impaired during the rainy season. The long-distance traffic industry shows the typical characteristics of a still-young branch of economy, such as disregard of safety and insurance regulations, overloading, the bad condition of the means of transport vehicles, loss of goods during transport, non-observance of time-tables — in short, irregularities in goods traffic are deficiencies to be met everywhere. The entrustment of the goods transport to such firms therefore constitutes a great risk to the trading enterprises. Under such conditions it is no wonder that part of the trading enterprises prefer to take on the transport of goods themselves. Trading enterprises which have their function of bridging distance carried out by independent transport enterprises often have to put up with considerable disadvantages in comparison with their competitors.

The central transport problem of Tanzania, however, is the short-distance transport, i.e. the transport of goods from the agricultural areas of production into the trading centres or to the traffic junctions, or, alternatively, the transport of consumer goods from the trading centres to the rural consumer markets.
On account of the bad condition of the approach roads considerable traffic impairments and losses often occur.
A short-distance traffic industry practically only exists on the periphery of the major trading centres. It reveals the same deficiencies as have already been mentioned in connection with the long-distance industry, the only difference being that they appear in a still more marked way here. This applies more particularly to the reliability and the regularity of the transport performance. More isolated areas are either not at all developed by the transport industry, or transports are offered so rarely and irregularly so as to be useless for any trading enterprise. It is therefore quite obvious that under such circumstances the function of bridging space in short-distance transport has almost exclusively been taken over by the trading enterprises themselves, so much so that the taking-on of goods transport is not rarely the basic prerequisite for the operation of a trading enterprise.

II. Regrouping of Quantities

The quantities of products yielded by the individual enterprise as a rule do not conform with the quantities required by the individual user. The task of the regrouping of quantities on the part of trade therefore consists of the changing of quantities accruing on the procurement side into quantities conforming to the purposes of their use. Typical for the first instance is the buying-up of agricultural products by the agricultural produce trade, whereas in the marketing of industrial goods, more particularly of consumer goods, a regrouping of larger quantities into smaller ones occurs.
The production of agricultural small-holdings is quantitatively small and rather diversified as well. Moreover, the production is qualitatively very different from enterprise to enterprise, which fact additionally increases the tasks of regrouping quantities on the part of trade on account of the delivery of largely homogeneous (fungible) goods. Contrarywise, the production of plantation enterprises is specialized, voluminous and of uniform quality, so that it often can be sold through a produce broker directly to the user, or at least to the exporter.
In sharp contrast to this stands the situation in respect of the finished goods trade. Whereas in the agricultural produce trade small quantities on the pro-

curement side are opposed by relatively large quantities on the marketing side, in the finished goods trade great quantities of supplies are opposed by relatively small marketing quantities. In a similar manner this applies to goods traffic between trading enterprises within the trading levels but also to trade between the trading enterprises and the consumers. Since the ultimate demand with its buying power is limited, the quantities purchased in each buying transaction are very small, i.e. frequently only the daily requirements are purchased.

The low incomes as well as the purchasing power dispersed on account of the extensive manner of settlement on the part of the population are causing relatively small sizes of business in the retail trade of consumer goods. On the basis of statistical records and of investigations made by the author, the average turnover per annum of a retail business is estimated to amount to 1,500 pounds[3].

The size of the retail enterprises has a direct influence upon the size of the orders. Taking into consideration an average profit margin of 15 per cent, an average annual purchasing quantity of 1,275 pounds results. The frequency of procurement depends on the distance between retail and wholesale trade and the difficulties ensuing during the transport of goods as well as in a strong measure on the financial means available. Generally speaking, the more distant retail businesses procure more infrequently than those in the immediate vicinity of wholesale enterprises. Also the wide-spread shortage of capital is responsible for more regular procurement of goods.

On account of the facts mentioned above it should be clear that the function of the regrouping of quantities in Tanzania is larger than in industrial countries as a result of the different structure of demand and supply.

III. Regrouping of Goods

The character of the function of regrouping goods is the reformation of the range of goods more or less defined by the disposition set up by nature into assortments defined by requirements. This transformation is an essential task of trade.

The importance of the regrouping of goods in the raw material trade lies in the fact that the qualitatively very heterogeneous supply of goods, 60 per cent of which originate, as is well known, from farming enterprises, have to be regrouped into a homogeneous quality suited to a mechanized production process. In the case of the consumer goods trade things are different; this

3 Urban retail shops which import directly remained out of consideration in this account.

trade occupies itself with rendering suitable to the requirement structure of the heterogeneous population of Tanzania (Africans, Indians, Europeans) the imported goods from the industrial states in respect of quality, product design as well as packing. The African population, requiring the smallest task of regrouping of goods, plays the largest role in respect of its purchasing power. The European and Asian minorities should altogether not be able to command more than 40 per cent of the total demand for consumer goods. The function of regrouping goods of the consumer goods trade in Tanzania should accordingly not play such an important role as that of the consumer goods trade in developed national economies.

IV. Equalization of Time

The function of equalization of time consists of bridging the gap between the dates of production and consumption. Essentially, trade fulfills this task by means of storage. This function is relatively unimportant in Tanzania, because on the one hand the time lags in respect of the production of foodstuffs for climatic reasons are not as great as in regions with a moderate climate, and on the other hand due to the fact that producer and consumer (of a large part of the agricultural production) are very close to each other.
With regard to character and scope of the function of equalization of time, it is of importance whether the goods are transported overseas or consumed domestically. In the first case the bridging of time plays a small role because practically the entire agricultural export production is already bought up during the harvest, or at least immediately afterwards — mostly by way of auctions. In the second case there are state organizations, the Marketing Boards, which, in respect of the most important foodstuffs, undertake the storage.

V. Granting of Credit

In the development countries, more particularly in Tanzania, shortage of capital exists in all fields of entrepreneurial activity. Next to the low average incomes, the reasons for this can preponderantly be traced to social-cultural facts which are adversely opposed to the accumulation of capital. This general shortage of capital is opposed by relatively large capital requirements, not in the least on the part of agriculture. Since they cannot offer sufficient security, the owners of agricultural small-holdings cannot obtain loans from the banks. Public credit programmes are too limited in size, and for this reason trade is the only source of credit for the large number of small and medium-sized urban enterprises, most of all, however, for those situated in the country; moreover, trade is also responsible for the granting of consumer credit.

VI. Contact, Information and Consulting Function

The contact, information and consulting function of trade serves the overcoming of the "knowledge gap" between the spheres of production and consumption and thereby also the increase of the market transparency for the participant people. Trade exercises this function not only on the marketing but also on the procurement side. Special importance must be attached to the fulfillment of this function by trade in Tanzania. Its task is to make contacts with foreign enterprises and to promote such contacts. Since a considerable part of the population cannot be reached by newspapers, radio or other means of communication, it is encumbent upon trade to improve the knowledge of the consumer in respect of the market and of goods.

B. INFLUENCE OF ECONOMIC AND TRADE POLICY UPON TRADE

I. Economic and Trade Policy under British Administration

During the period of British rule, no structural-political inroads were made on the part of the state trade policy; it was assumed that trade fulfilled its tasks in an optimal way considering the circumstances. A certain influence, however, was exerted by the British administration upon trade structure in restricting the Indian and Arab minorities to the trade centres as well as the major trading posts. This caused Africans with savings from the sale of agricultural products or from employment to be able to establish a trading business in rural districts, protected against the competition by Indian and Arab traders.
Of considerably greater importance was the influence on the part of agricultural development policy upon trade, more particularly trade with agri-

cultural products. To an increasing measure there occurred consolidations on the part of the agricultural small-holders on a co-operative basis for the purpose of marketing their products.
The assistance rendered by government to the co-operatives consisted in part — and this was of special importance to private trade — of vesting in them the marketing monopoly, as far as such action seemed to be opportune to it. Thereby in many cases the main trading object was taken away from many of the hitherto private Indian produce dealers.

II. Economic and Trade Policy after Independence

The transfer of political power by the granting of independence in 1961 by the British administration to African politicians resulted also in a reorientation of economic and trade policy.
The supreme goal of the economic policy of Tanzania, i.e. the increase of economic welfare, consists of economic and extra-economic components.
The extra-economic conceptual targets of economic policy, as far as influencing trade policy is concerned, are

- Entrenchment of the co-operative economic principle
- Accelerated Africanization.

The economic targets consist of

- Increase and improvement of production and productivity by industrialization as well as structural reformation of agriculture
- Safeguarding of supply with basic foodstuffs
- Increase of export yields.

1. The Extra-economic Targets and Measures for their Realization

Entrenchment of the co-operative economic principle

The economic-political objective aspired to by the government of Tanzania is the socialistic-co-operative economic order. In this is seen the form of economy which renders possible the economic and social reformation without thereby destroying the traditional values of Africa. Looked upon as such, a traditional value is the pronounced community thinking which has developed from the tribal order. The co-operative societies are looked upon as a medium for maintaining this sense of community or to revive it, respectively, where it has already become partially buried by colonialization, and also to educate

the people to the adoption of a sense of responsibility as well as a sense of duty towards the community.
In respect of a change, first priority was given to trade, which was looked upon as the prototype of an economic form educating the individual to become an egotist and in which the prosecution of the principle of maximizing profits takes advantage in turning lack of knowledge and conditions of distress to one's own benefit.
It is the target of trade policy to put onto the market the entire production of agricultural small-holdings in Tanzania by means of co-operative societies by 1970; by that time it is intended to have the whole of Tanzania covered by an uninterrupted network of marketing co-operatives, entailing a further establishment of about 400–600 co-operatives. In this connection, the co-operatives are nominated buying agents by the state Marketing Boards.
It is intended to build up by 1970 the consumer co-operative societies to such an extent that they will concentrate upon themselves 10 per cent of the trading turnovers. In a long-term view, a proportion of 30 to 40 per cent is envisaged. For the purpose of realization of this target the Co-operative Supply Association of Tanganyika (Cosata) was established in 1962, intended to function as a wholesale organization for the co-operative societies to be established on the retail level.

Accelerated Africanization

Another important target of the new government consists of the increased and accelerated Africanization of trade. The laissez-faire policy of the British administration on the trade sector had caused trade at the time of independence in very strong measure being vested in the hands of the non-African minorities, i.e. Europeans and Indians, who, moreover, employed hardly any Africans in their trading enterprises. Although in 1961 more than two thirds of all licenced dealers in the consumer goods trade in Tanzania were Africans, they concentrated upon themselves, however, hardly more than 20 per cent of the turnover of the entire finished goods trade[4]. The social tensions resulting from the opinion of the majority of being "taken advantage of" by a minority embodied a danger for continued economic progress. In agricultural trade, the Africanization is promoted by the establishment and advancement of marketing co-operatives. In the finished goods trade, however, where, contrary to agricultural trade, African private trading enterprises occupy an important position, it is intended to achieve Africanization primarily via the consumer co-operatives, since all efforts made to advance the African traders by training, councilling and granting of credits are not successful in a satisfactory measure.

4 G. E. Kommissar: *Increased African Participation in Commerce and Industry.* Manuscript 1963.

2. Economic Targets and Measures for their Realization

Increase and improvement of production and productivity

It is intended to achieve the increase and improvement of production as well as of productivity through reformation of the structure and control of the agricultural production as well as through an increased industrialization of the economy.

The agricultural small-holdings primarily geared to grow their own supplies are working with but small productivity, since the "production programme" is very diversified, and they in no way make use of the potentially available production possibilities. A decisive improvement can only be reached when the achievement has been accomplished to specialize the agricultural productive small-holdings and, connected therewith, to gear stronger to market production. This structural reformation entails a mental process of transformation of the farming population which necessitates a large educative expenditure and which in Tanzania should primarily be achieved by the co-operative societies. Preconditions must be the reduction of the marketing risk to a measure bearable for the producer (which is already being done by the Marketing Boards) as well as the establishment of a well-functioning trade in consumer goods, with a broad range of offerings in goods, sufficient storage capacity, attractive prices as well as good service.

The growth possibilities of the economy of Tanzania are restricted even if success is achieved in the transformation of agriculture from a subsistence production into a marketing one. Unless in a long-term view the danger of an economic stagnation is to be encountered, Tanzania must become industrialized. For this reason, the government brings special pressure to bear on such industrialization. In order to achieve this target, the realization of the following prerequisites is considered necessary:

- Improvement of the functioning of the trade apparatus
- Increase of incomes of the people in agriculture
- Opening of new sources for the accumulation of capital.

Safeguarding of supply with basic foodstuffs

In Tanzania, the agricultural production is subject to strong regional and periodic fluctuations. The equalization between supply and demand did not always "function" in the past, so that in certain districts extreme situations of scarcity often occurred. Thus, Tanzania was forced to import basic foodstuffs in years with a sub-average harvest in order to safeguard the sustenance of its population. Quite apart from the humane side of the problem, this led to an undesired outflow of foreign exchange and also hindered the process of structural reformation in agriculture.

In order to obviate such supply crises and the price increases entailed thereby, the Marketing Board competent for the most important basic foodstuffs keeps central stock-piling depots. The financing of such stocks is achieved via the price (compulsory marketing).

Increase of foreign exchange income

The industrialization, the improvement of the infra-structure as well as the steps towards modernization in the economy require the importation of capital goods, which in coming years in all probability will considerably increase. It may be taken for granted that the imports in terms of money shall grow faster than the exports so that the picture of a today still active balance of payments may very soon undergo a change. By the Marketing Boards, which monopolize the offerings of the agricultural exports, it is intended to achieve better prices on the world markets and thereby increase the income of foreign exchange. By the interposition of Marketing Boards, moreover, it is aimed to prevent any transfer of profits to overseas countries by vertically-integrated enterprises with capital ties.

C. TRADE WITH INDUSTRIAL PRODUCTS

I. Institutional Forms of Trade

In Tanzania, the marketing of industrial consumer and capital goods is performed almost exclusively by institutional trading enterprises. An industrial character of an enterprise within the meaning of the establishment of sales branches of its own is restricted to some few cases. For purposes of expediency the institutional trading enterprises are being sub-divided into private, state and co-operative trading establishments. On the one hand, this distinction seems to be suitable because in Tanzania private, state and co-operative trading are understood as contrasts, on the other hand, because there exist some considerable structural differences between them.
As characteristics of distinction the following criteria shall be decisive in the case of

private trading:

- The entrepreneurial policy is geared to the principle of maximizing the profits or to the appropriate yield of an income.
- The entrepreneurial policy is defined by the private owners of capital in accordance with the amount of their participation.

state trading:

- The entrepreneurial policy is defined by the government. As a rule there will be some participation with capital, but should not be looked upon as necessary. State trading can take place in competition with private and co-operative forms of enterprise; it can, however, also be vested with certain privileges, such as, for instance, with a monopoly.

co-operative trading:

- Equal rights of members in defining the entrepreneurial policy; the amount of capital participation is irrelevant.
- Maximizing of profit of the members.
- Self-administration by the organs of the co-operative society.

For reasons of considerations of expediency, the characteristic of voluntariness of the members shall be waived.

II. Trading Chains

1. Trade with Consumer Goods

As a rule, the trading chain in the marketing of industrial consumer goods consists of importer — domestic wholesale — semi-wholesale — retail trade. A clear delineation of the individual links of the trading chain between one and the other, however, is only possible in the case of state trading. In this case, imports are carried through exclusively by the State Trading Corporation (STC), and the marketing takes place via the state's own wholesale and semi-wholesale depots as well as retail trading businesses. Functional overlapping in the sense of one preceding trading level fulfilling the functions of a succeeding trading level, hardly occurs, apart from semi-wholesale trading. Within the scope of the state and co-operative trading, there therefore exists a clearly definable succession within the trading chain.
The trading chain of private trading is immeasurably more differentiated. In principle, the level classification of importer — domestic wholesale — semi-wholesale — retail trade exists here also, but the various trading levels

can by no means be delineated as clearly against each other as is the case in respect of state trading.
Practically all wholesale levels are geared to retail trade. The sale to the ultimate consumer is in part specially promoted by the smaller wholesalers as well as by the semi-wholesalers, because the profit margin in this connection is larger.
Inversely, larger retail enterprises are reselling to small retail shops or to street-hawkers and peddlers, thereby undertaking wholesalers' functions. Just as fluid were the delineations in respect of the importations between the now nationalized import houses, on the one side, and the domestic wholesalers as well as major urban retailers on the other. Both last-mentioned groups are in part importing themselves, and not infrequently the procurements of goods from abroad exceed those from domestic sources. Functionally unequivocally definable are therefore only the small retail businesses (the dukas, so-called).
Another essential characteristic is the lack of constant business relations of the trading levels amongst one another, i.e. under certain preconditions, one level — mostly the semi-wholesaler or the wholesaler — is by-passed. This, for example, is the case during the annual turnover peak. The increase of demand renders it possible for the smaller wholesalers to omit the central wholesaler of the district or of the region and to purchase directly from the importer on the coast. Likewise, it becomes profitable (costs of transport) for medium-sized retail enterprises to leave out the semi-wholesaler from whom they order during the period of small turnover and to purchase directly from the central wholesaler. In other words: in times of strong demand the number of links of the trading chain involved decreases; during periods of weak demand, however, an increase of chain links takes place.
The system of distribution in the private sphere is nothing else but the logical adaption to the environmental conditions of the country. It guarantees an optimum of flexibility and utilizes optimally the available trading establishments, since every trading enterprise represents a potential point of supply for the population. On the other hand, this extensive inter-merging of trading levels exerts negative results upon the efficiency of the trade.
State and co-operative trading as well as private trading function almost independently from each other. More particularly, it was state trading, which was inaugurated with the express purpose of reducing the dominating position of private trade. Both forms of enterprise enter into mutual business transactions only in the event of one of them possessing monopoly rights. The state trading organizations, for instance, have the import monopoly for a number of important products which preponderantly find their way into the African consumer households (e.g. Khangas [5], condensed milk, sugar). In

5 Square cotton cloths.

the event of private trading enterprises not wanting or not being able to waive the trade with the monopolized range of goods, they are forced to acquire such goods from the state trading organizations. The reverse case will occur when private trading enterprises possess contractual monopoly rights.

2. Connecting Links in Trading with Production Materials

In the main, the trading chain in respect of the marketing of materials is defined by the type of product concerned and the amount of users. Large aggregates (e.g. factory equipment, machines) are procured by the domestic users mostly directly from overseas, in which case pursuant to the special circumstances an agent/representative can act as an intermediary. The latter is always the case when overseas manufacturers vest the rights of sole agency on an agent in order to safeguard their interests. Standardized capital goods of lower value (e.g. smaller agricultural machines) as well as mass-produced goods (e.g. building materials, fertilizers and spraying agents) as a rule are stored by the importers and sold in their own businesses. To larger customers (plantations, missions, government agencies) goods are sold mostly directly or by the mediation of wholesale agents with storage facilities who have their registered office in one of the trade centres. The supply of the rural smallholdings takes place either via the agricultural marketing co-operatives, whose procurement organs are the STC or one central co-operative society, or, in the event of a territory not yet being developed by co-operative societies, by major general dealers, who carry materials as a sideline (e.g. cement) and who as a rule obtain their supplies from the urban wholesalers.
After this short review of the trading organizations to be met with in Tanzania, the various links in the trading chain in private trading as well as in state trading will now be described.

III. Private Trading

1. Specialized Importers

After the nationalization of the four largest and several smaller importing firms in February 1967, only the so-called specialized importers can be counted amongst the importing companies.
Amongst the specialized importers the following categories can roughly be distinguished:

- Importers of materials for industrial and agricultural users (iron and steel, machines)
- Importers of building materials and hardware
- Importers of motor vehicles and spare-parts
- Importers of durable consumer goods
- Importers of food, including luxury food, beverages and tobacco
- Importers of textiles
- Importers of medicaments and cosmetics.

Overlapping and inter-merging of the range of goods occur relatively frequently. No clear separation between importers of consumer and capital goods can be ascertained. An importer of consumer goods as a rule will not hesitate to introduce materials into his range of goods carried if an overseas producer offers him the sole marketing rights; this will not even happen if the prerequisits for the marketing of such products have so far been lacking to him. The reason for this lacking specialization in the range of goods carried on the import level can preponderantly be traced to the small purchasing power of the Tanzanian market. It causes the firms to tend to enlarge their range of goods for reasons of a degression of fixed costs. The disadvantage of this entrepreneurial policy can be found in the fact that in the case of a wide range of goods the same attention is not paid to individual groups of goods as is done in the case of specialized importers.

As a rule, the specialized importers do not have a wide distribution network of their own. Only the largest of them have opened up branch offices in the towns of the country (Tanga, Moshi, Arusha, Mwanza). In the other localities, the specialized importers are represented by so-called agent/wholesalers or major urban retail enterprises, in whom has been vested the sole agency for certain products in a specific territory.

The turnovers of the more strongly specialized importers can be assessed in the neighborhood of £50,000 and £600,000 to £700,000; this top limit just mentioned can in exceptional cases be exceeded by far (e.g. motor vehicle trade). It can be taken as a general rule that enterprises concentrating their business on mass-produced goods with fast turnover may well be found in the upper brackets of the scale, whereas importers geared more strongly to products with generally slow turnover may achieve turnovers between £50,000 and £150,000, in special cases (special products) even less.

Whereas the European trading firms are as a rule conducted according to modern business principles (active selling policy, modern accounting methods, etc.), the management of the Indian import dealers is conservative. Their dominating business principle consists of the minimization of expenditure with regard to the individual production factors (family enterprise). The decreasing of unit costs by enlarging the turnover, in other words, cost-consciousness in terms of efficiency, is foreign to the Indian merchant. The

static mental attitude of the Indian importers finds its expression in their entire entrepreneurial attitude and marketing policy.
The use of incentive pay figuration as an instrument of management policy, such as is in part commonly applied by European concerns, can hardly be observed in the case of Indian importers. Although account books are kept and annual balance sheets compiled, this is generally only done in order to comply with the Company and Income Tax Laws. Selection of a range of goods, definition of stocks to be kept, quantities and dates of orders, calculation and price-formation take place largely by way of intuition, i.e. without system. Thus it is not rare that the composition of the range of goods is not optimal (too large stocks of slow-selling goods and too small stocks of readily-saleable articles); this decreases the competitiveness on the selling market and causes difficulties of financing. Fixed prices, i.e. prices calculated in advance, exist only in the large — mostly European — importing firms; otherwise the price is in each case negotiated between vendor and buyer, in which case the quantity to be purchased, mode of payment as well as current financial situation of the importer play a decisive role.

2. Indent Merchants

On account of the large distance between the markets, necessarily coupled with the lack of information as well as the small purchasing power of the market in Tanzania, the indent business has assumed relatively large importance. From the point of view of the inland trading enterprises, the efficiency of such agents consists preponderantly of their knowledge of the sources of procurement overseas and of their being informed by continual contacts on the most favourable offerings of goods at any time. This function is more distinctly expressed in the case of the large indent houses, which often represent several producers from various countries in the case of one and the same article. They are thus able to select the most favourable price offer and, simultaneously, on the basis of their mediating position, to exert a certain pressure upon the producer. Very frequently, this is met in the case of mass-produced goods, such as, for example, iron and steel goods or building materials.
From the viewpoint of the overseas offerer (who could either be a producer or an export trading company) the work of the indent merchant mainly consists of being represented in a country with small purchasing power, in which a branch office or trading organization of his own would not be profitable, and also proves its value in being kept abreast of the happenings on the market. Such firms as a rule obtain the right of sole agency. Many indent firms carry a dozen or more agencies. The range of goods thus represented can accordingly consist of several hundreds of articles. Usually the indent

firms specialize in various groups of goods (e.g. clothing, building materials machines), their registered offices being situated in the trade centres of Dar es Salaam and Tanga.
The commission paid by the overseas suppliers on an average amounts to 5 per cent of the invoice value. These rates, however, differ according to groups of goods and generally run between $2^1/_2$ per cent and 10 per cent.

3. Brokers

The domestic counterpart to the indent merchants are the trade brokers. They act as intermediaries not only in the marketing of agricultural products, mostly with the buyers in the interior of the country and the exporters, but also in the selling of industrial finished goods, in this case with the importers and the wholesalers in the interior of the country. The majority of brokers have their offices in the harbour towns. The reason for their mediation lies in their better knowledge of the market situation and market development as a result of their proximity to the market. They function primarily to safeguard the interests of the trading firms in the interior. For the agricultural produce dealers they ascertain the best marketing possibilities, for the wholesaler with industrial finished goods the most favourable procurement possibilities — a fact of greatest importance for the concerns involved because of the frequently fast-changing prices. The importance of the broker in the field of agricultural marketing has declined in recent years, although in the marketing of industrial finished goods it has remained virtually unchanged.
For his services, the broker usually receives a commission between $^1/_4$ per cent and $^3/_4$ per cent of the invoice value in respect of finished goods, the seller normally paying $^1/_4$ per cent, the buyer between 0 per cent and $^1/_2$ per cent. In the marketing of agricultural products the commission amounts on the average to 1 per cent of the invoice value, as a rule paid by the buyer.

4. Wholesalers and Semi-wholesalers

The independent wholesaler occupies a central position in the total distribution system of Tanzania. Although some distribution organizations are run by local producers, these also almost without exception make use of the services of independent wholesale firms, giving them the status of agents — often with the sole rights of distribution. Only very few industrial firms keep delivery depots of their own. The import firms have also, as has already been mentioned, established themselves — though only on a small scale — on the level of domestic wholesaling.
The preponderant number of wholesale concerns in Tanzania also conduct

business with the ultimate consumer, and in the case of a considerable part — if not the majority of them — the retail turnover may be higher, in part far higher than the wholesale turnover. The functional gradations of these "wholesale firms" are thus considerable. They run from trading concerns with a wholesale turnover of 90 per cent and more to trading concerns which sell hardly more than 20 per cent to resellers. Trading firms concentrating on the retail turnover shall in the following be designated as semi-wholesalers.

In the trading chain, wholesalers and semi-wholesalers are only seldom found on the same level. Frequently the semi-wholesalers procure from the genuine wholesalers, and a levelling occurs only temporarily, e.g. during the season when the sizes of the orders warrant a direct procurement from the importer and no obstacles arise on the financial side. The semi-wholesaler is usually a connecting link between the urban wholesaler and the small — mostly rural — retail businesses.

The genuine wholesale firms mostly have their offices situated in the towns. Only in economically more strongly-developed areas (e.g. Sukumaland) they are in isolated cases also to be found in so-called trading centres. Semi-wholesalers, on the other hand, can be found in the towns, in the larger trading centres as well as in smaller settlements. The participation of the semi-wholesaler during the sale to re-sellers in the towns, where the semi-wholesaler has to work in competition with the "genuine" wholesaler firms, is due to the fact that he sells units in smaller quantities, under certain circumstances gives credit to customers who otherwise would have to pay cash, and in part takes over the transport to more distant parts of the country.

On the basis of investigations conducted by the author, it is possible to convey approximate ideas of the sizes of the enterprises of wholesalers and semi-wholesalers. In towns with a rich hinterland (Mwanza, Moshi, Arusha) there exist some very few wholesale firms with an annual turnover of £200,000 to £300,000. The majority of the wholesale enterprises in the towns of Tanzania achieve turnovers in the amount of £30,000 to £150,000. In the case of wholesalers with turnovers of less than £30,000 these are generally specialists, such as traders in motor car spare parts and accessories. The turnovers of the semi-wholesalers in the towns average between £15,000 and £25,000 per annum, in some cases also beyond that figure. In the case of semi-wholesalers with turnovers of less than £15,000, either the proportion of retail sales is very large or the enterprises specialize in goods with a slow turnover. The semi-wholersalers in the major trading centres and smaller settlements may well achieve annual turnovers of approximately £5,000 to £10,000.

The large and medium-sized wholesale enterprises are exclusively Indian family enterprises. In former years, there existed some European enterprises on this trading level, which, however, could not hold out against the strong competition and have disappeared during the course of time. Even semi-wholesale businesses were conducted generally by Indians. Only in traditionally Arabic settlements areas (on the coast and along the central railway line, more particularly in Tabora) Arabs operate on the semi-wholesale level. African participation in semi-wholesale trade is similarly still very limited.

As is the case with import trading, the Indian management of the firms leaves much to be desired with regard to wholesale and semi-wholesale trading. Marketing-conscious thinking as well as up-to-date management methods are practically unknown. The arrangements with regard to the policy to be followed by the firm generally do not extend beyond the limitation of expenditures and the discovery of the most favourable sources of supply. The wholesaler considers himself primarily as supply organ and distributor. This is expressed most clearly in the marketing attitude and in service policy towards customers.

Only few wholesalers engage in active sales promotion, for example, by having their customers called upon by commercial travellers or travelling salesmen, by "pushing" certain articles by means of advertising methods, etc. The taking up of contacts in principle takes place on the part of the customer by their visiting the wholesaler's office. In the stockroom of the wholesaler, the retailer is not confronted by a range of goods displayed in a manner promoting sales in the sense that the retailer would be able to obtain a survey of the supplies offered. Neither is he told of expected developments of the market, informed of novelties, nor expertly advised (e.g. with regard to selection of a range of goods, possibilities of financing, etc.); nor even is he treated in a friendly way. The paramount theme of the sales talk is the price, which, contrary to developed economies, is not fixed, but which in part is subject to strong periodic fluctuations, varies according to customer, quantity to be sold, mode of payment, etc., and — apart from some few articles — is again and again the subject of intense haggling.

In order to create on the part of the purchaser the impression of an optically favourable price, weight manipulations are frequently carried out. This is made all the easier on account of the fact that home produce such as maize, rice, sugar, etc., is generally sold by the sack and not according to weight. Within the scope of any business transaction betwen the wholesaler and his customers, a similar importance as to the price attaches to the question of credit. The grant of a loan is often the prerequisite for the realization of a selling transaction. From the viewpoint of the wholesaler, credit serves a means of tying the retailer and thereby to side-step the sometimes strong competition.

The consideration that competitiveness and efficiency lastly depend on the sound credit standing of the customer and that it serves his own interests to advance this standing in the best possible way, is largely unknown to the wholesaler in Tanzania. The relation of the two "market partners" can — at least at the present time — can be considered like the relation of two contracting parties, of whom each one attempts to cheat the other. It is clear that this business policy does not serve to create a relation of confidence between wholesaler and retailer.

The figures ascertained with the wholesaler pursuant to fiscal aspects can hardly be made the basis of an overall calculation of performance and output, which should reveal sources of loss within the enterprise, neither are they looked upon and applied as such by these enterprises. A systematic compilation of the entrepreneurial operations is unknown even to the major wholesale enterprises.

Trading firms as multi-product enterprises frequently try to achieve the target of their management policy of maximizing profits and income by maximizing turnover. This applies also to a large extent to the trading enterprises in Tanzania. The dominating method of maximizing turnover is the enlargement of the range of goods, which is very often implemented without particular target, i.e. without paying regard to considerations of marketing and of costs.

This entrepreneurial policy of the wholesale trade in Tanzania led to the carrying of very wide ranges of goods, partially even to the carrying of hardly homogeneous groups of goods or to articles, which presumably already during a very rough analysis of the outlay in question could be proved as loss bearers.

A conscious specialization in the range of goods carried could hitherto only rarely be observed; it is largely restricted to wholesalers in the towns or major trade centres. "Specialized wholesalers" exist among the groups of goods such as food, including luxury foods, beverages, and tobacco, textiles and clothing, motor car spare parts and accessories, building materials and hardware as well as motor vehicles. A specialization in absolutely pure form, however, is rare. Very frequently, other groups of goods are carried as sideline or marginal ranges of goods. Relatively frequent combinations of goods carried consist of foodstuffs and textiles as well as foodstuffs, textiles and cosmetics. On hand of a few examples an impression of the wideness of the range of goods carried as well as the possibilities of variation shall in the following be given [6]. The groups of articles mentioned in the following compilation in the first and second place form the keypoints of the range of goods carried:

- Food, including luxury food, beverages and tobacco, shirts, shoes, pharmaceuticals and cosmetics, stationery, radios, blankets, mattrasses.
- Food, including luxury food, beverages and tobacco, pharmaceuticals and cosmetics.
- Food, including luxury food, beverages and tobacco, motor car accessories,

6 In the three towns of varying size, Tabora, Iringa and Korogwe the range of goods carried by all trading enterprises was ascertained. The data of the above compilation are based on the results of this investigation.

tires, bicycles, electrical goods and spare parts, sports goods, music instruments, watches, radios, sewing machines (agency), arms, fishing nets.
- Textiles, haberdashery, jewellery.
- Building materials, hardware, tires, shirts, shoes, radios, miscellaneous articles.
- Motor fuel, oil, tires, foodstuffs, textiles, cosmetics.

The management policy, trying to achieve an increase of turnover mainly through broadening the range of goods carried, the seasonal fluctuations of demand, the general distance from the supply markets, the bad and in part insufficient means of communication, the transport problems as well as the general scarcity of capital coupled with the few possibilities of procuring funds from outside sources, are making great demands upon the organization of stocks, more particularly upon the stock-planning of the wholesale enterprises. In order to achieve and maintain an approximately optimal stock-keeping policy geared to the viewpoints of costs and marketing, a careful reconciliation of the procurement policy to the possibilities of selling, all above-named aspects would have to be taken into consideration. This, however, does not apply to the present date. The quantity and date of procurement is fixed by the entrepreneur on a purely intuitive basis. It is thus no exception that the stocks carried do not conform to the selling requirements. In respect of articles with a quick turnover, the stocks are often insufficient, in articles with slow turnover they are frequently too large. Repeat orders, on account of the complete lack of a systematic stock control, are frequently placed only upon the occurrence of stock deficiency. The formulation of an estimate of the sales potential, even though only a rough one, is as good as unknown. In his procurement policy, the wholesaler allows himself to be guided more strongly by viewpoints lying outside considerations pertaining to stocks and sales economy, i.e. by favourable conditions of procurement (e.g. high discounts), favourable transport possibilities, credit possibilities, large profit margins in respect of the article concerned, but also by speculative considerations.
Although also the technical-organizational side of the stock economy is not found to be in the best state, considerable frequencies of stock turnover are in part nevertheless achieved. In spite of the lacking management qualities on the part of the wholesale enterprises, these enterprises are in a certain sense efficient. This is mainly based on the fact that almost exclusively family enterprises are involved. These enterprises dispose of a maximum of flexibility both with regard to the timely and the relevant employment of labour and with regard to the cost of labour. It is this very angle which will make it difficult for other entrepreneurial forms, which, although managed by more modern principles, have to rely on "outside" labour, to come in on this trading level under such competitive conditions. Unproductivity on

account of insufficient business management will always — even in a long-term view — be attempted to be equalized by such family enterprises by means of increased labour performance (in the physical sense) as well as the waiving of income, all the more so as qualified personnel is scarce in Tanzania.

5. Urban Retail Trade (without town dukas)

In the towns, in which or in the surroundings of which lives a sizeable number of Europeans, relatively large retail shops have sprung up. Although small in number, their influence is considerable especially with a view to the future development.

These urban retail shops in part are using modern management methods and merchandising techniques; in their case also the building up of a specialized range of goods is relatively far advanced. Financial accounting is a matter of course for such enterprises; apart from this, the first trends towards a systematic control of the range of goods carried and of stocks as well as accounting in and calculations of groups of goods have become visible. Some of these enterprises operate in the form of self-service stores, thus necessitating a clearly displayed and sales-stimulating arrangement of goods as well as fixed prices. The attempts to improve service, to give advice to customers, to serve courteously, etc., cannot be overlooked. A certain problem is posed by the granting of loans. For reasons of rationalization, the attempt is increasingly made to restrict the credit sales in deals with ultimate consumers. The consumer — hitherto accustomed to credit sales — does not seem to be willing or to be in a position to accept the cash sale. In relation to this, a cautious procedure would be required on the part of the trading enterprises.

A specialization of the range of goods carried occurs as a keypoint in the case of foodstuffs, textiles as well as drugs, pharmaceuticals and cosmetics. The range of goods carried by the urban retail businesses generally comprise qualitatively high-value goods and demonstrate in each range of goods an astonishing breadth and depth. In every sense, they are comparable to the ranges of goods in Europe. Retail shops thus characterized can mainly be found in Dar es Salaam, Arusha, Moshi, Mwanza and Tanga.

The turnovers of these enterprises are in part considerable as far as Tanzania is concerned. According to their sizes they may well have turnovers of between £50,000 and £150,000 per annum in Dar es Salaam, in part even more; in towns like Tanga, Arusha or Mwanza approximately between £20,000 and £100,000 (as a comparison, the turnover of medium-sized urban wholesale enterprises: £30,000 to £150,000).

The urban retail shops supplying the "Europeanized" market, procure either from the import firms — generally through the mediation of indent merchants — or directly from the producers or export houses overseas. The trend

towards direct procurement is strong in respect of the retail businesses, because by the by-passing of the import trading level their profit margin improves. Of influence is also the fact that a number of articles is, on account of the small demand, not kept in stock by the import enterprises, and that thus only a direct procurement by importation comes into question.
The mark-ups in the calculation may well on an average be higher in the case of the urban retail businesses than in the case of the traditionally conducted retail shops. These enterprises, however, cannot be compared with regard to range of goods carried as well as service policy — if only to mention the two most essential factors.

6. Urban and Rural Dukas

The preponderant number of retail enterprises in Tanzania are so-called duka enterprises (derived from the Indian Dukawala). A typical characteristic of these duka enterprises is the wide range of goods carried, geared to the daily requirements of the African population. Only in the towns shops specializing in food can sporadically be found, including luxury food, beverages and tobacco, fabrics sold by the yard. Generally, the composition of the range of goods stocked conforms with that of the rural general dealers in Europe, with the only difference that this range in the various categories does not reveal the same breadth and depth on account of the considerably simpler requirements of the population and that in Tanzania such enterprises can be found not only in the country but also in the towns. Principally, two kinds of duka enterprises can be differentiated:

Larger enterprises with an annual turnover in the neighborhood of £1,500 to £5,000, with a very large range of goods

It comprises the groups of goods: food, including luxury food, beverages and tobacco, textiles, medicaments, detergents, cosmetics, haberdashery, hardware and household goods (crockery and cutlery), stationery, cheap jewellery, shoes and footwear, etc. With regard to the goods selected for stock, there may hardly be an article which — bearing in mind the scale of requirements of the African — is not to be found in such a duka. The larger dukas are as a rule Indian, and partly also Arab businesses. More recently, African enterprises of such dimensions are to be met in the economically less developed parts of the country, though these are by and large exceptions.

Smaller enterprises with an annual turnover of up to approximately £1,000

The range of goods carried by these enterprises is considerably smaller and consists chiefly of such goods as food, and special commodities such as beverages and tobacco, pharmaceuticals, cosmetics and detergents. This limitation has almost always financial reasons. These enterprises are almost without exception run by Africans.

The dukas are generally family or one-man enterprises. Only in rare cases does one come across companies on this trading level. These usually do not survive very long, as the distrust between the parties concerned normally seems to be too pronounced.

With respect to education, considerable differences exist between the owners of the large Indian and the small African duka businesses. Nearly all Indian merchants have as a rule passed through eight classes in the primary school and have behind them a more or less long period of learning in an Indian trading enterprise, usually in one belonging to a relative. At the time of establishing their own firm or taking over some business they already dispose of a minimum measure of mercantile training, practical experience in management, as well as a sufficiently comprehensive insight into the procurement market. The African, on the other hand, possesses on the average a considerably lower standard of education; generally he stems from quite different occupational groups and thus — at least at the beginning — has very little experience in business matters.

Very many African traders formerly were artisans or occupied themselves in agricultural work (subsidiary enterprises). The share of business owners, however, who already at a prior time had engaged in trade as hawkers or market dealers, is surprisingly small.

The fact that the African, before opening up his own business, does not pass a "commercial apprenticeship", is less the result of lacking desire than lack of opportunity. The Indian enterprises, which primarily would come into question as training enterprises, are almost exclusively family enterprises. As a rule the families are so large that not even all members of the family can find an occupation in the firm. Thus, for non-members of the family there hardly offers itself a chance of a "training period" — apart from purely subaltern manual services. Another reason rendering it difficult for outsiders to find employment in an enterprise is the widespread fear in these circles that the person in question could divulge business secrets.

The lacking or deficient commercial training causes — especially in the early stages — a comparatively high quota of closures in the case of the African enterprises shortly after opening up. Many a firm can only be kept going because of the availability of other sources of income (e.g. from agriculture). The African duka businesses therefore represent for the wholesalers and

semi-wholesalers a great credit risk, which they are rarely willing to take. Out of 40 evaluated answers of African retailers, 35 stated that they do not receive credits from their suppliers. The remaining 5 enterprises had credit lines amounting to £50 to £100. For the Indian duka businesses, however, it is generally not difficult to obtain credits from their suppliers, and nearly all Indian retail businesses are to a considerable part conducted on a credit basis. Because of this different treatment with regard to the granting of credits, the conclusion is often drawn that the Indian wholesalers or semi-wholesalers were discriminating against the African dealers. This reproach may well be unjustified on the whole. In respect of granting credit the decisive criterion for each supplier is the question of the credit standing of the customer. If the risk is too large, no supplier will be prepared to extend credit, never mind whether a European, Indian or African is involved.
The credit risk is unequivocally smaller in the case of the Indian than concerning the African customer. Next to the superior commercial training and the generally more extended experience in business life, the circumstance preponderantly plays a role that the wholesaler as a rule is sufficiently well informed or can inform himself on the history as well as the family background of his Indian trading colleague, and that in the case of a suspension of payments, he can avail himself — apart from the purely legal but generally unsuccessful measures — of social pressures of the most varied kinds (the religious communities as well as ties of relationships can be taken into account in this connection). This usually does not apply in the case of African traders. In the event of an African suspending payments the amount usually can be written off as a loss. Another reason for the reticence of the suppliers in granting credits to Africans can be found in their lacking debtor's ethics.
For financing, therefore, the African traders have mostly to rely on their own resources, which are generally very small, and on account of which considerable competitive disadvantages necessarily arise for them. Their range of goods carried must remain restricted to the most important articles, the amount of stocks being determined more so by the funds available than by the possibilities of sales.
The key problem of the duka firms — Indian as well as the African — is management, which is extremely undynamic. This finds its expression in its most poignant way in the attitude towards the customer. In the eyes of the duka owner, the customer is an opponent and not a partner in the market. This attitude causes a striving towards maximizing profits relating to the individual sales transaction and not to the entire enterprise. Prices are fixed only in the case of standard articles. In respect of other goods, they are as a rule freshly negotiated in every individual case. In arriving at the price, factors not immediately connected with the cost as well as the demand and supply situation (e.g. ignorance on the part of the buyer) are not infrequently

playing a role. Although, as HAWKINS[7] expresses it, this policy may "increase the overall profit of the trader by a small amount, this additional profit should hardly suffice to compensate the distrust built up thereby between traders and consumers".

Competition between trading enterprises today exclusively still consists of price competition, the value, preponderantly the advantage of service competition for the enterprises themselves, not being appreciated at all. It is surely true that on account of his low income, the consumer is very price-conscious, i.e. that he desires low prices. As could frequently be observed, there exists, however, on the part of the customers at least an equally large desire for information and advice in respect of quality of goods, characteristics of their mode of employment, etc. Not only for the sake of his own interests, the trader should much more strongly than hitherto endow the goods by his services with a higher utility value beyond their purely material value, and concentrate more on quality competition at the expense of price competition. Together with this should also go an attractive and well-arranged display of the goods in the store, a polite service, paying attention to customers' wishes and problems, the change-over to fixed prices — in short, measures capable of creating a relation of trust between retailer and consumer.

The range of goods carried by the duka businesses is primarily governed by the financing possibilities available. A selection of goods to be carried pursuant to principles underlying the conduct of business (e.g. frequency of turnover, profit) is as good as unknown. In the case of the Indian retail stores, for which there exist only few restrictions on the financial side, this leads to a very wide range of goods offered. Very often the ranges of goods carried are "puffed up" with articles, the turnover of which is only very slow. The goods offered by the African dukas, on the other hand, are essentially more restricted and are concentrated on food and special commodities, such as beverages and tobacco, other articles like detergents and cosmetics, medicaments as well as household goods; in each category only the most important of these are stocked.

On the basis of examinations of the ranges of goods stocked it can be assumed that in rural districts with exclusively or predominantly African tradership the range of goods offered — measured by the potential requirements of the population — is too small and that on account of this restricting influences are exerted upon the economic development in that the customers as a result of "lack of stimulation" are hoarding their financial income or that the desire for increased monetary earnings is not awakened in them; this would of necessity lead towards increased efforts in production.

Amongst the African tradership, more particularly the duka owners, having

7 H. C. G. HAWKINS: *Wholesale and Retail Trade in Tanganyika.* New York–Washington–London 1965, p. 143.

been occupied in this vocation for some considerable time, hopeful trends towards better management can be ascertained in spite of the bad initial conditions and the complete lack of suitable possibilities of training. Although a long distance will still have to be covered before satisfactory conditions are reached, the efforts to improve matters have become apparent and have already found expression in isolated cases in accounting for simple occurrences pertaining to business. It is remarkable that of 41 enterprises investigated, 9 carried a daily receipt book, 2 of them a receipts and expenditures account and one enterprise even possessed a complete accounting system with a daily receipt book, a journal as well as a general ledger (the latter, however, was an African semi-wholesaler). The opinion often to be heard that the present-day tradership was in principle not capable of development on account of its largely lacking commercial capabilities, mostly, however, the lacking open-mindedness as well as the will to self-help, is wrong in its categorical denial. There exist quite a number of traders who would be capable of development under expert guidance (e.g. by a leading wholesaler).

The profit margins of the duka stores vary according to locality, size of enterprise, key goods stocked, procurement partners (wholesalers and semi-wholesalers) as well as proportion of wholesale turnover in the overall turnover. The average mark-up in a large Indian or Arab duka business in Dar es Salaam or another major town in Tanzania amounts to approximately 15 per cent, in which case, however, considerable deviations from this figure can occur according to the frequency of turnover of the goods concerned. Similar businesses in a trading centre with a wider range of goods stocked and a larger percentage of articles with slow turnover, on an average mark up their goods by between 18 and 25 per cent, whereas the general dealers in smaller settlements are working on margins of 25 to 30 per cent, in special cases operating even on higher margins.

The difference of profit margins between towns and the country also exists in the case of the smaller African duka shops. With reference to the town-dukas, an average profit margin of 28 per cent was ascertained, as far as the rural dukas are concerned, on the other hand, this profit margin proved to be 36 per cent. In this connection, however, it must be taken into consideration that often considerable transport costs must be met by rural dukas.

7. Itinerant Trade

The by far predominating part of the peddlers and hawkers are Africans. From a viewpoint of their function and their range of goods carried, they can be sub-divided into two categories:

- Street dealers and hawkers with agricultural products — mostly fruit and vegetables — as well as fish. They supply the urban population as well as the rural population, which has already more closely assimilated itself to financial economy.
- Hawkers with industrial finished goods, either calling upon the rural population in the villages and smaller settlements or offering their goods on local consumer markets. Their range of goods carried is mainly made up of articles being able to support higher profit margins than the standard goods normally stocked by the stationary trading enterprises. In general, they carry clothing, cheap jewellery, haberdashery as well as small household articles.

In areas of settlement traditionally populated by them, Arabs also operate as hawkers, measured by the overall number of itinerant traders, their numerical importance, however, is small. Primarily they can be found in the cattle trade; in isolated cases they also occupy themselves as hawkers of industrial finished goods. As a means of transport these traders generally use a bicycle or an omnibus.

After the transfer of the buying monopoly to co-operative societies, Indian merchants may hardly operate any more as itinerant merchants. Before the monopolization, a number of stationary Indian trading enterprises sent small delivery cars into neighbouring districts, selling industrial finished goods and buying agricultural products. On account of the elimination of this opportunity of buying up agricultural products, this practice proved to be unprofitable.

A regional breakdown of peddlers and hawkers shows that they are chiefly to be found in districts with a comparatively high density of settlement as well as a population with high purchasing power; they are also to be met where stationary trading enterprises are well-represented. Thus about a third of all itinerant traders and hawkers can be met in the districts of Lushoto, Tanga and Dar es Salaam; also in other densely populated, "rich" areas such as Arusha, Moshi or Bukoba they are relatively numerous. In districts underdeveloped in respect of trading facilities, for example, in Nachingwea, Masai, Mpwapwa or Manyoni, no itinerant traders, or only a few of them, exist.

IV. A Note on Tanzania's State Trading Corporation

(by Michael J. H. YAFFEY)

1. Foundation of the STC

The STC was created by nationalising seven existing trading enterprises in Tanzania. It commenced business on 13th February, 1967, one week after the nationalisation of the banks.

The enterprises taken over, though seven in number operationally, were of more complex legal structure than this figure suggests, and legally it was necessary to acquire the entire share capital of eight companies incorporated in Tanganyika plus the Tanzanian assets and liabilities of nine others mostly incorporated elsewhere. Compensation was eventually paid to the former owners by the Tanzania Treasury as and when settlements were agreed upon, in 1968 and 1969.

The seven trading enterprises may be characterised as follows:

- Co-operative Supply Association of Tanganyika Ltd. (COSATA) — the only wholly Tanzanian of the seven. Having run into a loss-making position, it was placed under the management of INTRATA and was undergoing a pruning operation when nationalised. Thereafter it was wound up. Essentially it had been concerned with the importation of staple commodities.
- International Trading and Credit Company of Tanganyika Ltd., 60 per cent Government-owned when nationalised, 40 per cent owned by a Netherlands firm. It had pioneered state trading in the export business, concerning itself with vital specialised markets. After nationalising all STC exports were transferred to it and it became the Export Division.
- Smith Mackenzie & Co. (Tanganyika) Ltd., was the largest of the seven. It might be described as the main vehicle for the importation of British merchandise into Tanzania; in early 1967, 40 of its 66 regular agency suppliers were British. It was strongly organised, with almost military discipline, and very old-fashioned in its accounting system and in its purchasing policies. It dealt also in "local purchases", principally cement, cigarettes and beverages. Ultimately it formed the nucleus of the General Merchandise Division.
- Dalgety (Tanzania) Ltd., was a smaller, weaker version of Smith Mackenzie and was about to be taken over by the latter when nationalisation supervened. It eventually lost its identity though its expertise in shipping problems proved very valuable.
- Wigglesworth & Co., with various subsidiaries, was another British organisation, an outgrowth of the sisal business in which it still retained considerable interests. It was essentially a sisal exporter, with general trading

(importing) to counterbalance, and a clearing and forwarding section. Its shipping department was agents for several shipping lines, but not for the large U.K. lines which were held by Smith Mackenzie or Dalgety; likewise its import agencies were mediocre, chiefly "technical" items to service the processing side of the plantation sector. It had an excellent workshop, however, and ultimately formed the nucleus — albeit a weak one — of the Agricultural Machinery and Technical Equipment Division.

- Twentsche Overseas Trading Company (Tanzania) Ltd., was a Dutch company engaged in importing and exporting a wide variety of products. When nationalised it was loss-making, partly due to inefficiency and partly due to high Head Office royalties which served to avoid East African tax. Like COSATA, it was wound up without being judged capable of forming the nucleus of a Division.
- A. Baumann & Co. (Tanganyika) Ltd., was a British company with three related activities: the importing of British electrical and mechanical equipment; large-scale refrigerating (on a contract basis); and the importation, stocking and up-country distribution of frozen foods and liquid milk. It was well-conceived, run with low administrative overheads, and highly profitable it became the nucleus of the Grocery Supply Division.

2. Comparison with Kenya and Uganda Counterparts

The STC, unlike its counterparts in Kenya and Uganda, thus started life with a ready-made organisation, having nearly 1,300 employees. It will be evident from the foregoing, however, that the inherited organisation was not considered satisfactory, and indeed subsequently, organisational change has rivalled commercial activities in its claims upon managerial man-hours. In addition the inherited cash position was not satisfactory, there being a net bank overdraft of Shs 35 million. Despite the difficulties caused by this, especially in the sharp recession of 1967, the Treasury did not inject any additional funds into the STC.

A second peculiarity of the STC was that its main inherited activity was the importation of goods for the expatriate sector, i.e. capital goods and high-income consumer goods. Only one of its seven constituents, COSATA, had concerned itself particularly with the mass market, whereas the KNTC and UNTC are, metaphorically speaking, extended COSATA's in essence (so far as market coverage is concerned). This expatriate-market activity is in the main competitive in nature whereas the handling of staple commodities for the mass market tends to be organised on monopoly lines by virtue of a Government decree. The following table illustrates the differences; commodities handled by KNTC and UNTC are all monopolies, whereas those handled by STC are monopolies only if marked with the letter "m".

	STC	UNTC	KNTC
Barbed wire			×
Bedsheets	× (m)		
Bicycles	× (m)		×
Bicycle tyres	× (m)		×
Blankets	× (m)		×
Cement	× (m)	×	×
Corrugated iron sheets	×		×
Edible oil		×	× [a]
Fishnets		×	
Ghee	×	×	
Gunny bags	× (m)		
Hoes	×	×	
Hollow-ware		×	
Louvres	× (m)		
Matches	× (m)		
Milk, tinned	× (m)		
Nails			×
Natural fibres	× (m)		
Onions		×	
Razor blades			×
Rice			×
Salt		×	
Secondhand clothes			×
Shirts		×	×
Sugar	× (m)	×	×
Sweets, biscuits			×
Synthetic fibres	× (m)		
Textiles	× (m)		× [b]
Torches			×
Torch batteries		×	×
Weighing machines	×	×	
Wines, spirits	× (m)	×	×

[a] Not ghee.
[b] Cotton and khaki drill only.

The above list is comprehensive for UNTC and KNTC (based on data collected in early 1969) but for STC imports several hundred items are not listed[8].

The only monopolies enjoyed by the STC are:

- those inherited from COSATA and INTRATA;
- cement, since the seven enterprises between them enjoyed the entire market;
- wines and spirits, and tyres and tubes, these monopolies given later to the STC with the aim of gearing the import programme to the needs of nascent local production;

8 Its catalogues weigh over 1 kilogram.

- textiles produced in Tanzania, by voluntary agreement with the manufacturers to deal with the threat of over-production of grey sheeting and other primitive forms of cloth.

All these are included in the list above.

In addition to these differences, the STC is peculiar in making no effort to promote African (or any other) private enterprise. It does not give preference to any particular class of retailer, nor does it provide guidance or any other extension service to Africans seeking to enter retailing, whereas the KNTC and UNTC will go to the lengths of depriving the former retailer of supplies, and extending trade credit to the newcomer far beyond his commercial credit-worthiness. Nor does the STC enter into joint-ownership ventures with private businessmen [9].

The STC in fact is unique in equatorial Africa. There is in Rwanda a co-operative run rather like INTRATA, and in Congo (K) there is an organisation similar to COSATA in its darkest days. Zambia has a competitive, state-owned importation of building materials. Otherwise importing is essentially a private activity.

3. Commercial Results of STC

The suppliers, or Principals, for whom the STC was appointed Agent, in 1967, had a British bias shown by the following country-wide breakdown:

STC Agencies, by Country, 1967 [a]

United Kingdom	223	Pakistan	10
German Fed Rep.	55	Austria	9
Kenya	46	Australia	8
India	46	Belgium	8
Netherlands	36	China	7
U.S.A.	36	U.S.S.R.	4
Japan	25	Korea, North	4
France	19	Uganda	3
German Dem. Rep.	19	Yugoslavia	3
Tanzania	15 [b]	Canada	2
Italy	15	Denmark	2
Switzerland	15	Singapore	2
Hong Kong	13	Sweden	2
Israel	13	U.A.R.	2

[a] Based on lists compiled in June, 1967.

[b] Including Business Machines (T) Ltd., not a Tanzanian manufacturer; E. A. Oxygen Ltd. (ditto); and Holland Africa Line Agency Ltd. (ditto).

9 Except temporarily, in one case, when forced to set up a joint venture in hides and skins to acquire European expertise. No Tanzanian private capital was involved.

Also *one* each in: Norway, Luxemburg, Poland, Zambia, Hungary, Czechoslovakia, Bulgaria, Turkey, Taiwan, Kuwait, Malaya and Jamaica.

Total of E.E.C.	=	134 or 20%
Total of E.F.T.A.	=	228 or 35%
Total of East Africa with Zambia	=	65 or 10%
Total socialist countries	=	37 or 6%
WORLD TOTAL	=	654 (100%)

It will be evident that Britain could scarcely claim to be the cheapest supplier of the materials concerned, which cover virtually the entire range of consumer and standardised capital goods, a fact which was admitted later in that year by the forced devaluation of the pound. The dominant position of Britain in the import list, with one-third of the agencies, must be for institutional, political and historical reasons, rather than the unintended outcome of any scientific, cost-saving purchasing policy operated in the interests of the Tanzanian customers.

The bias was given attention in the months after the sterling devaluation, when the STC struggled, with roughly a 50 per cent success rate, to take the benefit of the devaluation (so far as sterling imports were concerned) for itself by discouraging price increases in sterling terms. Many U.K. suppliers particularly in the traditional older sectors such as textiles and machinery parts showed utter disregard of market circumstances and of the possibility of serious competition from non-U.K. sources. The STC severed relations with the most intransigeant U.K. suppliers and seriously began to plan a purchasing strategy which would tap the entire world market. Managers were sent to various countries and a start has been made to overcoming consumer resistance to brand changes, especially in tinned foods.

The STC has also made use of its negotiating position to insist on improvements in terms of trade, usually ancillary to the price. An example is the bargaining with a large European food compary. An important buyer of one of Tanzania's export crops, this company had compelled the exporter in Tanzania to hold stocks of worth no less than Shs 1,150,000, equivalent to 14 months' supply. This was stopped after nationalisation, and at the same time the company reduced the price for a product, which was imported into Tanzania to the level of another leading brand. Another producer ultimately extended his credit terms to cover the extra month required for ships to round the Cape of Good Hope instead of passing through the Suez Canal.

In 1969 the STC ceased to issue licences for the importation of tinned milk and took over the function itself, with a major depôt at Tanga. All up-country milk prices were equalised down to the Dar es Salaam level, with no increase in the latter and no loss of profit to the STC. This was done by a scientific purchasing policy involving placing very large orders at strategic times in the year.

As representatives of shipping lines, the STC had inherited about 35 per cent of the shipping agency market which by 1969 had risen to about 45 per cent. The rise was due to successful promotion of the lines concerned and being awarded a new line. There is no cost in directing STC business to STC lines, whereas other (private) companies bear considerable promotional expense and even run unprofitable exporting sections to bring business to their clearing and forwarding departments.

In other areas the commercial impact of the STC has been less successful. These are especially:

a) *Exports:* The STC has not yet acquired a body of citizen experts in specialised overseas markets.

b) *Imports:* The STC has not yet organised public information media to develop public price-consciousness and quality discrimination.

c) *Domestic trade:* The STC has not opened any new branches nor found any way of penetrating rural areas with wholesale trade.

d) *New lines:* Important commodities not yet dealt with by the STC include petroleum products and motor vehicles.

4. Financial Results of STC

The financial results are shown approximately in the following table:

	12. 2. 67—30. 6. 67 million Shs	1. 7. 67—31. 7. 68 million Shs
1. Profit before tax	1.2	11.6
2. (1) as annual rate	3.2	11.6
3. Revenue	138.1	365.3
4. (3) as annual rate	368.3	365.3
5. Total net assets at end	100.9	93.8
6. Net worth at end	25.1	27.3
7. (1) ÷ (3)	*0.9%*	*3.2%*
8. (2) ÷ (5)	*3.2%*	*12.4%*
9. (2) ÷ (6)	*12.8%*	*42.1%*

1967 was a difficult year because of the recession (political changes, bad weather, monetary disturbances) and it was also a period for writing down superannuated inventories, identifying bad debts, and streamlining accounts receivable. By mid-1968 total assets were actually smaller in the books than on Vesting Day. Yet the net worth (from which ultimately the Treasury must be reimbursed for the compensation to be paid to former owners) showed an improvement. Revenue revived strongly in 1968 while overheads rose only moderately, and from being only marginally profitable the STC arrived at a satisfactory standard of profitability.

About 40 per cent of the net profit is payable to the Treasury as Corporation Tax, together with any such further sum as is not to be reinvested in the STC (e.g. compensation). The absolute amount of profit remaining is therefore, while sufficient for normal commercial standards of corporate growth, barely adequate to allow the STC to develop in line with the economy as a whole, and certainly not adequate to finance a spectacular programme of major acquisitions. Should a rapid expansion of the STC's functions be found necessary, it will therefore have to be backed by law rather than by commercial aggressiveness.

Bibliography

BUDDERBERG, H.: *Betriebslehre des Binnenhandels.* Wiesbaden 1959.

HAWKINS, H. C. G. *Wholesale and Retail Trade in Tanganyika.* New York–Washington–London.

KOMMISSAR, G. E.: *Increased African Participation in Commerce and Industry.* Manuscript 1963.

OBERPARLEITER, K.: *Funktionen und Risiken des Warenhandels.* 2nd Edition, Vienna 1955.

Studies within the African Research Programme of the Ifo-Institut für Wirtschaftsforschung, Munich

Published:

a) in the series "Afrika-Studien"

(No. 1–18 by Springer-Verlag, Berlin – Heidelberg – New York; No. 19 ff. by Weltforum-Verlag, Munich)

No. 1 **Development Banks and Companies in Tropical Africa**
By Naseem Ahmad and Ernst Becher, 1964, 86 pages, in German

No. 2 **Agricultural Development in Tanganyika**
By Hans Ruthenberg, 1964, 212 pages, in English

No. 3 **National Accounting Systems in Tropical Africa**
By Rolf Güsten and Helmut Helmschrott, 1965, 69 pages, in German

No. 4 **Contributions to Internal Migration and Population Development in Liberia**
By Hans W. Jürgens, 1965, 104 pages, in German

No. 5 **Annotated Bibliography of Social Research in East Africa 1954—1963**
By Angela von Molnos, 1965, 304 pages, in German

No. 6 **The Political and Economic Role of the Asian Minority in East Africa**
By Indira Rothermund, 1965, 75 pages, in German

No. 7 **Land Tenure Reform in Kenya**
By Hanfried Fliedner, 1965, 136 pages, in German

No. 8 **Taxation and Economic Development in East Africa**
By Lübbe Schnittger, 1966, 216 pages, in German

No. 9 **Problems of Economic Growth and Planning: The Sudan Example**
By Rolf Güsten, 1966, 74 pages, in English

No. 10 **African Agricultural Production Development Policy in Kenya 1952—1965**
By Hans Ruthenberg, 1966, 180 pages, in English

No. 11 **Land Use and Animal Husbandry in Sukumaland/Tanzania**
By Dietrich von Rotenhan, 1966, 131 pages, in German

No. 12 **Land Legislation in the Cameroons 1884–1964**
By Heinrich Krauss, 1966, 156 pages, in German

No. 13 **Investigations into the Productivity and Profitability of Smallholder Sisal in East Africa**
By Hermann Pössinger, 1967, 172 pages, in German

No. 14 **The Attitude of Various Tribes of the Republic of Togo, Especially the Ewe on the Plateau de Dayes, towards the Problem of Commissioned Cattle Herding by the Fulbe (Peulh) of West Africa**
By Julius O. Müller, 1967, 124 pages, in German

No. 15 **The Role of Co-operatives in the Economic Development of East Africa, and Especially of Tanganyika and Uganda**
By Margarete Paulus, 1967, 156 pages, in German

No. 16 **Gabun: History, Structure and Problems of the Export Trade of a Developing Country**
By Hans-Otto Neuhoff, 1967, 273 pages, in German

No. 17 **Continuity and Change in the Division of Labour among the Baganda**
By Jürgen Jensen, 1967, 297 pages, in German

No. 18 **Trade in Tanzania**
By Werner Kainzbauer, 1968, 239 pages, in German

No. 19 **Problems of Agricultural Development in the Coastal Region of East Africa**
By Sigmar Groeneveld, 1967, 124 pages, in German

No. 20 **The Monetary and Banking Systems of the Countries of West Africa**
By Heinz-Günter Geis, 1967, 428 pages, in German

No. 21 **The Role of the Transport Sector in the Development Policy – with Special Reference to African Countries –**
By G. Wolfgang Heinze, 1967, 324 pages, in German

No. 22 **Ukara: A Special Case of Land Use in the Tropics**
By Heinz Dieter Ludwig, 1967, 251 pages, in German

No. 23 **Applied Economics of Education – The Example of Senegal –**
By Werner Clement, 1967, 224 pages, in German

No. 24 **Smallholder Farming and Smallholder Development in Tanzania – Ten Case Studies –**
By Hans Ruthenberg (ed.), 1968, 360 pages, in English

No. 25 **Smallholders in the Tropical Highlands of East Africa. The Usambara Mts. in the Transition Period from Subsistence to Market Production**
By Manfred Attems, 1968, 168 pages, in German

No. 26 **Attitudes towards Family Planning in East Africa**
By Angela Molnos, 1968, 408 pages, in English

No. 27 **Smallholder Production under Close Supervision: Tobacco Growing in Tanzania. A Socio-Economic Study**
By Walter Scheffler, 1968, 184 pages, in German

No. 28 **The Kilombero Valley/Tanzania: Characteristic Features of the Economic Geography of a Semihumid East African Flood Plain and Its Margins**
By Ralph Jätzold and E. Baum, 1968, 147 pages, in English

No. 29 **Investigations into Internal Migration in Tanzania**
By Hans W. Jürgens, 1968, 166 pages, in German

No. 30 **Studies in the Staple Food Economy of Western Nigeria**
By Rolf Güsten, 1968, 311 pages, in English

No. 31 **Agricultural Development in Angola and Moçambique**
By Hermann Pössinger, 1968, 284 pages, in German

No. 32 **Rural Economic Development in Zambia, 1890—1964**
By J. A. Hellen, 1968, 297 pages, in English

No. 33 **Small Farm Credit and Development — Some Experiences in East Africa with Special Reference to Kenya —**
By J. Vasthoff, 1969, 144 pages, in English

No. 34 **Crafts, Small-Scale Industries, and Industrial Education in Tanzania**
By Karl Schädler, 1969, 264 pages, in English

No. 35 **Money and Banking in East Africa**
By E.-J. Pauw, 1969, 278 pages, in German

No. 36 **Reorganization of Land Use in Egypt (three case studies)**
By E.-S. El Shagi, 1969, 175 pages, in German

No. 37 **Energy Supply and Economic Development in East Africa**
By H. Amann, 1969, 254 pages, in English

No. 38 **The African Settlers and how They Organize Their Life in the Urambo-Scheme (Tanzania)**
By Axel v. Gagern, 1969, 130 pages, in German

No. 39 **Irrigation in Kenya's Agriculture with Special Reference to the Mwea-Tebere Project**
By R. Golkowsky, 1969, 149 pages, in German

No. 40 **Economic Statistics in Developing Countries: the Example of Uganda**
By Hanns Hieber, 1969, 244 pages, in German

No. 41 **Problems of Land-Locked Countries: Uganda**
By W. Fischer, 1969, 274 pages, in German

No. 42 **Investigations into Health and Nutrition in East Africa**
By H. Kraut/H.-D. Cremer (eds.), 1969, 342 pages, in English

No. 43 **The African as Industrial Worker in East Africa**
By O. Neuloh a. o., 1969, 440 pages, in German

No. 44 **Rice Cultivation in West Africa — A Presentation of the Economic and Geographical Differences of Cultivation Methods**
By B. Mohr, 1969, 163 pages, in German

No. 45 **Structure and Growth of the East African Textile and Garments Industry**
By H. Helmschrott, 1969, 130 pages, in German

No. 46 **Social Change in Kiteezi (Buganda), a Village within the Sphere of Influence of the Township of Kampala (Uganda)**
By E. C. Klein, 1969, 160 pages, in German

No. 47 **Balance of Payment Problems in a Developing Country: Tanzania**
By M. Yaffey, 1970, 284 pages, in English

No. 48 **Fodder Plants in the Sahel zone of Africa**
By R. Bartha, 1970, 306 pages, in German, English und French

No. 49 **Status and Use of African Lingua Francas**
By B. Heine, 1970, 206 pages, in English

No. 50 **Cultural Change and Anxiety Reaction among the Yoruba of Nigeria**
By Staewen/Schönberg, 1970, ca. 430 pages, in German (with an English Summary)

No. 51 **Studies in Production and Trade in East Africa**
By P. Zajadacz and Contributors, 1970, 441 pages, in English

No. 52 **Planning Processes: The East African Case**
By R. E. Vente, 1970, 224 pages, in English

To be published shortly in the series "Afrika-Studien":

No. 53 **Financial Aspects of Development in East Africa**
By P. Marlin and Contributors (in English)

No. 54 **Administration and Economic Exploitation of German East Africa before 1914**
By D. Bald (in German)

b) in the African Studies special series "Information and Documentation"

No. 1 **Africa-Vademecum (basic data on the economic structure and development of Africa)**
Prepared by F. Betz, 1968, 163 pages, in German, with additional headings in English and French

No. 2 **Development Banks and Institutions in Africa**
By H. Harlander and D. Mezger, 1969, 211 pages, in German

c) as mimeograph (African Research Reports)

Economic Planning and Development Policy in Tropical Africa
By N. Ahmad, E. Becher and E. Harder, 1965, 283 pages, in German (out of print)

The Human Factor in the Development of the Kilombero Valley
By O. Raum, 1965, 56 pages, in English (out of print)

The EEC Market Regulations for Agricultural Products and their Implications for Developing Countries
By H. Klemm and P. v. Marlin, 1965, 95 pages, in German (out of print)

The Impact of External Economic Relations on the Economic Development of East Africa
By P. v. Marlin, 1966, 110 pages, in English (out of print)

Crop Cultivation on the Island of Madagascar with Special Reference to Rice Growing
By Alfred H. Rabe, 1965, 346 pages, in German (out of print)

Economic Research in Tropical Africa. Results of an Informatory Trip to Egypt, Ethiopia, Kenya, Uganda, Tanzania, Malawi, Zambia, Congo (Kinshasa), Nigeria, Ghana and Senegal in April and May 1966
By Hildegard Harlander, 1966, 193 pages, in German

Israeli Aid to Developing Countries with Special Reference to East Africa
By F. Goll, 1967, 189 pages, in German

The Economy of South West Africa (a Study in Economic Geography)
By Axel J. Halbach, 1967, 210 pages, in German (out of print)

Co-operative Farming in Kenya and Tanzania
By Nikolaus Newiger, 1967, 157 pages, in English (out of print)

Game Protection and Game Utilization in Rhodesia and in South Africa
By Wolfgang Erz, 1967, 97 pages, in German (out of print)

Zoological Studies in the Kivu Region (Congo-Kinshasa)
By Fritz Dieterlen and Peter Kunkel, 1967, 138 pages, in German

Recent English Economic Research in East Africa. A Selected Bibliography
By Dorothea Mezger and Eleonore Littich, 1967, 383 pages, in German (out of print)

The Attitude of Various Tribes of the Republic of Togo, Especially the Ewe on the Plateau de Dayes, towards the Problem of Commissioned Cattle Herding by the Fulbe (Peulh) of West Africa
By Julius O. Müller, 1967, 187 pages, in French

Examination of the Physical Development of Tanzanian Youth
By H. W. Jürgens, 1967, 152 pages, in English

The Chemical and Allied Industries in Kenya
By Hans Reichelt, 1967, 182 pages, in English

Traditional Farming and Land Development in the Kilombero Valley/Tanzania
By Eckhard Baum, 1967, 150 pages, in German

The Organization of Milk Markets in East Africa
By Helmut Klemm, 1967, 164 pages, in German

Botanical Investigations in the Masai Country/Tanzania (an Example from the Semi-Arid Areas of East Africa)
By H. Leippert, 1968, 184 pages, in German

Evaluation of Aerial Photography in East Africa (an Inventory)
By K. Gerresheim, 1968, 225 pages, in German

Manufacturing and Processing Industries in Tanzania
By K. Schädler, 1969, 55 pages, in English

Agricultural Development in Malawi
By H. Dequin, 1969, 248 pages, in English

Development Aid to Africa – with Special Reference to the Countries of East Africa
By K. Erdmann, 1969, 186 pages, in German

Vegetable Cultivation in Tropical Highlands: the Kigezi Example (Uganda)
By F. Scherer, 1969, 227 pages, in English

Science and Development Policy. The Problem of Application of Research Results
By M. Bohnet, 1969, 35 pages, in German

Importance, Volume, Forms and Development Possibilities of Private Saving in East Africa
By G. Hübner, 1970, 343 pages, in German

Operational Concepts of the Infrastructure in the Economic Development Process
By H. Amann, 1970, 203 pages, in German

In preparation:

The Present State of Legislation in East Africa
By G. Spreen

Development Possibilities of the Pig and Poultry Industry in East Africa
By H. Späth

Comparative Investigations into the Efficiency of Utilizable Ruminants in Kenya
By Walter/Dennig

Farm Management Systems in Kenya
By v. Haugwitz/Thorwart

Problems of the Transport Economy in Tanzania with Special Reference to Road Transport
By R. Hofmeier (in English)

The Influence of Urbanization upon the Development of Rural Areas — with Special Reference to Jinja (Uganda) and Its Surroundings
By Gerken/Schubert/Brandt

The Interrelationship between Man, Nature and Economy: the Example of Madagascar
By W. Marquardt

The Implications of Tanzania's Administrative System for Her Economic Development
By K. v. Sperber (in English)

Autonomous Institutions in East African Agricultural Production
By H. Blume (in English)

Applied Research in East Africa and Its Influence on Economic Development
By M. Bohnet and H. Reichelt (in English)

Co-operatives in the Sudan: Their Characteristics, Functions and Suitability in the Socio-Economic Development Process
By M. Bardeleben

Mining and Regional Development in East Africa
By T. Möller

The Economico-Geographical Pattern of East Africa
By K. Engelhard

Iraqw Highland/Tanzania: Resource Analysis of an East African Highland and its Margins
By J. Schultz (in English)

Methods and Problems of Farm Management Surveys in Africa South of the Sahara
By H. Thorwart

The Mau-Mau Movement: Its Socio-Economic and Political Causes and Implications upon British Colonial Policy in Kenya and Africa
By J. Muriuki (in English)

Beef Production in East Africa with Special Reference to Semi-Arid Areas
By K. Meyn (in English)

The Requirements for the Means of Transport in East Africa with a View to the Economic Expansion of these Countries
By H. Milbers

Population Trends and Migration in Malawi with Special Reference to the Central Region of Lake Malawi
By U. Weyl

Population Trends in Kenya and Their Implications for Social Services in Rural and Urban Areas
By M. Meck (in English)

Education's Contribution to Economic Development of a Tropical Agrarian Country — the Example of Tanzania
By H. Desselberger

Agrarian Patterns in Ethiopia and their Implications for Economic Growth
By V. Janssen

Development of Law in Malawi
By F. v. Benda-Beckmann (in German)